SEAN PENN

SEAN PENN

His Life and Times

RICHARD T. KELLY

CANONGATE U.S.
New York

First published in Great Britain in 2004 by
Faber and Faber Limited, London, England

Photoset by Faber and Faber

Printed in the United States of America

FIRST AMERICAN EDITION

ISBN 1-84195-623-6

Canongate U.S.
841 Broadway
New York, NY 10003

04 05 06 07 08   10 9 8 7 6 5 4 3 2 1

For Rachel Alexander

Our society has spent so much time and has achieved such startling results with the discovery of new mechanical processes of communication, but we have somehow forgotten that the process of living demands the ability to respond, to make contact, and to communicate one's experience to another human being . . . It is my firm belief that the discoveries and procedures essential for the actor's capacities are equally, if not more, necessary for the layman . . .

Lee Strasberg, *A Dream of Passion: The Development of the Method*

A journalist asked Sean while in Baghdad, 'Do you think this trip will change you?' And Sean said something like, 'I'd like to think that every moment in our lives is in some ways an aggregate of every moment before, in terms of all that's gone into who we are now . . .'

Norman Solomon, Executive Director, Institute for Public Accuracy

Contents

A Note to the Reader

This book is massed in the form of an 'oral biography', but it is not an entirely pure endeavour in that line. Passages of prose are interspersed throughout by way of segue and explanation. There are a couple of reasons for the mixture.

Firstly, Sean Penn is alive – very much alive; whereas oral biography is more often employed as a sort of multi-voiced valediction for uncommonly lively individuals who are, alas, no longer among us. Still, the form is undeniably well-fitted to any individual whose character and behaviour inspires – even demands – the telling of stories by those who have known the pleasure of his company. Which is where, in this case, we come in.

Secondly, the working process of oral biography has rather more in common with that of documentary film-making than 'writing a book'. In essence, you shoot for as long as your schedule allows, then you trim and order the rushes in the cutting room. At times, the temptation to add voice-over, if only for narrative purposes, is irresistible.

This book does its best to be accurate to the major events of its subject's life to date. In order to reflect the many facets of Sean Penn, I needed to allow witnesses to speak in their own voices. The transition from tape to print has required a certain measure of trimming and chronological reordering, as well as the clarification of syntax, but otherwise the verbatim text has been edited only to ensure that any details therein – dates, proper nouns, et cetera – are correct. In some cases, participants requested the right of review. In any case, I have taken care to ensure that both content and manner of expression have been carried over intact. In the event of any questions arising in respect of same, necessary corrections will be included in further editions.

It's at least my hope that this book has something to offer the reader on three different levels: firstly, as a portrait of an artist, and a detailed tour through a body of work that is continually challenging and accomplished, if not always well-known or indeed well-received. But then Sean Penn's abilities as an actor require no endorsement from critics: his fellow practitioners, I'd argue, are the best judges in this field, and some distinguished such fellows are present in these pages. From their words, and those of Penn himself, perhaps something useful may be taken about the whys and the hows of acting – and indeed writing and directing – for the screen.

Secondly I hope you will find some fun to be had from all this anecdotage, and thirdly that, in back of it all, something more might be discerned about the United States of America, and the strange times through which Penn and his family and friends have lived. The subtitle of *His Life and Times* may sound portentous for a book about an actor still in his forties. Let me try it on you this way: motion pictures can't help but speak of their times, and occasionally, if we're lucky, *for* them. There's just something about photographing stories acted out by real persons in pre-arranged places that betrays an era, its manners and preoccupations. Any significant film career will partake of such wider meaning, and Sean Penn, through his very singular choices in film, has actively encouraged that process. He has also sought to make a meaningful life for himself that is quite divorced from celluloid: what he has referred to as 'having the dots of your life connect to each other'. It's only natural: his father, after all, was a witness to and participant in some of the crucial events of the so-called 'American Century'. Sean Penn too has got in harm's way over the years, under very different circumstances but more often than not in the pursuit of a just cause. He is a man who, as Norman Mailer once wrote of one of his hard-wearing protagonists, 'can stand up when the trouble is brightest.'

Richard T. Kelly
June 2004

The Cast List

WOODY ALLEN: Writer/director, actor and comedian, b. Brooklyn, 1935. Among his many acclaimed features are *Love and Death* (1975), *Annie Hall* (1977, Academy Awards, Screenplay and Direction), *Zelig* (1983), *Hannah and her Sisters* (1986, Academy Award, Screenplay), and *Crimes and Misdemeanors* (1989). Directed Sean Penn in *Sweet and Lowdown* (1999).

DAVID BAERWALD: Singer/songwriter and composer, b. Oxford, Ohio. Recorded the album *Boomtown* (1987) with Dave Ricketts as David + David. Solo releases include *Bedtime Stories* (1990), *Triage* (1993), and *Here Comes the New Folk Underground* (2002). Has composed for films including *Loved* (1997), *Hurlyburly* (1998), and *Moulin Rouge* (2001).

HAROLD BECKER: Director, b. New York. Features include *The Ragman's Daughter* (1972), *The Onion Field* (1979), *The Black Marble* (1980), *Taps* (1981), and *Sea of Love* (1989).

RICHARD BENJAMIN: Actor and director, b. New York, 1938. Acting credits include *Goodbye Columbus* (1969) and *Portnoy's Complaint* (1972). Features as director include *My Favorite Year* (1982) and *Racing With The Moon* (1984).

BONO: songwriter, lead singer of U2, b. Dublin, 1960. U2's albums include *October* (1981), *The Unforgettable Fire* (1984), *The Joshua Tree* (1987), *Achtung Baby* (1991), *Zooropa* (1992), and *All That You Can't Leave Behind* (2000).

LINDA LEE BUKOWSKI: Née Beighle, partner of the writer Charles Bukowski from 1976, married to him from 1985 until his death in 1994. Subsequently the executor of his literary estate.

JOHN BYRNE: Painter and playwright, b. Paisley, Scotland, 1940. Authored the trilogy of plays *The Slab Boys* (1978), *Cuttin' A Rug* (1980), and *Still Life* (1983). For television, wrote the series *Tutti*

Frutti (1987) and *Your Cheatin' Heart* (1989).

R. D. CALL: Actor, b. Utah. Befriended Sean Penn at Group Repertory Theatre, LA. Film credits include *At Close Range* (1986), *State of Grace* (1990), and *Last Man Standing* (1996).

JAY CASSIDY: Film editor. Credits include *The Indian Runner* (1991), *The Crossing Guard* (1995), *The Pledge* (2001), the 'USA' segment of *11'09"01* (2002) and *The Assassination of Richard Nixon* (2004).

KEVIN CHAPMAN: Boston-born actor, in films since 1999. Credits include *Blow* (2001), *Mystic River* (2003), *21 Grams* (2003), and *Ladder 49* (2004).

BOBBY COOPER: Actor and retired bookmaker, b. New York, 1955. Appears in *The Crossing Guard* (1995), *She's So Lovely* (1997), and *I Am Sam* (2002).

PETER COYOTE: Actor and writer, b. Colver PA, 1942. Credits include *E.T.* (1982), *Jagged Edge* (1985), *Bitter Moon* (1992), *Kika* (1993). Author of *Sleeping Where I Fall* (1997).

BENICIO DEL TORO: Actor, b. San Germán, Puerto Rico, 1967. Raised in rural Pennsylvania, studied with Stella Adler. Credits include *The Indian Runner* (1991), *The Usual Suspects* (1995), *Traffic* (2000, Academy Award), *The Pledge* (2001) and *21 Grams* (2003).

ERIN DIGNAM: Writer/director, b. 1957. Credits include the feature films *Loon* (a.k.a. *Denial*, 1990), *Loved* (1997), and *The Last Face* (pre-production, 2004).

TONY DRAZAN: Writer/director, b. New York, 1955. Credits include the feature films *Zebrahead* (1992, also wrote), *Imaginary Crimes* (1994) and *Hurlyburly* (1998).

DENNIS FANNING: Detective, Los Angeles Police Department, b. Chicago. Befriended Sean Penn while acting as consultant to *Colors* (1988). Appears in *The Crossing Guard* (1995), *She's So Lovely* (1997), *I Am Sam* (2002).

JAMES FOLEY: Director, b. Brooklyn, 1953. Graduate of USC film school. Features include *Reckless* (1984), *At Close Range* (1986), *After Dark, My Sweet* (1990), *Glengarry Glen Ross* (1992), *Two Bits* (1995) and *Confidence* (2003).

GISELA (MARTINE) GETTY: Photographer and film-maker, b. Kassel, Germany, 1950. Ex-wife of J. Paul Getty III. Acted with Sean Penn at Peggy Feury's Loft Studio, 1978–80.

JERRY HANNAN: Singer/songwriter. Performed music for *The Late Henry Moss* (2000), contributed song to *The Pledge* (2001). Has recorded the albums *Madly In Love With You* (1997, as The Mad Hannans) and *Sounds Like A Story* (2003).

WOODY HARRELSON: Actor, b. Midland, Texas, 1961. Acted with Sean Penn on film in *Cool Blue* (1988) and *The Thin Red Line* (1998) and on stage in *The Late Henry Moss* (2000). Credits include *Natural Born Killers* (1994), *The People vs. Larry Flynt* (1996), *The Hi–Lo Country* (1998).

AMY HECKERLING: Director, b. Bronx, New York, 1954, graduate of NYU and AFI film schools. Credits include *Fast Times at Ridgemont High* (1982), *Clueless* (1995) and *Loser* (2000).

DENNIS HOPPER: Actor/director/artist, b. Dodge City, 1937. Acting roles include *Rebel Without A Cause* (1954), *Apocalypse Now* (1979), *Rumblefish* (1983), *Blue Velvet* (1986) and *The Indian Runner*. Directorial credits include *Easy Rider* (1969), *The Last Movie* (1971), *Out of the Blue* (1980), *Colors* (1988).

ANJELICA HUSTON: Actress/director, b. Santa Monica, 1951. Credits include *Prizzi's Honor* (1985, Academy Award), *The Dead* (1987), *The Grifters* (1990), and *The Crossing Guard* (1995). Directed *Bastard Out of Carolina* (1996) and *Agnes Browne* (1998).

ALEJANDRO GONZÁLEZ IÑÁRRITU: Director, b. Mexico City, 1963. Credits include *Amores Perros* (2000), the 'Mexico' segment of *11'09"01* (2002), and *21 Grams* (2003).

STANLEY JAFFE: Studio executive and producer, b. New Rochelle, New York, 1940. Appointed President of Paramount Pictures in 1969. Later credits as independent producer include *Kramer vs. Kramer* (1979, Academy Award), *Taps* (1981), and *The Accused* (1988).

NEIL JORDAN: Writer/director, b. Sligo, Ireland, 1950. Credits include *The Company of Wolves* (1984), *Mona Lisa* (1986), *We're No Angels* (1989), *The Crying Game* (1992, Academy Award, Screenplay), *Michael Collins* (1996) and *The Butcher Boy* (1997).

DR EDWARD ('EDDIE') KATZ: 'Gentleman's gentleman'.

HELENA KATZ: Wife of Dr. Katz.

NICHOLAS KAZAN: Screenwriter, b. 1950. Son of Elia Kazan and Molly Day Thatcher. Credits include *Frances* (1982), *At Close Range* (1986), *Patty Hearst* (1988) and *Reversal of Fortune* (1990).

KATHY KELLY: Peace activist, coordinator of Voices in the Wilderness. Met Sean Penn in Baghdad, December 2002. Sentenced to prison in January 2004 for civil disobedience at the US Army's 'School of the Americas', Fort Benning, Georgia, and ELF nuclear facility, Wisconsin.

ANDREW 'DAULTON' LEE: Convicted of espionage in 1977 with Christopher Boyce. Their story became the subject of the book *The Falcon and the Snowman* by Robert Lindsey, filmed in 1985 by John Schlesinger. Employed by Sean Penn as personal assistant, 1997–8.

BARBARA LIGETI: Producer, b. New York. Co-produced the plays *Goose and Tomtom* (New York, 1986) and *Hurlyburly* (LA, 1988). Produced the feature film *Hugo Pool* (1997).

ART LINSON: Producer and author, b. Chicago, 1942. Credits include *Melvin and Howard* (1980), *Fast Times at Ridgemont High* (1982), *The Untouchables* (1987), *Casualties of War* (1989), *We're No Angels* (1989), *Heat* (1995), and *Fight Club* (1999). Author of *A Pound of Flesh* (1995) and *What Just Happened?* (2002).

ELIZABETH MCGOVERN: Stage and film actress, b. Evanston, Illinois, 1960. Engaged to Sean Penn, 1983–4. Credits include *Ordinary People* (1980), *Ragtime* (1981), *Once Upon a Time in America* (1984), *Racing with the Moon* (1984), and *House of Mirth* (2000).

MIKE MEDAVOY: Agent, studio executive, and producer, b. Shanghai, 1941. Senior VP, United Artists, 1974–8. Co-Founded Orion Pictures, 1978. Chairman, TriStar Pictures, 1990–4. Co-founder and chairman, Phoenix Pictures, 1995–.

COLE MILLER: Los Angeles-based writer and web content designer, founder of NoMoreVictims.org website.

DAVID MORSE: Film and TV actor, b. Hamilton, Massachusetts, 1953. Credits include *Inside Moves* (1980), *Desperate Hours* (1990), *The*

Indian Runner (1991), *The Crossing Guard* (1995), *The Green Mile* (1999), and *Dancer in the Dark* (2000).

SAMANTHA MORTON: Actress, b. Nottingham, England, 1977. Credits include *Under The Skin* (1997), *Sweet and Lowdown* (1999), *Minority Report* (2002), *Morvern Callar* (2002) and *In America* (2003).

ADAM NELSON: Screen actor, befriended Sean Penn after role in short film *Hotel November* (1987). First major role in *The Abyss* (1989). Credits include *Dead Man Walking* (1995), *The Pledge* (2001) and *Mystic River* (2003).

JESSIE NELSON: Director, screenwriter, producer. Credits as co-writer include *Stepmom* (1998) and *The Story of Us* (1999). As director: *Corrina, Corrina* (1994), *I Am Sam* (2001), *The Night I Followed The Dog* (2004).

JACK NICHOLSON: Actor, b. Neptune, New Jersey, 1937. Three-time Academy Award-winner, major roles including *Five Easy Pieces* (1970), *Chinatown* (1974), *The Passenger* (1975), *One Flew Over The Cuckoo's Nest* (1975), *The Shining* (1980), and *Reds* (1981). Directed by Sean Penn in *The Crossing Guard* (1995) and *The Pledge* (2001). Directed *Drive, He Said* (1971), *Goin' South* (1978), and *The Two Jakes* (1990).

MEEGAN OCHS: Political activist, daughter of folk-singer/songwriter Phil Ochs. b. New York, 1962. Personal assistant to Sean Penn, 1983–5. Subsequently went to work for the American Civil Liberties Union (ACLU).

MATT PALMIERI: Film-maker, b. Malibu. Befriended Sean Penn at Malibu Park Junior High, 1969. Attended Stanford University and Harvard Business School. MGM executive, 1988–91. Wrote and directed Penn in short *Cruise Control* (1992, Academy Award nomination).

CHRISTOPHER PENN: Actor, b. Los Angeles, 1965. Younger brother of Sean Penn. Film roles include *Rumblefish* (1983), *Pale Rider* (1985), *Reservoir Dogs* (1991), *Short Cuts* (1993), and *The Funeral* (1996, Best Actor, Venice Festival).

EILEEN RYAN PENN: Stage, TV and film actress, b. New York, 1927.

Mother of Sean Penn. Film credits include *At Close Range* (1986), *The Indian Runner* (1991), *The Crossing Guard* (1995), *Magnolia* (1999) and *The Pledge* (2001).

SEAN PENN: *passim*

DON PHILLIPS: casting director, producer, b. New Jersey, 1939. Founded Talent Services Associates with Michael Chinich, later cast *Fast Times at Ridgemont High* (1982), *The Crossing Guard* (1995), *The Game* (1997), and *The Pledge* (2001). Produced *The Indian Runner* (1991). 'Creative consultant' on *Hurlyburly* (1998).

LOU PITT: Agent at International Creative Management until 1998, represented John Cassavetes until his death in 1989. Producer of *Hollywood Homicide* (2003).

DAVID RABE: Playwright and screenwriter, b. Dubuque, Iowa, 1940. Plays include *Sticks and Bones* (1972 Tony Award, Best Play), *The Basic Training of Pavlo Hummel*, *The Orphan*, *Streamers*, *Goose and Tomtom*, and *Hurlyburly*. Screenplays include *Casualties of War* (1989).

BOB RAFELSON: Director, b. New York, 1933. Features include *Head* (1968), *Five Easy Pieces* (1970), *The King of Marvin Gardens* (1972), *Stay Hungry* (1975), and *The Postman Always Rings Twice* (1981).

JORDAN RHODES: Stage, TV and film actor, b. Maryland, 1939. Directed by Leo Penn in TV shows including *Bonanza*, *Little House on the Prairie* and *Matlock*. Directed by Sean Penn in *The Indian Runner* (1991).

TIM ROBBINS: Stage and film actor and writer/director, b. 1958, W. Covina, CA. Acting credits include *Bull Durham* (1988), *The Player* (1991), *The Shawshank Redemption* (1994), and *Mystic River* (2003, Academy Award). Wrote and directed *Bob Roberts* (1992), *Dead Man Walking* (1995), and *Cradle Will Rock* (1999).

RICK ROSENTHAL: TV and film director, b. New York, 1949. Feature films include *Halloween II* (1981) and *Bad Boys* (1983), TV credits include *Buffy the Vampire Slayer*.

JAMES RUSSO: Stage and film actor, b. New York, 1953. Film credits include *Fast Times at Ridgemont High* (1982), *Once Upon A Time in*

America (1984), *We're No Angels* (1989), *State of Grace* (1990) and *Donnie Brasco* (1997).

SUSAN SARANDON: Actress, b. 1946, New York. Met Sean Penn while performing on Broadway in *Extremities* (1983). Film credits include *Pretty Baby* (1978), *Atlantic City* (1980), *Bull Durham* (1988), *Thelma and Louise* (1991), and *Dead Man Walking* (1995, Academy Award).

JON SCHEIDE: Assistant director, producer. Production assistant on *The Crossing Guard* (1995), First AD and Additional Photography on *The Pledge* (2001), Produced Sean Penn's 'USA' segment of *11'09"01* (2002).

GARRY SHANDLING: Writer, actor, and comedian, b. Chicago, 1949. For television, wrote and starred in *It's Garry Shandling's Show* (1986–90) and *The Larry Sanders Show* (1992–98). Film credits include *Hurlyburly* (1998) and *What Planet Are You From?* (2000).

DANNY SHOT: Poet and co-founder with Eliot Katz of the poetry magazine *Long Shot*, which published work by Sean Penn in 1987 (#5) and 1989 (#8).

NORMAN SOLOMON: Executive director of the Institute for Public Accuracy in San Francisco, and co-author of *Target Iraq: What The News Media Didn't Tell You* (Context Books, 2003). Accompanied Sean Penn to Baghdad in December 2002.

KEVIN SPACEY: Stage and film actor, b. New Jersey, 1959. Film credits include *Glengarry Glen Ross* (1992), *The Usual Suspects* (1995, Academy Award), *LA Confidential* (1997), *Hurlyburly* (1998), and *American Beauty* (1999, Academy Award).

HARRY DEAN STANTON: Actor, b. Kentucky, 1926. Credits include *Pat Garrett and Billy The Kid* (1972), *The Missouri Breaks* (1976), *Wiseblood* (1979), *Repo Man* (1983), *Paris, Texas* (1984), *The Last Temptation of Christ* (1988), *She's So Lovely* (1997), and *The Pledge* (2001).

DAVID SUCHET: Film, TV and stage actor, b. London, 1946. Credits include *Oppenheimer* (TV, 1980), *Freud* (TV, 1984), *The Falcon and the Snowman* (1985), *A World Apart* (1988), and *Poirot* (TV, 1989–)

JOHN SYKES: Cable television executive, friend of Sean Penn since 1985. Head of Programming at MTV (Music Television), later chief executive of VH-1, then CEO of Infinity Broadcasting.

CAMERON THOR: Acting teacher and film/TV actor, founder of the Carter Thor Studio in Los Angeles. Directed Sean Penn in *Terrible Jim Fitch* (1979).

LARS ULRICH: Drummer, songwriter with Metallica, b. Gentofte, Denmark, 1963. Albums include *Kill 'Em All* (1983), *And Justice For All . . .* (1988), *Metallica* (1991), *Load* (1996) and *St. Anger* (2003).

THOMAS VINTERBERG: Director, b. Copenhagen, Denmark, 1969. Co-wrote and directed *The Biggest Heroes* (1996), *Festen/The Celebration* (1998, Jury Prize, Cannes), *It's All About Love* (2003) and *Dear Wendy* (2004).

JOSEPH VITARELLI: Composer, b. New York, 1960. Befriended Sean Penn at Santa Monica High School, 1977. Film scores include *The Last Seduction* (1994), *The Substance of Fire* (1996), *She's So Lovely* (1997), and *And Starring Pancho Villa As Himself* (TV, 2003).

CHRISTOPHER WALKEN: Actor, b. Queens, New York, 1943. Roles include *The Deer Hunter* (1978, Academy Award), *Pennies From Heaven* (1981), *The Dead Zone* (1983), *At Close Range* (1986), *The Comfort of Strangers* (1990), *The Funeral* (1996), and *Catch Me If You Can* (2002).

ART WOLFF: Theatre and television director, b. 1938. Directed Sean Penn in *Heartland* on Broadway in 1981. TV directorial credits include *It's Garry Shandling's Show*, *Penn and Teller's Cruel Tricks for Dear Friends*, *The Wonder Years*, *Dream On*, and *Grace Under Fire*.

DONNA WOLFF: Wife of Art Wolff.

ROBIN WRIGHT PENN: Actress, b. Dallas, Texas, 1966. Married Sean Penn in April 1996. Leading roles include *The Princess Bride* (1987), *Loon* (1988), *State of Grace* (1990), *Forrest Gump* (1994), *Loved* (1997), *She's So Lovely* (1997), *Hurlyburly* (1998), *The Singing Detective* (2003), and *The Last Face* (pre-production, 2004).

Fade In . . .

1 Sean Penn on location for *The Indian Runner*, 1990

ANJELICA HUSTON: Everything has kind of gone retro lately: it's like we all have this idea of what a 'diva' is, as opposed to what the word used to mean. And, in a way, everything is devalued by that. Our heroes – at least, the ones I look up to – are people who went before me. It's hard to be a legend in these times. And I think Sean *deserves* to be a legend, you know?

I remember when Sean became a fixture on the LA landscape: there was a moment where he and Charles Bukowski were hanging out. And I think I thought then that it was a pity, in a way, that Sean had been born after his proper time – that maybe he should have been born a bit earlier, say, the early to late forties; that he missed out on a moment that was more receptive to exploration, or a certain sort of breakthrough. You know the book *Rock Dreams*?[1] I kind of see Sean in that book: that's my emotional visual place for him, the particular heroic of that moment, the fifties and sixties. I see Sean with Kerouac or the young Bob Dylan. But I don't really see him in corporate America, 2004.

MEEGAN OCHS: My father died at thirty-five: many people live much longer lives with much less experience in them. But Sean has definitely lived an incredible life already. He's never ever said to me, or to anyone as far as I know, 'Don't talk about me.' But I think there is a tremendous feeling of protection among everyone who loves him, because he's been so misperceived by the press.

JERRY HANNAN: Before I met Sean? I don't subscribe much to pop culture and I hadn't seen many of his movies, but I knew what I'd read in the tabloids – that he's a prick, right? Going out with Madonna and punching cameramen . . .

WOODY HARRELSON: One time me and Sean were hanging out, he was talking about the public, and he said, 'The thing is, they love you no matter what you do. But they *hate* me.' I kind of disagreed with that . . . And I think Sean still feels tied to some stuff, just because the press coloured him as 'the bad boy' years ago. But whatever made him say that, I always felt that whatever qualities made him the bad boy – and [*laughs*] he certainly had some that I can see would contribute to that – I always resonated with *all* of them . . .

---

1 Fantasy-tribute to the legends of rock 'n' roll and R&B, drawn by Guy Peellaert with text by Nik Cohn, first published in 1973.

DENNIS FANNING: Sean don't just talk the talk, he walks the walk: I've been there. I don't know if he ever got his ass kicked . . . but I know that when he finds things offensive, when trying to get a consensus through intellectual or verbal means don't work – he don't mind throwing a punch.

DAVID MORSE: Sean acquired a reputation as a fighter early on, but what he fights for is so much deeper and more interesting than what people think. He fights for the kind of stories he wants to tell and the characters he wants to play, but also for the kind of life he wants to lead. He has a vision about his life and about the work he does, and he doesn't let many things stand in the way of that.

ART WOLFF: There may be people who dislike Sean. I think people get upset in the business, because they think you're not supposed to bite the hand that feeds you. I don't know where it says that. I've never met anyone on any of Sean's sets who had a problem with him: his crews all seem to really enjoy him. But there are producers and development executives who think he's a royal pain in the ass. And why? Because he won't be bullshitted.

JAMES FOLEY: That's the key thing about Sean, that he's done 'consequences be damned'. And, certainly, anybody of lesser talent with that attitude would be gone and buried in Hollywood by now.

ALEJANDRO GONZÁLEZ IÑÁRRITU: There is one quality that defines him, which is integrity. Integrity, because there is congruence in what he thinks and what he does and what he expresses. You can like it or not, but that's *very* difficult to find nowadays in this industry. And in this world.

ROBIN WRIGHT PENN: If I had to pick one – loyalty. It's how I would define Sean. He's loyal. To people, to his word. And he expects that of you.

GARRY SHANDLING: 'Courageous, courageous, courageous.' That's what'll be on his gravestone. Why three times? Because he's *more* than courageous, in my eyes. He's a man on fire. Like a flame. And I'm one of the moths . . .

ART LINSON: The best actor of his generation. Period. No contest. There is nobody as good. If you look at the myriad of roles that are so different and so extraordinary – the range becomes frightening, actually.

CHRISTOPHER WALKEN: You know, the Elizabethans called the profession of acting 'the mystery', and there's a lot to be said for that. I know that good actors very rarely talk about it. There's very little shop-talk, I guess . . .

BENICIO DEL TORO: I'll say this – it's good to have secrets. I've never really sat down with Sean to talk about acting choices. I think we'd be bored to death . . . But we can talk about *other* actors: Jack Nicholson, Christopher Walken. De Niro, Pacino. Jon Voight. Marlon Brando. Harry Dean Stanton. Because Sean really, truly understands and loves actors. And I think he really cares about acting – not just his own acting, but acting as a form of expression.

BOBBY COOPER: Robin will say to me, 'Coop, he's got no fear.' And it's true, that's why he's a great actor. No fear of trying something, no fear of failure. The average guy will say, 'I can't do that, I'll look like an asshole.' Sean's like, 'Call me Mr Anus.' And he'll just go for it.

DAVID RABE: The truth is, Sean in many ways is a character actor. It's an extreme version, say, in *I Am Sam*, or Meserve in *Casualties of War*. But then he can be a character actor in *Hurlyburly* where he just looks like himself and doesn't have any particular gimmicks. He has to have a slant on the part that separates it from himself in some way. And then his imagination takes over, and he's free.

KEVIN SPACEY: On the one hand, you know – acting, it's not bricklaying. But every time Sean puts himself on screen, he's giving a part of himself, and I find it brave – brave, in actors who are not interested in presenting an image but in serving a writer and understanding what the function of a character is in a piece.

SUSAN SARANDON: I mean, if you trace the evolution of Sean's acting career just in hairdos *alone*, you'll see that he's pretty brave and out there. I don't really know anybody else apart from Cher who's done so much to their hair as Sean has. So, clearly, he's willing to sacrifice his ego and his vanity in order to jump into a character . . . I think Sean came under the wing and the tutelage of Nicholson certainly early on and was exposed to Brando – those people who have always been on the edge, never worried about whether they were *liked* or not, and had a great sense of irony and humour, all of which is there too in Sean's work, if you look. And I think those are the cornerstones for any actor who's, first, going to have a long career, and then also an interesting one.

DENNIS HOPPER: Sean's a terrific storyteller, has a wonderful gift for the gab – in that respect, he reminds me a lot of Jack. And it's just a pleasure to be around those guys, because they've always got a tale to tell and a song to sing.

JACK NICHOLSON: When you've known someone for a long time and you're both sort of *lively* . . . Sean and I can have a good time together, no doubt about that. I remember when we were scouting for *The Pledge*, I got up the next morning for breakfast and there was Sean asleep under the piano. I thought, 'Here's another reason we get along. Another Irishman who don't wanna get up in the morning . . .'

DAVID RABE: The real thing about Sean, the guy I've known and admired, is that he has an appetite for life. That's kind of a cliché, but then I don't mean it in the normal way: he has an incredible interest, and a willingness, to take the risks that are involved in learning about something or knowing somebody or having this or that kind of friend.

TIM ROBBINS: You know, it's always interesting if Sean calls up and says, 'Hey, I'm at this restaurant. You want to come over?' *Always* interesting, to see the diversity of the people at the table with him once you get there . . . It's part of the adventure, right?

JOHN SYKES: Sean can sit down with Steven Spielberg and Dustin Hoffman and a studio head and talk about a major motion picture at five in the afternoon; then at two in the morning he's holding court with Hell's Angels and some cops at a club in downtown LA. But he can walk both sides of the fence.

CAMERON THOR: Sean has that underlying quality of 'I won't live another minute unless I'm exciting myself and everybody around me . . .' And actors who aren't on the margin of their experience are wasting everybody's time. Sean's a great actor, but he's even better at getting your attention. Like when he went to Iraq – I thought, 'Of *course* Sean would go to Iraq. What else would make things go jiggedy-jiggedy . . .?'

ALEJANDRO GONZÁLEZ IÑÁRRITU: What I love about Sean is that he is kind of the last outsider in his country, you know? He can understand America from a very good perspective because he knows other countries and other cultures, and he honours the differences, and likes them. So he can criticize his country so precisely.

BONO: The first thing that strikes you about Sean is – he's very funny. The second is a sort of relentless intellectual curiosity. He gangs up on a subject. So then he *knows* more than you, about what you're talking about. Which is . . . annoying, if, say, it's music. Or politics. Or your wife. But he's sharp. And you will cut yourself.

MEEGAN OCHS: Sean was always very intrigued by politics, much more so than his public persona would have suggested. He did do things over the years: during the LA riots, or when Geronimo Pratt asked him to go down to Alabama, he stood up and said his opinions. But he wasn't one of those actors who get totally identified with their activism. I think he's always been selective about when he's stood up, because he wanted to be effective when he did it.

DAVID BAERWALD: I'd call Sean an old-fashioned unsentimental leftist. I think he's also of the 'Where are we going? And why are we in this hand-basket? And why is it getting so hot?' Party. He's a Roosevelt Democrat, I'd say, and a decent person who hates seeing people suffer unnecessarily.

DR KATZ: I've seen Sean talk to studio heads and heads of *state*. I've known three people who are brilliant like him. And all of them, they're brilliant in ninety-nine different ways – but when it comes to women, the domestic thing, they're worse than I am, Jesus Christ . . .

HELENA KATZ: Sean and Robin are the best thing that ever happened to each other. It just took them a long time to realize that.

ELIZABETH MCGOVERN: He was a guy who grew up on sets, with a father and mother who were both professionals in the business. I don't know if that has anything to do with it, or whether it's the fact he has this particular kind of . . . genius. Because, god knows, there are enough guys who grow up around movie sets and can't do *anything* of what they want to do.

DON PHILLIPS: Sean is a crazy mixture, in that Eileen is Irish and Leo was Jewish. What a combination! I don't know if the world truly understands what that's like. You wake up in the morning and you don't know whether to *sell* something or *steal* something. The irony

is that Leo was more like an Irishman, while Eileen was very protective and nurturing, more like the Jewish-mother type. So I just
think some kind of reversal happened . . . What I love about the Penns
is that I think it was instilled in them at a very early age how strong
the family is. Sean roots for his brothers Chris and Michael more than
you could imagine: he's their biggest fan, and vice versa. Eileen is in
The Indian Runner and *The Crossing Guard* and *The Pledge*. I don't
think I'd put *my* mother in a movie . . . And that's what I think
attracted Sean to Bruce Springsteen's song 'Highway Patrolman'.
Like the song says, 'Nothin' feels better than blood on blood.' And
that's Sean's credo.

BONO: You always got a sense from Sean of a resentment of the plate-
glass life – that he wanted to smash that, and screw the air-conditioning,
and walk on the other side. He liked Irish people, liked a row, liked to
drink . . . and there's that Irish melancholy that he shouldn't have, but
has. It doesn't rain in Los Angeles, so I don't know where he got it
from. But I think that's why he leans towards those characters on the
fringe, who have that blue note. He's not a gospel singer, that's for
sure. You're talking Robert Johnson here. And how that devil got a
hold of his heel, I'll never know . . .

ART WOLFF: Sean is well brought up, in the best sense of the term, by
good folks. If you dig deeper, in terms of where Sean's stuff comes
from . . . his father was blacklisted. And that had a real effect on him,
much more than I've ever seen written about. I think it manifested
itself, for one, in an enormous respect for his father's integrity – that
his dad was a stand-up guy, a real American. And part of why Sean has
a jones about Hollywood is because of the way his father was treated,
and then their pretending it never happened.

JOSEPH VITARELLI: Leo was a remarkable man: a decorated war hero,
flew numerous missions over Germany. This man survived unbelievable
shit. Then he comes back to the United States, and he's blacklisted. What
could be more offensive than that? How does that happen? As it was, he
was a brilliant stage actor, he became an enormously successful television
director, he directed *everything*. He raised three really smart boys, stayed
married to Eileen for forty-one years, built a beautiful estate out in
Malibu. But you have to wonder what would have happened had Leo
Penn not been blacklisted. Who knows what he could have done?

ONE

Leo & Eileen

2 Leo Penn

EILEEN RYAN PENN: I'm half-Irish, half-Italian, I'm a practising Catholic, I was married to a non-practising Jew for forty-one years, and I'd have been married to him until the day I died, except he died before me. We adored each other, we had a great marriage.

The original family name on Leo's side was Piñon: it means 'nut' in Spanish, so there had to be some Spanish in the family, way, *way* back. But they were Russian Jews: Leo's mother was a Russian Jew, his father was a Lithuanian Jew, and they're practically the same country. So Sean is Russian–Jewish/Irish–Italian–Catholic.

Leo's father, Maurice – 'Poppa', my kids' grandfather – came to the United States when he was fourteen, his sixteen-year-old brother brought him over from Russia. They asked for his name at Ellis Island, he said, 'Piñon,' with his accent, and they said, '*What?* OK, Penn.' I wish they'd kept Piñon, it's a pretty name. I would have preferred it to Penn. But then Sean's made it mean something. 'Sean Piñon' would have been very different . . .

Between the two of them, those two young boys brought their whole family over. Maurice never got an education, but he worked to put his brothers and sisters through school, and they were all pretty successful. His sister Sonia got degrees and PhDs, and she became a very successful psychoanalyst in New York. But Maurice was basically working in orange fields until he managed to get his own bakery.

Leo was born in Lawrence, Massachusetts, 27 August 1921. He was an only child. Leo's grandmother was the matriarch – she was a horror, I guess. Leo told me how his father took him to the circus as a boy, on one of the big holidays when you're supposed to fast, and Poppa bought Leo an egg-salad sandwich. He comes back and the grandmother says, 'Oh, Leo, you must be hungry. Now we can eat, the fast is over.' Leo says, 'I'm not hungry, Grandma! I had a sandwich!' Well, she wouldn't talk to her own son-in-law for years after. They'd sit at the same table and she'd say, 'Tell *him* to pass the salt.' So that's what *she* was like: a tough cookie. But she was involved with theatre, and she loved theatrical people, so the genes go back there on that side.

SEAN PENN: I have my dad telling this story on tape. About two years before he died, he spoke to Women in Film [WIF], and they taped it for public-access television. On Father's Day every year, I show my kids ten minutes of it, because it's very much the him they remember. To keep that memory alive . . . once a year, ten minutes.

LEO PENN (WIF recording): My grandmother owned a dry goods store in Lawrence, Massachusetts, and she also wrote one-act plays – in Yiddish. And I was drafted to be in one of her plays. She was also a devout socialist, so you can imagine what the content of that play was . . . I was four, maybe five – I had a pistol in my hand, and my line in Yiddish was, 'Der volk zenen vild, sie missen essen,' meaning, 'The people are wild, and they have to eat.' I think that conditioned a lot of my personality since . . .

SEAN PENN: My dad stayed in Massachusetts with his mother, and my grandfather came to Los Angeles to make money to bring his family out and start a life for them. East Los Angeles was all orange groves then: right below City Terrace was the start of it, and it just went on for ever. And he squeezed oranges for a year to make the money to get a roof over their heads and get them out on a bus.

LEO PENN (WIF recording): I'll never forget that trip. That had a large impact on my life, because it was so joyous. This was during the Depression, when the gap between rich and poor was not what it was now: we were all in the same boat, and we all had a blast on that Greyhound bus – people playing guitars and singing songs and relating to one another, liking one another . . .

First house we moved to was in East Los Angeles – dirt road, barbed wire, and thousands and thousands of acres of open range: cows, horses, screes, caves. And in twenty-four hours I went from being a tenement kid to Huckleberry Finn . . .

My father was an extraordinary man: very quiet, gentle, sweet man, who was a news nut. And he was a socialist. But we used to argue all the time, because I was much more radical than he was – and, of course, he was right and I was wrong . . . He loved this country. But he was terrified about taking the exam to become a citizen . . . And he was on the Attorney-General's List, because, as a young man, he was a member of the International Workers' Organisation.

SEAN PENN: My grandfather started a leather shop, and that went all right for a little while. And then he wound up opening a bakery of his own on what used to be Brooklyn Avenue in East Los Angeles, which was largely a Jewish area at the time. My dad grew up in the last of that. By the time I was born and visiting there, they were the *only* Jews in the area; it was all Hispanic already. But my grandparents stayed there while everyone else moved out.

EILEEN RYAN PENN: How did Leo get the acting bug? His grandmother, I guess, was always enamoured of acting. And he had an uncle who ran a movie theatre in Massachusetts. But then how did *I* get the acting bug? My father was a dentist . . .

LEO PENN (WIF recording): I had a unique gift, for mimicry. And so, when I was playing ball, I was the shower-room clown, I could make everybody laugh. But then when I got hurt, I didn't know what to do with my energy or my time, and there was a man – his name was Ernest Wennig – and he did plays with the Dramatic Society at Lincoln High School. And there followed a series of misadventures.

The first thing was in a Community Chest project, and I was playing a doctor, because there was a lot of tuberculosis going on at the time, and people had to be made aware. And there I was on a stage, and I had a stethoscope and I had to listen to somebody's heartbeat. And everybody laughed, and I didn't know why – I thought I was wonderful. But I forgot to put the things in my ears . . .

Then we had Lincoln's birthday, and I was John Wilkes Booth. I had this cap-pistol, there was Lincoln sitting there, and I had to shoot him. And the damn thing wouldn't go off. So I clubbed him to death, and changed the course of history . . .

Then I went to UCLA. It had no drama department, no film department – just the University Dramatic Society. There was one man there, his name was Ralph Freud, after whom one of the auditoriums is named now. Ralph Freud came from the Pasadena Playhouse; he was a wonderfully gifted actor himself, and he taught some courses and he managed the University Dramatic Society. And it was a wondrous time. But I never, even then, never once thought that I would want to become a professional: I really didn't know what I wanted to do – maybe come back and teach at UCLA. And then I went to war, and I was away for four years.

CHRISTOPHER PENN: Dad was in the Eighth Air Force, stationed in England, on the coast. And he flew thirty-one missions with the Eighth.[1]

EILEEN RYAN PENN: Myron McNamara was the captain on all those missions, and Leo always said the reason he came back alive was because of Myron. When he became ill, he started writing a lot about it – his experiences, and the friends he had there. But before, he didn't want to think about the past too much.

SEAN PENN: I think my dad was a pretty classic World War II veteran: I wouldn't say 'stoic' on the issue but . . . he had about ten years of hardcore flashbacks and sleeplessness, and using things to stay awake and things to go to sleep; and then the nightmares that were probably enhanced by those pharmaceuticals. Because there was nobody who really knew how to deal with all that stuff. He was a tail-gunner and a bombardier. And as a tail-gunner, you saw the face of your enemy:

1 Leo was attached to the 458th Bomb Group, 755th squadron, and assigned to Horsham St Faiths, Norfolk, on April 12th 1944. He would receive the Distinguished Flying Cross for his service.

you waited for them to get in range, they came right up to you. And so you saw the devastation of the rounds at the end of your gun. That was a big thing for him.

Courtesy of Sean Penn

3 755th Squadron, 458th Bomb Group, US Eighth Air Force: Leo Penn, standing, second from right

LEO PENN (WIF recording): Came back on overseas leave – I was invited to do a play at UCLA, and Ralph Freud directed it. I played a fella my age now . . . it went very well and suddenly I was getting phone calls from agents. 'Jesus, is it possible to turn this into a profession, to live by?' And suddenly I had a call from Paramount Pictures – war was still going on – would I be interested in doing a screen test? Why not? And to my amazement, they put me under contract. There was nothing I could do, 'cause this was while I was on overseas leave. I then had to go to Midland, Texas, to become an instructor in dead-reckoning navigation – to Chinese cadets, some French cadets, and always through an interpreter – in the air. And I thought I would go quite mad . . .

I spent the last part of the war at the Air Force Motion Picture Unit, which was the most hilarious time I've ever spent in my life. You had

all these actors – Lee Cobb, Ronald Reagan – who hadn't gone overseas, they hadn't done a goddamn thing except make training films,
and they'd get pissed off if the Navy was doing a training film at
MGM and they weren't sent there on loan-out. They were so frustrated about getting on with their careers . . .

I figured, 'Well, I think I'll hang out around this business.' And I did.
And life was very rosy for a while. For my first few years as an actor, I
worked in the theatre at night. Also at the time I had a soap opera on
the radio. And now I was under contract to a B-movie company called
Monogram. I did one picture.[2] They didn't like my name and I refused
to change it. I thought 'Penn' was perfectly fine so I changed my first
name to Clifford, 'cause I liked Clifford Odets. They didn't like
Clifford 'cause they said he was a communist . . .

*Conservatives are fond of quipping that, while there may have been no
witches in Salem in 1692, there were undoubtedly communists in
Hollywood in 1947. Many Party members, such as the screenwriters
Albert Maltz and John Howard Lawson, were indeed of a mind that
the Party then constituted 'the best hope for mankind'. But in that
extraordinary post-war moment, there were perhaps a greater number
of enthusiasts for simple social welfare than there were apologists for
the crimes of Stalin. The degree to which this stew of reforming
instincts constituted a subversive threat to the United States is debat-
able; but the 'Red Scare' that then erupted made a wreck of umpteen
livelihoods, including that of Leo Penn.*

EILEEN RYAN PENN: It was all brought back to me when Jeff Corey died
in 2002, and I went to his testimonial. Jeff was often at our house in
Malibu: Point Dume is full of people who were blacklisted. Jeff was
actually a member of the Party, but even the ones who were card-carrying like Jeff . . . He didn't believe in the Party after a while. It was an
idealistic thing. And Leo was never a card-carrying communist; he was
a Democrat, all his life. He was just lumped with everybody else
because he went to some meetings and was interested in what they had
to say. Not that he didn't agree with some of it . . . And I guess
Franklin Delano Roosevelt would have been called a communist:
social security was very communistic . . .

2 *Fall Guy* (1947), directed by Reginald Le Borg, adapted from Cornell Woolrich's story
'Cocaine'.

LEO PENN (WIF recording): God, it was simple – all you had to do was shuffle the wealth around a little bit. Whatever's fair, you know? Living wage, people have a right to have a house, enough to eat. What's so difficult about that? Oh-ho-ho . . .

The US government established a House Un-American Activities Committee in 1938 as a watchdog of subversive tendencies among the citizenry, under the chairmanship of Martin Dies. After the war, it became a permanent congressional body under John E. Rankin. In May 1947, a sub-committee headed by Rep. J. Parnell Thomas landed in Hollywood to investigate suspected 'communist infiltration' of the film industry. Republicans had gained control of the House in 1946, and many of them disdained Hollywood's fairly recent progression to unionization and guilds, redolent of Roosevelt's socialistic 'New Deal'. (Leo Penn, as it happened, belonged to the Screen Actors' Guild, the American Federation of Radio Artists, and the Actors' Equity Association.) Studio bosses were no happier about organized labour, and Rep. Thomas found 'friendly witnesses' easy to come by, from Walt Disney to Jack Warner.

Thomas called forty-five industry people in all, and an 'unfriendly nineteen' announced they would not co-operate: among them, Alvah Bessie, Herbert Biberman, Lester Cole, Edward Dmytryk, Ring Lardner Jr, John Howard Lawson, Albert Maltz, Samuel Ornitz, Adrien Scott and Dalton Trumbo.

Philip Dunne, William Wyler, John Huston and Alexander Knox then formed a Committee for the First Amendment to challenge HUAC's blunt question 'Are you now or have you ever been a member of the Communist Party?' as being 'disloyal to both the spirit and the letter of the Constitution'.

HUAC narrowed its investigation from nineteen to the ten named above. On Monday, 28 October, the members of the 'Hollywood Ten' took the chair, one by one, pleaded the Fifth Amendment, and were angrily dismissed.

The following Monday, a progressive actors' group took a full-page ad in the Hollywood Reporter, *entitled 'The Thomas–Rankin Committee Must Go!', expressing solidarity with 'the Washington protests against the star chamber and others who broadcast their indignation . . . We are proud that they are upholding the finest traditions of our profession and our country.' Concurrent with HUAC, a*

California Legislative Committee under Jack Tenney was also involved in the hunt for 'subversives', and Tenney's fourth official report of March 1948 noted the names of all signatories to that advertisement, including Leo Penn.

On 24 November 1947, *the Ten were cited for contempt of Congress. The next day, the heads of the major studios assembled at the Waldorf Astoria hotel in New York and issued a joint statement, saying of the Ten, 'their actions have been a disservice to their employers and have impaired their usefulness to the industry'. The studios now pledged to refuse employment to communists, and one by one the Ten were either fired or suspended without pay. Subsequently indicted on the contempt charge, eight were then sentenced to a year's imprisonment, the other two to six months.*

Leo Penn was also tainted by his association as an occasional performer with the socially conscientious Actors Laboratory Theatre of Los Angeles, traduced by the FBI as little better than a communist cell. The 'Actors Lab' was founded in 1941 largely by members of the Group Theatre,[3] with the avowed purpose of organizing entertainment for WWII servicemen. But many of its members had broader social interests. In October 1945, some joined the picketing of Warner Bros during a strike of skilled labour by the Conference of Studio Unions, which led to a studio lock-out. On 9 November 1945, the Hollywood Reporter *declared the Lab to be 'as red as a burlesque queen's garters'. In February 1948, the Lab premièred a new play entitled* Declaration, *which drew comparisons between the HUAC investigation and the Alien and Sedition Acts of 1798. Later that year, the IRS revoked the Lab's tax-exempt status, and its funding for veteran training was withdrawn the next. It closed shortly thereafter.*

By 1949, lists of alleged 'pinkos' in the acting profession were being compiled with extra-zealous help from American Legion publications Firing Line *and* Legion, *and the anonymously edited* Counterattack *and* Red Channels *put out by American Business Consultants. These became bibles to the radio and fledgling TV industries, and a blacklist mushroomed into being: any imagined 'Red sympathizer' contaminated as a 'Red front' any organization to which he or she belonged, and all its fellow members were henceforward considered Red by association. This circuitous route made for a ludicrously large and supposedly*

---

3 Founded in New York by Lee Strasberg, Harold Clurman, and Cheryl Crawford.

sinister cabal. But certain ex-Communists, whether as a skin-saving exercise or a belated repudiation of the Hitler–Stalin Pact, would 'name names' of other sinners and were themselves saved: perhaps most prominently, in 1952, the director Elia Kazan.

EILEEN RYAN PENN: The names were definitely listed for all the agents. 'You wanna work? You don't put *this* one up.' So they were all disenfranchised.

LEO PENN (WIF recording): To my knowledge, nobody named my name. But I know why I was blacklisted . . . There would be these meetings concerning the Hollywood Ten, and Albert Maltz, Dalton Trumbo, various people would speak at these meetings. They would try to get 'names' – well, every once in a while, a 'name' would drop out. And I'd get the phone call: 'Will you speak?' And I did. So I sometimes shared a podium with all these people . . .

© Emerald Productions, Inc

4 Leo Penn (Steve) and Sally Forrest (Sally) in
Not Wanted (1949, dir. Ida Lupino)

Then I did a movie for the best director I ever worked with in film, whose name was Ida Lupino . . . a film called *Not Wanted*.4 Ida was a considerable person, and way ahead of her time, and fell victim, I think . . . to a kind of prevailing male chauvinism . . .

4 Lupino co-wrote this 1949 drama of lonely single motherhood with Paul Jarrico. Penn is a hip, coldly charming piano player for whom Sally Forrest falls, the source of her subsequent woes . . .

Then I was cast opposite Gregory Peck in a film called *The Gunfighter*. And I never got to do it. Because before we went to start shooting, I had a phone call from a friend who was at their last production meeting and said, 'Leo, I don't know how to tell you this, but, uh, one of the guys there said, "What are we doing? Why are we hiring this dirty little Red?" So you're not going to do the picture.'

So I was blacklisted. Here, in California. This was before it had spread all over the place. My agent at the time said, 'Don't fight it, don't try to get your money' – because the deal had been made – 'because it's gonna spread like wildfire. Get your ass to New York.'

EILEEN RYAN PENN: I think Ronald Reagan had a lot to do with Leo's blacklisting, as I understand. Leo always hated Ronald Reagan.[5] He had a meeting with Reagan, and Reagan really put the final stamp on Leo.

Photo by Charles Caron

5 Eileen Ryan

EILEEN RYAN PENN: I was born 16 October 1927. My maiden name is Annucci, but my mother's maiden name was Ryan, so when I act I'm Eileen Ryan. When I paint, I'm Annucci – the Italian is for the paint-

5 Reagan was President of the Screen Actors Guild from 1947 until 1960.

ing, the Irish is for the acting. I also sold a screenplay once, and for that I was Eileen Ryan Penn. So I have quite a few a.k.a.'s . . .

My grandparents were immigrants. My father was born Amerigo Giuseppe Annucci, but he didn't use any of that: he called himself 'Bill' or 'A. William'. And DDS after his name, because he was a dentist. He always wanted to practise law, but the Depression hit just after he passed the bar, and he had three kids. And back then, people didn't need lawyers as they do today, but they did need to get their teeth fixed.

My mother was Rose Isabel Ryan. She came from a farm in Flatsburgh, upstate New York, and at sixteen she was the teacher for the whole town in a little red school house. The only way to get out of there and come to the city was to be a secretary or a registered nurse. So she came as a nurse, and somewhere she met my father.

I'm the middle of three girls: my younger sister was Joan, my older sister Virginia. I think I knew I wanted to be an actress from about the time I was four. I was always dressing up and being theatrical. My sisters, especially Virginia, had no patience with me at all. They'd all be in the car ready to go on a long trip and I'm still putting on lipstick or a feather boa or a hat that was too big for me. Then I'd be sent back in the house: 'You can't wear *that*! Dad, she's not gonna wear *that*, is she . . .?'

Starting from my last year in high school, I did eight seasons of equity theatre summer stock. It was a great training, because you were working in a play at night after all day long rehearsing one for the following week. You learn your lines fast, I can tell you that. I loved it. A lot of different companies and places. So, every summer I was acting, and my father was always there with flowers and gifts, very proud of me being up onstage. I don't think my mother ever saw me do anything. My father was creative: he could draw, he had a beautiful singing voice – he had that side of the brain. But my mother, she was Irish and very practical, and to her, being an actress was about one step down from being a whore. Right after high school, I took a test to qualify as a registered nurse. Not only did I pass, out of 10,000 people who took it, I was in the top ten. And I told my mother, 'OK, I've shown you I could be a nurse, but I'm going to go to NYU, I'm going to take all of the Drama courses, and I'm going to be an actress.'

I was seventeen when I went in, in 1945. We had to get our Bachelor of Science degrees because our professor wanted his actors to have a broad education. But I did plays there: I played *Miss Julie* and shocked the hell out of the audience. The teacher who put it up and rehearsed it with us was fired. All the symbolic stuff in the dialogue, sexual and violent: I guess it was pretty shocking. I heard some of these teachers in the audience saying, 'Oh my god . . .!' But I thought it was wonderful.

I got my degree in 1949. I was twenty-one, and I went straight into a stock company at Keesler Airbase. That was hilarious. Carol, the ingénue, and I were the only girls there, both very pretty at the time. So we had to take four or five airmen on each arm every time we went out at night. All the guys would say, 'You can't just date *one* . . .'

Then she and I went to New Orleans, which is close to Biloxi. So exciting. I'd just been a college girl, studying. Now we looked at each other and we said, 'Yeah, we gotta stay here just a little bit . . .' We got an apartment in the French Quarter, and I sang in a club, the Hotel Roosevelt. Carol got me that by telling the owner that I was better than the girl they had. But then I was supporting the two of us. Finally I had to say, 'You know what? This was a lark, but I'm not staying.' 'Oh no, no, no!' she said. 'You can't go! How am I going to survive?' I said, 'I'm sorry, Carol, I'm going back to New York to be an actress.' And I don't know what ever happened to Carol . . .

So I got back to New York and started taking classes with Lee Strasberg.[6] I was studying voice and ballet and working two different jobs. And my poor daddy, he wanted to help me but I wouldn't take five cents. I was living in a cold-water apartment, and I would always meet him outside for lunch so he wouldn't know.

There were people who just stayed in Lee's class for ever. It was like, if you didn't have religion, Lee became your god – pathetic, some of them. But the sense memories were terrific, and I still use them when I work. It doesn't matter what sense memory you use – it could be the opposite emotion, the other actor doesn't know – as long as you know it's giving you the look that the audience can interpret. I was playing Masha in *Three Sisters*, in a scene with a radio actor playing Vershinin. I looked at him, and tears and love and life came to my eyes as I said the lines. And I was thinking, 'You are *such* a terrible actor, it's unbelievable . . .' I did the same thing years later with Chris Walken in *At Close Range* for a scene where I'm staring at him. Chris said to Sean afterwards, 'Your mother scares me. She looks at me like she

6 In 1948 Strasberg became Artistic Director of the Actors Studio, recently founded by Cheryl Crawford, Elia Kazan and Robert Lewis.

hates me.' You know what I was using? 'Oh God, he's so sexy. If I was thirty years younger? Oh boy . . .' That's sense memory. And that's what Lee's classes did for me.

Right away I got work, I did some live television. Then I started doing a lot of off-Broadway and Broadway. My first Broadway play was *Sing Till Tomorrow*,[7] and all I wanted was to see my name up in lights, above the title, which I did. But the play was so bad, you couldn't even understand what it was about. Angela Lansbury was coming out of the star dressing-room when I was walking in. She said, 'Oh, darling, I hope you'll be more successful than we were . . .' I'm thinking, 'If you were doing *dog-shit* up there we'd still be worse than you . . .' Brooks Atkinson was the most famous critic of the time. I remember he wrote, 'If Eileen Ryan could read, memorize and subsequently deliver the lines in *Sing Till Tomorrow*, she could probably do the same with a telephone book . . .' But I had a lot of wonderful experiences, particularly off-Broadway. It's funny – in 2000 I did *Arliss* with Ed Asner, and when we were introduced, he looked at me and said, 'You're introducing me to Eileen *Ryan*? She was the Queen of off-Broadway!' And there was this time in the fifties when I was doing all the leads. I played a lot of Russians for an Irish–Italian girl: Masha in *Three Sisters*,[8] Grushenka in *The Brothers Karamazov*.[9] I also did Blanche Dubois in *A Streetcar Named Desire* at Princeton in 1957, with Peter Falk. Art Wolff is one of the few people who saw me, and I always like running into Art because he remembers that performance of mine. It's nice to have someone *alive* who saw it.

ART WOLFF: I was nineteen, in college, but home for the summer, working. I had been in high school with Suzanne Pleshette, and she told me she was playing Stella in *Streetcar* with the University Players, the group that goes all the way back to Henry Fonda. So I went, for Suzanne. But I was just blown away by Eileen Ryan. She was haunting. I was so impressed by the emotional life she brought to it and the way she handled the language – because that play is not kitchen-sink drama. So I was enamoured by her, and wrote her name down, and thought, 'I'm really gonna watch out for her.' And then she just disappeared . . .

* * *

7 Opened at the Royale Theatre in December 1953.
8 Opened at the Fourth Street Theatre in March 1955.
9 Opened at the Gate Theatre in December 1957.

LEO PENN (WIF recording): So I went to New York. I was one of the lucky ones, because [the blacklist] didn't catch up with me in New York right away, so I was able to do all the live television shows, and I was working in the theatre.[10]

And then it took roughly two years, and I was dead in New York too. So for years I was out of the loop as far as film was concerned. I couldn't do either film or television. And I was lucky enough to be able continually to work in the theatre.[11]

In early April 1954, Penn's own stage play, Flak House, *concerning a group of WWII fliers recuperating in an English country house, was staged at the Neighbourhood Playhouse, directed by Sanford Meisner. The young Sydney Pollack was among the cast. Then Leo had a considerable success in Alfred Hayes'* The Girl on the Via Flaminia, *in which he played Robert, a culpably naive US soldier in post-war Rome who inadvertently condemns an Italian girl to prostitution.*

ART WOLFF: Leo won a Theatre World award for *The Girl on the Via Flaminia*, the Clarence Derwent Award for Most Promising Newcomer, named after an English actor who came to live in America. Still given today . . .

LEO PENN (WIF recording): When things got tough, I started writing, under another name, and was very lucky. Marty Ritt directed me in *Golden Boy* and *View from a Bridge*,[12] and became a very good friend. And Marty was producing a show, and he started buying scripts from me. He bought two of them. I thought, 'Jesus! I never knew I could do this! I could do this!'[13]

EILEEN RYAN PENN: In 1957, I did *The Iceman Cometh* at the Circle on the Square. I was in with Jason Robards as Hickey, and then Leo took over Jason's part.

10 Leo acted in several episodes of NBC's live *Philco Television Playhouse* between 1950 and 1952. In November 1951, he played in Joel Wyman's *Dinosaur Wharf* at the National Theatre.
11 In June 1953, Leo acted in two pieces jointly at the Theatre de Lys in Greenwich Village, playing Charles in Sheridan's *School for Scandal* and a Norwegian sailor in Simon Gantillon's *Maya*.
12 *View from a Bridge* played at The Coronet from September 1955 to February 1956.
13 For the *Studio One* series, Leo wrote an episode entitled 'For the Defence' (tx. 27 June 1955) and an adaptation of *Julius Caesar* (tx. 1 August 1955).

Leo was thirty-six then. I was twenty-nine, going on thirty. I had seen him do several things onstage and thought he was wonderful. But he wasn't aware of me. Before we had our first rehearsal, he was standing on a street corner, talking to a mutual friend from the Actors Studio. This friend called me over and said, 'Eileen! I want you to meet Leo Penn, he's going into your play.' I said, 'Yeah, I heard about that . . .' And I had the nerve to say to him, 'You know, this is a very good thing for you to be doing at this time in your career.' Basically, I was saying, 'You're not a juvenile any more: you *should* be thinking about parts like Hickey.' Well. He hated me on sight. He just thought, 'Who the hell is *that*, to be saying that to me?' I'm still accused of that – with affection. I have a lot of friends who'll say, 'Eileen, we can always count on you to call a spade a spade . . .'

Well, we had one rehearsal. He saw how good I was, called me up that night and asked me out. Two months later, we were living together. So I guess hate turned to love . . .

Leo had been married, ten years before I met him, to Olive Deering. Her brother was Alfred Ryder, and they were all well-known on the Broadway scene, so Leo was married into that family.[14] Now he was separated from Olive and in the process of getting divorced. Leo and Olive never had children – I wouldn't even have dated him had there been any children, because that was my rule.

I was almost thirty, I'd had a lot of relationships, plenty of proposals. One guy was very handsome and tall and rich, which wasn't true of Leo – he was handsome, but short and poor. And Jewish. But the other guy, what he really wanted was a hostess for his parties, somebody to point at – 'Look, she does this and she can do that . . .' And it was clear to me that Leo was right for me. It wasn't only the falling in love, he was just very gentle and good and kind, and he seemed like he'd be such a great daddy. I used to get severe dysmenorrhoea when I had my period. From the time I was thirteen, I'd be hanging over a toilet, terrible pain. And Leo was so sympathetic. I never wanted to see anybody when I was like that; if I'm in pain, I like to go through it alone. But Leo wouldn't take 'No' for an answer – holding my head while I'm puking, even. And I realized, after a while, that this guy really loved me. For all the right reasons.

Leo used to wear chukka boots, and when my mother first met him

14 Deering, née Olive Korn, made her stage début aged fifteen in 1933. She and Leo married after a week's courtship, Leo having gone in Ryder's stead to collect her from an airport.

she said to me, 'Not only are you marrying a Jew, but who ever heard of a poor Jew? What are those shoes he wears? Doesn't he even have money to fix his shoes?' And she said, 'Oh, honey . . . Oil and water. You'll never mix.' Well, we mixed pretty good. And my mother finally fell in love with him.

So I went to see the Bishop of the Archdiocese of New York, and he said, 'OK, he's Jewish, he's divorced, and what else? You can't marry him.' I said, 'Wait! He never got married in a religious ceremony, so you would consider that like having an affair, it's not like a marriage to you.' He said, 'That would be true if *she* was Protestant or Catholic. But she's Jewish like he is, so that's a marriage that lasts for ever.' I said, 'The Jews don't say that, so how can you?' He says, 'Canon law.' He made me so mad that I left the church. And I was away a long time . . .

Leo had no money but he had rich and famous friends – I never figured that out. I guess he was just so charming; and a good actor, of course. Anyhow, he had a friend, Jerry Lurie, a lawyer, who had a penthouse apartment right next door to the Russian Tea Room, and the owner would let Leo eat without paying when he had no money. So we had our wedding in Jerry's apartment, and the Russian Tea Room supplied all the food and booze.

Olive Deering was very strange. She used to call us up to pay for her teeth or something. She had a guilt thing over Leo that he had to take care of her, and the funny thing was that the money at the time was mostly mine because Leo wasn't able to work. But he'd take some of these calls, because she was always saying she was going to commit suicide. After years of her calling us and bothering us about money for this and that, I finally had to say, 'Look, you take one more of her calls and I'm out of here with the kids.' 'But she's gonna jump –' 'So let her jump. Gimme the phone, *I'll* tell her to jump.' She never jumped. It's a kind of pathetic story, the two of them, Olive and Alfred Ryder: they had a horrible mother who treated them as if no one could compare, made them think they were king and queen of all time. I think when you fall from that, it's pretty far.

I had natural childbirth with Michael, my firstborn. 1 August 1958. We'd seen Jean Gabin in a movie about natural childbirth[15] so Leo and I went to the classes. And, of course, there was nothing natural about it – it was twenty-four hours of hard labour. Maybe because I

---

15 *Le Cas du Dr. Laurent* (1958).

was thirty, I don't know . . . The nurses hated me, wanted to knock me out, but I wouldn't take anything, I was so determined. Leo told me, 'You know what you yelled at the end, when the baby was coming? "If it's a girl, push it back in! I'm not going through twenty-four hours of hard labour for any woman!"' And it was so exciting to see a boy come out of me – with his parts, his penis – out of a girl's body. Birth is amazing enough, but this was so powerful. It's funny, I've said this to other women who've had boys and they say, 'My god, I never thought of that.' But I sure did. I only wanted boys. My father was so loving and sweet and good. But he was so protective of us, so worried if I ever did something that he thought was dangerous. So I just wanted boys, who could go out there and do anything they wanted in the world, you know? Girls were limited in what we could do. Even today, there are certain things that they think it's OK for boys to do, but not for girls. Less and less, of course, but still . . .

We were all in one little room in a Village apartment, the baby and us. But Michael was always calm. He would wake up after we'd been up late with friends the night before. I would look over and say, 'Honey, Mommy and Daddy are *so* tired. You go back to sleep . . .?' And he would smile and go back to sleep. But we suffered for those first few months in 1958. The blacklist still affected us, Leo couldn't work, and now we had a little baby. I did *The Verdict Is Yours*[16] five days after giving birth to Michael. We needed the money to pay the hospital bill. No kidding.

The worst part for me was I then had to go off and do a play with George C. Scott, a terrible play called *Comes a Day*.[17] It didn't last, but it made George – he had a great role, very flashy. We were trying it out for six weeks out of town, and Michael was two months old. Leo said, 'You've got the work, you've got to go.' But you can imagine how that felt to a mother with her first baby. After that, I really wanted to quit. The baby didn't suffer – Leo was mother and changed the diapers. And when we finally got into town, it was great, because we now had the money to have a nice apartment about a block from the theatre, 51st Street. I could be with Michael and play with him all day long. Michael I think I brainwashed, because I put my father's guitar in his hand when he was ten months old and pushed his little

16 A daytime courtroom drama show on CBS.
17 Opened at the Ambassador Theatre in November 1958.

fingers onto the strings – I just thought it was fun to do. I look back in retrospect and think that must have always been a comfortable thing for him, that guitar in his arms . . . [18]

LEO PENN (WIF recording): I got really drunk one night and wrote a letter to Frank Stanton[19] at CBS, going into the whole aspect of the blacklist and how it affected me and how dare they? And what the hell was the war all about? What were we fighting for? And probably told some lies, I don't know, about the war record and so on. And I mailed it. And I was astonished to get a reply. They said, 'Come talk to us, we'll set up a meeting.' Well, I didn't talk to them, [but] I went to CBS and I spoke with a fella who dealt with these matters. I had talked to such people before. I had done *Girl on the Via Flaminia*, and the people in New York Columbia wanted to sign me, Harry Cohn said, 'Forget it, forget it! Don't talk to him.' Then they sent somebody to talk to me and would I give names? And I didn't.

In any case, this guy at CBS, he was an air-force veteran just as I was, and he was very sympathetic. And he said, 'Do you know why you're blacklisted?' And I guessed why. He said, 'Let me show you something.' And he pulled out a file, and there was a telegram that had been sent years before from an American Legion post in Chicago. 'Is this Leo Penn who appeared on such-and-such a show, is he the same Leo Penn who spoke at such-and-such a meeting, blah-blah-blah? And if it is, why do you continue to hire him?' And I hadn't worked since that day when that telegram had been received. In any case, I left that office encouraged. That very day, a director friend, Sidney Lumet, called me and said, 'Leo, I got a part for you.' But that was just CBS. Not ABC or NBC. Until I did the movie . . .

EILEEN RYAN PENN: We came out to Los Angeles to show Michael off to Leo's folks; he was ten months old. We stayed with them; we barely could pay for the trip to come out, but they were thrilled. And one night we went out – Leo's mother and father babysat for us. We hadn't been able to do that with Michael at all and now it was like, 'Oh! We're going *out*!' We went to dinner at Frascati on Sunset Strip and ran into Clifford Odets' sister, Florence.

18 Michael Penn's subsequent recordings include the albums *March* (1989), *Free-for-All* (1992), *Resigned* (1997) and *MP4: Days Since a Lost Time Accident* (2000).
19 President of CBS Inc. from 1946 until 1972.

LEO PENN (WIF recording): I hadn't talked to Clifford for maybe eight years, wouldn't talk to him because he spilled his guts in front of the committees . . .[20]

The next morning the phone rang – again, serendipity – and it was Florence Odets. She said, 'Leo, I just had breakfast with Clifford. He wants to know if you'll talk to him.' 'Why? Why would I talk to him?' She said, 'Well, he's written a film at Twentieth Century Fox and he's going to direct it. He wants to know what you look like now, and he thinks there's a part in it for you.' So . . . so much for integrity: I looked at my wife and I said, 'Yeah, I'll talk to him.' And I went to see Clifford, who was very uncomfortable, a lot of hemming and hawing, but I walked out there with a six-week guarantee in a big feature film with Rita Hayworth. And curiously enough, that film broke the blacklist for me: it was called *The Story on Page One*.

EILEEN RYAN PENN: Clifford put him in this picture, and then finally when they edited it he was cut out of it . . . But at least it gave us some money to get going. So we never went back to New York. We set up home in Ben Avenue,[21] North Hollywood, a teeny little house – I think we paid $17,000 for it. I was with the top agent in New York, Peter Witt, and he recommended me to a very good agent in LA called Lillian Small. And I started working. I'd get work, Leo would get work, we'd take turns with the baby. So, finally, things were really working out for Leo.

And then John Frankenheimer called and asked me to do a movie with Burt Lancaster. I told him, 'No, I've quit. And anyway, I'm pregnant with my second baby.' John said, 'That's absolutely perfect for the part. She's *supposed* to be pregnant.' I still said no. Afterwards Leo was really shocked. He said, 'You've been waiting your whole life for this, a big part in a movie. How could you turn it down?' I said, 'Well, *you're* working now . . .'

The fact is, I didn't want to be a 'mommy sometime' and have somebody else raise my kids. I was always a natural mother. And all the passion I had for acting went into being a mother.

---

20 Odets was named by Elia Kazan in April 1952, and duly followed suit in the naming stakes.
21 In the Valley Village district of LA, conveniently close to Universal Studios.

TWO

1960–1978

Bob and I share a birthday. His mother and my own shared the belief that
August 17 is the birthday of gods . . .

Sean Penn, 'AFI Tribute to Robert De Niro', June 2003

EILEEN RYAN PENN: Sean was born 17 August 1960 at St Joseph's in Burbank – that's where the doctor was, but we were still living in our first little house in North Hollywood. With Sean, I gave in to a caudal, where they numb you from the waist down. So, although I was still awake, I wasn't in that terrible pain.

Michael had been easy; he was always calm, could sleep for ever. Everybody said to us, 'Oh my god, that baby is so *good!*' And I thought, 'Ah, it's because of us.' Then came Sean . . . Not that he was a crying baby: he just couldn't sleep, still going at midnight. He's still got that problem – up until all hours. And by the time you're on to your second child, you're tired. But he was a good baby, oh yeah. He walked – and I mean really *walked* – at nine months. And before that, when he was tiny, he was the one who was always reaching for things, had to grab everything and look at it . . .

SEAN PENN: The first home I remember? City Terrace, my grandparents' house.

I remember this very culturally rich neighbourhood, where the people my grandfather worked with were the same people he lived amongst. All of his employees, of course, were Chicano. And it was, unbeknownst to me at the time, a major gang area. I remember seeing graffiti. But it wasn't dangerous to be there: at that time still in Hispanic gang culture, if you wanted to be a 'vato loco' *and* a man of respect, you didn't go 'Bang-bang'. You got up close and personal, it was the intimacy of using a knife. Not random stuff like there is now, kids on drugs shooting out the window . . .

So I liked to go there. My grandfather had an old house with a basement, and so many things that were cool from a kid's point of view, like a magnet he had in the soap so it stuck. And because he was his own boss, he would make his own deliveries to the restaurants he had deals with. If we were staying over, my grandmother would put me to bed with a spoonful of honey – *that* was cool: didn't happen at home, never *thought* to have it happen at home – then my grandfather would wake me up at three in the morning and I'd go on the bread-runs with him.

And when I say 'my grandmother', I'm speaking of my *step*-grand-mother, Mary Shore. When my grandmother Elizabeth brought my dad out here, the roof over his head at that time was shared with their best friends, the Shores. Mary's husband died, followed by which my grandmother died.

EILEEN RYAN PENN: Elizabeth had cancer even when I came out with Michael. She had been fighting it, successfully, for many years, but she died soon after Michael was born. And as Elizabeth was dying, she said to Leo, 'Make sure your father sees a lot of Mary . . .' She was matchmaking as she was dying of cancer, because she knew Maurice couldn't survive alone. And he did see a lot of Mary. And, after, I think, a respectable number of years, they married . . .

SEAN PENN: So that was the first house I remember. Brooklyn Avenue, where the bakery was, is now Cesar Chavez Boulevard – and deservedly so.[1]

In 1961 and 1962, Leo made a number of guest appearances on Ben Casey, *a TV drama centred on a neurosurgeon played by Vince Edwards. Leo had now hit forty. After all his career vicissitudes, he now had to consider his future options.*

EILEEN RYAN PENN: Leo was getting older and he wasn't getting the parts – 'not a juvenile any more', as I would keep telling him. So I think he knew it was time to get on the other side of the camera. Matt Rapf, a TV producer, gave Leo his first opportunity. Leo was visiting on the set of *Ben Casey*, and Sam Jaffe[2] was very unhappy with the script. Everything's very fast in television: you have to get the actors to do what you want them to do. Leo was a writer too, of course, and he was just visiting, but right then and there he sat down and rewrote something and showed it to the director. The director showed it to Sam, and Sam loved it: it solved the problem. And so Leo wrote a little more that night. Then Leo got together with Matt, and Matt was

1 Cesar Chavez (1927–93) was the founder of the United Farm Workers Union.
2 Jaffe played the role of Dr David Zorba.

impressed by him and put him on a salary to help out on the show, and then a few months after that he gave Leo a first chance at directing an episode.[3] Then we fixed up our house and sold it for $28,000 and moved to Sherman Oaks.

SEAN PENN: Where my full memories begin is in Sherman Oaks, starting in kindergarten, so I'm probably three years old. There are three experiences I had that would be more appropriate to tell a shrink, but I'll tell you for whatever they're worth. I remember sitting on top of my mother's wood-panelled station wagon, on the back of the car, in the driveway. We were on the corner of an intersection of two residential streets, and I could see through the trees to the street. And from there, I saw two fatal accidents when I was a kid. Once, I was called in by my mother; the other time, it scared me and I just stayed where I was. For a long time . . . And then there were ambulances and the clean-up.

There were a lot of screeches and near-accidents too, as I remember. But I used to sit out there, always wondering if that was going to happen.

Then there was a Saturday morning, I think, and I was the first one up, and I was out playing in the front yard. I remember my back was turned and I heard a sound like an approaching aircraft. And suddenly it was so loud, and I *saw* on the ground the shadow of the plane. And I remember getting down on the ground and thinking it was going to crash into my house . . .

Then, I remember having my mom make costumes for me: one or two superheroes and, most importantly and memorably, Robin Hood.

EILEEN RYAN PENN: I sewed as much as if I'd had girls. I made capes for them; then they were Indians, and I made vests. Michael would be Superman, and he always made Sean the lesser character. But Sean was Robin Hood, yeah.

SEAN PENN: But I can't wear my Robin Hood out anywhere. You know how some kids will go out in their costumes when they're really young? I wasn't interested in the world seeing me in it: I was interested in just *being* in it. And I was always OK with my family – it was true, until very late in my adolescence, that I was always able to be expressive at home, but not particularly outside the home.

---

3 'And Even Death Shall Die', aired on 19 November 1962.

6 Sean Penn, aged four

One day we went to Bullock's Shopping Square – used to love to go there because there was a Jolly Roger, a pirate-themed restaurant, and they had this thing called 'The Monaloa', a big sundae with a cookie on top that they'd light on fire. That was always an adventure. Well, on this particular day, I had an agenda. *Tarzan* on TV had an elastic white bathing suit; I wanted a bathing suit just like Tarzan. And I got it. I went into the dressing room to put it on, and I looked at myself. I'm five years old, if that. And I thought, 'Yep, that's just like Tarzan. But I can't wear it out anywhere, because it looks like underwear. But I *can* wear it at home, like one of my costumes.'

So I'm at home. And there was a junior high school up at the top of our street, and all the kids would walk by our house at the end of the day. Sometimes, that's who I'd be watching that led to a traffic accident . . . So now I'm playing Tarzan out in the backyard, and I want to go out front. I go to the front door and, literally, as I'm in motion, pulling that door open in my Tarzan bathing suit, down by the front gate a pack of junior high school girls are walking by. And this is what I hear: 'Aww! Look at the little boy in his *underwear*!'

I . . . I just wanted to be packed into the space shuttle and sent far,

far away. And I had no possible excuse, because I'd seen it coming – I *had* X-ray vision, I *saw* through the door, saw those girls there. I saw them there from *Bullock's*. I saw them there through the fire on the *Monaloa*. I fucking *knew* it . . .

EILEEN RYAN PENN: I really wanted about twelve kids, all boys . . . but it got so Leo couldn't have any more babies. I think the sperm count got low because of the cigarettes. But we were determined to have at least one more. And the doctor said, 'If you want to, you'd better hurry up and do it.' So we went to the Sportsman's Lodge that night and made Christopher. He was born on 10 October 1965. Chris was an easy baby, regular. There was more difference between Michael and Sean. Still is . . .

Then Leo directed a picture with Sammy Davis Jr, *A Man Called Adam*. Not so long ago I was at a party at my friend Veronica Brady's, and a friend of hers, a black actor/writer, said to me, 'You know, that movie is practically required viewing for young black actors. I watch it over and over again.' And I was thinking as he was talking, 'Gee, honey, are you listening, wherever you are? You've got a cult movie out there . . .'

SEAN PENN: I got hold of it again on *Mystic River*. Larry Fishburne gave me a tape.

A Man Called Adam starred Davis Jr as Adam Johnson, a gifted jazz trumpeter wrestling with his talent and his temper; Ossie Davis, Cicely Tyson and Peter Lawford co-starred as the butts of Adam's alternating fury and affection. The script is rich in hipster lines ('Blow your soul,' Adam exhorts his loyal protégé, Vinnie, played by Frank Sinatra Jr) and there are a pair of extraordinary spats between Davis and Lawford, anatomizing the racism of the business. The moral of the story arrives when Adam tries to go straight for The Man, and fatally loses his edge.

EILEEN RYAN PENN: We were all out there in New York while Leo was shooting. We had a newborn – Christopher was two months old when we left. We came home to the coldest winter we'd ever known in California, and we all got sick. I was alone; there was nobody there to help me. Leo was very busy shooting. And I had us all in one room because I couldn't get people to come fix the heat-pump that wasn't working, and I wasn't driving yet. An unbelievably horrible time, very stressful with two little kids and a tiny infant. And then my brain just . . . exploded. I had an aneurysm.

SEAN PENN: I remember Michael calling me, going into my mother's room, and she was bleeding from ears, eyes; she was blind – that was what scared me the most.

EILEEN RYAN PENN: Michael was seven and he was like a little genius. He called our neighbour and said, 'Anita, my mommy's dying, get over here right now!' She said, 'I just saw your mother this morning. She was waxing the floor, she's fine.' He said, 'She's lying on the floor! Please come!' He then called the obstetrician, Dr Smith – he knew the number. The doctor said, 'Get her right over to St Joseph's, Michael, I'll meet her there!' He's talking to a seven-year-old . . . But Michael got Anita to take me to St Joseph's and by then I was throwing up and pretty much out of it. Anita told me later, 'The little one, Sean? He went and got a pan for you to throw up in.' When Leo saw me in the hospital that night, he passed right by me: he thought I was some ninety-year-old woman, that's how bad I looked.

SEAN PENN: Nowadays, my mother and I will have disagreements on things, but I can see why, as a parent, she remembers them a certain way. This one, I really remember it the way that I say it. It's just that, as a parent myself now, it would have struck me the way that it struck them. I went into her hospital room; there were louvres on the window, and the sun was in my eyes and it made me cry. I had to hide under the bed for shade. I wouldn't come out. And you can imagine the other side of that story . . .

EILEEN RYAN PENN: I knew Michael was OK; he was very grown-up for seven, and everyone had told him how brave he'd been. But Sean was five, and shy, and he was absolutely petrified looking at me. I was thinking, 'If I die, Michael's OK, and the baby doesn't know anything, so he'll go on with whoever Leo goes on with.' But I was very concerned about Sean. I had to get back for him, no matter what. I remember thinking that, through excruciating pain – 'Gotta get back . . .'

SEAN PENN: It was quite a statistic that she lived, at that time. But my dad wasn't saying, 'Your mother's going to die.' And my mom, you're going to have to run her over with a *tank*, three or four times, before she's going to say, 'I'm gonna die.' Or panic, even. She's particularly good in tough situations; equally so in her own tough situations.

EILEEN RYAN PENN: They thought at least I'd have brain damage. So that became my excuse. I'd tell the kids, 'OK, you got a problem with me? I have brain damage. Leave me alone . . .' But I wasn't too clear for a long while after: I'd look at a tree and I knew the word but it didn't translate into anything to me. It was a bad year.

June 1966, I had to move directly from the hospital into a new house we had already bought in Woodland Hills. We just kept making more money on our houses each time we sold; and this was a big home, two-storey, beautiful pool and lawns.

SEAN PENN: Now, Woodland Hills: this is where we find out where, you know, I came from, OK? 5833 Lubao Avenue. A nice neighbourhood, much nicer than North Hollywood or Sherman Oaks. Very typical setting, lawn to lawn, house to house, low fence to low fence, 'Hey, neighbour, want to use the barbecue?' Vicky lived across the street, Vicky Gerlich. Girls got prettier and prettier. There was something about blonde girls . . .

So now I'm living a blissful life in a certain sense. But I begin First Grade in Woodland Hills, Calvert Street School. And I hate school. It's a school that I walk to, like my own kids would. Michael is there, two years older, and we're not talking about anything weird happening – yet. But this is 1966. Come 1969, there was a guy named Charlie . . .

Around that time, LA City School District started forced bussing: bringing in kids from the ghetto to different schools in the public-school system. This is the story of a guy named Lynn Milner. Lynn was being bussed from South Central Los Angeles, and he ended up my best friend in elementary school, third grade. That was the beginning of a new-found confidence, that friendship with Lynn.

EILEEN RYAN PENN: Lynn was smart in school, a good basketball player, very nice, clean-cut, polite kid, and they used to have a really nice time together. I would have the kid over to stay, because they were walking distance from the school, and I wasn't going to have Sean stay overnight at Lynn's house in Compton. Then many years had passed after elementary school, and Sean had become an actor – he hadn't seen Lynn since he was 17. And then the trouble happened . . . 4

4 See chapter 4.

Courtesy of Sean Penn

7 Third Grade, 1968-69, Calvert Street School, Woodland Hills: Penn is in the front row, far right. Lynn Milner is back row, second from the left

SEAN PENN: But Woodland Hills was also where a lot of actors were, among them Wally Cox, somewhat famously known as the best friend of Marlon Brando5 – bespectacled guy, thinning hair, seemed like a nerd; but he was also quite the outdoorsman. Wally was a friend of my dad's, and he took a shine to Michael and I and introduced us to a lot of things. We were really interested in mini-bikes, and Wally was into motorcycles and dune-buggies – very big in the sixties, everyone's driving a dune-buggy. And Wally took us out in his.

Wally was a self-taught botanist; he knew every plant up in the hills and he turned me on to that. Then my mother and my dad would take us out fossil-hunting, a very successful practice for kids. The history of

5 Cox and Brando were Lincoln schoolmates, New York roommates, and lifelong friends. Cox had a hit TV show, *Mr Peepers* (1952–5), and was directed by Leo Penn in the TV movie *Quarantined* (1970).

this area is the ocean, so you'd find fossils and it was *dramatically* clear what they were. So I got very into rock-hunting, and wanted to be a geologist. And because of that, and motorcycles, the desert became my favourite place during that time. My dad would take me to Agua Dulce, on the way out to the Lancaster–Palmdale area: he knew the area because he'd shot there – it was often used for other planets in movies and TV; *Star Trek* used it a lot. And then, as I got older and I had a car, I went beyond it, and that's when I discovered Mojave. I took girls there, I've written things there, *Indian Runner* among them.

Agua Dulce has rock formations 150-feet high, and you can climb up the side of them and literally sit up there on this perch. In fact, the night I wrapped *Fast Times at Ridgemont High*, I brought Eric Stoltz and Anthony Edwards out, and we sat up on a rock and watched the sun rise. Then I brought my son to Agua Dulce when he was the same age I was when I first went. And he loved it.

So I've marked a lot of occasions in a lot of ways in the desert.

EILEEN RYAN PENN: Leo's focus was family, and he wasn't going to travel all over and leave us. So he ended up being a television director – hundreds and *hundreds* of hours of television. He enjoyed the camaraderie of directing, and he was very much loved by everybody. He was never out of work. All the doctor shows he directed, *Ben Casey*, *Dr Kildare* – he made a joke that he could probably operate . . .

SEAN PENN: We did a little bit of visiting TV sets: *Gunsmoke*, *Bonanza*, *Mod Squad*. I liked the actors. I remember Sugar Ray Robinson – because he was Sugar Ray Robinson . . . He came over to Woodland Hills because he was in *A Man Called Adam*. And he taught me how to box on one of those things that kids have with the punchbag on top of the wire: bam-bam-bam. My dad directed him and Ben Gazzara in an episode of *Run for Your Life*.[6]

Then, movies. The beginning of movies for me was when I went with my grandmother in City Terrace in the summertimes to the movies my parents wouldn't let me see: *Bonnie and Clyde* and *Bullitt*. *Easy Rider* and *A Clockwork Orange*, my parents wouldn't let me *near* – I remember the advertisement in the newspaper, the knife and the eye and the bowler hat. And I remember looking at my mother in the kitchen and not even *asking*. But I know my parents loved *Bonnie*

6 NBC series that ran from 1965–8.

and Clyde and *Easy Rider*, so I thought, 'If they're so great, why can't I go and see them?' Thirty years later I'm keeping my kids away from *21 Grams* . . .

And I remember Zeffirelli's *Romeo and Juliet*. I remember being asked if I wanted to see it, knowing that there was a breast or something in it. I had seen a picture of Olivia Hussey. And just the *idea* of Olivia Hussey, and her breast, separated me from my attachment to blondes – for the moment. But then the thought of acknowledging that was . . . unacceptable. So I turned down the opportunity to see the movie on that basis, because I assumed that my desire would have been singularly clear.

Then my dad wanted to take me out to the movies, and the only thing playing was a double bill of *Romeo and Juliet* and *Charly* with Cliff Robertson. We go, we see *Charly*. I'm tired. Dad says, 'Do you want to stay for *Romeo and Juliet*?' Do I want to say, 'I want to see Olivia Hussey's . . . '? No. We leave. And by now my friends had seen it, and I thought, 'I had a chance! I could have, but I didn't . . .' I end up *asking* to see it.

And I don't remember her breast. But I remember the movie, the way the zooms worked. I was very young, but I was noticing this stuff – and just loving the life of the movie, and the character of Mercutio. What they would now call a 'pro-teen-suicide movie'. But, for some reason, it didn't make me kill myself. For all my heartbreaks, nonetheless, here I stand . . .

Before we'd even left Sherman Oaks, I remember going over to a friend's house and hearing on the radio the news of our clear engagement in Vietnam.[7] And that's when the war shows started on television – every night. The significance of that war – it only gets deeper, to this day. And as it did, I re-evaluated my youth. 'What was the impact? Am I projecting an impact?' But back then, it looked pretty bad. I mean, we saw images of *that* war that you don't see from *these* wars. And we had Walter Cronkite, and you could believe him – to a large degree, anyway. And my parents clearly were against the war, my father in particular.

Hippies were cool. The hippie *movement* was cool – the drugs were *not* cool, but my father never passed comment on the drugs. My mother did. And the drugs were scary to us, the whole idea. But Nehru jackets were cool, head shops were cool, Black Light posters

7 On 5 June 1965, the engagement of US troops in Vietnam was publicly confirmed.

were cool, incense was cool, The Beatles were cool. Hot Wheel Cars were cool. This was all exciting stuff. Charlie Manson . . .?[8] *That* was a problem. So now I don't want to walk home from school, not with Charlie doing his thing. And I don't like school anyway. Then there was the fucken *Zodiac* Killer[9] . . . And they never caught him. So he could be my neighbour today.

EILEEN RYAN PENN: Every four or five years we'd fix a place up and then move. And every four years I was squeezing Leo closer and closer to the beach. Christopher had asthma and he would turn purple-blue. The paediatrician was giving him shots every week but, of course, they want you to keep coming. I knew it was from the smog and the dirty air. You're with your child all day long, you know. Twice in one night we had to have him in Emergency. I said, 'That's it, we're getting out of this smog.'

SEAN PENN: The beach was somewhere we'd go to with my mother when my dad was working, through the tunnel of Malibu Canyon. And I just loved it, *loved* the beach. So there was no concern about lost friendships or anything when it came to the idea of moving. 'You guys are thinking about moving to the *beach*? Let's *do* it . . .'

EILEEN RYAN PENN: It was 1969. I put the kids in the car and drove out to Malibu. There was a little real-estate office on the corner. The guy said, 'Oh, Mrs Penn, I don't have anything nice like where you're living in Woodland Hills.' I said, 'All I care about is clean air. Can you get me anything?' He said, 'People don't move from here. I've got one thing on this street, Zumirez.' And, really, it was like Tobacco Road – a terrible little house, infested with weeds.

SEAN PENN: We all go the next weekend as a family to see the house. Dan Benes was the realtor, dressed up like Clark Gable, same pencil moustache. But I'm hearing scary stuff about the family who lived there, the main thing being their son Corky. And indeed we do find a syringe in the house. They had all kinds of problems, and they couldn't afford the place any more.

EILEEN RYAN PENN: Leo's father thought I'd gone out of my mind. But I brought Leo out and I said, 'Look! We can clear a trail and go to the

8 Saturday, 9 August 1969 saw the foul murder by the Manson 'Family' of Roman Polanski's pregnant wife Sharon Tate and four others on Cielo Drive, Benedict Canyon.
9 'The Zodiac Killer' was suspected of thirty-seven murders between 1966 and 1974.

39

beach. And the clean fresh air for Christopher . . .' And he agreed. He thought, 'This is wonderful.' So we moved in July 1969. We added to the place, we potsied, this and that. And Chris would say to me, 'Mom, don't I have to go for my shots?' I said, 'No, honey, you're cured.' He never had an asthmatic attack again. And I put him in Pop Warner Football to expand his chest. You've seen him: I guess his chest expanded, right?

SEAN PENN: That house was bought for $49,000. The neighbourhood has jumped since – even since I left. Now, Barbra Streisand lives there. But if you looked at Point Dume from the sky now and took half the streets and three quarters of the houses away, you'd guess what it looked like then. It wasn't considered a commutable area. It was rural; I could get to my school without touching pavement – all trails and gullies, and you'd pass girls riding horses, bareback. Girls discovered things early . . . I immediately discovered surfing, within days of arriving. I fell totally in love with it. I still am. And that would be almost every day for the next seven years.

Matt Palmieri – one of my oldest friends – was the first friend I had who had been outside of the country. We played a lot of sports together; surfed together, but not much because he was Malibu Colony. He was a rich kid – there was a sense of class – but he was an unprejudiced rich kid.

Matt Palmieri's father, Victor, was one of the world's foremost corporate restructuring gurus and crisis-solvers, soon to turn around the colossal bankruptcy of the Penn Central railroad; he had also served Lyndon Johnson as deputy executive of the 1967 Kerner Commission into the race riots of the day. Matt's mother, Martha Cooley, was a gifted abstract painter, peace activist and philanthropist.

MATT PALMIERI: Sean and I lived at different ends of Malibu and went to different schools, so the first time we met was when he walked into the dugout of the Malibu Little League Dodgers in 1969 and sat down at the end of the bench. We just nodded at each other . . . He was a pretty good athlete, not a leader, but not a follower either, very competitive but always pretty reticent. He was a scrappy, slim, compact kid: very quiet, very to himself, very self-contained – we were both sort of tough kids who didn't take a lot of shit. He did it in a quiet way, I did it in a big loud way . . .

Courtesy of Matt Palmieri

8 Pacific Palisades/Malibu YMCA basketball, 1972: Penn is front row, far left; Matt Palmieri back row, second left

CAMERON THOR: I knew Sean at elementary school and first year at Malibu Park Junior High. I lived on Escondido Beach, five miles north of the Colony. There were communities in Malibu where kids sort of congealed, but on Escondido Beach there was just me, a lonely beach kid. So I'd wander down the beach to Point Dume, and there was this other guy who was sort of an outsider. That was Sean. We'd hang out and talk. And I liked going to their house because his brother had a drum set.

EILEEN RYAN PENN: Michael always figured he was the odd man out because everybody else in the family was an actor. Christopher said a very funny thing just a few years ago: he said, 'I just got to really know Michael lately. And he's a really nice guy. Growing up, he was just that guy in the room with his guitar who Sean and I would pass if we were going outside to throw a ball around . . .'

CHRISTOPHER PENN: Michael was always into music. Sean had played Little League, and I got into the game. And he had wrestled, and I wrestled. So first of all Sean was more like my older brother; we were

41

closer in age. And I didn't even understand Michael at all. Then Michael and I got closer, and Sean and I argued . . .

But Sean was always looking out for me, always backing me up in an emergency – that's his nature. I'll tell you a story: this is self-effacing . . . I used to pee in bed when I was a kid, till I was about six or seven. And it was embarrassing, because I was out running around the neighbourhood, and one of Sean's friends had seen the bed wet, and he said, 'Ha-ha, Chris, piss-in-the-bed, piss-in-the-bed!' Sean wasn't going to let me take the heat for it. He says to his friend, 'Nah. That was *me* pissed in the bed. You got a problem with that . . .?' That's my big brother . . .

SEAN PENN: Meanwhile, and before I was even thinking about drinking in my life, I knew that my mother went through a fifth of Smirnoff a night, and my Dad went through a fifth of J&B. It was noticeable, but not a negative thing to me, even now. My father never had a reaction to it. Maybe he'd just go a little quieter, but he was pretty quiet to begin with – unless there was a story to tell. It's like the saying, 'Wise men speak because they have something to say, and fools speak because they have to say something.' When my dad had something to say, he said it fully and enjoyed saying it. He was a raconteur that way. And my mother would become a little more flamboyant and full of life when she'd drink. But then she'd ultimately nod out.

He liked her an awful lot. He'd get home late; we'd see him right before going to bed or right after. And if you sneaked out for a snack or something, they'd just be sitting there, lights out; she'd be sound asleep with her head on his lap, and he would be rubbing her hair. And that was very common – nearly every night.

EILEEN RYAN PENN: We had so much in common. We never were bored with each other – we grew together. I think that's very important in a relationship, that one person doesn't outgrow the other.

SEAN PENN: My mother's father had died before I was born, and my mother's mother came and lived with us. She was charming and funny. But we were aware that it took an enormous amount of forgiveness on my mother's part to accept her into our home. There was a lot of drinking going on there when my mother was growing up.

EILEEN RYAN PENN: My mother was an alcoholic. She never showed affection; I said that to her while she was living here, because I'd never been able to get to tell her that. Before, she was with my younger sister Joan, who was then so ill for many years that she couldn't stay there any more. So then we took her.

SEAN PENN: My first drink was related to her. I had copped out of school one day because I wanted to miss a test, and the next day I really was sick, woke up with a bad headache. But I couldn't justify two absences to my mother. She was in another room, and my grandmother was outside in her wheelchair, a blanket over her lap. She wasn't meant to drink. But she pulled the blanket down a little and showed me a bottle of I. W. Harper bourbon. And she said, 'Take a swig of this and you won't even know you have a head.' So I did. And then I went to school.

Now, there was another thing about this surfing culture, which is that I remain today the only living surfer of that age who doesn't smoke pot. So I drank, pretty early on. My parents became aware of it when I started to get into dirt-bike riding. I could not get them to buy me a dirt bike. I tried like hell one Christmas. They said it was too expensive and too dangerous. Meanwhile, I was riding other people's dirt-bikes every day. Jerry Connelly was the best motorcycle rider in the neighbourhood, and I'd ride my bike to his house, about six blocks away. So Jerry and I are at his house. Jerry's father had quite a collection of *Playboy* magazines. We split a bottle of tequila. I'm thirteen years old; I'd drunk beer, I never drank half a bottle of tequila. I could have fucken *died*. And I remember trying to ride that bike home: it was about three in the afternoon, summer, hot. I'm wearing Levi's and a T-shirt and a pair of hiking boots. Boots were going to be a problem . . . I took 'em off, went barefoot. But I'm falling off every forty yards, cutting myself, getting back up, sliding off of the pedal, cutting my bare foot. Just *drrrrunk* . . . I got onto my street, and there was a kid named Chris Wofford lived at the top, a surfing buddy of mine. I banged on his door; he wasn't home. So I grabbed a rock and broke the window. And I went in there, vomited all over myself and passed out on the broken glass.

The Woffords never did get home. It got to 6 o'clock and my family was in a panic, and my older brother was among those on the search party. He saw the window smashed and went in, and there I was. He carried me home, cleaned me up in the bath. My mom was there by then, but she let Michael follow through. And they put me to sleep. I had not had a good relationship with Michael prior to that. So I was pretty humbled. I got up the next day with the DTs, really poisoned.

My dad took me outside and talked to me. Very calm. He said, 'You wanna go drink some tequila . . .?' I just about blew my chunks all over again . . .

EILEEN RYAN PENN: Generally speaking, the education in Malibu was terrible. I think the kids were just bored, you know? What Sean was interested in he was very good at, and what he wasn't interested in, well – he didn't assert himself very much . . .

SEAN PENN: I hated school every day until the end, except for one year in junior high that was interesting because of Leonard Vincent.

MATT PALMIERI: Mr Vincent was the embodiment of the classic teacher/ mentor figure. He was an incredible man who made great efforts with every kid, wrote everybody personal letters, gave out awards. There was no student of his who ever left his class feeling like they hadn't been thought about and approved of and included. He taught American History, but within that curriculum, he brought in world affairs, culture, current as well as past. He'd do presentations on the death penalty, civil rights, *Inherit the Wind*, the story of the great Clarence Darrow Scopes trial. And during Watergate, every day, we got a running commentary on the hearings. He made us all very aware that it was a monumental event in American political history.

SEAN PENN: And that was all pretty interesting to me; school was interesting for the first time. Watergate, the end of the war, Nixon's fall. What is our government? Who do we believe? Why did those guys die? This was all getting louder. Over that summer, I was told to watch those hearings.[10] And I watched every day. Later, when I saw Fred Thompson in *Marie*, I said, 'That guy was on the Watergate team . . .'[11]

MATT PALMIERI: Mr Vincent would read the *Washington Post* and the *New York Times* to us every morning and ask us, 'What's the subtext here? Is anybody telling the truth?' He was teaching us to be sceptical, to read between the lines, which was a wonderful discipline to inculcate. At the same time, the whole experience, for Sean and me and everyone else in the class who managed to pay attention – it was ideal-

10 17 May – 7 August 1973: the Senate Watergate committee began congressional hearings, carried by all three networks and PBS, with repeats at night for prime-time audiences.
11 Sen. Fred Thompson (R-Tenn.), the committee's chief minority counsel. Played himself in the 1985 film *Marie*. He later acted in action movies such as *Die Hard 2*.

breaking, it busted our concept of what our country was supposed to be all about.

In our ninth-grade year, Sean and I ran student council together, along with a few others at Malibu Park. From the school, you could just walk across the street to Zuma Beach with your board and a girl and a joint, or whatever, during nutrition or lunch. We wore trunks and flip-flops and hang-ten T-shirts, the weather was always good, it was pretty much the good life . . .

SEAN PENN: Mr Cater, the crafts teacher, had a big storage closet; we could bring our boards, as long as we got there before the first bell. So one parent or another or an older guy would drive us; we'd have a 5.30 a.m. pick-up, they'd drop us off in the dark, we'd wait for the sun to come up so it was light enough to jump out in the water, and we'd surf until we could make it to class . . .

EILEEN RYAN PENN: My god, I'd be a nervous wreck on the beach while he was surfing. But Sean was in junior lifeguards, where they had to get out there in that cold water and swim for miles. He always put himself through tough stuff: very stoic like that, he can take a lot of discomfort. I think he was testing himself, you know? All through elementary school and junior high. He was preparing his whole life, I think, for what he became. Very quietly, but he was doing it . . .

SEAN PENN: My last year at junior high had some high spots. But I'm also a shy guy who couldn't tell a girl he liked that he liked her. Once a month, Saturday nights, they'd throw a dance. This was the time to connect with the girls. And this was a time, of course, when I was useless. If a girl liked me, she'd have to *really* tell me that, clearly. And gotta hope I like her too . . . Nonetheless: 'Oh, I'm glad you like me, I like you too.' And then: nh-uh! I didn't follow up.

But Matt was a popular guy, very much the king of his own kingdom in the school, outgoing, confident, athletic, good-looking, girlfriends – and he'll tell you happily tales of older women, probably some of the kids' mothers . . .

They had a girls' vice-president and a boys' vice-president. I was the boys' VP. I ran on a platform of getting a surfing contest going. And, of course, won. It just made sense: our whole culture was surfing, and they had every other contest, they had fucking *equestrian* events. So we'd say, 'Well, why can't –?' And they'd say, 'We don't have the insurance for it.' 'You've got insurance for kids on horseback. We're surfing every day and nobody's getting hurt.' Well, I went to every insurance company around, could not find one. And then one day it hit me. What insurance company did they use for the horses? It was their general coverage. I went back into it, and there was nothing there prohibiting a surfing contest; they just hadn't done it. That's politics, right? I pointed this out. And so we had our surfing contest. First Annual . . .

Higginbotham And Penn Tops In Surfing Contest

On Saturday, March 1, a strange happening took place; it was new, different, whatever you would like to call it, but whatever word you choose to describe this event, most of all, it was fun. The event was the first annual Malibu Park Junior High School Surfing Competition.

It was 7:45 a.m. on a cold Saturday morning at Westward Beach. The fog was rolling in along with several gusts of wind. There wasn't a soul on the beach and a surfing contest was to take place at 8:30. The waves, far from crashing, were about two feet and mushy.

At 8:10 a.m. people started filling in and the competitors began to group wondering whether or not the contest was going to take place due to the lack of surf. At 8:30 (the scheduled starting time for the first heat to enter the water) a decision was made to go on with the contest. At 8:45 the first heat was in the water and miraculously the waves began to pick up.

Each heat lasted approximately 15 minutes with a few exceptions due to minimal waves so the judges gave one to four minute extensions; semi-final heats usually lasted 20 minutes and finals, 10 to 15 minutes.

Head judge Pat Waind backed up by fellow judges Mark Waind, Tom Stelling, Mike Sprock and Brian Cousins kept the contest running smoothly.

The contest was divided into two separate divisions, "A" and "B". "A" was the upper and "B" the lower division. The winners are as follows:

"A"

1st place: Jeff Higginbotham, 97½ pts.

2nd place: Sean Penn, 96 pts.
3rd place: Kirby Kotler, 93½ pts.
4th place: Christian Anderson, 88½ pts.
5th place: Chris Phelps, 86 pts.
* Ride of the meet: Bingo Horner

"B"

1st place: Matt Higgins, 68½ pts.
2nd place: Jack Starr, 60 pts.
3rd place: Marlin Miller, 55½ pts.
4th place: Joe Keenen, 51 pts.
5th place: Jeff Keenen, 48½ pts.
* Ride of the meet: Matt Higgins

Trophies were handed out to surfers placing first through fourth and to the two surfers with the top ride in their division. The "Ride Of The Meet" trophies were handmade by Jo Jo Perrin.

Over all the meet was a success and there are already thoughts of holding another one in May!

Choral, Instrumental

Kiwanis Sponsor Musical Contest

What is Kiwanis? The Kiwanis Club of America is a mens' service club. One of the services it performs is sponsoring a solo contest for choralists and instrumentalists.

MALIBU PARK JUNIOR HIGH SCHOOL
VOL. VII, NO. 6   MALIBU, CALIFORNIA 90265   MARCH 21, 1975

JEFF HIGGINBOTHAM of the K-H surf team, (left), won first place in the "A" division, riding waves such as this one, with total control and precision turns. Sean Penn, (right), placed second in the "A" division, rid-

Courtesy of Sean Penn

9 News of the 'First Annual' Malibu Park Junior High Surfing Competition, March 21 1975

MATT PALMIERI: The surfing contest was purportedly the first officially sanctioned of its kind by a California junior high school. I think Mr Vincent had informed the Secretary of State or the Governor that we had done this, and we got this official letter back wishing us 'Congratulations'. So Sean – always thinking – decides that we now have some juice with the state government that we ought to put to good use. He writes a letter back to them saying that his next initiative – he would like to suggest very strongly – was that they reduce the school week from five days to four; that that extra day of rest would make us all much more effective students. He typed that up and sent it to the governor with high hopes. And he got a letter back some time later saying, 'Thank you very much for your thoughtful suggestion, young man. But . . .'

CAMERON THOR: Malibu was different then: little houses and mostly crazy people.

SEAN PENN: It *was* idyllic. But there's stuff that's unbelievable. And it makes an impression on you.

I was out at Trancas Point one day, surfing there – which is me not being local, and localism was a big thing: you don't surf other people's beaches. A guy I never liked much, Doug Jones*, pelted my car with rocks as I left, and I nearly lost control of the car. That afternoon, I came back looking for those guys with a baseball bat, couldn't find them, but I ran into their parents, and I told them what had happened. Next day I'm out in the school quad, waiting for the bell to go to first period, and I get a fist in my head that knocks me back over a berm. I get up and there's Doug Jones. I whack him. Then people intervened – those things get broken up before they start. Doug came to school with a shiner after that. Five or six months later, he was at home in his bedroom, took a .22, and shot himself in the stomach. And he just sat there and bled to death. Left a suicide note; I don't know what it said.

Bobby Herman* was a guy in our class. He was the portly guy: he was Piggy in *Lord of the Flies*. And a sweetheart, I got along with him just fine. But this is a guy who, throughout high school, I convinced that I'd got into helicopter-flying, and the helicopters he saw in front of his beach house were me.

HIM (*suspicious*): The yellow one?
ME: You saw me! Did you see when I banked?
HIM: Yeah . . .?

1981, three or four years later: I get a letter from Bobby Herman, from Hawaii. He's started a helicopter-rescue service for ocean swimmers and surfers. He sends me the brochure. And he's thriving.

1985, 17 August, the day I turn twenty-five years old. The day before, I got married. I stayed the night at my parents' guesthouse out at the back of their house – built after I left – with my first wife. The two of us get up in the morning and go for a jog on the beach. A six-

* These names have been changed.

foot-five Adonis is running towards us: it's fucken Bobby Herman. 'Piggy'. And it's like he grew ten inches up and sucked the rest in. He's cut and handsome . . .

[*baritone*] 'Hey, Sean. Oh, hello, Madonna. Nice to meet you.'

And, I must say, I was happy to see it. Wow. Good for you. I almost said as much. But this ain't no way to start your married life. So I'm gonna take my two-foot-shorter-than-you ass and head on out, OK? 'No, you too! See you again . . .'

Sometime in the nineties, Bobby Herman is back in Los Angeles from Hawaii. He jumps out of the car across from Moonshadows Restaurant, Pacific Coast Highway, butt naked, screaming something about Jesus, gets back in his car, intentionally murders a pedestrian with the car, jumps out again, runs screaming into Moonshadows. Gets sent to a psych ward in prison, starts writing me letters about how he's 'maintaining his masculinity' – no one's taking *that* from him. 'I'll be out soon.' He's out now, I don't know where. I stopped answering letters.

About the same time, my friend Dan's brother Pete* calls 911 to report that he's killed his mother. The cops get there and he's masturbating over her naked body. He stabbed her to death. Pete went to Camarillo.[12]

These are all Malibu kids . . . and I'm forgetting fifteen more of these guys. Matt Palmieri and I will get together now and talk about it. I think it's maybe about isolation, and the culture shock of what became a much faster-moving world. This list of the dead and imprisoned, it was Malibu and then they were out in the big world. The beach culture, it had an edge – it was like a gang, and that was all about localism. But basically there was a very idyllic, very peaceful solitude to it that, I think, got broken. It was a bunch of fish out of water, and I mean that literally, because these were all surfers . . .

Towards the end of junior high, I was getting into tennis. And that was really because I saw a girl who played tennis, and I wanted to have a reason to be on the next court. And then I fell more in love with tennis than with her. A blonde girl . . . I mean, it's not like I close my eyes and think, 'What's a beautiful woman?', and that's what I see. It just turns out that's how I end up . . .

12 Camarillo State Hospital for the mentally ill, Ventura County, CA. These names have been changed.

10 Penn, aged sixteen

Courtesy of Sean Penn

So, high school. Tennis. Bad academic situation. *Really* hated walking from our house to the street corner and waiting twenty minutes for a bus going twenty miles to school at traffic hour, with *AM* radio. And then the same thing back every day, and *late* in the day if there was tennis practice, which was most of the time. And looking out the window as we're driving along the coast when there was a great swell, incredible waves, and thinking, 'Why am I going to this factory, where I'm learning absolutely fucking nothing?' And I stand by that today – I wish I had not gone to school. Because I really missed a lot of great waves and good times, and everything I learned was outside of school – with the exception of Mr Vincent in junior high school. And I didn't learn much about girls at this time either, or anything else.

EILEEN RYAN PENN: Sean was one of the jocks at Santa Monica High. He was not hanging out with all the little guys in the drama department. Most of the kids in Malibu, they had tennis rackets in their hands from the time they were crawling, but neither Leo or I were into tennis. Leo liked to throw a ball around, and he liked to watch sports, but not like some men, you know – *really* into it. And, of course, Sean made the tennis team. I couldn't believe that.

CHRISTOPHER PENN: My father's pilot in the war was Myron McNamara, and they flew those thirty-one missions together. But he hadn't seen Myron in many, many years. Sean was playing tennis for Santa Monica High, and he found out that UC Irvine was having a game with Pepperdine in Malibu. Myron was the coach at the UC Irvine tennis team. He was known in the tennis world as one of the old-school guys. So Sean tells my dad, 'Hey, come to this tennis match with me.' Dad says, 'Why would I go to a tennis match?' Sean says, 'C'mon, just come with me, it's a favour.' So he brought Dad down there. And, like a silver bullet between them, Dad spotted Myron, Myron spotted him. And suddenly, wow, they were back together again after so many years and it was as if nothing had changed. The funny thing is, Sean said, 'I don't wanna tell these guys what I'm doing.' He could have just organized for them to meet. But he made it a surprise.

JORDAN RHODES: The big thought about Sean in those days, we all thought he was going to be a tennis pro. He was quite a player.

EILEEN RYAN PENN: Leo and I always encouraged our kids to be whatever the hell they wanted to be. I was never that ambitious for them. I never said to my kids like my mother did, 'Don't be an actor', or 'Be this or that.' As long as they were happy, I didn't care if they wanted to dig ditches. I had thought Sean wanted to be a lawyer, like my dad, because he would be reading *Black's Law* to all hours of the night. I would have to go in and say, 'Enough! Put the light out!' But Sean had his own private little world going from the beginning. I was the same in my family – separating myself from my sisters. And sometimes I would catch him looking at books that had pictures of Leo and I from the theatre . . .

SEAN PENN: At fourteen I was an extra on *The Little House on the Prairie*[13] That was the director's son getting a job . . . We wore woods clothes and it was summer time in the Simi Valley. I didn't believe in the principle of breaking for lunch: I thought you should stay with your character in the situation. So I stayed out in the middle of the day under the blazing sun. They come back and call 'Action'. I started doing a jig, and passed right the fuck out. Sunstroke. So that was my début on film . . . No, it wasn't. As a younger kid, I did a one-liner on *Marcus Welby M.D.* . . .

Going to the movies, that was big. There were impacting pictures; it was like every week was an event of some kind. I remember me and Matt going to see *Lenny*. I always had an interest in Fosse – took me a while to get onto it, but I think there was much more of a directorial interest in him than some of the other things I loved. And still is; he has a strong place for me. Friedkin's *Sorcerer* was a big one too: like with Fosse, there was something directorially interesting. In fact, I think *Sorcerer* was the beginning of a lot of the imagery that we're seeing in advertising as well as in the movies today. What I loved is it was a generation of film-makers who didn't put their stamp on things, then people borrowed from *them* to use their ideas as stamps. But whether it be Hal Ashby or Friedkin, the movies looked like the movies: they didn't look like whatever their last movie was – *French Connection* and *Sorcerer* have no relationship at all – they looked like the movie *this* movie was supposed to look like.

I have a very strong memory of *Badlands* the first time. I didn't see it when it first came out, because I already knew the legend of it. I caught up with it later, at a great re-run theatre two blocks away from

13 'The Voice of Tinker Jones', tx. December 1974. Eileen also appeared in the episode.

my acting school: the Beverly Cinema off of LaBrea on Beverly. Also the Fox, Venice. That was where I caught up with *Mean Streets*, *Scarecrow*, *Harold and Maude* . . . So anything I had missed when I was stuck on a surfboard, or in school, anything that I had a sense was of the cinema that I had fallen in love with, I could catch up with it there.

And I have a very strong memory of *Taxi Driver* the first time. I remember being a little bit embarrassed that I responded like I did to it, to that character. I just didn't think anybody else would agree with me about it. It wasn't a movie that you shared with surfers . . .

Then, Super-8 movies. My younger brother got real into them, wanted to write movies, learned *everything* about Vietnam.

EILEEN RYAN PENN: School was not something that interested Christopher. But he would get on the bus and go into Malibu, with his little Vietnam script under his arm that he wrote with the help of a next-door neighbour who had been in the war. He'd talk to people in stores, feel out what their view on the war was, pro or anti, and whatever it was, he'd tell them that the script was from that point of view. Then they'd give him money: he'd come home with twenty-dollar bills from this one and that one . . . He bought film and wardrobe and shot one long film;[14] he even got Martin Sheen to work for him. They had a scene at the cleaners on Point Dume: Martin all dressed up in a suit because he's playing the father of a son coming back from the war. Christopher was saying, 'No, Martin, you're going over the top, make it less.' And Martin was wonderful, treated him as the director, said, 'OK, Chris.'

Sean was interested in the films too, but I didn't notice it as much until later.

SEAN PENN: Charlie and Emilio: we all knew they were the kids of Martin Sheen, who I only knew as the movie actor jogging up and down the Pacific Coast Highway all the time. Emilio I know – he's not a surfer but he's a skim-boarder on the beach. And Christopher and Charlie were good friends. They go to the Philippines for the shoot of *Apocalypse Now*, come back, and they've got a hold of things like a prosthetic rubber severed hand and a few other props. They start making movies. Then I get to know those guys, and I go over to Charlie and Emilio's house to be in one of their movies. And out of the drawer came the hand . . . I decided I wanted to make a movie based entirely

14 Entitled *Nobody's Heroes*.

around this hand. And I did: about a group of kids who didn't like one amongst them, so they hang him off a cliff, and they're chanting, 'Cut it off, cut it off!' We left the hand on a fence and did a dummy-drop.

We end up making a bunch of movies, of varying lengths, five or six, from twenty minutes to an hour. This is where Joe comes in.

JOSEPH VITARELLI: My father moved our family from New York to Malibu in December 1977. Malibu was surreal to me. I was a New York kid, and suddenly I was living in Trancas Canyon. I showed up for my first week at Samohi in tweed pants and a silk shirt, with a rope chain and a fucking Samsonite briefcase. Then I discover kids in California go to school in shorts and cut-off T-shirts, carrying their surfboards. Fortunately I played Varsity basketball, so I guess that saved me . . .

Sean carried around a Snoopy lunch box, stuffed with film-making paraphernalia – notebooks, memo pads, squibs for wound make-up. There certainly wasn't anything to *eat* in it. So you can see why we were drawn together . . . He and I were inseparable in that period, best friends. We spent most of our days together and hung out at night, driving around Westwood, going to see movies. A lot of time at Winchell's Donuts. Sean and I have always said we went to 'Winchell's High'. But also a lot of time out making Super-8 movies. Chris did them with us, and we used Charlie. He was *so* little. Once they hung him inside a refrigerator for a scene, so when the mother comes home, she opens the door to find her son in there. Someone was always getting killed – we killed each *other* a number of times. Sean actually shot me once, with live ammunition, a .22. We were sitting in a closet, he was fooling around with a rifle, and the thing went off and right through the wall. So I'm the only friend he's ever shot.

SEAN PENN: I *almost* shot him. I missed. He still whines about it . . .

Emilio and I made one called *The Dog Movie*, which he still has a copy of, and which is great – it could be like a Corman late-night classic. But they all had a lot of irony in them – a lot more than my career has been touched by since then . . .

So I now find myself acting in these movies too, because they're night shoots, as such, and everybody else does homework. We don't. We stay up all night making movies. Go to school, sneak in to surfing, play tennis. Promise ourselves we're gonna talk to the girls, don't, and go start all over again.

JOSEPH VITARELLI: There was a silly game that we played, which you couldn't do any more, called 'She's the One'. We would drive my father's Cadillac around, and one of us would find a beautiful young woman on the street, complete stranger, jump out of the car, kiss her squarely on the mouth, say, 'You're the one', and then run away. And clearly something good had to come out of all this, because otherwise we'd all be dead – either that or failing miserably.

Samohi had a weekly or monthly newspaper, and they wrote several pieces about Sean and me. I remember one article entitled 'The Penn Film Technique' . . .

CHRISTOPHER PENN: Sean had a very clear concept of what he wanted to do, what the subject was, how it began, how it got fleshed out and then how it ended. So that became his thing; he was really focused on it.

SEAN PENN: I started liking directing movies. I made a forty-five-minute film, *Looking for Someone*. I acted in it too, and I spent quite a bit of time on that picture.

JOSEPH VITARELLI: *Looking for Someone*! I wrote a piece of music for that, actually – my first score. A really awful song. Sean loved it, though; he still asks me to play it. [*sings*] 'Are you the man . . .?' Sean probably knows it verbatim.

SEAN PENN: It's a detective story. Unfortunately the only copy of it burned, in the fire that took my house.[15] But it's a sort of psycho-drama/thriller, with some nice stuff in it, surrounded by *ridiculously* adolescent stuff – I should say ridiculously *American* adolescent stuff – of the seventies. Nonetheless, one of the great inspirations for it was the Peter Gabriel song: [*sings*] 'Looking for someone, I guess I'm doing that / Trying to find a memory in a dark room . . . '[16] And then *Solsbury Hill* was the next movie, about a guy exploring characters on Hollywood Boulevard because he dreamed of being someone other than who he was. Never completed. But *Looking for Someone* got screened at Santa Monica High. It was a big moment – not for the audience . . . But a big moment for us to explore the size of it. We projected as far a throw as we could, compromising quality for size: I would say we projected it about twelve-feet wide. So I was seeing that you could make a little movie on Super-8. And that was provocative. I

15 See Chapter 9.
16 From the Genesis album *Trespass* (1970).

was able to do something that wasn't sitting in a room watching television.

EILEEN RYAN PENN: I would have loved to have seen it but I didn't. Sean only told me after the fact. He was feeling himself out . . . But I think they got so much bigger a reaction than they'd expected, from the teachers and the other students. And I think Sean liked that: the laughter and the feeling of the audience out there. He was probably a closet actor up to that moment.

SEAN PENN: So Anthony Zerbe[17] comes to our high school Career Day to talk about acting. He's wearing a pair of zip-up boots that I like. I go get a pair: I think of them as 'actor boots'. And I wear them in a Super-8 movie. I look down at these boots and I think, 'Well, I guess I must be an actor now.' Then I start paying more attention to the actors in the movies I'm seeing: more and more and more . . . And then: 'I want to *do* this.'

---

17 Actor in films including *The Parallax View* (1974) and *Who'll Stop the Rain?* (1978).

THREE

1978–1981

The working, the working, just the working life . . .
Bruce Springsteen, 'Factory' (1978)

EILEEN RYAN PENN: It's true about actors that they're either very introverted or very extroverted. There are reasons for that. And when they're very introverted, they can open up by having a character. Christopher was more extroverted.

CHRISTOPHER PENN: Sean didn't have an innate sort of flamboyant or entertaining presence at all. He wasn't, in a sense, a natural actor. He was rather introverted, highly intelligent, very serious and sort of shy. But how hard he worked to become an interpreter of life – which is what an actor is, right?

MATT PALMIERI: I went away to high school in the east while Sean went to Samohi. We would see each other in the summers, around town or out in the surf. Then, the summer before I was leaving for college, we ran into one another at the local Malibu pizza parlour. We shot the shit, then he asked me what I was up to, and I told him that I was going off to study history and literature. He thought that was cool – even though it wasn't something he would ever want to do. I asked him the same question, and he said, 'I think I'm gonna be an actor. I'm studying with Peggy Feury, and I'm working on sets in theatres in town . . .' Sounded good to me – especially since Peggy lived on my street, so I knew he was learning from one of the greats.

SEAN PENN: My dad knew about the GRT – the Group Repertory Theatre – and I went over there, talked to Lonnie Chapman, who ran the place, and I got in as an apprentice. I stayed there a couple of years, learned the technical side of production.

And I met R. D. Call there. He did a scene from *Terrible Jim Fitch* by James Leo Herlihy, and I thought, 'Who the hell's *this* guy?' We just took a shine to each other and became great friends. R. D. had been a movie-admiring rodeo cowboy from Leyton, Utah – a Mormon – and his back was broken falling off a saddle bronco.

R. D. CALL: I had to change my life: so I decided to get into something stable, like acting . . . Then I realized I could do things onstage and get away with them, which in life they were trying to lock me up for. So it was like therapy; and it became something else. I literally flipped a coin on whether to go out to Los Angeles or New York. Then it was like *The Grapes of Wrath*, piled everything into a truck . . . In the fall of 1978, I joined the GRT. And Sean joined at practically the same time.

GRT was like an apprenticeship: a lot of building sets, a lot of tech work, you had to run lights and sound for the shows going on. Sean and I did that together. He was just out of high school, but I knew when I first met him he had this serious, committed part to him. He also liked to have fun and hang out. There was a bunch of guys we used to hang out with – like the Bowery Boys. And Sean was kind of a practical joker. We were working on a show, he and I were running the sound, and there was a girl, I'll call her 'Nancy', running the lights. It was a boring show. Right around that time, Sean had got into make-up and special effects. And midway through this show, Sean suddenly says, 'Ah, God, I can't stand any more of this . . . ', and made like he'd cut his wrist. Blood slapped onto the wall. He'd rigged his wrist and made it up so it would shoot blood if he pumped his fist. But Nancy thought he'd really done it – she screamed and passed out. It stopped the show: everybody in the audience, everybody *onstage* looking to the booth, as Sean's like, 'Oh, God . . .' But Lonnie loved shit like that. He had his favourites there, especially the guys – it was like *All My Sons*.

SEAN PENN: Group Rep was in North Hollywood, so I was either staying *in* the theatre or me and R. D. would crash at a big empty ranch house out in Sun Valley, owned by a friend of ours from GRT named Jake Harper. It was an unkempt spread, but it *was* a spread. I had a sleeping bag in a room, R. D. had a mattress on the floor, Jake had a bedroom but we never went in. He used the house as a shack-up place so he'd show up once a week, and he had a thing that, whenever he had sex, he had to blast the Rolling Stones. So if the Stones were blaring, we knew Jake was home . . .

I talked to my Dad and to Lonnie Chapman about who were the acting teachers around, because I wanted to do that simultaneously. I went down to sign up for the Strasberg Institute; my old man drove me to Hollywood Boulevard, and we were across the street in a hamburger joint. Who shows up there but Lee Strasberg? My old man knew Lee from years before. So I meet Strasberg, and my old man tells him I'm going in there to audition. He says, 'Good luck.' At that point he was married to Anna, who was pretty much running the school. The audition was essentially a conversation, and I was accepted, but I ended up choosing not to go.

Strasberg later participated in my Actors Studio audition at DeLongpre Avenue in LA. I got a girl from acting class to do a scene with me from *When You Coming Back, Red Rider?* It was one of those classic auditions where the lights are in your eyes and you can't see them sitting out there in the dark. And after we finished, all we heard was: 'The girl! Tell us about yourself!'

What I *did* do, I got into an extensive five-hour-a-day, five-day-a-week, two-year thing with Peggy Feury.

Like Lee Strasberg, Peggy Feury was a gifted actor who didn't cast easily and found her métier in teaching. She studied with Sanford Meisner and was a charter member of the Actors Studio, assisting Strasberg when he became artistic director. She then inaugurated the Strasberg Institute in Los Angeles, but in 1973 she left and later launched her own Loft Studio with husband Bill Traylor.

SEAN PENN: At Peggy's, I met someone I became very close with, a woman named Martine Getty at the time, now Gisela Getty – and she was Gisela before. But she was married to Paul Getty III . . . [1]

GISELA (MARTINE) GETTY: I got into a beginners' class of about fifteen people, and Sean was in that group. At first, while we were all sitting getting introduced and he hadn't said a word, you could think he was just a rangy Californian surfer kid. But in the first minute onstage, when we started doing improvisations, I saw there was a whole different dimension to him: an edge, a certain intensity. And I think very early on we connected, we became very close, because we recognized we were both like outsiders, interested in doing something different.

We both felt very supported by Peggy; she took a very personal interest in us and always put us together for scenes, which we wanted. She pushed you, she was open to taking risks: she did scenes and

1 After the nineteen-year-old Paul Getty III was subjected to a scandalous kidnapping/ransom effort in Rome in 1973, he and wife Gisela took flight, and made home in Los Angeles.

improvisations and exercises just so we could find out about ourselves and look at what was coming out. The first improvisation Sean and I did, we played a sister and brother with an erotic attraction to each other, and it ended up that he took a knife out and put it to my throat – very, very intense. At times with Sean we would get to scary places, expressing anger, getting physical. But we loved going there, Sean and I. Peggy saw that, and she worked with it a lot. It's funny, I also became friends with Sean's parents, and his mother would say, 'I don't know where it comes from . . .'

I remember too we did a scene from *Equus*. I played the psychiatrist, but as a woman. And we set up the stage elaborately, an office with a desk, which Peggy never liked us to do usually. But Sean and I were sitting up on the benches looking at the stage, and I could see him [*mimes chin-rubbing*] looking intently to see if it was all done. Then he jumped up and went to the desk where I would be sitting, got out a cigarette from a pack and started crumbling little bits of tobacco around the desk. I laughed and said, 'Nobody will see that!' And he said, 'But *we* know it's there . . .'

Anjelica Huston came to the Loft to study in 1981, a little after Penn departed.

ANGELICA HUSTON: Peggy was a very beautiful figure, quite small and delicate. She had that halfway-to-heaven look: pale eyes and light hair, she liked pale stockings and pearls, and sometimes she looked very angelic. She was extremely intelligent and mordant, Irish, with certain very visceral preferences: she could rhapsodize about food or a certain kind of glass or just something you brought in that day as a prop. But she was very visual, and she wandered around and sort of *tasted* everything.

She had a way of telling a story that was always instructive to what you were doing. And a way of commenting on a scene that was never destructive. Even if sometimes she would shoot you a sideways glance and you knew she thought it was pretty terrible, she had a way of translating it positively to the actors – her process was very reinforcing, I think. When I was lucky enough to get *Prizzi's Honor*, so much of that had to do with Peggy saying, 'Go on, just bite its head off.' I don't know what she was to Sean, but I'm sure many of the same things.

And occasionally she fell asleep, because she was narcoleptic. So I always felt that was a challenge. My aim was to keep Peggy awake . . .

SEAN PENN: You'd start a scene, she would doze off, you'd sit there, wait for her a couple of minutes. And she'd come up, and she would have gotten it all, had seen the whole scene and could talk about it – including the part where her eyes were closed and she was snoring. And I'm not making that up. To a man, other people will tell you that. Whether it was a half-sleep state or that she could tell where you were gonna go from where you started, I don't know. But she heard it . . .

Night class at Peggy's was more advanced. I moved into it pretty quickly, about a year in. Michelle Pfeiffer was there, Bruno Kirby, Annette O'Toole. Jeff Goldblum was sort of 'the guy to watch'. The night classes were great, because they would focus on one playwright for eight weeks, and largely they were living playwrights and often they'd be there a lot of the time. But we also did some of the classic playwrights. I workshopped *Romeo and Juliet*, got to play Mercutio. We did Proust, working from Pinter's *Proust Screenplay*. Chekhov was really significant: we did him in a director's class. We got professional directors coming in who were looking to learn how to work with actors better. I got Gene Reynolds, one of the creators of *M*A*S*H*. He later was among the guys who fucked me at the DGA[2] – not because he's a fucker, but because he's a very traditionally old-school guy.

So I would go right from Peggy's to the GRT, work there until midnight or one in the morning, pass out on the couch or go back to Sun Valley – or sleep on the stage bed at Peggy's. You could climb up a pipe on the back wall of the Loft, get in through a second-storey window that was always open, sleep on the stage bed – and god knows the DNA that was left on that by people doing 'rehearsals' late at night . . .

I was doing this job, that job, here and there: loading dock, roadway express, restaurant work. My friend Tom Levin got me a gig with 'Catering by Pierre', Beverly Hills. You'd either wash dishes, serve hors d'oeuvres, tend bar or valet-park. They thought my name was 'Champagne', so they sent me to work gay parties. One night we were up washing dishes in Beverly Hills – *not* a gay party. I'm rinsing. Tom's scrubbing. The soapy water turns blood-red. Tom says, 'Uh! Uh!' Sugar Ray Robinson had just walked in. Tom saw Sugar Ray and cut himself on a big knife. I go up to Sugar Ray, say, 'You taught me how to box!' He says, 'You're Leo Penn's kid!'

---

2 See Chapter 8.

But I could not get an acting job. Could not get an *agent*. Auditioned for every agent in town.[3] A manager named Ron Singer came to see a show, kept asking me if I wanted to go to the YMCA and wrestle with him . . . I never did. And I never had reason to believe he was odd in any way but that he liked wrestling. But he did promote me for a while. He'd seen me in a play at the GRT, because as an apprentice you could do workshop plays, then I became a member. I did *Earthworms*, that was quite an elaborate production, and a thing based on *Red Badge of Courage* that Lonnie Chapman wrote, *Bugle Boys*. And there was a stage version of *The Young Savages* . . .

EILEEN RYAN PENN: Leo and I saw him in that play. And he was just flying, going for broke. He probably had no direction at all. It was so interesting to us, because he'd been such a shy little kid. Boy, once he got on a stage it was a whole other thing! Once he put on that costume of character . . . And Leo and I really found ourselves holding each other's hands and exchanging glances, making faces at each other, like, 'And he wants to be an *actor* . . .?' We were just so worried for him. Well, saying that, the one thing in his favour was, he was brave. Too brave!

SEAN PENN: Was their approval important to me? Well . . . it was important to me when it was there. But, you know, like most kids – when the news is bad, they're wrong . . . I was not devastated. But I was struck by her, uh, candour . . .

EILEEN RYAN PENN: I realize now that to go in with that kind of guts, and do it so badly, but with bravura, is really a good way to start acting. It was big, what he was doing. But they say that Laurence Olivier started too big. It's better than being inhibited. If you don't have the guts to go for it and get up there in the first place . . . The thing Sean *had* was guts. All the talent came after. But he got better right away.

SEAN PENN: I did a piece from a James Leo Herlihy novel, *All Fall Down*, which, as I remember, my mother saw, and was a little less . . . well, she came around . . .

---

3 BOBBY COOPER: Sean and I are at the Four Seasons in New York, and this old guy is looking at Sean: he's foaming at the bit, he's got to come over. Sean didn't recognize him, guy had lost his hair. But he was the first agent Sean went to, way back. And he'd said, 'You don't have any talent, kid. You'd better get a new line of work.' Now the guy says, 'Sean, I've been waiting to say this to you for twenty years. And I've also said it to two other major stars. I'm so sorry.' Sean says, 'I *bet* you are . . .'

And I directed R. D. Call in Herlihy's *Terrible Jim Fitch*: we work-shopped it in Group Rep. I was fascinated by that piece of writing; I liked the language of it. And it seemed very tragic. One person erasing another person. It was touching to me.

R. D. CALL: *Terrible Jim Fitch* was a play I had known of through work-ing with Lee Strasberg and Charlie Shoal. Outsiders, misfits, guys in trouble, damaged men – I know these guys. I grew up with them. I am one myself, in a way. I understand them. The interesting thing about the piece is that Fitch spends the whole piece trying to get the girl, Sally, to talk, and she never does. I understand all that – that kind of frustration and rage. And so does Sean. I was talking to Sean about it one day, and he read it, said he'd like to direct this. So we did it. It was obvious then that he had that talent. For one thing, he already had the sign language that actors develop; he kind of intuitively already knew that a word or a gesture gets something across where somebody else would talk for forty-five minutes.

That was a project where we got to invite an audience. That's how I met Leo and Eileen, and they became almost like surrogate parents for me. Leo recommended me for my first real acting job, a rapist on *Barnaby Jones*, and that got me into the Screen Actors Guild. And then I was away, into all this madness . . .

SEAN PENN: At the same time, I was doing plays all over town: some full productions, some showcase productions where maybe you play it a couple of nights for an invited audience. I got into a star-studded pro-duction of *The Time of Your Life*,4 rehearsed out of the Actors Studio in Los Angeles and put on at the Beverly Hills Playhouse, starring Bobby Neuwirth, Marisa Berenson, Carlos Palomino and Penelope Milford, who'd recently had an Academy Award nomination for *Coming Home*, so I was among pretty high-pro people. It was a crowd that used to hang out at Roy's Restaurant on Sunset Boulevard, which was quite a Hollywood hang – where, coincidentally, Jessie Nelson was a waitress at the time.5 Roy, who owned the restaurant, directed this production. I was the newsboy who comes in and sings. I came out onstage and started singing 'When Irish Eyes Are Smiling', and Roy said, 'Sean? For this rehearsal, just *talk* the song, OK?' And that was the day I got fired.

---

4 Pulitzer Prize-winning 1939 play by William Saroyan, concerning a diverse set of char-acters who frequent a San Francisco dive-bar.
5 Later to direct Penn in *I Am Sam* (2001). See Chapter 12.

11 Penn aged eighteen

But then I did a production and played the part of *Terrible Jim Fitch* at Santa Monica City College, directed by Cameron Thor. I was taking auto mechanics there at the time – with speech and cinematography. I'd be surprised if I was there more than four months. Some time towards the end of that is when I got with Cameron. And once I got into rehearsals was when I realized I didn't want to put my car back together or do the speech stuff *or* the cinematography . . .

CAMERON THOR: I was standing out on the college quad and Sean came walking up, said, 'Whatcha doing?' I hadn't seen him in a while. But I wasn't surprised he'd started acting. As kids, we were both like outsiders, and now we were actors, and I thought, 'Oh, yeah. Of course. That's what we do.' Of course, he did it a lot better than me . . . He looked a whole lot like he was wearing Robert De Niro's costume from *Taxi Driver* – jeans and cowboy boots and an army jacket, eating seeds out of his pocket. He was obsessed with De Niro, had pictures of him all over his room.

SEAN PENN: I had seen *Mean Streets* and *Taxi Driver* and *The Deer Hunter*. And I had been on the set of *Raging Bull*. I snuck into Culver City studios in Los Angeles when they were shooting the boxing footage, just to see 'em work. That was before they shut down and De Niro gained the weight. Oh, he was significant for me, he was major. Primarily because – besides that he was great in the films, and the films were also great – one was aware of the discipline that he had and the commitment to what he did. That was inspiring. It's something I associate with ballet: I don't particularly like the aesthetics of ballet, you know, but when you see a great dancer and you know the sacrifice that went into it – that is moving to me.

CAMERON THOR: Sean introduced the subject of doing *Terrible Jim Fitch*. When I was nineteen I wouldn't know a good play if you shoved it up my ass, and I'm still hard-pressed. But I thought it was cool, and clever, and violent – all the things nineteen-year-olds like. And Sean was cool.

We spent one afternoon in a little room behind the stage at City College, a dressing room with a big cushy barber's chair so people could get made up. We closed the door. I said, 'OK, Sean, you sit there quietly with your eyes closed, we'll go through some relaxation exercises. And then I'm gonna talk to Jim, Jim Fitch. And ask you questions about your life. And you can't think of what you're gonna say, you have to answer with the first thing that pops out of your cabeza.' Sean was like, 'Cool.' I asked weird, random questions like, 'What was the name of the doctor who delivered you?' 'What was the weather like the day you were born?' – just going down the corridor of this life, picking out moments. And, after a few shaky minutes, Sean started answering every question like [*clicks fingers*], in a great rhythm. It was fascinating. That exercise taught me that, in the arts, the intuitive is far more intelligent than the intellect. And it was great that the first person I ever did that with [*laughs*] was Sean Penn. 'OK! I got it!'

Then we did the play, one afternoon only. The place was pretty much full. Sean's performance was really good: it was quiet and intense, but still had enough moxie in it to reach out twenty seats. Sean was studying with Peggy Feury and completely enamoured of her. And I think Peggy was very weighted in the psychology of living in the character. My experience of Sean is that he found the character by following a hunch with his body first and letting the psychology fill itself in through his very powerful imagination. And it was fascinating to watch the psychology of that character get seated in the actor. He created Jim physically first: he'd show up one day with a gun tucked in his boot, the next day with a bowl haircut he'd given himself; he'd dyed his hair and his eyebrows with shoe polish. He messed around with his walk. All to be Jim Fitch. Even then, he was a hair actor – starting from the hair and going down . . .

SEAN PENN: One of my other sleepover places at this time was Martine Getty's home with Paul in Laurel Canyon. I would often be rehearsing with Martine and then I would babysit her kids, Balthazar and Anna. And they were living a high life, a crazy life – this was before Paul paralysed himself with drugs.[6]

GISELA (MARTINE) GETTY: The acting community in Los Angeles had read so much about Paul and all we'd gone through, and they were very welcoming to us when we first came. I met Ryan O'Neal, Barbra Streisand, Kris Kristofferson . . . Dennis Hopper came by the house, raving mad, and my twin sister was there and he completely fell in love

6 In 1981 Paul Getty III took a near-lethal overdose and suffered a massive stroke, which left him completely paralysed and nearly blind.

with her. It ended that I eloped to New Mexico with Dennis . . . it only lasted maybe a month. But, being crazy myself, it seemed just the right thing. Then, through Dennis, I met Bert Schneider, and we were a group, Bert and Jack Nicholson, Bob Rafelson, Monte Hellman, Huey Newton, who Bert had supported. And I told them about this boy in my class . . .

SEAN PENN: Martine had a whole circle of friends who were either part of the sixties music scene or the war-protest scene or acting. So it was an interesting time in my life because I was being exposed to people – I met Wim Wenders, Leonard Cohen was in that circle, I spent a lot of time with David Blue. And I really only discovered as years went on how formidable some of these people's works were . . .

David was the best friend of Phil Ochs, had played at Phil Ochs' memorial concert, a beautiful song called 'Cupid's Arrow'. And he was part of *Renaldo and Clara*.[7] But I didn't know any of that yet, didn't know who Phil Ochs was. I just found David a real interesting guy. Sometimes I'd be babysitting the kids, and rather than go out with the gang, David would hang out at home, and we'd just rap and drink. I was back in Jerry Connelly Land, because we'd drink tequila all night and pass out.

Once in a while, I would go out with Martine and her friends, and that was like my entrance into a version of what everybody calls 'The Scene'. But it wasn't my generation's scene, it was the generation before me.

JACK NICHOLSON: Well, I guess the first time I was aware of Sean was at Helena Kallianotes' roller-skating party out in White Oak or Reseda . . . Helena kind of created the roller-skating boom in the late seventies, and we all went out there one night a week and skated around. Sean was a kid I was sort of aware of. But you could probably trace everybody back through that place . . .

SEAN PENN: It was Sherman Way roller-skating rink in the San Fernando Valley, and it was like a roller-skating Studio 54 with lights on, and a mirror-ball over the skating floor. This was a party where you'd see Jack Nicholson, Ringo Starr, Ed Begley Jr, Harry Dean Stanton, Leonard Cohen and his wife, the woman who was 'Suzanne', movie stars galore, young and old. Now, I wasn't going to get out on

7 Bob Dylan's filmic document of his seminal 1975 Rolling Thunder Revue.

fucken roller skates . . . but I was invited along with Martine a couple of times and I was a wallflower at those things. I used to see Harry Dean, and he was doing *The Black Marble* at the time – I know, because he had a perm. The perm made me think he was gay. Later I saw the movie and reoriented myself . . .

GISELA (MARTINE) GETTY: I had always taken pictures of people I liked, so I took some of Sean. I thought he had the James Dean quality: introverted, deep; you could feel the intensity. I also thought he was very beautiful. I went to all my friends, gave them pictures, and said, 'You have to put this kid in a film, he's going to be good.'

12 Penn by Gisela Getty

R. D. CALL: Sean went out and got his first 8 x 10s done: kind of a glamour shot, with windblown hair and dramatic lighting, and his hair long and blond. I tacked that up on the wall at Sunland. The place was empty, there was no furniture, so the only thing hanging on the wall was this picture. I crossed out his name on the bottom of it, and we decided to make up a name like the old movie stars, Rock Hudson or Tab Hunter – his was 'Fortune Hunter' [*laughs*], that would be his screen name. The irony of the joke was Sean was never interested in being a movie star or money or being famous or any of that shit. That's why we did it. Because it was ludicrous.

SEAN PENN: So things are going well in class, going well at GRT. But

I'm tired of just, you know, hand-to-mouth. And nobody's interested in me as an actor. Ron Singer got me to every agency, big and small – everyone passed. It didn't matter what I auditioned for, the only thing I could get was plays. I did *Summerspell*,[8] a real independent film, in the sense that they had about $12 to make it. The producers made a deal with the Group Rep similar to Equity waiver theatre, and I had a small part, but it meant going on location for the first time, up to Stockton. But I was jumping fences at the studios when I'd read something in *Drama-Logue* or it was out on the nexus. I didn't get any of those jobs, but I got some interesting meetings: one with Robert Redford for *Ordinary People* and one with Bob Rafelson, who was doing *Brubaker* with Redford at the time. Oh, and *The Blue Lagoon* [*laughs*]. Then on my nineteenth birthday I got a gig: an episode of *Barnaby Jones* with Ed Harris and Madeleine Stowe and Buddy Ebsen. And I got my SAG card off of it. But I *still* couldn't get an agent.

JORDAN RHODES: I was talking to Leo about Sean's career. He told me, 'Ah, my kid wants to be an actor . . .' He had called Ken Gilbert, who was a friend of both of ours, and Ken had given Sean a small role. Ken had said, 'I don't know, there may be something there . . .' But if you're relegated to those roles, no one's gonna know how good you are anyway.

JOSEPH VITARELLI: I don't remember a steady woman in Sean's life until Meg Tilly, briefly. Meg was really special, I always liked her.

SEAN PENN: Oh, that's right . . . I skipped a lot of personal stuff, girls and things. The first person I lived with was Meg, which was a bizarre period of time. Nice-as-all-hell girl, but . . . God, when you're that young, you don't know who anybody is. She was a serious ballet dancer who got injured. Then she started getting interested in movies and became one of the chorus dancers in the movie *Fame*. And then moved to California to get into acting in a serious way and ended up in a production of *The Girl on the Via Flaminia* at the Gene Dynarski Theatre, where we met. I was a young drunk soldier at the beginning of the play. And then I brought Meg into Peggy's.

R. D. CALL: Sean and Meg got involved, and then I got involved with

8 Directed by Lina Shanklin, a forty-five-minute piece expanded into a feature three years later.

Meg's sister Jennifer. They were both living in a place over on Franklin and Normandy, little studio apartments one above the other. Jennifer lived upstairs and Meg lived below. Sean and I used to go over there in the middle of the night and throw rocks at the window to get 'em to open up and let us in . . .

SEAN PENN: In the mornings we'd put our heads out the windows. R. D. would look down, I'd look up, we'd see each other. 'Good morning, Larry!' 'Good morning, Moe!' 'The girls go yet?' 'Yup. Let's go get a coffee . . .' I ended up moving over to an apartment on Stanley that Meg kind of moved into for a little while. But she kept her own place. And shortly after that, I was off to New York.

CHRISTOPHER PENN: I think Sean was very serious, tried to get a couple of parts, didn't get 'em, and said, 'You know what? I'm going to try another venue, and try to do this from the ground up, instead of taking advantage of personal connections in Hollywood. I'm going to go do theatre in New York.' Any parents who care are nervous when their kids go away. But I never got the sense that they didn't approve.

JOSEPH VITARELLI: I had left Malibu and gone back to New York. I was playing piano in bars and lounges. I had started that when I was twelve or thirteen; parents used to invite me to their cocktail parties and I would sit and play requests all night long in a ruffled silk shirt and a velvet jacket. Then Sean came out and joined me.

SEAN PENN: I'd been there once before when I was five years old, for *A Man Called Adam*. I've got $800 – that's it. Joe's grandparents had a guest room for each of us, but they could only give us about two weeks to stay. And Jordan Rhodes was also friends with a director, Art Wolff, who was casting an off-off-Broadway show.

ART WOLFF: I was teaching at NYU and I had a student called Larry Nicks, who came to me and said, 'If I found a really good play that had a role for me, and got the financing, would you direct it?' And so came *Heartland* by Kevin Heelan.

Heartland *is set on a dilapidated front porch in a Midwestern town where a killer is at large. Skeet, an unemployed nightwatchman, guards his homestead, sharing beer and prejudice with his meek buddy Earl as he polishes a shotgun. For the killer, Skeet likes Tiny Baker, the town loon, whom he once assaulted on suspicion of molesting his teenage son James. James is slow-witted and timid around his father but surprisingly adept with a rifle. Skeet's wife, James's mother, has long since taken to her bed, near-catatonic.*

ART WOLFF: It wasn't that big a cast – two guys, the kid, the town sheriff. The first person we found was an actor I'd worked with before, J. C. Quinn, who was perfect for Skeet. We saw dozens of kids, but I was about halfway into the process and we still hadn't found anybody. And I got a call from Jordan. I had sent him the script because I thought he'd be just right for the sheriff, but he was busy.

JORDAN RHODES: Sean had told me he was going to New York, and I said, 'Well, I have some connections there with people in the soap operas.' But he was absolutely adamant he didn't want to do any of that. Then I had this script, and I called Art and asked him if he had cast the son yet. He said, 'No, we're still reading.' I said, 'There's somebody I'd like you to audition: a friend of mine, Leo Penn's son, Sean. He's very talented.' Art said he'd be happy to, and I called up Sean, said, 'Do you want to audition?' and he said, 'Oh man!'

ART WOLFF: This was early November 1980. We were working out of an apartment on 90th and Madison. Kevin Heelan and the stage manager were helping us read. Sean walked in the door and immediately Kevin and I were thinking, 'If this kid can act, then it's perfect. He looks so much like J. C. Quinn, he could *be* his son.' We talked a little, looked over his résumé. I could see he was well-trained. And then he read. And he was awful. Just the worst. I stopped him, we went outside, I gave him some adjustments, said, 'Take some breaths, you seem a little nervous.' Then he read again. Still terrible. We thanked him and sent him off. And after he left, Kevin and I both said, 'Can you believe it? He was so physically *right* . . .'

JORDAN RHODES: That night, I got a phone call from Sean, and he was really down. He said, 'Ahh, I didn't do well, Jordan . . . I know I can do it, but I didn't read well.' I said, 'Stay at your number there a few minutes.' I called Art and asked him what he was reading in the next day or so. And I said, 'Do me a favour, have Sean back and have him read with the other actors. Then you won't have to have the stage manager do it . . .'

ART WOLFF: I've never met Bob De Niro, but the word always was that if he had ever had to audition to get roles he would never have worked – that he mumbled, was cold, couldn't put two words together, and only got work because Martin Scorsese and Brian De Palma knew him. People would say, 'Why are you casting *him*?' They'd say, 'He'll be fine.' And clearly, he was . . .

The next morning, Sean was there at about a quarter to nine, waiting outside the building for us. We started work, hung out, had lunch, joked around and got to know each other. And he began to relax a bit. As the day wore on, and I saw him get more and *more* relaxed, I said to Kevin, 'Why don't we have him read again?' There was one last guy reading for the sheriff, the last scene of the play. And I asked Sean to read the kid, James. He did it, and it was electric. Our sheriff left – it was the end of the day. I looked at Sean, told him to stay where he was, and said, 'Kevin, will you get up with Sean and read the father, up to the end of the play?'

SEAN PENN: And Art stood up afterwards, all welled up and everything, came and put his arms around me and told me right there and then – he didn't look back at his producers or anything – 'You're doing the play.' I . . . oh, I could not fucking believe it. I was just flying. I called home. Joe and I were in a Village apartment down in the gay area on Christopher Street, and I ran from 90th and Madison all the way down to that apartment. I finally caught up with him at the Racing Club where he was playing piano. And Art turned out to be a lifelong friend, a great guy.

ART WOLFF: To this day, if we're together, when he introduces me Sean never fails to say, 'I'd like you to meet Art Wolff. This is the guy who gave me a career.' I don't know that's really true, but it's one of the things that I love about Sean – he is a decent, loyal guy.

JORDAN RHODES: Ten years later, I acted in *The Indian Runner* for Sean. Then he invited me to a screening, and there was a little party afterwards. I went over to Sean to say thanks. He reached up and grabbed me round the neck, and I gave him a hug. And in my ear he said, 'I've never forgotten what you did for me . . .'

JOSEPH VITARELLI: *Raging Bull*, I remember Sean and I went to see that together in Times Square.

SEAN PENN: Saw it when it opened, couldn't wait. There was a huge billboard of the poster painted on the side of a building right near our apartment. And that was an experience. Just an incredible poem, that movie . . .

The character in *Heartland* was not only fourteen but also . . . frail. And I was a physically oriented guy at that time. So I had to lose weight. I came back out to California, to Sun Valley, and I was running around a dirt corral with no horses in it.

R. D. CALL: He put himself on a real strict regimen, diet and exercise. His breakfast was half a bowl of cream of wheat, no milk. Maybe a piece of grapefruit later in the day. But he lost so much weight that people were concerned for his health; he looked like someone walking out of Auschwitz. He even used to taunt himself when he was doing it.

SEAN PENN: I wasn't eating, but I had a vicarious interest in eating. This was just at the end of the disco era, and R. D. was about the furthest thing imaginable from a disco. So I started making chocolate cakes that I would dress up and write 'Disco Cake' on, and I'd feed him. 'Eat more!' But that was [*laughs*] a sad and lonely time: I think I went down from about 175–180 pounds to about 119.

At the same time I got cast in a TV movie, *The Killing of Randy Webster*.9 And I think it was the last day of shooting – I was out on the Sierra Highway with Gary McCleary, who was playing Randy Webster, and Jennifer Jason Leigh – when it was reported that John Lennon had been shot.10

I get turned onto Phil Ochs at that stage too, because I visit back home and Chris is listening to source music for his Vietnam movie. And I read about Phil Ochs and become sort of immersed in him for a time.

SEAN PENN (sleeve notes to *A Toast to Those Who Are Gone* by Phil Ochs, Archives Alive/Rhino, 1986): '*I am the masculine American man / I kill, therefore I am . . .' There was a consistent sense of irony and humour along with his beautiful melodies. In laughter and tears, I listened through breakfast . . . I began to feel a disturbing familiarity with his sense of hope in its contrast to the ever present pain. I was in the midst of some 'to the brink' troubles of my own at that time; and it seemed, as it always does, that no one else could suffer to the degree we all claim as exclusive.*

9 A troubled teenager is shot and killed in an altercation with police, who then attempt a cover-up. Penn has a handful of scenes as Randy's loyal, bespectacled, slightly square friend Don.
10 Mark Chapman shot and killed John Lennon on 8 December 1980.

JOSEPH VITARELLI: Sean and I crashed at different places in New York for a while, then we got it together to rent a horrible little apartment on 48th Street between 8th and 9th. Half the size my living room is now, for the two of us, a mattress on each side. A kitchen I could barely fit in. Shitty old shower. Roaches were the primary tenants. $300 a month, which was huge money to us then. I remember saying I wanted to put plants in the place; Sean was completely against the idea. I think the Gulag motif appealed to him. He had got so thin, rail thin, *scary* thin. And it was a harsh winter in New York. Leo sent him a huge padded snowsuit that weighed almost as much as Sean did, the kind of thing you expect people working on pipelines in Antarctica would wear. But Sean walked around in it, because it was the only way to stay alive.

ART WOLFF: We originally planned to do *Heartland* off-Broadway, then we weren't able to rent any of the theatres we wanted. We did consider postponing. But in mid-December 1980 the producers found out that the Century, a mid-level Broadway house – 299 seats – was available. And after you get over everybody dancing around going, 'We're on Broadway!', you think, 'What are we doing on Broadway with this little off-Broadway play . . .?'

At the first reading, Larry Nicks had not only learned his entire role, he'd decided on every inflection; he was ready for costume and make-up and opening night. Sean, good Actor's Studio person that he is, now knows he's got the role and he's comfortable. So he's now going to throw out everything he did in the audition, because we've got four weeks of rehearsal and he's starting again from scratch. So Larry's standing up declaiming, J. C. is hung-over and just trying to get through it, and Sean is sitting with his face buried in the book, talking flat, mumbling . . .

One thing Sean did scared the hell out of me at first. He came to the second or third rehearsal wearing one of those collars for a strained neck. I thought, 'Oh my god, please, not some surfing injury?' And he said, 'No, this is Peggy's idea. She told me to wear this so I don't start hanging my head onstage and talking to the floor . . .'

SEAN PENN: Martin Sheen said something great to me when I was going to do *Heartland*. I had only played theatres that were ninety-nine seats, and I told him, 'I'm worried about getting to the back row.' He said, 'If you've got something to say, they'll hear you.' And I found that to be true. I mean, you've got to be heard. But I can sense somebody on a stage from a back row if they're *there*. I think of it this way: just because it's opera, does the acting have to be so bad?

ART WOLFF: You can tell by reading the play that it's not the most original concept: 'A father who mistreats a son, violence in the heartland.' But what I loved was how Sean turned round those clichés. The lines weren't there: the audience was going to have to get it in the way he behaves, his physicalization of his emotional life. He took a kid you thought you'd seen a hundred times and made a very particular guy. Take the stage directions at the end of Act One. All they say is, 'They get in the car. Exit. James sits. Nervous. Pacing. Picks up radio. Turns it on.' I said to Sean, 'So now you're alone, and it's your house to take care of. What are you gonna do?' With Sean, you can't be too specific – 'Nervous. Pacing' is meaningless. Onstage there were three chairs, plus the porch steps, plus the rails. And Sean moved around from place to place, with his gun, looking to see what was the right place to be to watch the house: sitting on each chair, then on the step, then leaning against the rail . . . trying on poses of how to be a man. There was such a mixture of bravado and fear in that. And a great end to Act One.

SEAN PENN: During the whole rehearsal period, I start hanging out at the West Bank Café right on Theatre Row, 42nd and 9th. Twenty years later, I took my daughter to New York on a trip, and we went down there on a walk. You wouldn't take a twelve-year-old to 42nd Street when *I* was there. It wasn't even called 42nd Street; it was 'Forty-Deuce'. And that was where all the little hooker boys hung out . . . Larry Clark's book *Teenage Lust* was out at the time, and it had a New York section that was very disturbing. So, the West Bank, it would be Joe and I and J. C. and Doc Katz . . . Katz was always the last to leave.

JOSEPH VITARELLI: Dr Katz is a book unto himself. And the scary thing is, most of it's true. He became a part of Sean's business, to varying degrees, in the late eighties. But he's a remarkable guy, who basically would say or do anything he felt at any given moment. There's a lot of Katz nakedness in this tale . . . And tough too, with a military background. So behind all the lunacy was a very serious guy.

DR EDWARD ('EDDIE') KATZ: I was in Vietnam, got a Purple Heart. If it wasn't for me, you'd all be speaking Vietnamese. I saved this world from Communism . . .

I was a pot smuggler from 1970 to 1980. J. C. Quinn was a friend of mine, and I invested $2,500 in the play for good luck for J. C. It wasn't that much to go to an opening night on Broadway. So I had 10 per cent of a Broadway play. I even rented a brand-new tuxedo – with an option to buy – hoping the thing would be my *Hair*. It wasn't . . . But I got to know Sean during the rehearsal period. A sweet kid, shy. And J. C. and I took him around . . .

SEAN PENN: So I'm at the West Bank, and there, every night, is Tennessee Williams, holding court with his group of about six people. I recognized one of them as Alfred Ryder. And always next to Tennessee was this ravaged old drunken woman, with beady, crazy eyes. I'm at a back table, just sitting there, and all that's on my mind is, 'That's fucking *Tennessee Williams* . . .' One night, the woman catches me looking at Tennessee. She gets up and starts to come over. And now I'm in a weird state of mind. I'm an actor. I *had* been a surfer and an athlete, but now I had gone from 180 pounds down to 119. So I'm suddenly feeling like a fourteen-year-old boy, and there's this woman coming over. And she says: '*I* was almost your *mother*!'

It was my dad's ex-wife, Olive Deering. I knew she was Alfred Ryder's sister, and she'd been the beauty queen of the De Mille pictures, but I hadn't ever seen anything of her. I'd only had her described to me. That was the only time I met her: she died not many years after that.[11] And so did Tennessee, and so did Alfred.

Heartland was written as a piece in which violence is passed from father to son, leaving a mother incapacitated and a son who goes on a small-town murder spree, culminating in his Dad. For Wolff's production, the ending was reworked: the killer is an off-stage character, and mother Pauline shoots Skeet from the house before he can inflict further violence on James.

ART WOLFF: I wanted it to be less of a thriller, more of an examination of what had happened to this family, as opposed to, 'Oh wow, James is the killer?'

HELENA KATZ: All of Sean's family came to the opening night. Eddie danced with his grandmother.

11 Olive Deering died of cancer on 22 March 1986.

Courtesy of Art Wolff

13 *Heartland*: from left, J. C. Quinn (Skeet), Penn (James), Larry Nicks (Earl)

DR KATZ: Chris had never been on an elevator before, and I lived on the 37th floor.

HELENA KATZ: Chris and some kids were doing some kind of Vietnam film, so they went through Eddie's closet looking for old army uniforms. But none of them fit . . .

ART WOLFF: I had met Leo before in Los Angeles. Chris, at age fifteen, came to the opening-night party with his movie he had made. This was the first thing he did: 'Here! Soon as you're able to find a videotape player, this is my movie.' OK, Chris, we got *that* straight . . . Eileen I had talked to on the phone during rehearsal, but the first time we met was opening night. And the first time I looked at her, I just had the feeling, 'I *know* this person . . . But Sean has her eyes, so that's probably what I'm seeing.' Then afterwards, at the party, we're sitting together schmoozing. I'm still looking at her. She says, '*What?*' I say, 'I *know* you.' 'Of *course* you do.' 'No, I know you from seeing you *perform*. You're an actress.' 'That's right.' And it suddenly hit me. 'Oh my god, you were the best Blanche Dubois I ever saw . . .' And, you know, looking back at it, I don't have any doubt that if there are genetic markers for acting . . .

DR KATZ: Sean's grandfather died during the run,[12] and he was pretty upset. He called and came over. He loves chocolate, so I went to the all-night delis and supermarkets and got him all different slices of chocolate cake. Tried to make him feel better . . .

ART WOLFF: It was an extraordinary début for Sean: certainly everybody I talked to felt that way. But he didn't get extraordinary reviews. Mel Gussow of the *New York Times* didn't like it, and after you lose the *Times*, it's very hard to get it going again. The only really rave review – which couldn't keep us open – was in the *Post* from Clive Barnes.[13] What there *was*, from my memory, were lots of letters and notes and phone calls from people within the business. So that's where Sean's big splash was.

SEAN PENN: And that's when a woman at the Brett Adams Agency in New York named . . . it's terrible, I should remember her name. It was a short-lived relationship, but obviously at an important time – but she saw me in the play. Shirley Rich was casting *Taps* and was told about me by this agent. They then came down and saw me, and got me in on *Taps*.

Taps was a motion-picture project generated by Stanley Jaffe, son of Leo Jaffe, ex-chairman of Columbia, himself president of Paramount by the age of thirty. Now a solo producer, Jaffe had acquired Devery Freeman's novel Father Sky *in manuscript.*

STANLEY JAFFE: The project was originally started at Columbia and went through a number of incarnations and finally wound up at Fox. James Lineberger started writing it, I think, then the bulk of the work was done by Bob Kamen and Daryl Ponicsan.

The script finally titled Taps *traces a rite of passage at Bunker Hill Military Academy. The school's head, retired General Bache, informs his devoted, whey-faced cadets that plans are afoot by the trustees to sell the grounds to real-estate developers. Then Bache is disgraced when a townie kid is shot and killed in a fracas at the school's end-of-*

12 On 4 March 1981, Leo's father Maurice Penn passed away.
13 'Sean Penn carries off the disturbed boy with a properly strange gusto.' Clive Barnes, *New York Post*, 24 February 1981. '[Penn] renders his emotional disturbance so vividly we forget he is only in a play. When he is playing with a rifle he becomes scary enough to make members of the audience feel personally threatened.' Christopher Sharp, *Woman's Wear Daily*, 25 February 1981.

year ball. Taken into custody, Bache suffers a heart attack, and the Academy board decide to close Bunker Hill post-haste. But Cadet Major Brian Moreland elects to mount an armed occupation of campus and repel external forces, assisted by his seconds: thoughtful, steadfast Alex Dwyer and wildly gung-ho David Shawn. And so the boys don fatigues and muster, bringing the National Guard to the school gates . . .

HAROLD BECKER: The story was not at all far-fetched: the head of the school where we shot was a general who had commanded the Americal division in Vietnam, so he didn't exactly come from a field of glory. While I was scouting, they had a summer camp where a lot of parents sent their unmanageable kids to give them some 'discipline'. So they had ten-year-old kids drilling in the noonday sun. I see a big colonel, wearing bars that represent his serving rank, and he literally lifts a kid up – the kid's arms are like skinny pipes – and drags him to the general, who says, 'What did he do wrong?' The colonel says, 'Breach of discipline, sir. We're going to have to send him home.' The general says, 'Interrogate him first . . .'

I liked the idea of a film about zealotry: in this case, impressionable young people who get caught up in the romanticism of the military outlook, believing in things to the point where they can be led right over the edge of the cliff. The school had a cult-like quality: Bache is retired and now he's created another universe in the school, at odds with the one outside his walls. That happens with cult leaders too. And finally, of course, it leads to catastrophe, and the scales fall from these young men's eyes. I felt it was a good premise for a drama. And in George C. Scott I was casting a great actor as Bache, with enormous charisma, who could convincingly lead those kids in a charge up the hill.

STANLEY JAFFE: We made one radical departure. In the book, there was a lot of attention paid to the outside world, what was going on in the governor's office and with the parents. About eight weeks before the picture was to go on the floor, we made a decision that, in fact, all that mattered was what was going on in the minds of the boys. So we deleted everything of the outside world except what the boys could potentially see on a TV inside the school. That for me was what made the picture come to life. It also meant we now had to find a lot of very good young actors. And we spent a lot of time looking for them . . .

HAROLD BECKER: I fell in love with those kids. I still love 'em. Kids! Most of them now forty years old, gaining on me . . . But they went on to such distinguished careers. It's sort of a Cinderella story. For Brian I had Timmy Hutton: they were still cutting *Ordinary People* at the time, but I had already heard great things about him. And then I was looking for that little group around Tim.[14] Shirley Rich would go see a lot of plays, and she mentioned *Heartland* and a young actor who she thought I should see. So I went down there, and I was blown away by Sean: it really seemed like he was heaven-sent to play Alex, the surviving character, who for me was the lynchpin of the piece. He then came in and did an audition for us. We gave him the licence to do whatever he wanted; and it was so off-the-wall, it was hypnotic.

SEAN PENN: I did one of those jump-up-on-the-desk deals – it wasn't planned, I just ended up that way. It was a scene where I'm addressing a lot of people energetically, acting out. It's in the movie.[15] But it was better in the audition . . .

I met Hutton at my second audition, the call-back. I did it with a reader before, and they were going to cast me from that first one – I didn't know this yet. But Tim had been specifically called in to be asked, 'Are you gonna have a problem with this guy?' So I went back in there. 'Hey, how are you?' Did the scene with Tim. I go outside, they're still talking inside. Tim comes out and walks by me – he's got his hat and his cigarettes, he was a big chain-smoker at the time – and as he passes, he says [*sotto voce*] 'I'll see you later, Sean . . .' That was how I knew I'd got the part.

HAROLD BECKER: Then I put the kids through what I called a 'basic training': a four-week rehearsal to turn them into cadets. Half a day would be rehearsing the scenes, and the other half would be drilling and marching, so that, by its end, these actors would feel like the characters they were playing and it would have that authenticity.

STANLEY JAFFE: You couldn't just have a kid show up on the day of

---

14 Hutton played Conrad, a youth recovering from a failed suicide attempt, in Robert Redford's directorial début. It was only months after the death from liver cancer of his father, Jim Hutton.
15 As morale falls in the occupation, Dwyer does an inspired mimicry of a TV reporter sticking an imaginary microphone under the nose of 'Private Bleeding Heart' and imitating 'Colonel Adolf Kerby' of the National Guard, decrying the use of force while rubbing sweaty palms in glee.

shooting and have him look, sound, walk like any of the real kids. We had permission to have the boys stay in the dorms with the actual cadets at the school. And they needed to know how to march, how to ride – in the case of Sean, he's first introduced on horseback.

SEAN PENN: Was it useful? Yes and no. There wasn't enough of it, and it was too generalized. Sometimes they just want to feel like they're getting it done. And I think things should have been done a little more towards what each of us was actually going to be doing onscreen. The care was not taken to make sure those things were accomplished on the day. You couldn't say, 'Oh, could I get another one on that?' We were treated, I feel, a bit as one . . .

STANLEY JAFFE: It was a very good shake out to find out who could do the job. They mostly shaped up. One boy didn't, and he was replaced. And during the course of that boot-camp/quasi-rehearsal, another boy who was selected to play Shawn fell by the wayside.

HAROLD BECKER: I had cast a talented kid from a Shakespeare youth theatre in Tennessee. But he couldn't cut it, which was heartbreaking. Shawn is a 'war lover', as in the book by John Hershey. And I needed someone with that power, someone who could walk the walls. Then I noticed this kid, Tom Cruise. Now it's almost a joke to say it . . . Tom was a kid from New Jersey, he had the build of a wrestler and very little acting experience. I had hired what I called a 'cadre' to surround my principals. There was something in Tom that attracted me: I can't say I thought, 'This kid is going some place.' But I put him in. Now I noticed he was already out-marching the other cadets on the parade field. I auditioned him for Shawn, he auditioned well, and I offered him the part. He asked me, 'Well, what about . . .?' Because he and the other boy had become friends already – and that was nice to see in a young actor. But I explained to him the reality of it: I had to replace this boy, it was my responsibility, so if he didn't want the part, I would just continue my process. And he took it.

SEAN PENN: And that was that. Boom. He was *there*. This was a guy who was ready for his chance, no question about it. He wouldn't have known that himself – he was second-guessing everything all the time. But that didn't stop him from committing when it was time. Cruise was *so* . . . like he was training for the fucken *Olympics*. I think he was the first person I ever said 'Calm down!' to. A fun guy, too.

HAROLD BECKER: I think Sean had a terrific influence on Tom. Tom was coming from a totally unsophisticated background; he didn't have Sean's experience and depth. But what he learned from Sean was that amazing work ethic in the character. I was blessed by Sean's intensity, because it communicated itself to other actors. When actors are young, they're more easily distracted. But Sean helped me that way.

14 On location for *Taps*: Tom Cruise, Timothy Hutton, Penn

15 'I thought at one point on camera they were going to kill each other . . . ': Cruise (David Shawn), Penn (Alex Dwyer), Hutton (Brian Moreland) in *Taps*

Penn's Alex is the conscientious rebel of the group who wants it done by the book. 'My sense of honour may be a little ragged round the edges,' he tells Moreland, 'but I don't walk out on a friend.' As such, he butts heads with the brazen loose cannon Shawn. Their first encounter

on a stairwell is an exchange of jibes, and their differences become more pronounced as the occupation goes on.

HAROLD BECKER: There was an element of tension, because Sean and Tom were playing such opposites. That carried over often. Some of their contretemps Stanley Jaffe had to deal with, not me . . .

STANLEY JAFFE: The boys were very interesting . . . they were play-acting and yet deadly serious about performing their roles as real cadets would. And inside those roles there was supposed to be a discipline and an organization, who was on top and so forth. Sean wanted to be addressed as his character. His intensity that you see today was there then. And that's a joy to find. Ain't easy sometimes, but a joy to find . . . And Tom Cruise was *as* intense as Sean, and I thought at one point on camera they were going to kill each other. It was the scene where the boys go into town to load up with supplies. Tom's character shoots off a rifle, and when they get back to base Sean's livid with him. Now, Sean likes to push buttons. And he said something to Tom, and suddenly they're chasing each other around the place until we got them to stop. But that's the way they were: they were supposed to not like each other. So Sean found a way to have Tom not like him for a moment . . .

Such is the slow-burning resentment between Dwyer and Shawn that we come to suspect the denouement will be a little war between them. Instead it is Moreland who takes most umbrage at Dwyer's dismissal of the dwindling mission and the baleful influence of Bache, and the friends have a brawling punch-up in front of the company.

HAROLD BECKER: I remember choreographing the big fight scene between Sean and Timmy. It was one of those intense fights, something that can happen so easily in adolescence, even between good friends, where things can escalate. So we wanted to find the truth in it. But it had to be done carefully.

STANLEY JAFFE: Sean and Tim come up to me. Don't forget, they're nineteen, twenty years old. 'Can we talk to you? We talked to Harold, he said talk to you.' I said, 'Sure, what's it about?' 'Can we really fight?' I said, 'Excuse me?' They said, 'You know, can we really go at it?' I said, 'And then what do we do for take two?' There was a breath, and then they went back and did it the way it's supposed to be done. They weren't being silly: that's just how intensely involved they were in the roles.

HAROLD BECKER: But they were close friends outside. They lived together, hung out together, ran after girls together. You get a bunch of young kids and they're going to enjoy life.

SEAN PENN: Yeah, there was a lot of rock and roll going on on that floor. It was like I'd gone to high school and now *Taps* was college for me. And it was Fraternity Row . . .

After the accidental death of one small soldier – first seen talking to his mom on the phone, hence dead meat – the resistance ebbs away. Moreland breaks down, confessing his failings to a tearful Dwyer, who compels him to end the lock-in.

MEEGAN OCHS: Sean told me later that, when they were filming the last scene in *Taps* and basically they're about to go out and give up, he kept playing my father's song, 'That Was the President', on a blaster before each take, and by the time they'd got the scene, the entire set was in tears.

Dwyer's surrender plan, however, is thwarted by mad Shawn, who starts strafing from an upper window, inciting Colonel Kerby's tanks to roll in. Moreland and Dwyer go to restrain Shawn, Moreland first through the door as bullets hail in from outside. Kerby finally enters to find Dwyer cradling the lifeless Moreland.

HAROLD BECKER: When Sean wept over Tim's body it was a dark moment, a tragic moment. And Sean was *there*. There was no sense of his having to squeeze the tears out. I would never say to an actor, 'You gotta cry right here.' It's the kiss of death, it makes it too tough – tears on command. I just needed Sean to carry the emotion. But the tears came from him.

We ended with Sean carrying Tim's body out of the building. I had the whole scene planned out. I wanted a long continuous shot, the camera pulling back in a helicopter as Sean walked out, so that in the end you see the entire field of carnage as they walk towards the ambulance. I wanted to shoot in 'magic hour', so I brought the helicopter in an hour early and we went up in it and planned the move. We go to our first rehearsal. I'm sitting up in the helicopter, I call 'Action'. Sean walks out, carrying Timmy. And the wind from the helicopter blows them straight back through the door . . . Now I have about forty minutes left to get this supposedly great shot. Fortunately we had a crane, and a wonderful Steadicam operator, so I had him start on Sean and Tim, walk back, step onto the crane, and the crane lifted him up into the air. But talk about necessity being the mother of invention . . .

SEAN PENN: I felt very restricted the first time I made a movie – very restricted by the movie-making process. I had done some television stuff, so I knew that it's a scene here and a scene there, and you work within those restrictions. But *Taps* was my first time actually being a storytelling character, where you further the plot by your choices. And I was frustrated by the style that later became known to me as 'traditional film-making'. It was not very spontaneous. The whole thing of the actor's camera sense: that was the essence of my problem. For me, acting was about freedom of movement and trusting that things were being heard and witnessed enough not to be displaying them, or having to be careful – just to have them seen, and to really listen, watch, hear, play moment-to-moment, and find freedom in that.

STANLEY JAFFE: The thing I liked about Sean, you can't just tell him, 'Do this!' He wasn't being the Actors Studio 'Tell me *why* my character would' guy. But he did need more than 'Do this'. And he also told *you* why he thought it should be something.

HAROLD BECKER: I had to be on my toes with Sean to ensure that the motivations were honest ones. It was a challenge, and that was good for me. But he wasn't an easy actor to work with, because he had very strong opinions. Sometimes his opinions ran ahead of his film experience. The first day on the set, Sean was speaking very low. And I think there is something to that, in that it can sometimes carry more emotion. But I saw my soundman pointing at his earphones, signalling to me that he wasn't able to pick it up. Sean said, 'He could pick it up if he wanted to.' I said, 'Sean, let's get it halfway between. I don't need to hear everything, but just give me *something*.'

SEAN PENN: I remember Robert Duvall saying one time somebody told him to be louder, and he looked at the actor he was in the scene with and said, 'Can *you* hear me?' The guy said, 'Yeah.' 'Well, *that's* who I'm talking to . . .'

Harold Becker's a really good guy and a smart guy who I did not get along with on *Taps*, but I think I would say that it was an issue primarily of my inexperience, so that I would fight the director rather than finding a middle ground where we could have a dialogue as opposed to an argument. Harold wasn't that experienced either at the time. He'd made two or three movies, none of them with quite the demands of structure this one had. So structure took over, and much between was kind of . . . lost. I asserted myself, but only in anger, which gets you nowhere; and also without properly respecting the things Harold could bring to it. I think he recognized what that was – my immaturity as an actor and as a person – enough not to take it too hard.

HAROLD BECKER: There is an anger in Sean, and a pain in him, and clearly they come from the same wellsprings that feed his talent. Even working with him at that age, I felt that in him – a certain rage. It fed his work, and he's not alone in that. But where does it come from?

SEAN PENN: I beat myself up in my head much worse than I beat up anybody else. I was literally suicidal at that time. Or I should say, 'often pondering it'. I mean, I was so invested in Phil Ochs, who *had* done that.[16] And I remember I would take long walks and think about every possibility . . .

At that time in your life, I think, you begin to romanticize weaknesses; you idolize those things. And when one is feeling hopelessly self-loathing and loathing day after day of work . . . I mean, I was having a ball with the guys on the movie, but not really finding risk in the work. It was the disappointment that here I was in this place where I thought I would function – and movies and I, we don't get along. I'm not able to do what I do in the company of movies. In fact, that was not the case. It was just some fear and confusion; and inexperience.

And, of course, then came *Fast Times at Ridgemont High*, where I was able to find the music of the character enough to be absolutely freed. And the director, Amy Heckerling, was so laid-back and young and female, and comfortable with it. And I would go to dailies, and that was a learning ground for me also. I saw some dailies on *Taps*, but they weren't that sharing of them – they should have been. But I went all the time on *Fast Times*. And all of a sudden I'm thinking, 'So I can feel that free, and move, and you still get it? Oh! OK. Now I'm getting it. Now I'm getting there . . .'

16 Ochs had committed suicide, severely depressed, in 1976.

FOUR

1981–1983

Ninety-eight per cent of creation is accident. One per cent is intellect, and one per cent is logic. And it's about making the accident work for you, right? There's a way to create the accident; and it comes down to playing on a level of moment-to-moment reality, rather than a presupposed 'How is this scene going to end?' Your conclusions are already written, basically. But your moment-to-moment reality isn't. And Sean lives in that moment-to-moment – any really good actor has to.

Dennis Hopper

JOSEPH VITARELLI: I had come back from New York to LA, and I was living in an apartment on North Hayworth in West Hollywood. So I picked Sean up from the airport when he came back from doing *Taps*, June or July 1981. And Hutton had his Academy Award for *Ordinary People* in a duffel bag . . . Cruise came to LA around the same time. He was spending some time at Zumirez, some time at my place in West Hollywood. Then Sean and Cruise both signed with CAA, and off they went. Leo saw it happening, though. I remember him saying to me at the time, 'You know, a couple of good things happen, and you could all be in for a hell of a roll . . .' Then Cruise did a really bad movie in Mexico called *Losin' It*.

SEAN PENN: That was when his tension started to go. I said to him, 'What are you doing? You're gonna destroy your career . . .' I now had a pretty invigorated focus on the potential to get work. I had been scrapping long enough: now I had a real job on my résumé. I signed up with CAA and Todd Smith. So that period of time was a little more energetic.

Penn's next project, though, was not earmarked to be one of the more widely seen entries in his own oeuvre.

SEAN PENN: Have you seen something called *The Beaver Kid*? I'd have thought that would have told you everything you needed to know. That one's a friendship test. If people don't like you after that, they won't like you later. And if they do . . .

After I finished *Taps*, I got asked to do a project by an old friend of mine from GRT, Bob Burgos. He said, 'I'm at the AFI now, a friend of mine is casting this thing. I think you would like to do it, you should audition.' So I came. I didn't audition – I had just finished a movie, this was a little twelve-minute video project: I don't think I'm gonna *audition*, but I'll *do* it. And Trent Harris was an interesting guy . . .

Harris had elaborated The Beaver Kid *from a singular experience two years previously when, as an assistant TV cameraman in Salt Lake City, he was buttonholed in a parking lot by 'Gary', a seemingly average, if highly strung, young American male from nearby Beaver. But Gary had worked up a flabbergasting talent-show act in which, clad in black leather, blonde wig and full make-up, he murmured his way through Olivia Newton-John's 'Please Don't Keep Me Waiting'. Ecstatic when Harris agreed to videotape his act, 'Gary' then acquired some piercing sense of how his rapt private world might come across to a wider audience, and called Harris to request, haltingly, that the tape not be aired.*

*   The Beaver Kid *faithfully restaged Harris's experiences with 'Gary', Penn smartly imitating the guy's jangling nerves while introducing some notes of melancholy. Over three days' filming, Penn inhabited the role as was now his wont, even when introduced by Harris to friends as a cousin. 'It was funny,' Harris later recalled, 'because a year later, when he became a big shot, some of my friends came up to me and said, 'Hey, your cousin is really doing well for himself . . .* '[1]

Penn's authentic 'breakout' role originated in the journalistic vigour of Cameron Crowe, wunderkind of Rolling Stone *magazine, who was interviewing Led Zeppelin while still in his mid-teens. A fellow* Stone *alumnus, David Obst, had crossed over to publishers Simon & Schuster and enticed Crowe to write a chronicle of contemporary high-school mores. In 1979, Crowe went undercover and enrolled for a semester's study at Clairemont High, San Diego, whereupon he took copious notes and identified a number of near-archetypal characters: the young managerial type, the classroom beauty, the hustler, the loser, the perpetually stoned surfer. He also formed the notion that adolescents were being made to grow up too hastily into a dangerous world*

---

[1]   'Nice "Beaver!"', Paul Callum, *Salon*, 1 March 2001.

of financial and sexual responsibilities. Fast Times at Ridgemont High *was the result.*

Universal Studios took an option on the book before it was written; Crowe, however untested, was the obvious screenwriter. Producer Art Linson, who knew the music business and had the unlikely smash of Car Wash *behind him, came in to develop it.*

ART LINSON: I was producing *American Hot Wax*, about the disc jockey Alan Freed, when Cameron was a young reporter at *Rolling Stone*, and he came down to do a story on the movie. We met, and I liked him – in fact, we gave him a small role as a guy delivering Chinese food to a recording studio. Then I heard he was writing this *Fast Times* book and got involved. He came to New York, and I tried to sort of supervise him in writing the screenplay, because he had never written one before. But he did a fantastic job. Cameron was painstakingly into the detail of what he was trying to do. He took the slightest moments very seriously – how kids look at each other, how they feel about each other. At the same time, he wanted to capture all the dreams of adolescence: whether it's having sex in the baseball dugout or masturbating to Phoebe Cates or being the surfer who doesn't give a fuck about school and won't play by the rules – it just hit all of those nerves. It was unabashed, in a certain way . . .

Linson then brought in twenty-nine-year old Amy Heckerling, a graduate of both NYU and AFI film schools. Her AFI thesis film Getting It Over With *treated a teenage girl's determination to lose her virginity in the last eight hours before she turned twenty.*

AMY HECKERLING: Art was a really cool guy, and he saw my short and liked it. There were a lot of young people working at Universal at that time: I think the feeling then for film-makers was that there were all these 'Studios' making 'Movies', and then there was Universal, making the stuff that was Our Stuff. First of all, Art, no matter what age he is, he's a teenager. And me and Cameron were in our twenties, and so were the cast of *Fast Times*, if not younger. So it was a very adolescent movie . . .

Art showed me Cameron's script, and I really liked it and told him various thoughts I had. Then he showed me the book, and I *loved* the book, and I really thought they had been doing a disservice to it. Cameron knew all these people, and in the book he'd recorded very accurately everything that was going on with them, and it was very funny because of that; whereas I felt like Universal were possibly trying to make more of a regular teen movie. I had written a scene in a movie at another studio, where a girl teaches her friend how to give blow-jobs. Then I read something similar in Cameron's book, but it wasn't in his script. I said to Art, 'You *gotta* use this.' This was before I was involved in *Fast Times*. He said, 'Don't you want that scene in your movie?' I said, 'Screw it, this one's *happening*.'

The character that I personally related to was Mark Ratner, the hopeless case in high school – that was me. Even though he's a guy, I know what it's like to feel like the person who'll just never get it together with anybody . . . But one thing everybody agreed on was that the surfer character, Spicoli, was going to break through.

SEAN PENN: Here's what I remember: I'm in the garage, working on a motorcycle. There's a phone in the garage, and I get a call – Paula Wagner, from CAA. She said, 'There's this young director, she's very sensitive.' I say, 'Uh-huh?' 'And they're making this movie . . .' I say, 'Well, let me read the book before you throw me the script.' So I read Cameron's book. And I had a feeling who the guy was.

EILEEN RYAN PENN: Sean was always a great observer. Even when he was a little kid and we would have parties, Michael and Chris would get in there and mix and talk. But Sean was always studying the people, like he was making mental notes – observing human nature. And there were plenty of guys he had watched at the beach over the years . . .

DON PHILLIPS: When Sean came in to interview for *Fast Times*, his hair was still unbelievably short from *Taps*. But no one had seen it; they were still editing. So I said to him, 'Tell me about *Taps*. What role did you play?' Sean looked at me and said, 'I play the conscience of the film.' Well, for a twenty-year-old to say that . . . Immediately I was thinking, 'Who is this young man?' Usually I spend about half an hour with an actor; Sean, I think we talked for an hour and a half. And afterwards I said to Art, and to Thom Mount, 'I've found Spicoli!'

SEAN PENN: Then I go in to audition: no script, but they give me some sides. I'm sitting down against a wall next to Nic Cage, and he says something funny and we talk a little bit. They called me in and I auditioned. It was Amy, Art and Don. And Don was warmer than anybody else.

DON PHILLIPS: Sean was awful. Just God-awful. He gave us no sense of Spicoli's stoner image whatsoever. I don't think he had a clue where he was going. In that, all three of us were agreed. So then it was my job to walk him out of my *lonnnng* office and say goodbye.

SEAN PENN: Don came out with me and said, 'I want you to do it again', and he gave me a different scene. So I sat out there for an hour until they called me back in. I don't remember feeling that I'd blown it. I don't remember doing anything different. I've only heard the stories. Believe me, between Art and Don, you'll never know . . .

DON PHILLIPS: I said, 'Buddy? You're on.' I went back to my place, and Sean walked in. The looks I got from Art and Amy . . . I didn't say a word. Sean, in one move, pulled his T-shirt off over his head, *à la* Spicoli, and started in on what you would have to call a rap. Some of it was Spicoli's lines, but by the time he was about a minute into it, we were all agape. He had the stoner thing down, it was genius. He went from being the absolute worst I had seen to the very best. The rest is history. And he never ever stopped paying me back for having had that faith in him.

ART LINSON: I can tell you this: Don is a very, very good casting director and has a great eye for talent . . . Indeed, Sean did read badly. And maybe we were somewhat inexperienced in that we were thinking, 'Boy, we'd be really nervous about this guy playing the surfer', because we knew Spicoli had to be the big comic relief. But it's a hard thing to explain. When I met Bob De Niro on *The Untouchables*, had I not known it was Bob De Niro, I'm not sure I'd have thought he could play Al Capone. He was thin, quiet, reserved, thoughtful – hardly menacing. You would cast him as Al Capone's *barber*. But by then I had enough experience to go, 'I'm not concerned . . .' There was something special about Sean, and you can always tell that in the room. 'Maybe he's not right for Spicoli, but he's obviously great, let's put him in *something*.' But he made it known Spicoli was what he wanted to do. And so we went, 'Fuck it.'

R. D. CALL: I was in a coffee shop with my friend Charles Shoal, who I'd been studying with. Sean came in and said, 'Hey, I want to talk to you. I just got this movie, *Fast Times*.' He told us a bit about it, then he left, and Charlie made the comment: 'You know what? He's already doing that role. He's already in the process.'

SEAN PENN: I met Cameron Crowe early on, and he took me to my first Hollywood party – sort of. It was for Fleetwood Mac. This is where I said to Stevie Nicks, 'You look so much more . . . ' – and I couldn't find the word 'angular' – '. . . so much more *pitch-faced* than I thought.' And as it came out, I thought, 'Oh God . . .' But it was all that came to mind. Was I being Jeff or Sean? It felt like there *was* no Sean. I was *immersed*.

EILEEN RYAN PENN: As well as getting inside the character, Sean's always had a little feel for something external, whether it's wardrobe or make-up. Sometimes the external aspect helped him go inside – the faith of looking like the character. It's called the Delsarte Method – I doubt he even knows that. It's the opposite of what Stanislavsky taught: Delsarte[2] started with the external, always – the look, the vocal thing, the clothing, the carriage – and then he went in for the emotions and the sense memories. Sean uses both, really. But he just comes by it naturally, I think.

He chose his whole outfit for the movie: the wig and the white sun-block on his nose and the chequered sneakers – which became worth millions after the movie came out. Everybody wanted them. I said to Sean, 'Gee, why didn't you have a piece of it? You'd be a billionaire now.'

JOSEPH VITARELLI: Sean lived as Spicoli for months. He was driving between Malibu and an apartment in Brentwood, and he was living that life: surfing probably every single day, drinking plenty. And I saw him . . . randomly. When we were together, he was himself to some degree – he was a variation on the theme, I think.

AMY HECKERLING: He was a nutty kid, he was funny. He would leave me little notes in my office, addressed to 'Ame': one of them was after he worked with the costume lady, and he said, 'Costumes went very.' Just 'very'. That was it. So I assumed that was good . . .

I was told, 'You have X amount of days of rehearsals.' This being my first film, I never did rehearsals before . . . So I said, 'All right, we'll go to Van Nuys High School.' They let us have an empty classroom. And I just said, 'Everybody, bring in an object to talk about, like in English class – but in your character. Then we'll just have lunch and

2 Francois Delsarte (1811–71). His 'chart' for actors was acknowledged by Strasberg as a fit means of finding the appropriate gesture to represent an internal state.

16 *Fast Times at Ridgemont High*: Penn as Jeff Spicoli

hang out.' Sean comes to me and says, 'I don't wanna do the assignment. I wanna, like, *disrupt* things. In my character . . .' So we were
having this class when Sean and his buddies came in late with Chinese
food and started bothering everybody. Then, during lunch, he just
kept trying to pull up Phoebe Cates' skirt and generally harassing her
and Jennifer. Just being a nuisance. In his character . . .

I had seen this punk skinhead in *The Decline of Western
Civilization*, and I said, 'I need that kid for the dance scene.' Because
we wanted to get that starting-to-happen thing going on there. And
Sean just decided to start harassing him, just because he knew this was
the one guy with the shortest fuse. Just being Spicoli . . . But then when

we were shooting the dance scene, there were some extras playing chess, big tough guys, and Sean decided to mess around with their pieces. One of them got up and started to swing at him, and an AD had to fly in and intercept.

DON PHILLIPS: All through the shooting, you could not address him by name; you had to call him 'Spicoli'. It was written on his trailer. He made all the kids do that, even though *Taps* had still not come out, so nobody knew who the fuck Sean Penn was.

AMY HECKERLING: People were acting like, 'Who does he think he is?' And I'd say, 'What's the big deal? Who cares?' It seems to me like that's an *awfully* minor thing to ask: it's not like he wants a *limo* to come get him every ten minutes. So, yeah, write SPICOLI on his chair, big deal . . . I mean, Sean's own vocabulary, the slang he brought to the part, was instrumental in making it as popular as it was. The day we shot the school trip to the hospital where the teacher pulls out a human heart and Spicoli reacts: I just kept the camera running and said to Sean, 'Just keep doing it, say whatever comes out.' So where the line was 'Bitchin', Sean would say, 'Gnarly!', 'Tubular!', 'Awesome!' . . . a whole list. Finally I said, 'Cut', and everyone on set bust a gut.

ART LINSON: The famous scene where Spicoli comes late to class and Ray Walston rips up his card, and Sean says, 'You *dick*': Ray Walston didn't know who Sean Penn was. So he says his line: 'I think you know where the principal's office is.' And Sean says, 'You *old, red-faced motherfucker . . .*' Ray Walston turned beet-red and got crazy pissed off, like, 'How dare this kid?' But Sean, even then, was trying off-camera to get a rise out of him that would be great for the moment. That's a pretty audacious move for a kid who no one had heard of yet.

Such moments would be the seed of a Fast Times *cult, perhaps drawing the eye from the more substantive plot of the picture: in the role of Stacy Hamilton, Jennifer Jason Leigh (who had shared the briefest of scenes with Penn as the distraught girlfriend in* The Killing of Randy Webster*) was called upon to venture several smart impersonations of a teenage girl experiencing penetration for the first few times and enjoying variable returns that culminate in unwanted pregnancy.*

ART LINSON: About the second week, we looked at dailies, and I called Cameron and said, 'Look, Spicoli's just ripping it up. We've gotta add more of him.' And so Cameron wrote so many things: the dream sequence of him talking to Stu Nahan,[3] the scene in the coffee shop with his buddies. And then we took the scene where Jimmy Russo tries to rob Judge Reinhold at the 7-Eleven, and Spicoli says, 'Awesome! Totally awesome!' and moved it to the end of the picture. Originally, it happened with twenty minutes to go, but when we screened it to an audience, that was kind of like the high point for them. When he said that, the place went crazy . . .

JAMES RUSSO: I knew nothing about the movie. I read, got hired, showed up, walked into the 7-Eleven. And this kid was hanging out, with this blond wig. But you could see something was going on there, for sure. He stuck out like a sore thumb as far as the aura was concerned. And this was the thing: when he started talking, he was in *character*. I'm like, 'Who the fuck is this nitwit?' Then it was like, 'This nitwit's *got* something . . .' Then, when I saw the movie, this guy's the fucking *star* . . .

AMY HECKERLING: Sean was very smart about what he was up to. I'd get these edicts from the studio: 'More Spicoli!' And we'd try to figure out stuff to do, but to Sean it just seemed too much. He'd say, 'But that'll step on *this* joke' or 'This will just be a repeat of that.' He said, 'I'd rather there be less. I want them to want more of me.' I mean, there are actors in their forties who still haven't figured that out . . . But I think Sean likes to have a certain amount of control: even though his performances can be extremely daring, the back-of-the mind part of him that edits and judges also likes to have its say.

The morning after we wrapped, Sean showed up very nicely dressed in slacks and a shirt and jacket, and went around introducing himself to everybody as 'Sean'. And he gave me, Cameron, Art and Don each a chequerboard Vans sneaker he had sort of varnished. That was really sweet. But for a long time after the movie, people would ask me, 'What's Sean like?' and I would say, 'Well, I only know Spicoli . . .'

---

3 Penn was summoned from the Chicago set of *Bad Boys* to shoot a scene of Spicoli dreaming he's being interviewed by sportscaster Nahan after a surfing-contest triumph, bikini babes on each arm. Some of Crowe's dialogue ('Those guys are fags!', 'It's a way of saying, "Hey bud! Let's party!"') became schoolyard classics, the latter memorialized as the one-liner for the movie's ad campaign.

DON PHILLIPS: Sean was kind of stand-offish with the other kids on *Fast Times*. With one exception . . . He met a girl on the movie, a girl in a small part as one of the cheerleaders, by the name of Pam Springsteen – Bruce Springsteen's sister. She was the Boss's sister. And in America right then, that was a pretty cool thing.

AMY HECKERLING: Pam wasn't in that many scenes but, yeah – Sean was into her. One day I needed a girl with a nice butt to be walking away from camera, and I got Pam. And Sean was suddenly standing right next to me behind the camera, just making sure, you know, that I wouldn't go too far. And if I'd been a guy, I'm sure he would have been *really* pissed. But, me being a woman, I guess he figured I thought the shot was essential to the movie . . .

* * *

SEAN PENN: The friendship with Lynn Milner went through from Woodland Hills to Malibu, but not the schooling. He and his parents would come out to visit sometimes. But by high school, I was very much otherwise engaged. And then when I started working, I lost track of him, couldn't get him on the phone. And I was findable – my parents' number stayed the same. So you just figured you were both starting your lives. I think I was doing *Fast Times at Ridgemont High*, and it had been three or four years since I'd last spoken to him. Then his parents got in touch with me. He had been inside for those three or four years, and on Death Row for most of them.

EILEEN RYAN PENN: Lynn got into such terrible, terrible trouble. He was in jail for murder. And his mother called me and asked could Sean do anything to help?

SEAN PENN: I went and visited and saw him. And the parents were so convinced he was innocent, as he claims to be. It was shame, to them, that they were dealing with, and so they hadn't reached out until they had used up their writs of habeas corpus. It's not something I have made a judgement about one way or another, guilt or innocence. I only know that Lynn was and still is my friend. One man was dead, a white guy. Lynn was found, according to his defence, unconscious at the scene, with a lump on his head, many yards away. So the story was that it was others. One of the primary issues was medical: had he been knocked in the head, and how hard, and at what angle? Those things were not well documented. And one of the big problems he had on his conviction was that there had just been a really awful black-on white crime – I think a rape-murder – in the same court right before, and the political atmosphere where he was tried was terrible. So then I went through the stage of finding lawyers and people to look into this case. There was a feeling that the case was mishandled by his own representation, and by the courts; but not evidently *criminally* mishandled. And so he was locked up in that system . . . 4

As Fast Times *wrapped, before Christmas 1981,* Taps *was released in US cinemas. Its one-sheet poster – a low-angle on Tim Hutton, shooters on a gantry behind him backing up his requisition of the school armoury – was dressed with the slogan, 'This school is our home. We think it's worth defending.' The image, disliked by Stanley Jaffe for its Wild West genre connotations, nevertheless summarized the film's fairly chilly assessment of the spirit bred in such forcing houses, and rhymed with Colonel Kerby's assertion in the film that the outside world views the boys not as heroes but as 'home-grown terrorists'. Although* Taps *was itself somewhat coldly assessed by critics, it prospered over the Christmas-holiday box office of 1981. Hutton, it seemed, could sell tickets, not least to a teenage audience younger even than the film's cadets. Jaffe's instincts about purging the film of adult relations had been borne out. Penn's performance, too, was widely commended.*

His next commitment was Bad Boys *for Rick Rosenthal, director of* Halloween 2, *now hired by producer Robert Solo and Barry Spikings of EMI Films to helm this contemporary youth-crime picture. Mick O'Brien, a Chicago street kid, winds up in juvenile detention after a botched drug score ends in his running over and killing the kid brother of young Hispanic hoodlum Paco. Inside, O'Brien toughs his way to being top dog, 'barn boss', but outside his girlfriend J. C. is raped by Paco, who is immediately directed toward the same lock-up as Mick, and the inevitable face-off.*

RICK ROSENTHAL: The idea of *Bad Boys* was that we were going to make something that was really a B-movie, somewhat like those edgy Warner Bros movies from the forties or fifties. It would have some of that texture: 'Reform School Teens Behind Bars'. *Rebel Without a Cause* certainly came to mind as one of the potential prototypes – not as a take on that movie, more the genre and the style.

4 See Chapter 11.

For Mick O'Brien, we met a lot of young American actors: Tom Cruise's audition was phenomenal, but I had to say, 'I just can't see your looks as a kid from the street.' Then Sean came in and did a scene where Mick is talking to the prison advisor and confesses to the killing of Paco's brother. And he nailed it. We're thinking, 'How do we get EMI as excited as we are?' So we contacted Sean and told him we wanted to bring him back in and tape him this time. Sean says, 'I'm not taping any scenes from the film.' I ask, 'Why not?' He says, 'Well, if I tape the scenes, and then I go on to do the film – I will have already kind of committed to these particular scenes, I'll have sort of *done* them. And I'll never be able to do them fresh again.'

But we've got to do something. I say, 'Let's go in and improvise.' So we book a little rehearsal space and a video camera one Saturday morning. I said, 'You must have some monologue of some kind', and he did a five- or six-minute piece that was riveting. I asked him where it was from, and he told me – *Terrible Jim Fitch* by James Leo Herlihy. I showed the tape to the people at EMI and they all sat there for a moment, until finally one of the executives decided to speak up. And he said, 'You know, Rick, his mouth is kinda small . . .'

Once cast, Penn's devotion to representing the real kicked in. He grew his hair to shoulder length, acquired a wolf's-head tattoo on his bicep and contemplated getting some teeth filed and capped ('Grubby look-ing covers, maybe a few cracked ones,' he later told the press). Eileen, daughter of a dentist, suggested that wasn't a great idea.

EILEEN RYAN PENN: I was proud of him, that he would try things and tap into things. But tattoos weren't such a good idea . . . and he's done it since then too. And if you want to take 'em off, it's a major thing . . .

RICK ROSENTHAL: I was out in Chicago for a long time, and Sean came out early. We went down to St Charles, the reform school that we shot in, and he spent a lot of time with the inmates down there. Then I managed to convince the cops to let us go out with the undercover gang squad, two civilian-dress guys. So we're driving around, Sean and I dressed like guys from the street. Suddenly they get a radio call, they pull up outside a hotel and they're out of the car and running down to the basement. Sean and I looked at each other, kind of shrugged, and we got out and ran after them. By the time we get to the basement, they've got guys up against the wall, guns screwed to their

© Universal Studios. Courtesy of Sean Penn

17 *Bad Boys*: Penn as Mick O'Brien

heads, screaming. Total chaos. What Sean and I didn't know was that the back-up team were arriving on the scene when they saw our guys running in, and then they saw these two street guys – Sean and me – running in behind like they were giving chase. So they came in hot, ready for confrontation, and that's what happened. The door behind us flies open and three guys burst in. The first one says to Sean, 'Get your hands out your pockets and turn around.' Sean says, 'Gimme a –' And that's as much as he gets out before the cop throws him against the wall, drops him and starts cuffing him. The sarge is saying, 'Vinnie, take it easy, he's an actor!' But that was total validation for Sean – being mistaken for a real-life bad boy.

SEAN PENN: There are sometimes movies that you'll do where it's not because the script is dead-on, it's because you think you can make it work. Sometimes you're right, sometimes you're wrong, because film has its own life.

I spent time at St Charles's, but I didn't get to know enough. I wanted a lot more time and a lot more support in bringing something to that movie. I had a very difficult time with the director – and not due to lack of experience on my part. He and I just butted heads from the word go. He had no real . . . curiosity, about that socio-economic class and the music that comes from it. From his view, it was a movie based on movies, versus life.

I believe an audience knows the truth when they're being told the truth. They don't always know when they're being lied to. In *Bad Boys*, we lied that that's the nature of the street. We didn't lie about the truth of the character in other ways, but culturally we did. So for me, it was kind of like playing two different characters. One was a rehearsal of the text, where I could let myself go in what I had observed, which I thought had a poetry way beyond what we did: Rick Rosenthal would not trust it. And the other was a dismissal of the text – because I owned it enough that I could dismiss it. And the takes where I offered option in that area – to the degree that I was in any way able to accomplish it – were the ones that were used. So it was a movie made of 'One for me, one for Sean', and cut entirely as 'One for me . . .' And I was not pleased: not pleased with the picture, not pleased with my performance. But I was pleased with the performance that I gave that was not on the screen.

RICK ROSENTHAL: We were both young. I'm sure I'm wiser now and a little more into the psychology of directing as opposed to the pure authoritarian nature of 'I'm the director'. Early on in the film, Sean came to dailies, and my feeling is it's very hard for an actor to be objective at dailies. There were times where it led him not to trust me when I think he should have trusted me more. It led to a day when we were shooting a scene where Paco has come into the reform school. O'Brien is barn boss and he's handing out the work assignments. He hands out latrine duty to Paco, who spits on his feet. We had agreed that, no matter what Paco did, Mick would not look at him. And we shot the scene that way, a bunch of takes. Then I looked at it and I felt that it would be even stronger if what Paco does is so powerful that he *does* look at him. I explained this to Sean. He said no: 'If I do one take your way then that's the one you're gonna use in the editing room.' I told him he should give me more credit than that. I felt I'd been defied in front of everybody and that I had to fix this situation or I would quickly lose control of the set. Sean's agent was in Chicago at the time, and I suggested to Bob Solo that we have a meeting. I was pretty upset. She relayed that to Sean. And things pretty much cleared up.

SEAN PENN: I was still learning the whole thing about editorial privilege – and directors who wrongly believed they understood anything about acting – and what happens if you juxtapose two things. There's a huge trust issue there. To me, it's about not just scene-playing but recognizing that there are those inconsistencies of character in people. The possibility is there for all of it to happen in every scene, in some way. And that's when editing is a productive process: '*Now* let's see . . .' You're declaring the whole life in two hours – past, present, and the dream of a future. So if a director cuts out a nuance – say, 'This is where we're gonna see that he has a sense of humour' – it's a totally different character, a humourless character. Hence you get actors who just laugh it up in every scene. And then, of course, they lose the other. You make a movie three times – you write it, shoot it, cut it. You've got to kind of act it three times. So it's nice to have that keep growing and be as limitless as possible.

However Penn had envisaged Bad Boys *from the page, it was firmly cast within the reform-school genre as had been financed. Nonetheless, amid the crunchy violence that would spawn a fan base of its own were one or two scenes of unusual tenderness, in retrospect more typical of the wounded Penn critics would come to favour. Following the rape of his girlfriend J. C. (Ally Sheedy), Mick effects a break-out and races across the state by any means necessary so as to be by her side. Bursting into her bedroom, he sees her battered face and gasps: hot tears come to his eyes. An officer has lain in wait, but now gives him a few moments alone with J. C.*

RICK ROSENTHAL: The scene where Sean discovers Ally with her black eye was really powerful; they have such a bond there. And I think Sean had a great emotional life and wasn't scared of it: he understood that one of the signs of a really strong actor was the ability to convey emotion. The interesting thing is, I look at the scene and I feel like he's trying not to cry rather than vice versa – rather than seeking the audience's sympathy. I think that's the key – a distinction a lot of actors don't understand. I think Sean understood it early on.

Whilst in Chicago, Penn received regular visits from girlfriend Pam Springsteen, and on one such stay-over he proposed marriage to her. Her eminent brother Bruce was readying the release of a spare acoustic record called Nebraska, *a suite of songs about Middle America, poor families and violent crime. Springsteen had raided many a movie title in his time – 'Ramrod', 'The River', 'Point Blank', 'Badlands' – and was developing a lean narrative style to his song-writing. 'Highway Patrolman' was a* Nebraska *cut about a state sergeant regretfully striving to overlook the trouble-seeking tendencies of his younger sibling. 'Stories about brothers', Penn remarked in later years, 'seem to move me on another, deeper level than other stories.'*

SEAN PENN: Pam and Joyce Heiser, Bruce's then girlfriend, had an appointment on Sixth Street in Hollywood off Crescent Heights. And I was basically living there. Bruce had sent out a demo of *Nebraska*, and we had just heard it for the first time. That and the Clash, 'Rock the Casbah'. I'd had seven or eight Heinekens so I thought it would be a good idea to call up Bruce and tell him what I thought. In fact, I don't remember now whether I said 'Call Bruce!' or he just called. But I had a dissertation, and I laid it out. He listened patiently – he always does. I end up saying, 'Listen, I want to make a movie out of "Highway Patrolman" some day.' And he said the immortal word: 'OK . . .' [*laughs*]. Like, 'I have no idea who you are. I know that you like my sister. And that you're drunk. But go ahead, knock yourself out . . .'

In March of 1982, Francis Coppola had convened a crew in Tulsa, Oklahoma, to shoot a retro-styled film version of The Outsiders, *S. E. Hinton's much-loved story of soulful juvenile delinquency. He had a roster of new young actors, including Matt Dillon, Rob Lowe, Emilio Estevez and a chastened Tom Cruise, still recovering from* Losin' It. *While on location, Coppola read Hinton's moodier, edgier* Rumblefish, *and decided to stay on in Tulsa and shoot it back-to-back – albeit in a monochrome homage to Welles, Cocteau, Kurosawa and others. Rumblefish rolled over into the summer months. Among the cast members joining up were Mickey Rourke, Nicolas Cage, Dennis Hopper, Tom Waits and sixteen-year-old Christopher Penn.*

CHRISTOPHER PENN: My perception of acting was on a lower level than Sean's. It was really more of a hoot: 'Hey, I can play a part in a movie just like I act on the street.' It wasn't a real perception of a craft, though I think I grew into much more than that, years later, actually caring about what it meant to be an actor. And I intend on growing more. *Rumblefish* was my first real gig. Francis Coppola gave me the job, Nic Cage – Nic Coppola as he was – helped. Nic and I were in the Loft together that summer. There was a lot of turmoil in the movie business at the time. It was very hard to hire a kid under eighteen for a long movie because of the *Twilight Zone* incident.[5] But they did what they had to do, and I got a start in the business. So we were in Tulsa for the summer, and it was quite a blast for me, let me tell you. Everybody was hanging out, and whatever anybody said, I was on for. And Sean came for a social visit, a brotherly visit, a little of everything. 'I want to check him out, this guy, see what he's up to.' It was fun to have him out there. And I'm sure he was there to watch Francis as well. Who wouldn't, if they want to direct?

SEAN PENN: Francis is somebody I have great admiration for, so it was interesting to watch the process. I was a little alienated by it as an actor, technically speaking. Francis was in an experimental stage with it all, but his directions were coming out of a loudspeaker.[6] God spoke, you listened; and the actors heard 'em, but then so did the extras and the bystanders . . . So there were no secrets. And the secrets are important for actors: between director and actor, they're *very* valuable.

Francis was showing double bills of movies every night after dailies, no matter what time they wrapped. So I watched *Out of the Blue* until

---

5 On 23 July 1982, actor Vic Morrow and child performers Renee Chen and Myca Dinh Le were killed by a helicopter crash on the LA location of *The Twilight Zone: The Movie*.
6 Coppola was pioneering electronic film-making technology, directing from a customized Airstream trailer dubbed 'The Silverfish' wherein he could view video material and roughly edit 'off-line'.

five in the morning. And that is a *great* movie.7 I came back to the hotel after a couple of beers, and around 7 a.m. – which was call-time for Dennis – I saw him arriving at the hotel with a couple of friends in a taxi cab, clearly intending to run upstairs and wash his face and go straight to work. And I tried to compliment him and he walked right by . . .

DENNIS HOPPER: I didn't have a clue who he was. And I said, 'Hey, man, I can't really deal with this right now . . .' Then the second time I saw him was at a Fourth of July party at Carrie Fisher's. I had just got out of rehab, and he came up to me again. And I didn't know who he was then either. Bert Schneider said to me, 'Hey, that's Sean Penn, really talented young guy, you shouldn't be so rude to him, man . . .' Then I saw *Bad Boys* and *Fast Times*. My first impression? I thought he was a fucking incredible actor, man. Been a fan ever since . . . [*laughs*].

Fast Times at Ridgemont High *was released in August 1982. Would its imagined and sought-after youth audience prove willing to turn out and watch their hopes and vulnerabilities (crummy jobs, bad sex, accidental pregnancy) honestly portrayed? Or did they simply wish for the bathroom humour and generous nipple-count of those regulation teen movies Amy Heckerling feared? The sexual content of* Fast Times *was fairly frank and deglamorized, and could have been yet more so.*

AMY HECKERLING: I was angry about seeing so many movies with naked women and never seeing a naked guy. So when I shot the sex scene between Stacy and Damone in the pool-house, I wanted it to be real, I wanted it to be uncomfortable. She was naked, so I wanted to show the guy naked too. And the ratings board said, 'You do that and you'll get an X-rating.' I said, 'How come you can see all these naked ladies in movies?' And they said, 'Because the female organ is not aggressive, but the male organ is.' So what? Should we shoot it? Whatever . . . but I was a very cranky young lady, and the idea of compromising makes you crazy.

We were coming out at Universal after *E.T.*, so that had the bar set

---

7 Dennis Hopper assumed direction of this 1980 film, also playing a drunkard imprisoned for ramming a bus full of schoolchildren who, upon release, resumes his complex relationship with daughter Linda Manz.

pretty high. They released it in a couple of hundred theatres on the west coast: there wasn't even any advertising before it showed up on the east. Whatever, they quickly went a lot wider. And I don't know, but it seems to be a lot more well-known now than movies that made seven times as much.

ART WOLFF: *Fast Times* made Sean a *bona fide* movie star. Because he became this cult figure: everybody started 'doing' Spicoli . . .

DAVID BAERWALD: I'm still a sucker for Spicoli. When I saw that film, I was convinced that was who Sean Penn was – that was just him, and he wasn't acting. Because I knew so many people just like that, those kind of Malibu/Santa Monica/Pali dudes – they're everywhere, you know?

EILEEN RYAN PENN: A local kid came up to Sean after the movie came out and said, 'Hey, Sean, you were great as Spicoli', and Sean said, 'I was using you.' Now, Spicoli is this pot-brained idiot. But the kid wasn't insulted.

ART LINSON: Sean was *legendary* in that picture. He's still considered legendary, in the US, for Spicoli. It's like he can't get away from it. It's by far the most popular character he's ever created on film. And Sean knows it.

The fact that what Sean did was so great put us *all* on the map. You can't find anyone who doesn't think *Fast Times* is their favourite high-school picture, and a lot of them weren't even born when it came out . . . As soon as the movie is a hit, they always mention sequels, but with *Fast Times* it was never a serious conversation. What is the sequel? 'Spicoli Goes to College'? Spicoli couldn't have got *in* to college, except maybe Santa Monica City College. 'Spicoli Goes to Rehab'? Spicoli gets out of jail after fifteen years for pot possession and re-enters society? That *is* the movie, I suppose . . . Neither Sean or I have ever been so broke that we've had to think about it seriously. But frankly, if he ever wants to do it, I'm up for producing it. If Sean wants to do Spicoli the three-time loser, then I'm all for watching him getting a job at a fast-food place and trying to make it work: he's never going back, he's staying clean . . .

AMY HECKERLING: The next time I saw Sean after we'd done *Fast Times* was at the première of *Gandhi*, and he was doing *Crackers*, so now he had this little beard. And it was funny because, knowing Sean, you knew that now he was in *that* place, and you didn't know exactly who you were going to be talking to . . .

Louis Malle had been working with John Guare, playwright and screenwriter of Atlantic City, *on a film for John Belushi and Dan Aykroyd,* Moon Over Miami. *As of Friday, 5 March 1982, that aspiration was over: Belushi was found dead at the Chateau Marmont.*

Malle was then persuaded, against his every better judgement, into a remake of Mario Monicelli's caper comedy I soliti ignoti *for Universal. The cast was a splendid motley of dramatic/comedic talent: Donald Sutherland, Christine Baranski, Wally Shawn, Jack Warden and Penn. The plot was relocated to San Francisco's Mission District, where disgruntled Westlake (Sutherland) masses a team to rip off the run-down pawn-shop owned by Garvey (Jack Warden) where he is himself the alleged security guard.*

Penn was cast as Dillard, a skinny rockabilly/punk in a tiger-skin-print shirt and red blouson, topped with a blond quiff, wispy goatee and sideburns. A hopeless thief, Dillard's energies are largely devoted to wooing the honey-hued Maria (Tasia Valenza), sister of his best buddy Ramon (Trinidad Silva). Penn would tell Rolling Stone *that he considered Dillard as 'nearly retarded'.*

SEAN PENN: Louis saw *Fast Times*, and offered me the part in *Crackers*. I was a fan of his – *Lacombe, Lucien* I had loved. I read the script. I had an idea for the character. I won't comment on my sense of the success of that idea . . . but I sure followed through. I was going pretty outside-in; that's where I was at that point. And you see what the outside was . . . I told Louis how I wanted to play it, and he was thrilled. But then we met at Universal, and I said, 'I worry, though, that if I do that, can we then justify this girl's attraction to him?' And he said, 'Sean, let me tell you: women, zey either like you or zey don't . . .' And he was right. I hate hearing people use that term now, but I see women going for 'nearly retarded' people all the time . . .

I flew down to Austin, Texas, and checked into a hotel down there and asked at the desk if there were any young rockabilly players they knew of. 'Oh sure, Little Charlie Sexton, fourteen years old. He's playing at the Continental tonight.' So I went down there, and I just loved this guy and took pieces of things from him. It wasn't 'based' on him:

I had already made some choices that were very different to Charlie Sexton[8] . . . But I kind of did his hairstyle and more than a couple of things wardrobe-wise.

© Universal Studios. Courtesy of Sean Penn

18 *Crackers*: Penn as Dillard

Crackers was the first time I really spent time in San Francisco. My best friend in the movie was Trinidad Silva, and we used to hang out down at the bar in the Holiday Inn on the Wharf. He had such a way about him: he was Tex-Mex, very prideful guy, and loyal. I learned stuff from him, stuff to pay attention and aspire to, just as a man. And he had grown up in a country where there weren't invitations to the prom for Mexicans. But he was very fair, and he was a leader. Trinny and I went on to do *Colors* together, just as his wife had a baby. And just months after that, he was driving down the road, his wife and child in the car, and a drunk-driver T-boned him – his wife and child survived, but he was killed. Terrible . . .

'Crackers *was immediately dismissed – for good reasons, I must say,' Malle would later lament.[9] It has its moments, not least in Dillard's*

8 Within two years the hollow-cheeked Sexton had signed a huge record deal and was groomed as a teenage pop idol, but eventually found his métier in the nineties as lead guitarist for Bob Dylan.
9 *Malle on Malle*, ed. Philip French (Faber and Faber, 1995).

first test of the unlikely burglar alarm he has wired for Garvey, which sets off an unstoppable cacophony of televisions, tubas, vacuum cleaners and a cymbal-crashing toy monkey. Some of the performances – or is it the direction? – seem deficient in the needful comedic élan and definition. But the dialogue is novel in a manner that would shortly vanish from American films, and there is lovely irony in the climax. The incompetent thieves are disturbed about their work by Garvey and mount a pathetic alibi about rescuing the joint from 'black Mexicans wearing ski masks'. Garvey cottons on without malice, and directs his parting shot at a rueful Westlake: 'Friendship, that's what's important . . . But in the meantime you'll have to do.'

SEAN PENN: I think, at the time, *Crackers* was a fresh experiment for a real film-maker like Louis: I mean, that would be the way you might fool yourself . . . and in that fooling yourself, you're a little bit more vulnerable to people who are *not* film-makers imposing their will on you. The film-makers suddenly start saying to themselves, 'Maybe *they* know something I don't.' Well, then you cut to those other people at home alone that night, and they're thinking, 'I sure hope this guy knows a fucking thing or two about movies, 'cause he's listening to *me*, and I sure don't.' That might have been what happened . . . I think Louis was smothered by the studio, and he allowed himself to be smothered, I guess, from the get-go. He sure did some great work after that: *Au Revoir, les Enfants* . . . But it was a funny period. Not all of the sirens were blaring yet on the emergency that was American film, and so you saw a couple of what, at the time, were new ideas that were very charming and sellable, like Bud Light. And there's a whole section of time there that led us to where we are today, because of the economic success of those pictures, and because of the country's unwillingness to be uncomfortable.

I hadn't seen Louis for a year and then he wrote a piece about me in a short-lived magazine called *The Movies*. They had a motif of film-makers writing on other film-makers or actors, and he wrote a really nice thing, something I was very proud of.

LOUIS MALLE ('Sean Penn Rising', *The Movies*, July 1983): *Relaxed, and co-ordinated like a track-and-field athlete, he was always in the right spirit, in the right pace. And when he was not, it usually meant there was something wrong with the scene. Just like Pierre.*[10] *Above all, I think*

---

10 Seventeen-year-old woodcutter Pierre Blaise was the non-professional lead of *Lacombe, Lucien*.

Sean has something else that Pierre Blaise had – integrity. I cannot think of a higher compliment and I hope that success and agents will not make him another sacred egomaniac, like so many of his fellow actors.

Penn's regard and enthusiasm for the late Phil Ochs had not diminished in the two years since he first encountered this remarkable musician and the sweet, sceptical, polemical force of his song-writing. To Penn's thinking, Ochs's achievement – to have 'been at the centre of American activism and optimism throughout the sixties, totally uncompromising in his ideals' – was the stuff of a film project. The man himself was long-departed, but his daughter, born in 1962, was a red thread leading back to the radical moment of which Ochs had been an embodiment.

MEEGAN OCHS: In 1982, I was living on my own, cutting hair in Mill Valley, the town where I grew up. I was asleep at one o'clock in the morning and I got a phone call. The voice on the other end said, 'Sorry, wrong number', and hung up. And then about five minutes later, he called me back. This guy had a very thick Texan accent, and he apologized for waking me up and explained that there were two numbers on his desk, and he had called the wrong one, accidentally.

And so my introduction to Sean was also my introduction to his being such a great storyteller, because the first thing he said to me was basically a beautifully told lie. In fact, he *had* meant to call at one in the morning, he just thought I'd be awake.

He told me he was a huge fan of my father's, asked if I had seen *Taps*, which I hadn't, asked if I had seen *Fast Times at Ridgemont High*, and I said, 'Yes, I did.' And he said, 'Well, I was the surfer in that. And it would be my dream to make a film about your father.' So we made arrangements to have dinner. The next day I checked it out, thought it would be OK to hook up with him. But I had only seen him in *Fast Times*, and now here was this blond-haired Texan-accented guy in front of me.

Sean was interested in my father as a performer, but also as a man. How did he get to be the person who wrote those songs? My father died when I was twelve. And I think when someone dies when you're very young, particularly in the way my father did, it's too much to deal with. Someone who I loved had left me by choice. But Sean was very gentle in talking to me. It wasn't, 'So tell me all about your father.' He got to know me first; through that we developed a trust. I ended up talking about things I had never talked about with anyone. And in the process of it, we became fast friends.

19 Easy riders: Sean Penn, Christopher Penn, Tom Cruise c. 1982

Then, I think Sean developed a sort of older-brother feeling for me – I was very young and had lived in a very unchallenging place that didn't really expand my imagination. And I think Sean wanted me to have more of an experience of life, to explore the world a little more. He invited me to come down and spend New Year's with his family. Pam Springsteen was living up north, but we both flew down, and I stayed in his parents' little cottage by their pool.

With Sean, whatever you wanted to do, you could just go and do it: like, 'OK, let's go spend the day in the desert . . .' He and Tom Cruise had these motorcycles, and we would go out into the Mojave Desert, two people on each bike. The next thing you know, Tom Cruise and I are flying off into the hills and you wouldn't see each other for hours. It was such a blast. You know, what nineteen-year-old girl wouldn't be completely mesmerized by Tom Cruise? And they were *guys*! Guys on motorcycles, and they had guns, and they were teaching me how to shoot. There was a place they found, a huge dirt pit where you could do an incredible high jump, which you're not supposed to be doing at *all*, let alone with two people on a bike. And I was like, 'Well, at least I'm gonna die happy . . .'

Penn had not sighted a footlight since the four-week stint in Heartland that transformed his résumé. But with a couple of movies in the can, he was drawn once more to the possibility of Broadway. The Paisley-born artist John Byrne had crafted his first play, The Slab Boys, *from memories of his own indenture at the carpet designer A. F. Stoddart in Elderslie. Set in 1957, the play treats the discontents of smart, disgruntled nineteen-year-old Phil McCann, who dreams of art school while grinding pigments in a back room. He and sidekick Spanky are bad lads sporting DA haircuts and long paint-spattered coats, cheeking their superiors, bantering in various idioms – upper-class twit, American wise-guy – and sharpening their allusive knockabout style on their fellows: bespectacled Hector and new-boy-in-a-blazer Alan. The play was an immediate success at Edinburgh's Traverse Theatre in 1978.*

JOHN BYRNE: In 1980, *Slab Boys* went to the Hudson Guild Theatre in New York, off-off-*off*-Broadway, but it was seen by Jay and Laura Kramer, who wanted to re-cast it and mount a production on Broadway, or as near it as possible. Bob Ackerman had done a lot of directing in New York: *Bent* with Richard Gere, and *Extremities*, a very successful show with Susan Sarandon. And then the chance of the Playhouse Theatre on 48th Street came along. We had the casting process in late September, early October 1982. There had been a production at the Actors Theatre in Louisville, Kentucky; Kevin Bacon was Phil, and Bob got Kevin into ours. Then he said to me, 'There's a guy Sean Penn on the west coast, just finished a film called *Bad Boys*, really hot.' But I hadn't seen anything of him, I'd only Bob's word for it. Bob said, 'Should I get him to read for you?' I said, 'Aye, that'd be good . . .' Isn't that awful?

SEAN PENN: I read the play, and I liked it. But I had been forcing myself down people's throats as a movie actor for the last couple of years before that, and I guess they didn't get my overbooked résumé and had no sense of me as a theatre actor. So I had to audition, and I did.

JOHN BYRNE: He arrived in New York, looking very pale and slightly the worse for wear off his flight. And he did'nae say much. But I took to him, and I said to Bob, 'I think he's dead right for Spanky.' The next time I met him was in rehearsals, winter of 1983, with the snow about seventeen inches deep in New York. All the boys were very keen that they do it in what they called 'Glasgow accents'. And I thought, 'Aw, it'll just hold us up . . .' I mean, I've seen a version in Japanese, and the Japanese guys were just like guys from Paisley, the same attitude – just speaking Japanese. So we came to a compromise that it would be some kind of modification of the American accent, and they could take me as a model – a very bad one . . .

SEAN PENN: I couldn't understand a fucking word John was saying. But he was a supportive presence. And we soon got it. And then we toned it down . . .

JOHN BYRNE: They were all so young and so keen to get it just bang-on. The integrity of the text was everything to Sean: I remember one point in rehearsals – it was a mild wobbly – he looked at Bob and said, 'I've *got* to know where I'm coming from, man.' I did a poster for the show, a slab boy standing in a kind of rebellious, leering, laid-back attitude, with a pallet knife in his hand and a front tooth missing. And it was all we could do to dissuade Sean from going to have his front tooth removed [*laughs*], he was so dead serious. But I had to say, 'Well, there's dedication for you.' We'd a good laugh too, though. Val Kilmer was playing Alan, the new boy. He was going out with Cher at the time, and Sean and Kevin used to send Big Val up rotten. They'd say, 'You've got to dump the girlfriend, man. She's holding you back . . .'

We had sixteen previews from February into March – we were waiting, foolishly as it turned out, for Frank Rich of the *Times* to come back from holiday. Mel Gussow, who was his second, had given it a sensationally glowing review on radio. Then Frank Rich came back and gave it a betwixt-and-between job: wis'nae good nor bad, but it did'nae say, 'You've got to run and see this show.' And then it opened: and it was what is called a *succès d'estime* [*laughs*]. But, as Bob Ackerman said, 'Anybody who was anybody went to see it.' And Sean shone out, I have to say: everybody was good, but he did shine.

SEAN PENN: I remember getting pretty good reviews. And I got a couple of good jobs out of it. Richard Benjamin and John Schlesinger both came and saw the show, and it was out of that I got *Racing with the Moon* and *The Falcon and the Snowman*. The offers came at the same time, for different time periods, so I back-to-backed them.

JOHN BYRNE: Then, of course, the Kramers would not let the actors out. They'd signed a run-of-the-play contract, and the Kramers kept it running. Meanwhile, people were keeping films free: the story was that Paramount had closed down *Footloose* on the west coast and were waiting for Kevin Bacon, and Richard Benjamin was getting very frustrated about Sean. It was like, 'When are these guys going to be set free from this ailing play?' But the Kramers were determined to get their money's worth . . .

The only indication I got of Sean's, er . . . future temperament, was the official press night. We'd gone to the latest trendiest place in New York: I wanted to go to Sardi's and have all that stuff you dream about for a Broadway opening, but the producers all wanted to go to this non-event place and, of course, it cleared after a while, after the reviews started to filter in . . . Then Sean turned up late, having got into a fight and been thrown out of some bar. He was on a high, and I recognized it – that itching for a scrap. I thought, 'God, and he's so quiet as well . . .' He was going out with Pamela Springsteen at that time. We'd all gone together to see *Extremities* with Susan Sarandon. And the two of them, they were as quiet and shy as you could imagine any youngsters being: not one word could you get out of either of them . . .

MATT PALMIERI: You always knew Sean was there: there was always that force of intellect, force of character – but very quiet. But he can transcend that when he has to, very well. It was something he developed over time. In his early twenties, he used to hang around Café Central in New York, and he was around guys who were great storytellers, the Joe Pescis and Danny Aiellos of the world. You're the up-and-coming actor, you get in there and participate. And I think he learned he had a knack for it.

JAMES RUSSO: When I think of Sean Penn, I don't think 'Great actor', I just think of *laughing* . . . I was doing *Extremities*; when you're doing shows in New York your paths cross, and we all hung out at Café Central, which was *the* spot. You were seated according to your place on the totem pole: De Niro would get the best table and then it went down. Me, I'm lucky I got in the fucking door. But it was a scene, and it would go to three or four in the morning; and if a bomb had gone off in there, half the industry would have gone. There's a great story – Sean knows it, he might even have been there that night:

Courtesy of Sean Penn

20 *Slab Boys*: Penn as Spanky Farrell

Robert Duvall was trying to go take a pee, and every time he'd go up to the bathroom, the door was locked. This was going on quite a long time, and he was getting really flustered. So at one point he banged on the door like 'Get the fuck *outta* there!' And all of a sudden, out come Robin Williams and Christopher Reeve. And Duvall goes, 'This fucken *place*, I can't even take a *piss* but I got Popeye and Superman in there powdering their *noses* . . .'

SUSAN SARANDON: I met Sean when he was doing *Slab Boys*. Our paths crossed a number of times because I was doing *Extremities*, and this was before children, so I also had a night life . . . And in my limited dealings with him, it was clear that he was a nice hard liver – pretty intense in that way. But also serious about his work. I think Sean, as with all the actors who I really respect, started off more as a character actor than a leading man. Whether it's Nicholson or Chris Walken or Jeff Bridges or Jimmy Spader: they all did character parts – despite the way they looked. And considering that one of Sean's earliest parts was *Fast Times*, he could have just stayed doing that. But I think it was clear from the beginning that he was interested in the work and doing lots of different things, and all of that was evident in that he was doing theatre.

SEAN PENN: I'd *like* to say this: I was looking to attach what I had learned in film back to what I had learned as a stage actor. And, you know, that might have been the case. But I don't think of film and theatre as very different. Acting is acting – it's all interconnected and all coming from life in some way and going back to it. The theatre is easier in some ways, because depending on the play – a play can go back and forth in time too – but if you have a run at it, the emotional life, and it's linear, then the theatre provides what *you* have to provide in a more internal way in film. And I don't mean 'more internal' in performance: I mean understanding the bookends of a scene, the extensions in both directions.

The way they are truly different – and why I feel the theatre should now be preserved as a novelty – is because there are no longer, in the United States, audiences for theatre. And you need an audience. It's got to be participatory.

As Slab Boys *wound down*, Bad Boys *opened, on the same weekend – 25 March 1983 – as Coppola's* The Outsiders, *albeit on fewer screens and with less advertising. In interviews, Penn enthused about the kind of raw picture that excited him as a filmgoer: alongside the expected Scorsese/De Niro favourites were Rossellini's* Rome Open City, *Alan Parker's* Shoot the Moon *and Hector Babenco's* Pixote. *Rick Rosenthal's* Bad Boys *clearly did not fit this run of superlatives, but Penn's performance was sufficient to excite Pauline Kael. Moreover, the film's crunchy set pieces had teen audiences hooting, not least when Penn's O'Brien usurps the two goons who run the joint – 'Viking' and 'Tweetie' – by loading a pillow case with soda cans and beating the tar out of them when they least expect.*

RICK ROSENTHAL: The actors really sold it. No stunt doubles. The cans had been replaced by styrofoam balls, but when Sean swings that pillowcase – not only in the cell where he breaks Viking's nose, but outside, when he steps into an overhead shot and knocks Tweetie clean off his feet – man, you *feel* it. EMI had financed the film, but Universal was releasing it in the US only. Ned Tanen saw a rough cut with Bob Solo, me sat in the back. As soon as Sean started filling the pillowcase, Ned almost leapt out of his seat, and once he started to swing, Ned, very excited, started shaking Bob: 'This is great! This is great!'

The final fight with Sean and Esai Morales, too – it has a reality, it's messy, it's visceral, the way fights are; it's not a movie fight. And when Sean is stabbed in the side of the leg with that shop-made spike – it's not that hard to do in film-making terms, a retractable spike, but everybody feels it. Then, when Sean's on top and he brings down the spike: the moment of revelation – did he kill him or didn't he? We sneak-previewed in Philadelphia and Denver, and when it was revealed that he didn't, there was total silence. Then about half the audience cheered. And the other half went, 'Pussy . . .' But the last moment, when Sean's walking back to his cell and he's both laughing and crying – for me, it's incredible acting. That wasn't scripted as such. That was Sean working at his best.

I have a twenty-year-old son now and all of his buddies are impressed that I made *Bad Boys* . . . I've always felt that, because of our confrontational moments, Sean rarely mentions it. But, forget my involvement in it; I think *Bad Boys* is an incredible performance in the Sean Penn canon. And in terms of his iconography, let's say . . .

SEAN PENN: I would give in to that I was – relative to where I was as an actor at the time – effective enough for the story to be told. I think it was a very interior character, *both* of what I did: underplayed enough not to offend the realists. So it's not something I'm ashamed of, the performance in *Bad Boys*. But it's dangerous for an actor to underestimate or overestimate things that they've done. And you have to view the context of being perceived without baggage. Most of the smart people I talk to who like that performance, they saw it when it came out, and they didn't know me. I wasn't 'a famous actor', except in a kind of young, cult sense with *Fast Times*, and that was largely not the same demographic who would go to a dark picture like *Bad Boys*. And back then, you didn't have *Entertainment Tonight* saying, 'And the kid who played Spicoli is now . . .!' Those connections weren't being made as part of the pop culture. So basically I was being viewed in a purer way – like Mickey Rourke in *Body Heat*. 'Who's *this* guy?'[11]

ART WOLFF: When Sean's movies had their premières in New York, my wife Donna and I would always get invites. The *Bad Boys* première was like nothing I had seen before with Sean – I mean, girls with autograph books, screaming and yelling. All of a sudden, something was happening: I thought, 'He is a *big* movie star now.'

Then came the *Rolling Stone* cover, and he was really on his way.

That 26 March 1983 Rolling Stone *cover offered a moody colour portrait and a hostage to fortune: 'Bad Boy Sean Penn. The next James Dean . . .'. Journalist Christopher Connelly met Penn at Vinnie's Pizza in New York and got a candid interview in which Penn crisply dismissed comparisons with De Niro but made clear his passion for an unproduced script entitled* At Close Range *and a prospective screen life of Phil Ochs. Connelly grasped the nature of Penn's commitment: 'He doesn't want celebrity. He doesn't even care about audiences. He just wants to work.' Penn also shared some prescient words: 'I have some very specific things that I have to do. I can't describe it. You just have to do it. If I can no longer say what I want to say by being an actor, then I'll leave . . .'*

ART WOLFF: I was interviewed for the *Rolling Stone* piece and they called me for the dirt. 'Is he terrible to direct? Gave you a hard time?'

11 Rourke's two-scene cameo as an arsonist in Lawrence Kasdan's 1981 *noir* thriller had attracted even more critical favour than the lead performances of William Hurt and Kathleen Turner.

'No, that's not the Sean I know.' But that was the image they wanted to play up. And they likened Sean to James Dean, as they always do. But there was also a certain 'Irish working-class hero' thing that he found very easy to fall into. Not that he wasn't in his own way very authentic doing that, but did people really know his background? I don't think they really did. And, being in his twenties and being a black Irishman – I mean, what a combination, Irish, Jewish and Italian! – I'm not so sure that a certain part of Sean didn't want to live that kind of thing. I know he doesn't want to live it *anymore* . . . But I think at that point, Sean began to have to deal with the issue of the invasion of his privacy. Who could tell him how? It had never happened to Leo or Eileen.

Penn also spoke of his upcoming marriage to Pam Springsteen, making clear to Connelly that their romance had begun after Fast Times *was in the can: 'It's a permanent record when you make a movie, and it means too much to do your silly little playing around. I see a lot of that happen, and it's a shame.' At twenty-two, his commitment to acting was being mirrored in his views on the commitment of a lifetime; but inevitably there still remained some wisdom to be dearly acquired in both lines.*

DON PHILLIPS: To be honest, I felt Pam was a little too young. When I met Sean, he was just a few weeks shy of his twenty-first birthday, but I felt like he was twenty going on sixty. Some people are just born with what we call an 'old soul'. And Sean was an old soul. He *knew* stuff. Everyone else was very contemporary in their thinking and what they seemed to like. But Sean loved the older actors and movies, the older writers and poets. I'm not putting Pam down, because I loved her, but I think there was a little difference in maturity.

MEEGAN OCHS: Pam was wonderful, a total sweetheart. What Sean used to say about Pam, the thing he loved most about her, is that she would have loved him if he was a plumber; the problem was she would have *preferred* him if he'd been a plumber . . .

FIVE

1983–1985

All the fame one should look for in life is to have lived it quietly . . .
Michel de Montaigne (1533–92)

Twenty-three-year-old Steve Kloves had made his first successful studio pitch for Racing with the Moon, *a story somewhat akin to one of his favourite movies,* Summer of '42. *Its protagonists are Hopper and Nicky, high-school buddies poised to be drafted into the Pacific War. Hopper, son of the town gravedigger, romances local girl Caddie, whom he mistakes for a well-heeled 'Gatsby Girl' simply because her mother works as a maid in a big house. Nicky, a more feckless soul, pleads with Hopper to help him raise money for an abortion for his girlfriend Sally. Hopper is torn between loyalty to Nicky and his fine feelings for Caddie, whom he assumes could foot Nicky's bill.*

RICHARD BENJAMIN: I was finishing my first movie, *My Favourite Year*, and a producer called Alain Bernheim sent me Steve Kloves's script. What I liked was the metaphor of a steam train for what was happening to these two boys as life was rushing at them: what they were going to have to face by going off to war, and how they had to live intensely in these few months before they went.

I wanted Sean as Hopper from the beginning. I saw him in *Slab Boys*, and I just thought he was the real thing. I try to cast people for who they are, at least who I think they are, for what's inside of them. And Sean's intensity and innocence seemed so appealing, not to mention the acting ability. Then I met him, and the first thing he did was quote a line back at me from *My Favourite Year*, a line of The Kaiser's (Joe Bologna).[1] When he hurt someone's feelings, as he did on an hourly basis, The Kaiser would say, 'Get him something. Call my brother Harry and get him a box of steaks. Some tyres – whitewalls.' And Sean told me, 'Anyone puts a line like that in their picture, I gotta work with him . . . '

1 Bologna's character is a wiseacre perfectionist TV comic, modelled on Sid Caesar.

SEAN PENN: That cracks me up. It's like in *Time of Your Life*, when Kitty wants to call someone by a bad name, and she says, 'You, you . . . *dentist!*'

Stanley Jaffe and Sherry Lansing were Benjamin's executive producers; Nicholas Cage was cast as Nicky. Penn would be top-billed, but his female lead was a similarly well-regarded young performer, lately nominated for an Academy Award. Twenty-one-year-old Elizabeth McGovern had enjoyed a swift – and, to her, surprising – ascent. She arrived in Los Angeles from Illinois after her father accepted a post at UCLA. Her mother was also a teacher, so her background was scarcely show-biz. But she caught the fever from performing in plays at a small, creative high school, Oakwood, where she drew the eye of agent Joan Scott and soon auditioned, successfully, for Robert Redford. Milos Forman and Sergio Leone were similarly taken with her, in quick succession.

RICHARD BENJAMIN: Elizabeth I just loved. I'd seen her in *Ordinary People* and *Ragtime*. And to me she was like the girl on the Coca-Cola bottle – just the archetypal American girl, you know? Beautiful, like the fantasies you have as a kid.

ELIZABETH MCGOVERN: I don't think Sean's movies had made an impression on me at the time, but his reputation had – he was definitely incredibly highly regarded. Then I saw *Bad Boys*, and I was really impressed with him in that. I don't remember the *movie* as a work of genius, but I thought he had a really poetic grace, in what was a very dark film about very dark characters. Within that, I remember being struck by that grace of his. I think the first time I met Sean was sitting around a rehearsal table. My first impressions? There's the answer I think he'll love to hear, and then there's the real answer [*laughs*]. The real answer is that I thought he was kind of goofy and filled with a passion that was sort of ridiculous but endearing to me at the same time. I slightly had a [*rolls her eyes*] kind of feeling. But I was also really drawn to it, the 'in-the-moment'-ness of him. I thought he was really charming, I guess . . .

At the heart of Racing with the Moon *is a burgeoning love story: McGovern's Caddie has a kind of cool, poised wit that acknowledges and wards off the persistent, sometimes madcap, but always devoted attentions of Penn's Hopper. In real life, off camera, a twin-track process was afoot.*

21 *Racing with the Moon*: Elizabeth McGovern (Caddie) and Penn (Hopper)

RICHARD BENJAMIN: This is *totally* how directors think of their films. One day – we hadn't started shooting, it was a few days before – I was coming back from a location scout. And I saw Sean and Elizabeth away off in the distance, walking along a road, holding hands. And I thought, 'This is good. This is *really* good. I've got, what, forty days? Let this last . . .'

ELIZABETH MCGOVERN: You know, we were twenty-one and twenty-two, in this very intoxicating situation, in a sense. And so, you know, why not? [*laughs*] I couldn't see anything wrong with it. The blue eyes were definitely a part of it, I can't deny. I just can't tell you how naive I was. I mean, I had never even really had a boyfriend. It sounds a bit pathetic, I know. But I had been on my own for so long before we started that film, so in that aspect it was incredibly fantastic.

RICHARD BENJAMIN: It certainly wasn't a hindrance in any way. When they were working, there was no sense of anything other than professionalism. But it's like what I say about who people are – actors as good as Sean and Elizabeth, it comes through, what's really going on. Acting can't disguise what's really happening inside of somebody; it can read all that. And just as Sean and Nic Cage became good friends, I think the fact that Sean and Elizabeth became close to one another helped us get there.

Sean continually surprised me in the depth of everything he did, the full dedication to character. And it's *moving*, in a way, that somebody is so dedicated that they're actually giving you a gift continually. Hopper was meant to play the piano at the start of the picture, a bit of the *Revolutionary Etude*. And I hate the thing of where you shoot an actor at a piano and they're just vamping with their body, then you cut to somebody else's hands. I asked Sean if he could play, and he said no. I said, 'If you could learn a little bit, it would be wonderful.' And he learned the whole piece.

SEAN PENN: That took a lot of hours. But only a fucking dress rehearsal for *Sweet and Lowdown*. I never want to touch a guitar for the rest of my life . . .

ELIZABETH MCGOVERN: I learned a lot from watching Sean and from being around him, without a doubt. He was definitely very sophisticated about all aspects of the business in a way that was really impressive to me and that I was very far from; combined with what I felt – and still do, kind of, in retrospect – was a sort of immaturity about it too. He could make the camera work for him, he could decide what he wanted to do and do it. And yet that was coupled with this thing of 'I'm a method actor', which I still to this day think is bullshit. He would never *call* himself a method actor. But I never met a young actor who wasn't into that. And I don't think it helped him. It was just a bunch of *Sturm und Drang* all the time, in my opinion: a kind of creation of turbulence and mystique about the process that he couldn't resist. He would argue, 'If I'm playing a guy who stays out all night on a beach, I have to in fact stay out on a beach all night.' Whereas I would go home and get a good night's sleep. But not Sean, oh no!

RICHARD BENJAMIN: Sean wanted everyone to call him by his character name, which took some getting used to. But these crew guys, they've seen everything. We all thought, 'OK. If you want to. You know you're *really* Sean? But all right . . .' Elizabeth kind of joked about it. 'Sean? Oh, sorry – *Hopper*. I forgot.' I tended not to address him as anything. But it's all right – you're getting such good stuff from him, it didn't seem pretentious in any way. My feeling is that it's whatever works for you. And, certainly, he was totally involved.

STANLEY JAFFE: I thought I was old enough to call him 'Sean'. And halfway through the picture I looked at Sherry Lansing and I said, 'You know what? God help us if he plays a mass murderer any place, because they'll find bodies in the community after the film company leaves . . .'

ELIZABETH MCGOVERN: What is amazing is just how much of the time, more than anybody I met before or since, Sean would be able to exert this control, this will of iron, on his surroundings. For me, nobody ever wins that game, really – not in the end. But time and time again I would witness circumstances where Sean would *seem* to, where he would absolutely insist that a thing had to be done *this* way, in spite of the director or the cameraman. He was a more powerful presence on the set than Richard. Which is amazing, when you think about it: a twenty-two-year-old actor . . .

RICHARD BENJAMIN: We certainly pored over everything; we had extended discussions. But they were all informed, and they had nothing to do with ego; it was only to do with character and story. One big thing was stunts. Sean wanted to do them all. And he had a good point: 'You've got a moment where you're telling the audience it's me, and it's not. My body is different, my behaviour is different. I think that you affect the truth of the scene by doing that.' I said, 'Yeah, but there's danger here, Sean. If something happens, if you get hurt, then we're finished.'

SEAN PENN: For me, the principle is doing your own movement, in *any* picture. *She's So Lovely*,[2] when I jump through the window of the bar: I had to run down the bar – and it's three feet higher than the window – and come through blind: you have to close your eyes when you hit that glass. Then I had to land, hit the sidewalk, roll over, get up and run. I only did it one time, and we ended up using five cameras, and it

2 See Chapter 11.

was put together out of those angles. And it had to be the last day of shooting, for the insurance company. But you can do it in one – and you have *full* option, you can literally go with the character's movement.

So it's that. It's also *exciting*, and you should take every opportunity to do something exciting when you're working, something to look forward to, something new. There's times when you can't do it: either for insurance reasons or, in some rare cases, it's something only a stunt-man can do. But everything you could imagine motivating you to do it is in the same nature of what acting is. Otherwise you just feel like you didn't show up for work that day.

RICHARD BENJAMIN: The first thing that came up was the roller-skating scene, where Sean meets Elizabeth at a skating rink, pretending he knows how to skate, and he ends up flying out of a door. It was our second day of shooting. Stanley came to me and said, 'Don't let Sean do that stunt. If he breaks his ankle, the picture's over.' I said, 'But, Stanley, the camera's kind of close on him, and he says he can do it . . .' '*Don't let him do it!*' I told Sean, 'Stanley's kind of right.' Sean says, 'I can do this.' I said, 'OK, here's what, let's do it early, when Stanley's not here.' So we set it all up. Sean's on the end of a line of skaters, they swing him round and round and let him go, and he sails clean out the door, he's gone. I shout, 'Cut.' I'm thinking, 'Please, God, please . . .' I run out the door, and there's Sean, on his feet, giving me the 'OK' sign.

The train was a different story: Sean and Nicky had to jump out of the way of an oncoming train. And that scared me, because, of course, they waited, they were really testing each other: the characters were, and Sean and Nicky were, because they're both fearless. But I'm thinking, 'All you've gotta do is get a foot caught on that rail . . .' Then they're supposed to jump onto the train while it's moving, which again they both wanted to do. I couldn't let them. So Sean was upset by that. But my argument was, 'There's no stopping that train. And trains are deadly, they're unforgiving, and there are surprises.' And we had one. The stunt kid lost his footing on the gravel by the track and nearly went under the train. I got back and told Sean what had happened, and I think he knew then – that one was too much.

STANLEY JAFFE: When Hopper was supposed to be carefree and fun, there's nobody who can do that better than Sean. And then as the serious part of that picture – which was not meant to be terribly serious – falls into place, when Nicky gets the girl in trouble, Sean was *still* wonderful.

The best scene in the picture has Caddie comforting Sally in the back seat of Nicky's car as they drive tersely away from the trailer where her abortion was conducted. Caddie grows thoughtful and resentful, and asks to be let out. Hopper confronts her with what he considers to be her wilful avoidance of reality and is stunned when she bursts into angry tears and bitterly informs him that he is the more deceived.

ELIZABETH MCGOVERN: I think it was obviously a story that was close to me at that time: someone of that age having to face the consequences of their actions, having to say to somebody, or to themselves, in spite of all the promenading around, 'This is actually who I am, I'm not who you think I am.' It's a difficult thing for someone at that age to confess. And I really believe that Sean's passion and energy as an actor also made it totally easy. His combination of intelligence and commitment and humour and just this great, great heart – it just makes the job not a job at all. There are some people who are great actors who are not that great to work with, because you don't get that connection between you. A lot of actors, you'd be very surprised, they don't even need to look at the other actor – that's not a part of what they do. In a way, I think De Niro is a bit like that – he does it all for himself.[3] And it's brilliant, I'm not taking anything away from it. But Sean, at least when I worked with him, is so intoxicatingly engaged. And I much, much preferred working with it.

RICHARD BENJAMIN: To me, Sean, in playing Hopper, was the essence of an American kid with all these ideals, yet with edges to him. It was almost like he embodied that for the purpose of the part. But I also felt I was seeing some of Sean's own nature. Now, he may be such a great actor that, to him, he's just doing 'that kid', but as far as I'm concerned, there's a sweetness that I really see in there, and he was turning a light on that part of him. Certainly it's in him – otherwise how would he get it? That's the Sean I know and, I must say, whenever I've seen him since, I feel the same. But other directors might say different. Certainly, when I see him in other movies, he seems to be another person – that's what is so extraordinary . . .

3 McGovern played Deborah, the unrequited love of De Niro's Jewish gangster 'Noodles', in Sergio Leone's *Once Upon a Time in America* (1984).

MEEGAN OCHS: One minute Sean and Pam were together, and the next minute he was working on *Racing with the Moon* with Elizabeth, and they weren't . . . I ended up going to work for Sean as his assistant right after *Racing with the Moon*. He came back to LA, got a place, and I moved down there almost immediately. He and Elizabeth had just got together, and I started working for her too.

JOSEPH VITARELLI: He was committed to his work, so why wouldn't he be committed in his relationships? And we were all nuts in those days, so you would get engaged, and then you got disengaged – that's what young people do. I thought Pam Springsteen was great – she was sexy, and sweet, and sincere. Elizabeth McGovern, how could you not be in love with her? So beautiful – breathtaking.

MEEGAN OCHS: *At Close Range* was a script that for a lot of years had not been made. And Sean wanted it to be made so badly, and he worked for ever to get it made. One of the problems of being an actor is that you're very often excluded from a lot of the decision-making process. This was the first time Sean was involved from the start, and with every element.

It began with a newspaper story, spotted by producer Elliot Lewitt, about the Johnston family murders of August 1978. The brothers Johnston – Norman, David, and Bruce Senior – ran a larceny ring stealing farm equipment in rural Chester County, Pennsylvania. The 'brains', Bruce Senior, recruited youths, including his son Bruce Junior, and encouraged them to set up their own 'kiddie gang'. But when the FBI started closing in, the brothers began to worry that these kids were a liability. Bruce Senior's response was a two-week riot of carnage: six killings, including that of his stepson James. But Bruce Junior survived multiple gunshot wounds and testified before a grand jury, so sending his father and two uncles to jail for life in 1980.

NICHOLAS KAZAN: Elliot Lewitt brought the subject to me, and my first reaction was, 'I don't want to write about a father killing his kids . . .' But he just kept telling me how it was mythic, like Greek tragedy, and he finally persuaded me to read newspaper articles in the *Philadelphia Inquirer*. Then I saw what he was talking about, and it turned from something that repelled me to something that was a compulsion to do.

Bruce Johnston Senior killed his stepson, and he got his brothers to shoot his son and kill his son's girlfriend, whom he had already raped. I mean, the norms of human behaviour don't apply here. But, obviously, drama is about extreme actions . . . And Senior had his own moral code: the reason he tried to kill his son was because his son was ratting on him. Elliot and I went and met a member of his gang, who thought Bruce Johnston was a great guy. His actions belied that [laughs], so my sympathies lay with Junior. But I tried to make Senior as charismatic as I possibly could. His son had to idolize him and follow him, even as he began to see that his father wasn't a good person. I think Elliot gave the script to Sean, and Sean liked it right away, then the three of us met at Wolf's Deli in New York.

SEAN PENN: Here's where I will give Nick Kazan his due: I think *At Close Range* is one of the great scripts I've ever read. He's a writer who had his own conflicts – on the outside, one might say that they were thematically similar to his own life.[4] But that was not the heart of what he had done: he had done something as an independent writer that was magnificent. It's like a tragedy before you think of it as a film . . .

Bertolucci, Rafelson, Konchalovsky: these were all directors who wanted to do it – according to Elliot Lewitt. But it was Bob I started to work on it with.

BOB RAFELSON: I'd seen *Fast Times*, thought Sean's performance was brilliant. So I was expecting Sean to come over and be stupid and funny. And a guy comes in who is quiet and serious and super-hip. He knew the kind of people he respected and wanted to hang with: people who could teach him something about lifestyle or their craft, or a combination. And when he wanted to horse around, he was fun. He would bring Elizabeth McGovern; they would just sit around in my bedroom and we would talk or smoke a joint. I had made five movies; I believe Sean knew them. And we talked about *At Close Range* and movies in general. First of all, I said I would like to make it. All of my movies had to do with family or the acquisition of ersatz family – including *Stay Hungry*. *Five Easy Pieces* was a kind of study in a dysfunctional family; and *The King of Marvin Gardens* had dwelt more specifically on a brother-to-brother relationship. So the father–son story appealed to me.

4 Nicholas Kazan is the son of Elia Kazan by his first wife, Molly Day Thatcher.

SEAN PENN: We couldn't get it financed with Bob. We just ran out of options. He had been too recently in his altercations, and had alienated a lot of people. I don't think of Bob as someone who gets up in the morning and thinks, 'How do I make it easy on people to like me?' I like him tremendously. But he's . . . pretty relentless, in great ways and ways that get on people's nerves – and scare some people. He's a forceful alpha-dog . . .

BOB RAFELSON: Sean also had a kind of pugnacious side, and that particularly appealed to me – because I suppose I have that same quality, and I think that appealed to him also. I had tried to make a picture called *Brubaker*, and that's the time when I allegedly 'punched somebody out'. He was the head of the studio, and there was a lot of talk about it – and by the way, it was grossly exaggerated.5 But Sean clearly knew the story and it was that attitude that I think he liked. I don't like it in myself, I can tell you that, because the penalty is being unemployed for four years . . . *At Close Range* seemed a bit dour for many tastes, even though in the seventies 'dour' films were the governing taste. So I had the feeling that eventually it would leave me and go on to somebody else. And that's exactly what happened. But I was utterly intrigued by Sean. And that, by the way, has never stopped.

In the autumn of 1983, with At Close Range *stalled, Penn moved on to the second gig* Slab Boys *had earned him:* The Falcon and the Snowman, *another American true-life tale, to be directed by John Schlesinger from a script by first-timer Steve Zaillian, co-financed by Orion and Hemdale.*

Once again Penn was paired with Timothy Hutton, the first man into the project, who had swiftly become immersed in the real person he would play, convicted spy Christopher Boyce. Boyce was the son of an ex-FBI agent, raised on the picturesque Palos Verdes Peninsula. His best friend at elementary school was fellow altar boy Andrew 'Daulton' Lee. As a teenager, Boyce took up falconry; Daulton was a woodwork enthusiast, who also took up the use and sale of marijuana and cocaine. Boyce was twenty-two when his father swung him a clerk's job at aerospace company TRW, which built and operated 'black satellites' spying on Russia and China. Within months Boyce could access the most highly classified communiqués of US intelli-

5 A Fox executive had visited the set of *Brubaker* ten days into the shoot, 'something happened', and Rafelson was dismissed. He and Fox then filed lawsuits against one another.

*gence, and was struck in particular by the CIA's skulduggery even in
dealing with supposed allies such as Australia. Boyce began to smug-
gle out computer-programming cards and offer them for sale to the
Russian Embassy in Mexico City. His courier was Daulton Lee. But
such material as these unlikely spies could offer was never quite sufficient for the Soviets. Daulton wound up being arrested by Mexican
police and placed in a murder frame, from which his only resort was
to return to the US and stand trial for treason. Boyce was arrested
shortly thereafter. The two were tried separately, their defences incon-
gruent. Boyce got forty years, Daulton life, both beginning at Lompoc
Federal Prison in California. Boyce escaped and roamed free for two
years before recapture. Daulton committed himself to self-education,
reading and studying dentistry.*

ANDREW DAULTON LEE: The book *The Falcon and the Snowman* was
written by Robert Lindsey, bureau chief of the *New York Times*.
Lindsey was supposed to be writing an article, then he told me he was
doing a book. And I didn't want that. But he basically wrote it with
my co-defendant, and with me as the antagonist. So it put me in the
worst possible light as the guy that took this squeaky clean kid and
corrupted him. I saw that thing and I almost had a heart attack.

MEEGAN OCHS: The whole perception on the book, and the movie,
was that Chris Boyce is really suffering a crisis of conscience over the
things he had believed in so fervently as a child: first leaving the priest-
hood, and then ultimately betraying the government because he felt it
had betrayed him long before. Whereas Daulton's attitude is basically
like, 'Cool! Money-making scheme, let's go!'

ANDREW DAULTON LEE: Who knows what the real story is? I sure
don't. I'd just smoke another joint, sniff some coke, some heroin, then
get on an aeroplane and go talk to a Russian who's sitting there drinking out of a vodka bottle and asking me to sign a chit for our dinner.
That's not some serious people trying to put some serious plot together. It was a comedy of errors. I mean, John Belushi and Dan Aykroyd
should have been the characters in this.

So then this film comes along; it's adapted from Lindsey's book and
it's Hollywood taking the thing. I saw the script and, God, it was hor-
rid. I had lawyers on it, but they told me, 'It can't be stopped, they're
gonna make it.' Once you end up in the newspapers in the US, you're

public property, and the only way you can sue them is if they've written something that hinders your ability to work. Well, if you're sitting in federal prison, it's hard to claim that of *anything* that's written about you . . .

Then I got a phone call in prison: Sean Penn – who I didn't know from beans – had been chosen for the role, and he wanted to know if he could come up and we could meet? I said, 'Yeah. But understand, I'm not big on this . . .' So he arrived at Lompoc, walked in, and he had the sleeve of his T-shirt rolled up with a pack of cigarettes, showing a prominent tattoo. Now, I'm in prison surrounded by low-grade morons with tattoos. It's like carbon-dating yourself. So I looked at him and said, 'What you got that for? Only idiots get tattoos.' But I could kind of get it from his perspective. He was young . . . So we had this initial talk. And we did not hit it off well. I was just adamant against the film, and Sean was just, to my mind, part of that bad situation.

SEAN PENN: Clearly it was *not* good for him that a movie was being made: any kind of profile was gonna disturb his potential for release. So I negotiated with him, because he's a businessman, on the basis that the movie was going to get made with or without me, and if he wanted somebody to be the advocate for his concerns, I wanted his help. He agreed to that. So then I visited him frequently, and we talked on the phone. And he was very helpful.

ANDREW DAULTON LEE: He asked me a lot. And I did have quite a psycho-pharmacological background. Back then I had a foot-locker full of peyote buttons and bags of coke and heroin, bags of mescaline, hash and hash oil – I could tell you about it all. So I guess I was just a *spigot* of information [*laughs*]. At that point in time, I didn't really understand actors or 'method acting' or any of that stuff. But to Sean, it was imperative to get in tune with the character. And if he's going to portray a real person, it's the same thing: he wants to get into that person's head, study their voice inflections – all that. And he's *good*. Though I thought the voice he did for me was a bit whiney . . .

SEAN PENN: I was futzing around. I took some surgical tubing, wrapped some cotton around it, and some tape around that, and widened my nose. Then I went to a dentist in New York named Henry Dwork. He was recommended to me by Bob De Niro. He had worked with Bob on some films and had made Marlon Brando's piece for *The Godfather*, the 'plumper' for his lip. He was making appliances that you could eat with, and he made me a set of teeth. And then I futzed around with eyebrows and hair, and just bit by bit kept playing with this stuff and looking in the mirror . . .

EILEEN RYAN PENN: Sean was living down at Topanga with Elizabeth, and he came over to say goodbye to me because he was heading off to Mexico for *Falcon and the Snowman*. I said to him, 'You know, you don't *have* to do all of that, changing your hair and your teeth. It never really works. Why don't you just play the character?' He left, but he called me later and said he wanted me to come by his house. I said, 'OK, you want to see me again? I'll come.' I get out of the car, and this guy comes out of the house. 'Hi, Mrs Penn.' It's broad daylight and he looks vaguely familiar, like somebody I knew from Sean's school. He says, 'You don't remember me, do you?' So I came right up to him and looked him in the eyes. Then I said, 'Oh, for chrissakes . . .' He had done his whole make-up, the teeth, what looked like an old *rat* on his head. And he said, 'Gotcha, Mom . . .' So I saw his point.

DON PHILLIPS: Sean called me at 6.30 one morning, woke me up, and said, 'I got engaged!' I said, 'You did? Who was it this time?' I kind of knew it was Elizabeth . . . I said, 'Aw, that's great, Sean. Just be sure she's the right one. Don't be jumping into anything, you're still young.' But he was just so determined to be engaged. I think, in the back of his mind, he always wanted to be a family man.

SEAN PENN: I was in the Russian Tea Room with Elizabeth, and it had been printed somewhere that I would be doing the film with John Schlesinger after *Racing with the Moon* – we were in the window between. Dustin Hoffman came by our table and introduced himself – which was not necessary. But he did so very politely, and he said, 'You're going to work with John?' I said, 'Yeah.' He said, 'We need to talk.' I said, 'Really?' He said, 'John likes "acting" – in quotes.'

JACK NICHOLSON: Tim Hutton and I went out and scouted together in Kansas on a picture that we wound up not doing.[6] And I had talked a lot to Tim during that scout. Then he and Sean called and asked if they could come over and talk to me about *The Falcon and the Snowman*.

6 'Roadshow', loosely based on a novel called *The Last Cattle Drive* by Robert Day.

They were asking me how you work with a director you're not sure you're on the same page with. I knew John Schlesinger, so I told them they didn't have a lot to worry about. And they did a great job on the picture, they were wonderful together. I don't think it had much to do with my *advice*, but . . .

As 'Alex', Daulton Lee's contact in the Russian embassy, Schlesinger cast English actor David Suchet, having seen him play Shylock for the Royal Shakespeare Company. It was Suchet's first substantive film role.

DAVID SUCHET: I thought it was an excellent script, and I was sure that in John's hands it would be well filmed. I wasn't anticipating the tensions on the set that were to follow, with Sean and John.

SEAN PENN: I'd admired John's work enormously. But the differences manifested themselves fairly early. The problem I had with John was a disregard for the true story, which I felt was too high-profile to ignore, in terms of how I approached the character. And I didn't see a *reason* to ignore it, the way the script was structured. So I felt I was in the company of a disapproving father, in that sense. To begin with, John just didn't like the choices I was making physically – and sort of accepted them because he had handsome Tim there, you know? But I think he wanted us both to look our very best, like shiny new nickels: you can interpret what you like out of that. I think Tim's terrific in the movie, but I think he had a similar situation as the one I had in *Bad Boys*, in that there were a lot of extremely quirky, interesting choices he made as Chris that I think would have helped the film.

And I just don't think that John was on his game at that moment: I think he was getting safe. There was some room for political thrillers to be successful at that time, under certain kinds of 'traditional film-making' ideas that had nothing to do with what I loved about John. So he took a very interesting story about these two guys and turned it into an insert-picture in a lot of ways: too much information, too much teletype. And, for me, the 'espionage thriller' aspect didn't carry the picture.

DAVID SUCHET: We did a week or two's rehearsal in Los Angeles before we went to Mexico. John was very much a man of the theatre, and he

© Metro-Goldwyn-Mayer, Inc. Courtesy of Sean Penn

22 *The Falcon and the Snowman*: Tim Hutton (Boyce) and Penn (Daulton Lee)

liked to talk about 'moments'. But Sean didn't work that way: his acting was very instinctive, very in-the-moment, it's absolutely as it's happening then. I can see John rehearsing a scene, and saying, 'OK, we'll do it that way', and Sean saying, 'Well, it may change. I don't know what I'm going to do on the day. I haven't seen the location . . .' And Sean would suggest things initially, but ended up not suggesting things, just saying, 'This is what I want to do', because he didn't want to get into a debate about it. And once or twice I did find myself thinking, 'Oh no . . .'

ANDREW DAULTON LEE: Sean told me how they were shooting in the Camino Real Hotel near Chapultepec Park in Mexico City, and Schlesinger wanted him – in the movie – to go put a quarter pound of coke in the hotel safe behind the desk. Sean told him, 'This guy would *not* put his coke in the hotel safe, he's gonna keep it in the hotel room with him.' Schlesinger said, 'Well, I think this will play better . . .' So the two of them got into this knockdown drag-out, and Sean took the bag of fake coke and threw it across the lobby, and it came apart. White powder everywhere . . . I'm hearing these things, about a world I knew nothing about, and I'm thinking, 'Holy smokes . . . OK, I thought *I* had it bad going on in prison.'

DAVID SUCHET: When you watch Sean work, you can see he's in the moment, searching for the truth of a scene, rather than its effect, all the time. And an actor has to learn to fight for that moment. You can't safeguard much on a movie. The actor's only moment of control is between 'Action' and 'Cut'. That's where the difficulties arose: protection, on Sean's part. Therefore it's bang-bang-bang between them. Those things can grow out of all proportion, and tensions grew until there was very little meeting ground.

SEAN PENN: Again, it's a trust issue: as trust diminishes, it gets harder and harder to deal with. And neither John nor I were shy about speaking our mind. So, after about two weeks, we stopped speaking. And then we had this very childish situation where I'm standing five feet away from him, and John would say to an assistant, 'Will you please ask Mr Penn if he would be kind enough to come to his mark?'

'Excuse me, John asks if –'

'I heard him. Would you tell Mr Schlesinger that's not the mark from our rehearsal? That it's the mark he changed the camera for by whispering to his cameraman? And that I wasn't included in the reasoning behind that, and I don't understand it? And can you take my fucking mark and put it back where it was, until such time as I understand the adjustment, other than a technical thing for camera?'

And that would then be said to John . . .

It was stupid. Again, John is someone who I hold in high regard, but who I don't feel was on his game. And I think that he let my not occupying the part just as he saw it in the first place wind him out a bit, and he didn't come back from that.

DAVID SUCHET: Ultimately, I think Sean turned in one of the great screen performances; and I think part of that – Sean may not agree with me – was due to the conflict between him and John: that fight to win through on his level and do what he wanted to do with that character.

SEAN PENN: There's a funny thing about winning wars and winning battles, and in film you win a war together or you don't win it. You can win a battle as an actor and still not win anything. I think that I won the battle – I think I was right – about how to look and how to approach the character. But I think John, embittered by that loss, did somehow marginalize the character I was playing, as he perceived my choices.

ANDREW DAULTON LEE: After the film, Sean and I stayed in contact. I'd write him stuff every now and then. Occasionally I'd get something from him. He'd send me books, screenplays, saying, 'What do you think of this?' Kind of peculiar. There was really no reason or rationale to *have* to stay in contact with me. For him, it could have been just business. 'I've met this guy. I got what I want. I'm making films, he's in prison.' And that would have been fine, too. But it didn't turn out that way . . . 7

MEEGAN OCHS: While Sean was on location in Mexico, Elizabeth was in New York doing a play called *Painting Churches*, and I was at the house in LA. So all their stuff was living in the same house, and they saw each other, but they weren't physically together that much. Elizabeth very much wanted to be in New York and doing theatre, whereas Los Angeles is not really a place where you can have much of a theatre experience. So that was where their careers diverged. But they were definitely together, and very much in love.

ELIZABETH MCGOVERN: When I first met Sean, I think he was living in his car . . . I think he's easy to live with if you give him a lot of space, which I would tend to do. He also has this thing of liking to have people around him all the time. And I just personally like to have nobody around, unless I'm doing something. So that was a personal difference of lifestyle preference.

MEEGAN OCHS: Sean used to say that Tom Cruise ought to get an award for dealing with the press. His opinion was that Cruise decided early on a few things that he was going to share of himself with the public – his dyslexia, his lack of relationship with his father. Everyone felt they were getting this very sensitive insight and, because of that, he was golden with the press. But basically he just kept repeating these few things *ad infinitum* and never gave anything else up. Instead of what Sean did, which was just to try and keep things private. I think Sean's wariness of the press has always been because he wants the performance to stand alone, and anything that is known personally about him is going to detract from the ability of his audience to have a pure experience of that. He would read about some actor who would say, 'I smelled these dirty socks to get me ready for this scene', and then when you watch the scene, all you think about is the dirty socks. If you

7 See Chapter 11.

tell people your process, you've destroyed it. And if you tell people about who you're dating, it detracts from the work too.

23 Penn and Elizabeth McGovern, 1984

In early 1984, with Racing with the Moon *near release, Penn was asked to do a* People *magazine cover-story plus photo shoot with McGovern. He refused, having a low opinion of* People *in general, and a specific distaste for 'underwear stories'.*

SEAN PENN: I remember being a little bit embarrassed by the idea of a couple promoting themselves as a couple on the cover of a magazine: just feeling like we were about to add to a cancerous view of things – which hasn't gotten better since.

RICHARD BENJAMIN: I'm of two minds. If someone asks me to go out and sell a movie, I will. But I actually think the biggest thing is paid advertising: all the other stuff, the free stuff, is a small percentage of what gets attention for a picture. You go on the shows and you sing for your supper, but there's a trade-off: you're giving away some part of yourself, because you need to entertain. And I understand why an actor would say, 'Wait a minute, I didn't sign on for that kind of situation.' Because there is something kind of good about shutting up – being quiet, not spilling everything.

ELIZABETH MCGOVERN: Really, it was a problematic movie to sell. It wasn't a kid's movie; it was an adult movie with a young person's cast, and it fell between the tracks, I think. It wasn't the producers' fault. I don't profess to be an expert on marketing – in fact, I'm whatever the opposite is of that . . .

SEAN PENN: So they came up with about the worst poster in the history of graphic art and threw it out there badly. And the producers felt that it would be important for them to go on national television and say that I had let the picture down by not promoting it – despite the fact I was in Mexico City working eighteen-hour fucking days and had not been brought into the loop on the creative process outside of my own performance, and had nothing really to *say* in any interviews.

STANLEY JAFFE: I thought he should have been available to do press, albeit it could have been less than was normally asked for. I thought it was unprofessional. He knows it too. I was upset when he wouldn't do any, and we discussed that. We've long since gone past it. But I think part of the obligation is to help support the picture you thought was good enough to make. And we had very little to support that picture.

Racing with the Moon *ends in a lot of hugs: it was the lightest, most conventional piece Penn had yet appeared in, this despite the abortion subplot and the backdrop of young men going off to fight and kill and maybe die. Midway through the film, Hopper and Nicky get the news that a pal of theirs has perished at Guadalcanal. Gesturing to the horizon, Nicky shouts, 'There's a war out there somewhere!' Yet one doesn't quite believe him.*

ELIZABETH MCGOVERN: I think it's a very nice film myself. I feel proud of it. Not that anybody ever *saw* it . . . But I think Richard did a really good job, made a really nice film, and I think a lot of it is his. That's my opinion. I don't think Sean rates the film at all. I think he thinks it's wussy or something . . .

SEAN PENN: I would have assumed Elizabeth would think that . . . I think of it as a terrific, sweet movie. I don't think anything enormous was lost on it. The dramas that were dark in the script I read were included in the film – the abortion, the class issue. And they were treated in the way they were treated. But, you know, you put a certain score on a picture and it will go in a whole different direction . . .

EILEEN RYAN PENN: I loved Elizabeth. She was a very lovely, intelligent girl. But they weren't right for each other either, for different reasons. I remember Sean said to me, 'She should have married a dentist . . .' I said, 'Sean! My father was a dentist! Your grandfather! And he was a very creative, wonderful man!' But it was that 'conventional' idea: what he meant was that he scared her, he was too wild for her.

ELIZABETH MCGOVERN: Sometimes I think it's a miracle that Sean's still with us. It used to drive me crazy that he could never get into a car without driving it seventy miles an hour. But he has this absolute confidence he's going to land on his feet. He can get on a surfboard and stand up on a wave, and I think that's kind of a parable for his whole life. He's always riding the crest . . . I think, for us, it was as much a case of being in love with the dramatics of it as anything. I don't think that I really expected myself that, he at twenty-three, me at twenty-two, we were really going to settle down for the rest of our lives. I don't think that he would say he expected that either. But it doesn't take away from the fun that we had. I know I loved being with him. I just think that, for me, I needed a quieter life. I mean, Sean is brilliant, *brilliant*, at being the kind of reluctant celebrity, but he knows what he's doing: it's not an accident that some of his best men friends are Marlon Brando and Warren Beatty and Jack Nicholson. I do think Sean is an absolute Hollywood animal. He might hate to hear that said, but I mean it in the best sense of the term, I really do. And, in a way, I've always been envious of it.

SEAN PENN: I was in New York when they were shooting *Nine and a Half Weeks*, and I spent about a week with Mickey Rourke and Harry Dean Stanton, going out to nightclubs all the time. I was split up with Elizabeth, I was nursing that heartache. But I was a big admirer of Harry's work. He was definitely somebody who excited me. So it was kismet, meeting at Mickey's. Then Harry left, went back to Los Angeles.

Two weeks later I was back too, and I went up to what was a private club at the time, On the Rox. We used to go up there a lot; it was a great hang, because it was just friends – right on the Strip, very convenient. It was about eleven o'clock at night when I went in, and the only other person in the whole place, apart from Julie the bartender, was Harry Dean. And so I sat and talked to Harry, and he didn't remember me at all. No idea who I was. I'd just spent a week as a room-mate with him two weeks ago.

HARRY DEAN STANTON: I knew he'd done *Taps* with Harold Becker, I knew he was an up-and-coming actor. We talked a while, and he told me he'd been a big fan of mine, watched movies of mine when he was in high school. I'm always glad to be appreciated – like everybody else. I've always been kind of aloof, probably too aloof at times [*laughs*], too stand-offish. But I realized – I was affected by the fact – that he regarded me highly. And I was intrigued by him.

SEAN PENN: I found out he was on his way to Cannes the next day for *Paris, Texas*. And I had a passport from going to Mexico to work on *The Falcon and the Snowman*. I said, 'Can I go with you?' He said, 'Uh . . . OK.'

HARRY DEAN STANTON: Sean, all he brought with him was a passport and a toothbrush.

SEAN PENN: And I stayed in Harry's room for about five days in Cannes, then he said, 'Maybe you should find somewhere else to stay . . .'

By then I was friendly with Bob De Niro and Joe Pesci. They were involved in a movie showing at Cannes that Elizabeth was involved in too – *Once Upon a Time in America*. Elizabeth wasn't there, but De Niro got me a room at the Hotel du Cap and I started travelling around with them. I still saw Harry, now that he didn't have to live with me in his room, but he was busy doing his thing. And I had a fantastic time – nobody knew who I was in France, so I would just stay up all night, roaming the streets. But I stayed drunk a lot, because I was hurting.

I left Harry there, said I'd see him back in LA. And I found out later they won the Palme d'Or for *Paris, Texas*, which was great. I went to Paris with Bob and Joe. We had a couple of evenings there. I met Mikhail Baryshnikov; he and I became more friendly later. And Roman Polanski. He had offered me *Pirates* off of seeing *Fast Times*, but I had never met him, because we weren't in the same country.[8] Joe and I then went to Rome, and I left him after two or three days because I wanted to go visit Tom Cruise in England – he was making *Legend*. I went to London, saw Tom for a day – kind of a disastrous interaction . . .

---

8 Polanski was unable to enter the US without facing arrest, having fled to Paris in 1978 rather than accept a further prison term on his plea of guilty to unlawful sexual intercourse with a thirteen-year-old girl.

And that's when I first went to Northern Ireland. I thought, 'Take me somewhere *violent* . . .' And it was, at that time in Belfast. I saw a tower burning from the aeroplane, and I thought, 'This is where I want to be.' I needed to see a place like this now, I needed to see how people live somewhere that has this threat around it all the time, from all the stuff you'd hear about. And there was a lot going on; it was palpable. I landed in Belfast and I went originally to the famous hotel with the barbed wire round it, the Europa. But it was so forbidding-looking. I was travelling with just a shoulder-bag, so I walked and walked, right out of the town, and I found a bed-and-breakfast and got in there. And in the newspaper the next day, the bombing was reported, and I went to the scene. But I didn't really avail myself of people, I didn't go down to this or that community and ask them, 'What's going on?' I wasn't there journalistically or with anything other than an instinctive curiosity. And I'm still very shy at this time, not great at engaging anybody.

Then I started doing this drunken odyssey of the town. I found, after a certain level of consistent drinking for months previous, that I had an affinity for fat rosy-cheeked Irish girls. And then I would try to get arrested, in the sense that I would go by a police station and look suspicious. I was going into the shopping district through the army checkpoints, trying to shuffle past . . . just because I wanted to taste the system of it all. You know the term, 'Couldn't get arrested?' Nobody was interested. But it was a great trip. I left Belfast after a week, came back to New York, one more time trying to put my relationship back together – which I did, for a time. Then it didn't work.

ELIZABETH MCGOVERN: It wasn't like a devastating parting, I don't think, for either of us. This was very special in that respect – I don't think that either of us had done the other one wrong, I don't think either of us felt incredibly undermined or rejected. And it hasn't turned sour, in the way that a lot of times with old relationships you think about the person and it brings back a horrible feeling because of the way it ended. Whenever I see Sean, I still have this same surge of one-hundred-per-cent total affection – that hasn't changed one fraction.

SEAN PENN: Then I came back to Los Angeles and ran into Harry again, and now we really became friends. What made the difference? Him remembering who I was. They say elephants are slow to mate? Mammoths are slower . . .

Courtesy of Joseph Vitarelli

24 On The Rox: Harry Dean Stanton, Joseph Vitarelli, Penn

The late summer of 1984 saw the Broadway triumph of a play that would come to loom large in Penn's career, the strange tale of its genesis involving persons already dear to him and those very shortly to be. David Rabe's studies in drama at Villanova University were interrupted by a two-year service as a medical corpsman during the Vietnam War: that experience would inspire a sequence of magnificent, prize-winning plays through the seventies. Come the early eighties, Rabe was keeping some company in New York at the place that was The Place To Be.

DAVID RABE: Café Central was a cross-pollination of a lot of different worlds that were very comfortable there. The guy who ran it, Peter Herrero, had a great spirit. I would hang out there a bit, although I wasn't all that quick in a social situation. But then I met this actor and we had a drink . . . Sean was, I think, doing *Slab Boys*: I had seen it with Herrero so I was aware of who he was, and I'd been very impressed.

SEAN PENN: I love him. I think he's the best playwright in America, period. A great mind and a great guy. I knew *The Basic Training of Pavlo Hummel* and *Streamers*. And then I saw *Hurlyburly*.

Rabe's new hit concerned Eddie and Mickey, two pedal-to-the-metal casting directors whose condo in the Hollywood hills is a kind of divorcees' club, run on heroic doses of liquor and cocaine, attracting moths like producer Artie and ex-con/would-be actor Phil. Women come and go in this tale: Darlene, with whom Mickey dallies and Eddie rashly hopes for real intimacy; Donna, a teenage runaway waif whom Artie offers to his buds as a 'care package'; and Bonnie, an exotic dancer considered fair game for anything. Penn saw the play twice at New York's Promenade, so beginning a fifteen-year affair with its dark and drawn-from-life depths.

DON PHILLIPS: *Hurlyburly?* [*shakes head*] Ay-yi-yi-yi-yi-yi-yi . . . and I want you to write that too.

By 1975, my partner Michael Chinich and I had done *Serpico* and *Dog Day Afternoon*, and we decided we were ready for Hollywood. I had just been divorced, and Michael was separated at the time. I found a cute little guest-house on Carol Drive, perfect for the two of us. But because of my love of actors and directors, we made our place a haven – anybody at any time who wanted to could come over to Carol Drive and plonk down. We were poor, and we did some drugs, and we were all divorced and separated. David Rabe had written a play called *In the Boom Boom Room*, and I wanted to produce it as a movie. David was also out in Los Angeles. I told him, 'Come on out, I got a couch.'

DAVID RABE: I was working on *First Blood*. Pacino and Marty Bregman had hired me to do a draft, which I did and which they were appalled by and said, 'No, thank you.'

I'll go as far as saying, yes, I spent a lot of time on Carol Drive. I always felt it was a sort of aid station for divorced guys at that point. It was a fun place, you hung out. And there were certain events in *Hurlyburly* that are reporting.

DON PHILLIPS: In 1984, Michael Chinich said to me, 'You hear that David's got a new play? Mike Nichols is directing it. They're trying it out in Chicago.' And the cast is amazing – William Hurt, Christopher Walken, Harvey Keitel, Sigourney Weaver. So I call David and I say, 'Michael's told me about your play, we're gonna come see it.' He says, 'Don, I want you to read it first' . . .

As it turned out, I couldn't get out there when Michael went. But he called me afterwards and said, 'Don, you won't believe this. I walked into the theatre and there was this set that is the *exact duplicate* of Carol Drive.' 'What?' 'Then, there's you, there's me, there's Al Schwartz, there's Richie Foronji, there's our girls.' I said, 'You're shit-ting me.' He said, 'I loved it!' I say, 'Really? Who played me?' 'Bill Hurt!' I say, 'What kind of casting is that?'

A few months later, it opened on Broadway to rave reviews. I think I was there the second night. I walked out at the end of the first half. This is a play about three scumbags who should know better. And 'I' am the master scumbag in the play. It's not exactly 'me', but I would say I am the prototype. I don't think I can talk as intelligently as Eddie, and I don't believe that the coke was as rampant at the time as it is in the play. A lot of marijuana around, I remember that. And a lot of craziness. The kicker of it all was that Michael and I really did have a fifteen-year-old girl, and we brought her back to Carol Drive. I want this written: since I've come back to the Lord, I'm so embarrassed about those times – a lot of that stuff happened, and I'm not real thrilled about that. I don't think David tried to hurt me or anybody else. David is as honest as the day is long. He was just trying to show the underbelly of Hollywood . . .

There would be consideration of Penn taking over the role of Eddie from Hurt before the play closed in 1985. Penn's chance, however, was not lost, only postponed.

John Schlesinger's The Falcon and the Snowman *emerged in January 1985 as something of an Oedipal tale, mapping Boyce's estrangement from his disapproving ex-FBI dad (Pat Hingle) through disagreements over Watergate to the need for a good haircut and the perils of falling in with bad sorts. When Mr Boyce has a chance to reprieve his boy, he murmurs only, 'Let him be judged.' As the pair are led away in irons, big close-ups almost semaphore that it is the parents we might feel sorry for.*

The drama is also weighted by the speed with which Boyce comes clearly to disdain his comrade. An hour in, David Suchet's Alex speaks for the viewer in taking a quiet moment to ask, 'I'm curious, Christopher. Why are you and Daulton friends . . .?'

DAVID SUCHET: That's what I thought looking at the film: it didn't seem as though they were partners. And maybe that's the criticism. As I remember, it went very well on the east and west coasts, but as soon as it hit the middle states it got kicked out of court, as I suppose it was bound to. A film about traitors is never going to go all that well . . .

ANDREW DAULTON LEE: I was kind of happy when the movie opened and closed and didn't go anywhere. If that thing had turned into some huge blockbuster, I'd still be in prison. It's like Charles Manson or Sirhan Sirhan – other people who've committed murder are long out, but those people are never going *anywhere*.

Penn's performance at least had survived the turmoil of its making in blazing colours. His version of 'Daulton Lee' is a nerve-straining busi-nessman–addict, capable of quarrelling with the KGB about their manners in a Mexican restaurant before inviting them into a heroin deal. Whether trying to impress a blonde at a party or allay the despair of his Palos Verdes parents, he cuts a forlorn figure; but he knows as much and, in one splendid moment, snorts heroin in a bathroom before spitting at himself in the mirror.

JOSEPH VITARELLI: That was a breakthrough performance for Sean. It was just like, 'Wow . . .' That's sophisticated, isn't it? But sometimes 'Wow' is all there is . . .

ANGELICA HUSTON: We'd seen him in *Fast Times* and *Bad Boys*, and then all of a sudden he was in *The Falcon and the Snowman*. And then I think everyone just clicked in: 'The guy is great.' Sean has a very good physical framework in which to operate. But I don't think vanity comes into it. And I think Sean, in a way, has made that fashionable somehow, since that performance in *Falcon* – the fearlessness, to be unafraid to expose that ugly core, that thing that is the pathetic, ridiculous part of you. The part of yourself that – if you're a person like *me*, anyway [*laughs*] – you're always terrified will suddenly make the world turn on you. But Sean has done that again and again. Look at *Dead Man Walking* . . .

In May 1985, influential British style magazine The Face *selected Penn as the most promising actor in US movies, but they weren't alone in wishing to see him act in a movie that was as good as he was. True, Penn was still only twenty-four, but such was the age at which James Dean came to grief; it was also the age at which Marlon Brando first created Stanley Kowalski on Broadway for Elia Kazan, the director who then helped him up to the heights on film. Penn, a diligent student of the craft and the business, was not blind to the lessons of such col-laboration and had another, more contemporary exemplar in mind.*

SEAN PENN: I'd come to a place where I was looking for a continuous relationship with a director who I could make a series of films with. I felt that would be a productive thing to do, because I'd had enough inconsistent and disappointing relationships with directors. It had been provoked originally by an interview I had read with Olivier, talking about the value of the relationships within the RSC, the shared history they were able to bring to working together, and the shortcuts of communication you got. Certainly in film, Scorsese and De Niro had had a great model of that. And I was aware that Bob had 'worked' Marty a bit to do *Raging Bull*, and that there were productive relationships where people were nudged a little in one direction or another – not just, 'Oh look, we both want to do this.' So I was looking for that give-and-take a bit. We were already starting to finance things independently, so one also thought that if you did work you were proud of, there could be a strength that in terms of the financing: you could find people who were fans of the team.

I had seen a screenplay Jamie Foley had written, something kind of personal, called 'Cowboys of the American Night'. I don't remember what I thought of the script, but I loved the title. And I found him very energetic and interesting.

JAMES FOLEY: I was at USC film school, and we had a party where everybody got stoned and showed their movies on a white wall in the living room. It just so happened that my movie was showing when Hal Ashby walked by, in pursuit of a woman . . . Hal invited me to come meet his partner, Andrew Braunsberg, who essentially said, 'Hal loves you, write anything you want.' So I wrote 'Cowboys of the American Night'. In the eighties, you could drive down Santa Monica Boulevard and see all these teenage prostitutes, male and female, on the street corner. A lot of them, sadly, were the cliché of having come out on a bus from Des Moines wanting to be actors. Some would tell me about certain studio executives they had serviced . . .

By the time it came to make it, Hal had made two flops back to back, *Hamster of Happiness* and *Looking to Get Out*, and suddenly his ability to produce some young film student's film was diminished. But because I had been hired by Hal, it got me a certain entrée and attention. So I directed *Reckless*. I met tons of people for the lead, including Sean, who – as he always reminds me – was by no means committed to doing it should I want him to. And after *Reckless* was finally released, Sean was in New York and called me up, and very politely told me that he didn't think it was very good [*laughs*]. But he said it in a way that seemed to be without intent: he wanted me to know he had seen it, and, by the way, it didn't quite work. We kept on talking about wanting to do a movie together, and then Sean gave me Nick Kazan's *At Close Range* script and I responded to it strongly.

SEAN PENN: Jamie was in my casting office now. I was casting him as a director, but casting him, in my mind, into a working relationship that would continue, if he was the guy.

JAMES FOLEY: Sean was quite clearly the driving force in getting *At Close Range* made. He was extremely hot, and it was going to be financed if he agreed to do it. And he told the powers-that-be that I was the one he wanted to direct it. They clearly wanted Sean, didn't necessarily want me at all, and Sean said, 'I'll do it if you do it with this guy.' And they ultimately accepted me as director.

When Sean and Elizabeth McGovern broke up, Sean had been living with her, so he had no place to stay. I had recently bought a house. Sean came by and ended up staying several months on the couch in my living room. In fact, it was in that period of *At Close Range* pre-production and Sean's sleeping on my couch that his next relationship happened.

MEEGAN OCHS: After Elizabeth broke up with Sean, he used to say to me, 'I'm going to marry someone who doesn't speak English, because that way we won't have any fights and it'll work out great.' The joke of this was that Sean's car broke down around the same time, so we were driving around in my car and listening to my music. I had this Madonna cassette – my uncle had taped it for me, so it was just a blank cassette box with no picture on it. So we were listening to her, and meantime Sean would be saying, 'So who do *you* think I should marry?' Finally I said, 'Well, I think you should marry Madonna.' He said, 'Who?' I said, 'The singer we're listening to: she's really sexy and funny, she's got a great sense of herself.' So the joke became that we would get in the car and want to put some music on, and Sean would say, 'OK, play my wife . . .'

In the autumn of 1984, Madonna Louise Ciccone began her remorseless ascent from New York club act to worldwide pop-chart phenomenon. In the spring, she had recorded her second album, Like a Virgin. *That September, she filmed an eye-catching role in Susan Seidelman's* Desperately Seeking Susan *with Rosanna Arquette. In November,* Like a Virgin *was released, and just before Christmas its title track hit number one on the Billboard charts, staying put for six weeks. In January 1985, she shot the video for her next single, 'Material Girl', in Los Angeles, Mary Lambert directing her in a brazen homage to Marilyn Monroe's 'Diamonds Are a Girl's Best Friend'.*

MEEGAN OCHS: I had stopped working for Sean, a brief hiatus, and during that time Steve Zaillian's wife, Elizabeth, got me some jobs on music videos. I end up working on Madonna's video, 'Material Girl'. I called Sean up and said, 'Guess what? I'm working on your wife's video.' He said, 'You're kidding?'

JAMES FOLEY: Sean and I were sitting in my house watching this brand-new invention, MTV, and one of Madonna's videos came up. Sean knew Steve Zaillian from *Falcon and the Snowman*, and he told me that Steve's wife's sister was working as an assistant director on Madonna's new video, down in a studio in Hollywood. He says, 'Maybe we could go visit . . .?' I said, 'Sounds good . . .'

MEEGAN OCHS: Madonna's up there rehearsing away on an incredible sound stage, wearing an amazing pink dress. And they take a walkie-talkie up to her, and Simon Fields, who was the producer of the video, says to her, 'Sean Penn wants to come visit the set.' And she yelled into this walkie-talkie – and to the entire room – 'Only if he'll go out with me afterwards!' And my heart just dropped, because it never occurred to me that *she* would be interested in *him* . . .

So then Sean and Jamie Foley showed up, and basically spent the entire day playing with me, carrying me around piggy-back – not a word to Madonna, nothing. But at the end of the day, Elizabeth Zaillian brings Sean up to a room and they meet each other.

And then the next thing I know, Sean's on the phone to me saying, 'You know, your friend's *calling* me from Hawaii.'

'"My friend" doesn't know who I *am*.'

'*Oh* yes, she does . . .'

'That's only because you were carting me around on your back.'

'Look, your friend's calling me from Japan, she's calling me from *everywhere* . . .'

And so they started going out. And I'm thinking, 'This can't be happening: this is *so* not reality . . .'

JOSEPH VITARELLI: Well, on the other hand, she was – and is – incredibly attractive. And talented, and a great dancer, a great entertainer. She had a career that was taking off. He was single at the time. So why wouldn't he be attracted to her? Who wouldn't be? I liked her. She reminded me of girls I used to know from the neighbourhood.

EILEEN RYAN PENN: Sean brought her here after they'd had a few dates. I didn't know who the hell she was, nor did Leo. And she seemed like a sweet little girl. She wasn't loaded with make-up. She seemed shy and nice.

BONO: Los Angeles was one of the first places U2 went off in America, but before 'Hollywood' came to see us, Sean would come, early on, round the 'Unforgettable Fire' tour. He brought Madonna to see us. She was a cute cookie at that time. I don't think people realized she was as smart as she is. I'm not sure *I* did. But he spotted it from afar; and unless he's keeping that kind of company, he's gonna get bored.

Penn and Madonna dated in New York and Los Angeles, as suited their busy daybooks. While Madonna was captivating young males the world over, she was herself beguiled in no small part by Penn's formidable circle of friendships. Many were within his own profession; others were not so starry, but no less remarkable.

ANDREW DAULTON LEE: It was a year or so after the film. Sean and I had stayed in contact. When I first met him, I never said, 'If you want my help, it's gonna cost you.' I didn't go down that road. But now I said to him, 'Look, you're in New York. So is my mother. And she got left by two husbands. You want to pretend you're me, take my mother out to dinner?' It wasn't so much a *quid pro quo* – I just threw it out there. And Sean said, 'OK,' and it was a very nice, kind gesture.

This is how my mother tells it. They meet up at this restaurant. They sit down and Sean says hi and she says hi. Sean says, 'And this is my girlfriend, Madonna.' And my mother said, 'Hi, Donna! And what do *you* do, honey?' She said, 'I'm a singer.' My mother said, 'Oh, that's *nice*.' A couple of days later my mother talks to my older sister, who's got four teenagers. She said, 'Oh yeah, and I had dinner with Sean Penn and his girlfriend Donna. Says she's a singer?' My sister says, 'You mean *Madonna*?!?' And my little nieces are all a-flutter . . .

MEEGAN OCHS: Clearly that was the moment when everything changed: when Madonna got there, the world turned upside down. It had been happening a bit before that, with Elizabeth. But they put it in hyper-drive when he got together with Madonna. She was someone running at the limelight and he was running away from it. Oh my god, was that a conflict.

Selling records was one thing, but consolidation of a musical career meant touring the United States. As Madonna started rehearsals for her first such undertaking, The 'Virgin' Tour, Penn turned at last to the realization of At Close Range *and the role of Brad Whitewood Junior, unfortunate son of coolly psychopathic tractor thief Brad Senior.*

JAMES FOLEY: It seemed so organic that Sean and I were living in the same house, talking about the movie, going out to dinner and socializing. The movie just seemed like an extension of whatever the hell our lives were: as if Hollywood had nothing to do with it, not the studio nor the producers. Which is, I think, why, in retrospect, the producer and the writer probably felt excluded from the beginning. Sean and I would meet actors together and he would read with them. Knowing Sean meant knowing his family. I met his brother Chris over at the house, and Chris seemed like the best person to play Sean's brother in the movie.

EILEEN RYAN PENN: Sean got me back into acting: *At Close Range* was the first thing I had done since I had quit to be mama. He said, 'I want you to come and read the grandmother for Jamie.' But before I read, he introduced me to Jamie and the producers and we met for lunch. Sean called me after and said, 'Mom, you can't show up in a tweedy suit looking groomed. This is a backwoods woman you're supposed to play.' I said, 'We were going for *lunch*. I wasn't coming as the character. I can play old. Do they have no imagination?' He said, 'No, they don't. Now I'm going to insist they read you. But play it down, OK? Wear a house dress, no make-up.' So I came in, sat out in the waiting room, and Sean came out and saw me. He sidled up and he whispered to me, 'Perfect! You look like shit!'

Photo by Joyce Rudolph

25 *At Close Range*: Penn as Brad Whitewood Junior.

CHRISTOPHER WALKEN: I believe my playing Sean's father very much had to do with him saying that was what he wanted. I had met Sean socially in New York when I was doing *Hurlyburly*; clearly he was very taken with the play. I knew he was a terrific young actor. So we were pals. And as a matter of fact, it seems to me that we talked the n about how it would be great to look for something that we could do together. I think we even mentioned that we could play people who were related . . . The script had good language, and I found the father a very interesting character: somebody called him 'a hayseed Lucifer'. I saw pictures and read articles about the real family, and they're nothing like the people in the movie. They were, you know, repellent. Nobody in the *movie* was all that nice, but we were all much more attractive . . .

JAMES FOLEY: The reality of the script, as I envisaged it and as Sean did, that was the gold standard – who the real kid was, how he walked and talked was not pertinent, because they weren't famous figures.

  East of Eden was one of the seminal films that got me infatuated with film-making. When you think about how Elia Kazan used widescreen – James Dean on the train, going to see his mother – which up to that point was only thought of with spectacle, and Kazan used it for the first time in an intimate drama. And there's no question that I recognize the influence of *East of Eden* in *At Close Range*. Come to think of it, Sean's physical look is closer to James Dean than anything else he ever did, including the blond hair and being a bit thicker.

SEAN PENN: The true story was that 'Brad Junior' took, I think, thirteen rounds to the body and head. We narrowed it down to seven to sell it. And the idea was simply to make me sturdy, to make it believable and have somewhere to go, to be diminished, from *that* to how shrunken he is by the end in the court room.

JAMES FOLEY: I had this little shed out in front of my house, and Sean went to the store and bought heavy weights, brought them back and put them in the shed. And I remember he was so surprised, once he committed himself to that, how his body changed so dramatically, in a short period of time. But he had to eat an awful lot too, and that was hard for him, funnily enough.

CHRISTOPHER WALKEN: Instead of getting on a plane to go down to Tennessee, Sean had a pick-up truck, and so we drove together from

New York to Nashville. It was a great way to get to know each other: we were about to play father and son. And we went through beautiful parts of the country that I had never been to. Took a couple of days; a very interesting way to get to location. We didn't talk about the movie. Talked about a number of other things, though . . .

R. D. CALL: That film was magic. Especially for me, my first major film. And there was a real sense of . . . family, that I've never really had since then. It was a hand-picked cast, kind of a labour of love. And we were kind of isolated, secluded, off in the hills of Tennessee, a world within a world within a world.

MEEGAN OCHS: Sean and Jamie had talked so much beforehand, they were sort of finishing each other's sentences. Sean was there for everything – scenes he wasn't in. There was never anything that happened that he wasn't there for.

JAMES FOLEY: There was a scene where Mary Stuart Masterson[9] visits Sean in prison after she's been raped by Chris Walken. It's wordless, and very, very heavy. And beforehand you could feel the tension building in Mary, that she was having to go to this very tense, dark, complicated place. Sean came to me and said, 'Mary's so wound up, it's gonna paralyse her. Why don't you and me all of a sudden get very cold? Tell her we're getting kicked out of the location, just disconnect her from the solemnity of it, so she just has to dive in and do it.' So I started screaming, 'Sorry, guys, we don't have time to talk about this! Let's get in places, and action!' Mary was in it straight away. And that's the take that we used. It was something about directing actors that I learned from Sean directly, because he sensed it.

The other time I was really grateful was for my own under-heralded appearance in *At Close Range* as the Assistant DA, which was only because a day-player didn't show. It was Sean's idea. He said, 'Don't worry, I'll take responsibility.' And I trusted him. It was actually the worst day of my life – I couldn't stand being on that side of the camera, and I, of course, was terrible. But Sean comes up to me – he's the director now – and says, 'Just make believe that you're talking to a child, say the lines in that patronizing way.' And I thought, 'Make-believe? That's not Method acting.' But it gave me something to focus on, and we got through it. And that's the kind of practicality Sean has

9 Masterson, not quite nineteen, was cast as Brad Junior's ill-fated girlfriend Terry.

in his acting: he's got his own private universe he's dealing with, but he's also got a very practical discipline that shapes how he goes about doing it.

26 On location for *At Close Range*: Christopher Walken (Brad Senior) and Penn (Junior)

NICHOLAS KAZAN: I was on location in Tennessee. I was at the office, I just very rarely went to the set – they wouldn't let me. Sometimes I went anyway.

The scene in Kazan's script of which he was proudest was one set in a whorehouse, where, in a grotesquely misconceived bonding exercise, Brads Senior and Junior fuck in adjoining beds, the father exultant, the son plainly miserable.

NICHOLAS KAZAN: For me, the whorehouse scene elevated the stakes for the whole movie and indicated how outrageous it was going to become: it prepared you in some way for the killing of the kids. If a father could do *that* to his son, he'd do anything.

Drama is conflict, and the essence of the scene is that Brad Junior has always wanted to go into a whorehouse and he wants to impress his father – and he doesn't want to be there. The thing is, Jamie told me that Sean didn't want to shoot that scene. Years later, he called and asked me to do him a favour, and in the process confessed that when he had attributed feelings and statements to Sean, they were actually his own.

CHRISTOPHER WALKEN: A movie set is an artificial circumstance, and there are many things that operate against giving the illusion of reality and the sense that you sincerely mean what you're saying. Very often, actors do things to keep it alive. There are methods, techniques of creating spontaneity when it's not really there.

SEAN PENN: I don't think that I am guilty of trying to do that until I feel something has to change – that we need something else. I don't mind trying something and it not work: you've gotta fall on your face, on and off camera, if you're gonna make things work. So I'm not beyond distracting somebody or making something uncomfortable if something's not working in the first place, when it's comfortable . . .

MEEGAN OCHS: The first dialogue scene they shot was where Sean meets Mary Stuart Masterson and her friend at the town square. Sean was playing tapes and doing goofy dances, then he'd turn it off and walk up to them, and they were giggling like teenagers – which is what he wanted. There was a take during dailies where, at the end of that, Mary Stuart looked at the camera and said, 'Screw you, Peggy Feury.'

NICHOLAS KAZAN: When Rafelson was involved, he wanted me to write a father–son confrontation scene at the end, before the trial, and it is that scene that exists in the film, which in many ways is very effective. Though frankly I preferred the austerity of the original script. To me, when Brad Junior gets riddled with bullets but washes himself and drives over to his father's place, I leave the movie, because I don't believe it – it's too many bullets.

CHRISTOPHER WALKEN: In that scene, Sean points a gun at me. And I'm an absolute coward when it comes to that stuff in movies. I stay away from guns – I won't even get on a horse. Anyway, Sean ran out of the room, and I heard him say to the prop man, 'Give me the other gun!' He came back with what I thought was a different gun. And Jamie Foley said, 'Roll it', and Sean pointed this gun at me, near my eye, in fact. Of course, he hadn't done anything. But I didn't know that. And he created the doubt in my mind. He was just trying to scare me, and indeed he did. I think in the scene you can see that. It was not my cup of tea . . . But I'm very grateful to him – I mean, he made me good in that scene, so really it was generosity on his part.

SEAN PENN: I think Chris and I really trusted and liked each other. Some people you wouldn't fuck around with that way. But he fucks around all the time in certain ways, very spontaneously. And he's out there for what's onscreen.

JAMES FOLEY: Madonna came down to Tennessee, and I remember just pandemonium at Nashville airport upon her arrival, a horde of paparazzi following her. But she wouldn't come to the set, in order to keep the monsters at bay. She was very respectful of the process, very much not wanting to be disruptive.

MEEGAN OCHS: They got engaged on location: I was with Sean in his trailer and he told me that he had asked Madonna to marry him. He said, 'It scares me that you predicted this.' Then he told me, 'No one can know on the set or at home. You have to organize this wedding without telling anybody.' It was meant to be a secret until the invitations went out. Sean told me and Jamie Foley. And Madonna told Liz Rosenberg, her publicist – who never said a word, to her incredible credit – and Rosanna Arquette, who unfortunately told someone, who told *everybody*. And that was the end of that. My mother in northern California, completely disconnected from Hollywood, started getting calls from people about Sean marrying Madonna . . .

JAMES FOLEY: We were all staying in the same hotel, and these paparazzi were constantly outside, so that every time Madonna or Sean or the two of them together ever broached the idea of going out, there would be an attack. I was involved enough with them on that occasion, and later in New York, to understand what it's like to have people who physically confront you with heavy pieces of metal, hitting your head sometimes. It's like, 'Whoah, wait a minute.' You're being assaulted.

MEEGAN OCHS: There were weird things that were completely inappropriate: someone thinking that Madonna was pregnant and had had an abortion, sending her a huge bouquet of black balloons. As much as one can say Sean should have expected it, I don't think he was expecting how mean-spirited it was going to be. He was very taken aback by it, and felt very protective of her. She would become the master manipulator of the press, but she wasn't that yet, and I don't think even she realized how insane it was going to get when you're in some small town in Franklin, Tennessee. But the press descended. And that was the first time, I think, that he ever actually hit anybody.

Sunday, 30 June 1985: two reporters for Rupert Murdoch's British Sun *newspaper, then engaged in a tabloid circulation war that called for the most relentlessly door-stopping journalism, came to Nashville chasing the Sean-and-Madonna scoop. They spotted the couple hand-in-hand in the car park of the Maxwell House Hotel and, doubtless unaware of Penn's recent endorphin-pumping workout regimen, tried to push their luck. An altercation ensued in which Penn wielded upon the hacks a rock, his fists and their own camera. The hacks told all to a judge, police attended the Maxwell, and Penn was arrested. He went before the night court, was charged on two misdemeanour counts of assault and battery, and released on bail.*

CHRISTOPHER WALKEN: You know, it's amazing, in show business – whatever it was that happened took about five seconds, but somebody takes a picture and suddenly it's all over the world and never goes away. His life became intermingled with rock 'n' roll. And that's a different ball game.

JAMES FOLEY: I remember very clearly a photograph that got into the national papers – even the international papers – of Sean in mid-swing, hitting a guy. But his arrest didn't interfere with the shoot at all. I only knew about it after: Sean never said a word. The next day, this group of crew guys are standing round over a newspaper, and I say, 'What are you looking at?' I see this picture and I'm like, 'What!?'

MEEGAN OCHS: One thing this press experience created was that no one felt comfortable just walking up and talking to Sean. And he kind of liked that.

R. D. CALL: Everybody was kind of circling the wagons. And it was exciting, 'cause you didn't know what was going to happen from one day to the next.

The mounting public interest in pieces of Madonna's flesh reached a crescendo of sorts when on 7 July Penthouse *announced it would pub-*

lish some 'artistic' nudes taken in 1979. Playboy *followed suit and got to the stands first. On Saturday, 13 July, Madonna played the 'Live Aid' concert for Ethiopian famine relief at JFK Stadium, Philadelphia. She was escorted through the scrum by Brad Whitewood Junior, a.k.a. Sean Penn, in check shirt, old jacket and Ray-Bans, nursing a can of Heineken, his movie musculature and peroxide-job in full effect.*

MEEGAN OCHS: We flew off from Tennessee to go to Live Aid, into a whole storm where you *know* it's going to be craziness. My memories of the day seem like a silent movie – I'm there, but I can't really believe it's real. I remember Madonna and I flew separately from Sean. I remember walking backstage with them, and everywhere you looked were all these music legends. And I remember, when she was onstage and Sean was watching, that he had a big smile on his face . . .

27 Cartoon by Michael Penn for invitations to the wedding of Penn and Madonna, August 16 1985 in homage to Grant Wood's *American Gothic*

Back in Los Angeles with At Close Range *in the can, the couple rented a bungalow in Beachwood Canyon and prepared their nuptials. Michael Penn designed invitations calling the anointed 'to Sean and*

Madonna's Birthday Party on the Sixteenth of August Nineteen Eighty Five. The Celebration Will Commence at Six o'Clock. Please Be Prompt or You Will Miss Their Wedding Ceremony . . .'

MEEGAN OCHS: Their original thought had been to get married on the stroke of midnight of the sixteenth and the seventeenth, so they got both their birthdays . . . They knew everyone they wanted to use and made all the decisions. But it was pretty tight. No one was allowed to know where the wedding would take place, only the day. And then I personally spoke to every single person the day before – I was sitting there in my pyjamas, with Sean on my couch beside me telling me, 'You're not giving good enough directions.' I said, 'Sean, it's *Tom Cruise*, he knows how to drive a couple of blocks past your parents' house, don't worry about it . . .'

ART WOLFF: Meegan said, 'Sean wants you to come to his bachelor party', so I came early and hung out. It seemed to me that Sean was truly trying his best to ride the whirlwind – of both the excitement and total amazement that he'd hooked up with the world's most famous female at that particular moment. You couldn't look in a newspaper or a magazine without seeing something about Sean or Madonna. I went to have dinner with Leo and Eileen, and they were very bemused by the whole situation. I could see the looks on their faces. 'Well! I don't know, but . . . this is it!'

EILEEN RYAN PENN: Misgivings? No, you don't think that way then. You think positively – and I didn't consciously allow myself to think the negative things. I was hoping that they would grow together, not apart.

ART WOLFF: On the Rox was a place made famous by Aykroyd and Belushi, and all the young turks were there for Sean's bachelor party, the 'brat pack'[10] as they were called at the time. And there were three 'old guys' there: me, Duvall and – though he would bristle to be so described – Harry Dean. We just sat at the bar and commented wryly on all of the activity.

JOSEPH VITARELLI: Someone arranged for about twenty-five *Playboy*

---

10 June 1985, a *New York* magazine story by David Blum christened 'The Brat Pack', a gaggle of young actors then socializing and starring together in *The Breakfast Club* and *St Elmo's Fire*.

Bunnies to show up. And the interesting thing is that none of the men were schmoozing with the Bunnies at all – the guys in the room were just interested in talking to the other guys who were there. A lot of these men hadn't seen one another in a while – and, frankly, it was more interesting to talk to Harry Dean and Robert Duvall. So all these beautiful girls were sitting around kind of bored . . .

EILEEN RYAN PENN: They got married at the house of two very faithful friends of mine, Elda and Dan Unger. Sean wanted it to be in Malibu, and they had this huge place that was just right for a wedding: right next door to Johnny Carson, the next block over. Also it would be private, supposedly – this before the helicopters came.

CHRISTOPHER PENN: It's not like the press needed twenty helicopters there. They could have had one cover it and all shared it. But they made it a bigger scene, because Sean and Madonna didn't want it to be a scene. So it became this friggin' scene . . .

MEEGAN OCHS: That was when Sean made his announcement from the balcony, now famous: 'Welcome to this year's remake of *Apocalypse Now* . . .'

JAMES FOLEY: I was Sean's best man, and I remember being with him before the ceremony, and him being really mad, wanting to get a bazooka and shoot them down.
   The ceremony was on a promontory, and while the vows were being taken, I was standing right there with Madonna's sister, her maid of honour, and I couldn't hear what they or anybody were saying because the helicopters were so loud.

PETER COYOTE: I found myself under the helicopter drop-zone at the wedding, where Sean had written 'FUCK YOU' in the sand below the house so that the paparazzi would have a hard time photographing it. The next thing I knew, there was my and my wife's picture in *People* magazine as part of the celebrity entourage.

JOSEPH VITARELLI: The helicopters were dangerously close – too close to one another, and too close to us. One of those things crashes and you wipe out half of Hollywood . . . Andy Warhol, Cher, David Geffen, Diane Keaton, Cruise.

ART WOLFF: But it's indicative of Sean that, in addition to the celebrities that you'd expect – Chris Walken and Andy Warhol[11] with his Polaroid camera – there were a number of people who Sean wanted there just because of his affection for them. Including, as at every event I've ever been to that has been meaningful in Sean's life, his high-school teacher, Leonard Vincent.

CHRISTOPHER WALKEN: There were people I hadn't seen in a while and people I'd never met before. I had a pair of bronze African animal sculptures, and I gave them one . . . But aside from that there was almost like a Fellini movie atmosphere. They had a big tent set up, and there were literally people jumping out of bushes with cameras. Helicopters overhead like big dragonflies. I'm glad I saw that – once, anyway – because one sees it on *Entertainment Tonight* and so forth. But to actually be there . . . 'surreal', I guess, is the word.

MEEGAN OCHS: The party took place under a tented tennis court, and I think everyone had a blast. Just the usual wedding scene, except for much better dancing and much better food – Wolfgang Puck catered. No one at the wedding was allowed to bring cameras, except for Herb Ritts.

DR KATZ: I was standing around the back of this place and there was a hedgerow beside me. I look down and there's a guy there in camou-flage, dirt on his face. I thought I was back in Vietnam . . . He must have been there twenty-four hours. I told him, 'Be smart, leave with what you have now, they're gonna take your film if they see you.' He didn't leave. Bouncers got him . . .

DONNA WOLFF: After I'd had quite a few drinks, I thought I'd try invit-ing Madonna over to our place. I finally shook her hand and said – terrible thing to say! – 'Oh, you must come to dinner! You know, Sean always brought his girlfriends to visit at our place.' And she just sort of *slid* her hand out of mine and away . . .

HAROLD BECKER: I knew Madonna too from *Visionquest,* and I was at the wedding. I wished them well. It didn't surprise me what happened, because it's hard to live in a fishbowl. Nobody who hasn't could have an inkling of what it's like, the pressures of it and how they affect people, even people as strong as Sean and Madonna.

11 Warhol had not been invited, strictly speaking, but came out as the date of Madonna's close friend and ex-room-mate Martin Burgoyne: 'It was the most exciting weekend of my life. . .' (Warhol, *Diaries*).

JAMES FOLEY: But it was a blast: it was a whole moment in pop-culture history. And I think it was a union that was a real romantic love that neither would deny to this day.

I think back on it now . . . I was young and Hollywood was new, and that wedding was a kind of specific white heat of whatever the hell 'celebrity' was in the middle of the eighties, bearing down with this unflinching hot light. But it's like when you're shooting and sometimes the actor will complain, 'Does that light have to be so close?' I could feel it just walking down the street with them. And that light was such a pressure on Sean and Madonna.

SIX

1985–1987

My understanding of the direction that Madonna was choosing was a misunderstanding. And the degree to which she would be choosing, and chosen for, such an intense spotlight was not something I had seen on the cards. So that *was* a surprise. It was a *big* surprise . . .

Sean Penn, *Playboy* interview with David Rensin, November 1991

The newlyweds made home in a Spanish-style mansion in Carbon Canyon, Malibu, formerly the residence of Olivia Newton-John; they also took a New York apartment on Central Park West. Penn returned to Nashville on 17 October to face his outstanding assault charges. His lawyer Robert Sullivan told the court, 'A plea of "no contest" does not represent an admission of guilt on the part of Mr Penn. He simply felt it was time to resolve the matter and move on to more creative matters.' Penn received a ninety-day suspended sentence and a nominal fine. Madonna set to work on her True Blue album, its title-cut a paean to 'the coolest guy in the universe'.

The newlyweds were now inundated with film projects. Producer John Kohn owned and had co-written a script based on the 1985 novel Faraday's Flowers by Tony Kendrick: a retro-comedy concerning a missionary nurse who gets tangled up with an American grifter in pursuit of a notorious lost consignment of opium in 1938 Shanghai. Kohn sent it to English TV director Jim Goddard, who in turn passed it to Denis O'Brien of George Harrison's UK-based Handmade Films. Harrison wasn't hopeful for the material, nor were prospective financiers. But Kohn had a connection to Sean Penn, and in November 1985, Penn and Madonna committed to Shanghai Surprise.

SEAN PENN: Why did I do it? For love and money. John Kohn was someone who I had known on *Bad Boys* and liked. Getting us as a pair was attractive to them at the time. I have long been paid so little – relatively to others. And that movie was the first time that I was getting to a number where I could afford . . . well, put it like this, I was in a marriage with somebody who had a lot of money, and I didn't want to be the thing that limited the lifestyle too much. And I certainly did not want to be anything less than a full participant in anything that we did. But that was the number-two thing. The number-one thing was: I had just got married, and she was asking me to do it . . .

Then, a tragedy: one of the lodestars of Penn's young life was taken on Wednesday, 20 November 1985. Peggy Feury died in a head-on car collision caused by one of her narcoleptic episodes. She was sixty-three.

SEAN PENN: It shouldn't have happened. She had certain students who functioned as sort-of chauffeurs and right hands, but there were times where she made the choice to drive. I think it was generally considered a charming eccentricity – not by the families of those who were killed, and not by her, and not by her own.

Penn spoke at Feury's funeral service. Years later, Premiere *magazine canvassed her students by way of tribute and he reflected: 'She would have been just as helpful to Marlon Brando as Stella Adler was, or to James Dean as Lee Strasberg was. And probably Brando would still enjoy acting, and Jimmy Dean wouldn't be dead . . .'*[1]

At this moment, another significant elder entered Penn's life, an influence both literary/philosophical and social/personal. Charles Bukowski had, at the age of fifty, quit a job at the post office to become a writer. As he later remembered, 'It was my last day on the job. One of the clerks said, "I don't know if he's going to make it, but the old man sure has a lot of guts."'[2] *His first novel was* Post Office *(1971). Erections, Ejaculations, Exhibitions and General Tales of Ordinary Madness (1972), Factotum (1975) and Women (1978) followed for Black Sparrow Press. By the late seventies, Bukowski had a cult renown in Europe, helped by good translation and a splendid drunken performance on the French TV talking-shop* Apostrophe. *Such was his force: as Penn would later declare, 'Bukowski was not irreverent; he was without reverence. He was us, after a hard night of sex and drinking. He was us before the shower, on the toilet, sick, tired, broken-hearted and on the way to work . . .'*[3]

---

1 *Premiere*, 'Children of the Light', Nancy Griffin, October 1990.
2 *Film Comment*, September/October 1987.
3 *Inside the Actors Studio*, Bravo, November 1998.

SEAN PENN: I remember being at Art and Donna's apartment in New York, looking at the books on their bookshelf and seeing the name: Charles Bukowski. The first actual book I had was given to us at my wedding, a copy of *War All the Time*, with acrylics by Hank in it. I read through it, and I thought, 'I'm hooked.' And I started talking about him to everyone I met.

ART WOLFF: Now, the difference between Sean and everybody else is that he read the books, adored them, and made it his job to go search out Bukowski. Had to camp on this doorstep to meet him and really get to know him.

SEAN PENN: I ran into David Geffen, who mentioned that he was having a barbecue and said he was thinking about inviting this person and that person. Dennis Hopper was one, and I let David know that if Dennis Hopper was gonna be there I would be too – that I would love to meet him. Dennis showed up, David played Cupid, and we sat in the corner and talked. And I brought up all the Bukowski I was reading.

DENNIS HOPPER: I was absolutely a fan of Bukowski's writing. My father too worked in the post office . . . So I said to Sean, 'You like Bukowski? There's a script he wrote that you should really do, called *Barfly*.' He said, 'And you'll direct it . . .?' I told him, 'No, because it was really Barbet Schroeder who had Bukowski write it. And Barbet's going to direct it – he's not going to let it go.'

© Michael Montfort. Courtesy of Linda Lee Bukowski

28 Linda Lee Bukowski and Charles Bukowski

LINDA LEE BUKOWSKI: It was early 1977. Hank got a call from Barbet Schroeder asking if he could come over and talk to him about writing a screenplay. Hank said, 'Oh maaan, that's not my thing. I gotta go to the track, write my poems. You do a movie, you get everybody else's hands in there, it ends up it's not your writing any more.' But Barbet came, they hung out and talked. He was a great storyteller who'd had some unbelievable experiences in life, and he talked Hank into it. And once Hank made a commitment, he was true to Barbet: he had a great loyalty that way. So then Barbet went to all corners of the world – Germany, France, Russia, Japan – trying to get money. Finally, seven years later . . . Barbet got associated with these two Israeli guys, Golan and Globus, who were Cannon Films at the time. They were tough cookies, and Hank had to listen to a lot of absurd insanity from them. But they were the ones who agreed to make *Barfly*.

SEAN PENN: This was a movie nobody was touching, the fucken thing was just sitting there for years. The only reason it got going was 'cause I told people at Cannon I'd do it for a dollar. Barbet went public with that, and Mickey Rourke read it and called him.

LINDA LEE BUKOWSKI: I remember mentioning Sean Penn to Barbet and Hank. They had never heard of him. Hank didn't go to movies. But I'd been a huge fan of Sean's from when I first saw his work. I went out and rented *Fast Times at Ridgemont High*, and Hank and I sat down with a bottle of wine in front of his TV and watched it. And Hank loved it – he was cracking up, on the floor, thought it was a hoot.

SEAN PENN: So I tracked down Bukowski through his editor at Black Sparrow Press, John Martin. I said, 'I don't know if he knows who I am, but I really want to talk to him about *Barfly*.' I left my number with John. Then Bukowski called me and left a number. I was at Musso and Frank and I returned his call. I said, 'Sean Penn calling for Charles Bukowski.' He said, 'This *is* Hank Bukowski.' And then: 'Sean Penn? You're my *last* favourite actor . . .' And I never clarified that with him: did that mean I was last on his list? Or had he given up having favourites after seeing me?

But I suggested that we meet, and he said, 'Anywhere but a bar. There's nothing in 'em . . .' He ended up inviting me over to his house the following weekend. I went, and we had a great time; talked a little bit about *Barfly* but mostly about other things. And we ended up setting a date for the following Sunday. This would go on for nearly ten years, almost every Sunday I was in town . . . But we got to *Barfly*. I knew about it because of Dennis: I was with Dennis for a reason, in my view. And I wanted to make a movie with Dennis, so I wasn't going to do *Barfly* without him.

DENNIS HOPPER: I had confronted Barbet in Ma Maison and announced that he was going to ruin it, that he shouldn't direct it, that he shouldn't even be directing traffic, and I should be directing his movie. But I did this publicly, in a very loud and drunken speech to the whole restaurant. So there was no way in hell Barbet was going to let me direct this movie. And I tried to explain all this to Sean, but Sean kept saying, 'No, come on, we'll work this out, I'll work on it.' But nothing could happen straight away, because he and Madonna were on their way to Shanghai . . .

SEAN PENN: This is the chapter I'd like written in *blood* . . .

* * *

JOSEPH VITARELLI: Just don't write about *Shanghai Surprise*. Just leave it out, man [*laughs*]. Stick with the good stuff. Who the fuck cares?

SEAN PENN: We flew to Shanghai and spent a week there, in wintertime: bitter cold, great food. And then went to Hong Kong, then Macao, and then London, and made the alleged 'movie' . . .
I would say the poison on that picture was me and Denis O'Brien. He was diabolical – and later turned out to be diabolical in George Harrison's life – in terms of his deceit. He was playing games with money and nothing else, and it was just a drain on the picture. And I was letting myself get pissed off and drunk. It's the only movie I ever did drunk, other than a drunk scene where I had experimented. On this, I was drunk a lot. It was torture. *Torture.*
Did the drinking help? Well, it made so that what I've read and what I'm about to tell you are my only memories of the whole experience . . .
I arrived in Macao by jetfoil. As I recall, my then-wife had taken the jetfoil ahead of me and was there getting a hair change done for the next day's shooting. Hong Kong had been *insane*: mostly driven by my wife – not by her intention, but by her fame. So now, you finally had a little peace. I was five minutes inside the hotel, and a friend and I were charged with attempted murder . . .

© Metro–Goldwyn–Mayer, Inc.

29   On location for *Shanghai Surprise*: Madonna and Penn

I came with a fellow who I had hired as a sort of assistant/security guy. He had been my private kick-boxing coach. I had done some boxing, and I was trying to get myself back into shape. So he and I are greeted off the jetfoil pad and driven about three minutes to the Oriental Hotel. We're met by two security guys who walk us upstairs, very gracious, to show me the room. The doors are open, breeze blowing through from the balcony, fresh flowers – a very nice tribute from George Harrison. And as I approach the room, security drops back. There's a door to the left side of the corridor, and as we make a right into the room, somebody jumps out. We were not prepared for this. And both of us reacted. We grabbed the guy, ran him through the room to the balcony and hung him over – on the ninth floor – not with the intention of throwing him over. But those two security guys saw this, and saw what we had now come to see – which was that the guy had a camera. Not that that instantly meant he *wasn't* a freak. He had come out so abruptly. But I had come to feel he was easily neutralized, and an older man. We were pulled off him by the security guys, and we went willingly; it wasn't violent. And we got arrested for attempted murder. Five minutes later I'm in jail, sitting on a stone floor next to my friend, and now everybody's talking Portuguese. And only the hotel staff know we're in there, nobody from our group. So we're looking at each other like, 'What do we do now?'

The cell door was ajar. We took off, got out, ran to the jetfoil. And we were able to make a phone call to the production office. They then made a phone call, and they had everything stalled by their contact in the Chinese Triad who ran Macao. It was a delicate process with the Asian face-saving stuff, so the second-in-command from one had to ask the second-in-command of the other, 'If my boss asks your boss this, will the answer be yes?' And so, independently and without lawyers involved, some things were arranged so that we were able to work during the investigation and then flee. We went to England, finished the alleged 'movie'. A year later I got in the mail at my house a pardon from the Portuguese government on a crime of which I was never convicted – no explanation, but I was pardoned, I guess, for flight and anything else that followed. So I can go to Portugal. And Macao . . .

Penn and Madonna flew to London to complete filming at Shepperton Studios and various exterior locations, where the attentions of the

British tabloids naturally placed a further onus on the already listing production. George Harrison hoped to ameliorate the poisonous coverage with a press conference, from which Penn absented himself, and at which one hack exhibited a stunning brass neck in asking Madonna to apologize for her and Penn's behaviour towards the press. Nonesuch was forthcoming. Principal photography limped across the finish-line in March.

DENNIS HOPPER: Sean got back from *Shanghai Surprise*, and he invited me and Barbet Schroeder to have a meeting at Bukowski's place in San Pedro. I told him, 'This is not gonna work . . . ', but anyway, I went down there. And I had just stopped drinking, man, so it was like a scene . . . I mean, I get accused of a lot of things because I wasn't drinking – even more than when I *was* drinking [*laughs*].

SEAN PENN: It's recounted, not necessarily so fairly, in *Hollywood*.[4] It was the colouring of it. I can't read it objectively as a piece of literature because I was in it, and I certainly love everything else he wrote. Hank flattered his own directness a bit. And we all suffered in translation. But that's his privilege as a writer, I suppose.

LINDA LEE BUKOWSKI: Dennis showed up wearing a turtleneck sweater and a gold medallion, and I could see Hank thinking, 'What's this guy doing?' I don't know if Dennis was nervous, but Hank didn't know him and he immediately made some sort of judgement call. Also, Dennis was laughing all the time, like people do sometimes when they're nervous: 'Ah-ha-ha-ha!' There's nothing wrong with real laughter, but this was happening every two seconds . . .

SEAN PENN: I know Hank took issue with Dennis. And he had a lot of investment in Barbet, who had been very devoted to the film and showed a great passion. What I said to Barbet was, 'Nothing to do with you, Barbet, but if *I'm* gonna do it, I have to do it with Dennis. Would you consider doing it that way with you producing?'

LINDA LEE BUKOWSKI: It got a little bit heated. And finally Sean was loyal to Dennis, and Hank was loyal to Barbet. I remember the next day Hank said, 'See? This movie business, it's crazy, Jesus Christ . . .'

SEAN PENN: But the upshot of it was Hank and me and Linda stayed great friends.

4 A drawn-from-life novel by Charles Bukowski (Black Sparrow Press, 1989).

LINDA LEE BUKOWSKI: Sean would come over at least once a month, drive all the way from Malibu and come and spend a good long night. And Hank just didn't do that with many people; he wasn't a club member. So the relationship he and Sean had was really one on one, heart to heart, spirit to spirit. Hank's a great storyteller. And, as we found, so was Sean. Hank would talk about when he was a kid, playing baseball with some little guy then going into the basement of his house, drinking wine and getting sick. And then Sean would think of something. He has such a creative mind and a great wit and an ability to create a graphic event when he's talking – you visualize it, because he's animated, physically, when he talks. Whether it came from deep experiences of sorrow and suffering . . . I don't think so. But he and Hank bounced off of each other.

SEAN PENN: This is also when I first got in contact with Marlon Brando: after *Barfly* hadn't flown, I wanted to do Bukowski's *Women* with Marlon, and I would adapt it and direct it. Hank told me, 'There's this guy Verhoeven who wants it but it's yours for the taking, if you can get him . . .' Marlon didn't want to do it. But we met through that. And he's a brilliant guy, who I have a lot of love for.

LINDA LEE BUKOWSKI: Sean came over a couple of times with Madonna. There they were, a movie star and a rock star, and it was Hank they were coming to see. Then he brought Harry Dean Stanton, and Hank took a liking to Harry Dean – there's certain similar little curmudgeonly things about their personalities. They'd both been around the block. And Hank saw that in him, that endurance, definitely. Hank used to say, 'Endurance is greater than love.' Sean had that loyalty that Hank also had with his friends. I think Sean surrounds himself with people for whom he has a deep, intuitive caring and respect: people who have lived deeply and honestly, and in spite of themselves and the situations around them.

JOSEPH VITARELLI: Sean and Bukowski loved one another to pieces. And he was likeable and fun to be around. And maybe, in some way, a little bit like Leo . . . Not the drinking. Leo was a drinker but not like that – I mean, *nobody* was like Bukowski in that. But there might be some similarity, some qualities, about Leo and Bukowski. The intelligence, maybe . . . I'm not sure. But it's worth thinking about.

LINDA LEE BUKOWSKI: Sometimes Sean would call us 'Mom' and 'Pop', and we would call him 'Son'. He'd come to the door and it was like he'd been away at school or college or off somewhere. 'Hi, son, there you are!' We'd just talk about stuff that he might sit and talk with his parents about. This is not to take away from Sean's pure, dear love for his mother and father, because that family is close-knit and loving. But with Hank and me he could maybe expand upon it a little more . . .

SEAN PENN: Hank was the sort of guy who, a little drunk, would *say* things. Like, 'I'll kick your *asssss* . . .' But he was a *fantastically* sweet person, a beautiful guy. All the other stuff, you just let it go and went on with the show. One time he danced with my mother at a party at the house in Malibu. She said to him, 'Oh, you're just a big phoney.' And he says to me, 'I *like* your mom . . .' This was the thing: people called him a misogynist. Look what he says about *men*. He was a fair, balanced critic . . .

JAMES RUSSO: I moved to LA in 1985, and I guess the closest thing to Café Central out there at the time was Helena's5 – big place, everybody went, Jack Nicholson and the whole crew. Sean and I got into a couple of things together, but I never really saw him go off – that was always from a distance. I'm *glad* . . .

ANGELICA HUSTON: I do remember the whole brouhaha over a fistfight that went on at Helena's. And I remember thinking that was pretty cool. I'd like men to fight over me . . . Though, now I think about it, the thought is much nicer than the act.

SEAN PENN: I'm a year into my marriage now. And I want to just have an evening where I'm not gonna drive and I'm gonna drink. So I go to Helena's nightclub in downtown LA with my wife. There's a guy there, his name's Hawk Wolinski.6 The first week I was dating my wife, this guy had played pals-y with me. Then she got into the car with me after she was doing some work with him, telling me how he'd been trying to hit on her. Well, I wanted to go back in the house right then and flatten him. But she convinced me not to.

It's a year later: I'm walking out of Helena's. I'm with Madonna and Chrissie Hynde. Jack was there this night too. And who stands up to

5 Named for hostess Helena Kallianotes, she of the Sherman Way roller-skating party, *c.* 1979.
6 David 'Hawk' Wolinski, songwriter and keyboardist, played with Rufus and wrote 'Ain't Nobody', a hit record for Chaka Khan in 1983.

say hello – to *me*? Hawk Wolinski. He's in my space. And I say, 'Why would I shake your hand? You're a fucking liar.' He says, 'Who, me?' 'When I came over your house that day to pick her up, you'd just been hitting on her, and you're inviting me in with all your words of admiration. What kind of fucking respect is that, you piece of –?'

And then something . . . went wrong. He denied it. And I, stupidly, hit him. And he went down. And *then* I made the mistake. He was bigger than I was, I didn't want him getting up, so I picked up a chair – not thinking I just went from the misdemeanour handbook to a felony, assault with a deadly weapon – just thinking, 'I want to let him know not to get up.' And it was more of a threat than anything else, but I *did* make contact. And now I wish I'd fucking slammed him, because I went to jail like I'd slammed him, and I got sued civilly and lost like I'd slammed him . . .

The fall-out from this incident would consume a year's worth of legal manoeuvring, contribute to a sentence of incarceration, and inspire a scene in a later Penn-directed picture.

At Close Range *premièred on 16 April 1986. The fruits of the labour were clear: it was an immaculately styled piece, carefully lit for mood, elliptically edited, the camera moving sinuously, montage knitted together by umpteen musical variations on Madonna's ballad 'Live to Tell'. All in all, a horrendous true-life American tale had been given the toniest possible rendering. In a* Vanity Fair *interview for the picture, Penn thumbnailed it as* 'Paris Texas *goes to* Flashdance-land'. *Still, its final dramatic effect was an impressive traducing of the notion of family ties and values. Christopher Walken's Brad Senior lectures his gang on the inviolability of blood ('Don't say nothing against the family') but finally authorizes his son's execution to protect the 'family' business ('This is a group – you don't violate that').*

JAMES FOLEY: There was a tremendous conflict between myself and Elliot Lewitt and Nick Kazan. Their complaint was that the movie veered sharply from the real people, so its entire look, the look of Sean, was at variance with that. They'd had a different vision. And one of the things that cemented my view of Sean was that he instantly took a position in support of myself and my cut. I think Hemdale, without Sean, would have been happy to get rid of me and only didn't because Sean said, 'If you get rid of him then you get rid of me, for publicity or anything else.'

NICHOLAS KAZAN: I will say, I couldn't have more admiration for Sean as an actor, and I thought he was brilliant in the film. As far as its look is concerned, I thought Juan Ruiz Anchia did a fantastic job, and the film looked really beautiful. It was *not* the way I saw the film. And I honestly think that the director made a mistake in making the film too pretty. I think a more documentary style would have told the audience subliminally what regrettably never appeared on the screen, which is that it was based on a true story. They were so excited to get Madonna's song that they put up a title-card about it, but took off the card that said it was based on a true story . . .

Lewitt and Kazan aired their grievances in a piece for GQ *magazine written by Kenneth Turan ('Sean Penn Flexed His Muscle', July 1986), blaming Penn and Foley for the wilful perversion of the script. In later years, Kazan came to the view that he had fired too many guns.*

SEAN PENN: It ended fairly poorly between what became the two factions, though in later years Nick and I were absolutely able to patch it up.

NICHOLAS KAZAN: After Jamie called me up and told me that he'd attributed stuff to Sean that was his own doing, I wrote Sean a note saying that was what had happened, and I apologized for including him in my previous remarks. It was important to me to try to make amends for that interview. He sent me a note back saying, 'Accepted'.

SEAN PENN: Jamie Foley is a very gifted movie-maker. I'm proud of the movie. But in terms of the alternate ways of approaching something, even my own choices within it were moved in the direction of where the director was excited at that time and where we shared an excitement, whether or not a vision. Because at the end of the day, in the balance of it, it was to be his vision, and I supported that. There wasn't anybody in the group not capable of doing other versions. But there wasn't a group consensus. And rather than say 'That's a shame' I would only say that there are other versions of the movie I'd like to see. Is that diplomatic enough?

Having said that, now we're talking about the movie we made. Jamie and I agreed pretty well on everything. There was magic that was there that would not have occurred in another version: the version that I'm dreaming about does not include Christopher Walken. Now, that would only have made the movie we *did* make far less than it was. Let me give you an example: I think Tennessee Williams's play *A Streetcar Named Desire* is a masterpiece. I think that Marlon Brando, as a creature, is more poetic even than that masterpiece, and therefore what was Blanche's play became Stanley's movie. It's not hard to say what was gained; it's harder to say what was lost. Lost, in our case, would have been the magic of Chris Walken, which is a point of pride, because Jamie and I fought for that, and it made enormous sense in this context. I don't want to be revisionist, but it may be that I, right or wrong, was carrying a feeling that that version we're talking about wouldn't have suffered *me*, much less Chris. Me as an unknown? Yeah. But I am not the picture visually that I have in my head of Brad Junior, if I were directing it, in that context. The structure of his face is different than mine. I wouldn't want to ever have seen him before.

BENICIO DEL TORO: Before I started acting or even started to *understand* what acting was all about – Sean Penn was someone whose movies I'd go see. Me and my brother were both Sean Penn fans: you know, like other people have Tom Cruise . . . And I remember seeing *At Close Range* and being blown away. I grew up around where the story takes place, that Amish country, Harrisburg and Hershey, Pennsylvania. And Sean brought a reality to that part. He was dressed exactly like the kids dressed in that area: the way *I* was dressing at the time . . . and he made it seem like that kid was flesh-and-bone. To me, that's one of the best performances by any actor at *any* time, his performance in *At Close Range*. To this day, it's one of my favourites.

For all its final flurries, At Close Range *had been Penn's most crucial and involving experience in film to date, and he was more than willing to give interviews in which he extolled the work he, Foley and company had achieved. 'I feel this is my first movie not for hire,' he told* American Film. *And in the background was the consideration of an extended partnership with Foley on future projects.*

SEAN PENN: I know that Orion originally was willing to leap at Jamie, on the strength of *At Close Range*. I felt that way right through the movie to the end of it, and it was he who chose not to come into the original *Colors*. He chose a different path, and I was disappointed by that, because I felt that the way in which we invested in the thing was worth a follow-up, and that some of his concerns would balance as we went. Some of the concerns were, I believe, exterior concerns, and not necessarily in my view the most legitimate ones. But that was what he chose to do.

In the event, James Foley next signed up to direct Slammer, *a screwball comedy for Warner Bros to star Madonna.*

The press were now pre-programmed for certain kinds of Sean Penn stories, but it was somewhat out of the blue when on 8 July 1986 they were moved to report that he had given a reading of his poetry at the Eilat Gordon Gallery in Beverly Hills.

SEAN PENN: Hank influenced me to want to write poetry, no question. I wrote poetry as a drunk. I would drink, and write on napkins . . .

DANNY SHOT: *Long Shot* is an arts and literary magazine that Elliot Katz and I started in 1982, with help from Allen Ginsberg. He did a reading at Rutgers University and split the door, and that was enough to get us started.

I remember the *New York Daily News* had in the gossip or Page Six . . . they were sort of making fun of Sean Penn, the bad-boy actor, as a poet. And they printed one of his poems to show he wasn't really a poet. And I liked it. 'This is good! What are they talking about?' Somehow I found an address and wrote to him, said I liked his work and why didn't he send us something? He saw that *Long Shot* had published Bukowski, so I think it was an easy fit for him. And I was quite delighted by the poems he sent: 'Bazooka Joe', 'Leather Girl', 'This Water's Cold' . . .

LINDA LEE BUKOWSKI: I do remember Sean saying he gave Hank a bunch of his poems and he was wondering what Hank thought about it. As it turned out, the only one Hank read was this poem where a guy wakes up in the morning with his head up some chick's ass . . . He thought that was pretty funny. Probably related to it, from one night or other in his illustrious past. Some people wake up in funny places . . .

SEAN PENN: Was it 'This Water's Cold' about the shit on the chin? Yeah, he liked that one, that's right. *Only* that one . . . When I decided to write seriously, I didn't find myself a poet. I found myself much more interested in prose and screenwriting. I wrote a script for a movie called *Dominic and Eugene*.7 It was written for De Niro: not that Bob was involved, but it was something I wanted to do. And the producers did not want to go, let's say, as dark as the picture went, the way I did it. I asked David Rabe to do a rewrite on it. He was busy. But now he knew I was a fan of his. Soon after, he called me to do *Goose and Tomtom*.

Rabe's Goose *and* Tomtom *suffered a New York début in 1982 so poor that Rabe disavowed it. But the play was undoubtedly a strange beast. Its eponymous protagonists are a pair of cheap hoodlums in a grim apartment, pally and belligerent to one another by turn, incensed by the idea that they have been ripped off by mobster Bingo, and teased and tormented by a brassy dame named Lorraine. All this would be the stuff of hard-boiled* roman noir, *except that the dialogue invokes a sepulchral and supernatural world,* Goose and Tomtom's *fears encompassing not just gangsters and girls but also witches, ghosts, snakes and spiders.*

DAVID RABE: Where did it come from? I wish I knew . . . A religious friend of mine was taken by the play but didn't understand it, and he gave it to a scholar and said, 'What is this?' The guy said, 'Oh, it's a Gnostic myth . . .' When I first wrote the play, it was just voices, no stage directions. I just started hearing the exchanges, and one thing led to another. But as I became more conscious about the play, I did then describe the setting as 'An apartment in the underworld', and I used that word in reference both to a contemporary criminal underworld but, more importantly, to the mythical underworld, to Hades – which is where it *really* takes place, I think.

SEAN PENN: I'm gonna show you why I love this play. I read it and I want to do it again – seriously. Here it is:

TOMTOM: So this green goddamn witch come into my house. I was little. I could walk, I wasn't crawlin', but I fell over a lot. That was the age I was: where you fall over a lot. And so into this room I was in comes this green goddamn witch with eyes full of little bee-hive holes and she's got this snake in her hand: it's wigglin', hissin' like a witch's voice – you want cream? – and she stood lookin' at

7 Eventually made for Orion in 1987, the script credited to Alvin Sargent and Corey Blechman.

me. I was playin'; her face was green, her lips had these wrinkles like grooves. She was starin' at me. I fell over backwards. She scared the crap outta me and I fell over backwards. (*He sets the two cups of coffee on the kitchen table.*)
GOOSE (*moving to join TOMTOM*): A witch, huh?
TOMTOM: Yeah.
GOOSE: I saw a witch once. She wasn't green. She put me in a sack . . .

SEAN PENN: The whole play was written in about thirty hours. But there was stuff there that I found really cut close to the bone. I guess David must have been roughly the age I am now, early forties, so I understand it well: it deals with fears and how we attach them to things. And that's the distraction – they're not attached to anything. Fear lives by itself. 'Fear, fear, she's the mother of violence . . . '[8]

BARBARA LIGETI: Fred Zollo and I were going to produce *Goose and Tomtom* for David to direct, and we were going to do it at Williamstown Playhouse. And then Sean said, 'How about my wife as Lorraine?' 'Oh, your *wife* . . .?'

DAVID RABE: I entered into it with the two of them a little reluctantly, frankly – I always saw Tomtom as an older guy than Sean, and I wasn't sure what Madonna would come up with. But, on the other hand, I thought, 'This will be fun [*laughs*], it will definitely be interesting.' It was a very anomalous situation. Lincoln Center spent a lot of money on a workshop, and it could only be that, because Madonna was scheduled to go off and do *Who's That Girl?*[9] We had three weeks to rehearse it, then it would run for four days, and then she was gone. I look back on it and I think a large part of what was going on was that Gregory Mosher and several others running Lincoln Center were using it to get to know Madonna and Sean – they really had very little interest in the play. And it wasn't too long before Greg was directing Madonna in *Speed-the-Plow*. But they built a full set and we had a full production – lighting, costume were complete like you would expect if you were going to run it.

I had gone through any number of productions of the play that had failed, because there was a missing element in my understanding and

---

8 From 'Mother of Violence' by Peter Gabriel, from the 1978 album *Peter Gabriel II*.
9 Formerly 'Slammer'; the now-retitled Warner Bros picture with James Foley.

everybody else's. It only became clear to me through a conversation I had with Joe Papp. Previously, everybody, myself included, wanted to do the play as if Goose and Tomtom were like Beckett characters, buddies in a certain way, and their adversaries were outside the room. And it never worked. I remember Joe saying, 'No, no, Tomtom *hates* Goose.' First, I thought, 'What!?' Then it was like a flash. They're acting like friends, but deep down Goose is terrified of Tomtom, and Tomtom has an incredible rage and anger and a desire to dominate Goose. That's the core of the whole thing: the way in which they almost unconsciously war against one another, and the jealousy between them that Lorraine plays on. So, finally, in this production I came with that knowledge and, for me anyway, it was the first time the play made sense. And Sean certainly understood that when we talked. I looked at it as a father–son thing but I think he found the same relationship in a competitive thing between brothers: he was a middle brother, and he did talk about it in those terms. It didn't really matter, as long as it was clear between these two guys who was invested in being the dominant dog in the pack.

30 *Goose and Tomtom*: Penn (Tomtom), Madonna (Lorraine), Harvey Keitel (Bingo), Lorraine Bracco (Lulu)

Photo by Brigitte Lacombe

SEAN PENN: He cast the right boys for that . . . Barry Miller's a piece of work.

DAVID RABE: The play had a lot of almost slapstick physical action – if Goose said the wrong thing, he got whacked in the back of the head or whatever – to which Sean brought a kind of reality, at the same time as they were a little bit goofy. Sean has good physical control; nobody was getting hurt. But somewhere the line got crossed between Barry's sense of who he was in the play, in relation to who Madonna and Sean were. This crazed Oedipal dynamic that's loose in the play came to rest on him. Tomtom is very jealous of Lorraine's relationship to Goose, and I think that got turned into Barry feeling threatened that, because he had to flirt with Madonna, he was going to get killed by Sean [*laughs*]. It was good for the play, up to a point . . .

Then Barry showed up one day in what looked to me like hockey equipment: elbow pads, and shoulder pads under a big sweatshirt, and a helmet of some kind – he looked like the Michelin Man wandering in. Sean said, 'I can't act with this.' But Barry felt threatened. And on the one hand, you can say, 'Jesus, ridiculous.' But I had to take his concerns seriously enough to spend time talking about what he felt, then assure him that if he ever was hurt, he could stop rehearsing instantly and we would find a way to make sure it never happened again . . .

As a director/playwright, it was a weird thing to be discovering so much of what then became permanent about the play in terms of its physical life. Tomtom has a big speech to Lorraine towards the end, and what came in rehearsal was an idea of Tomtom drawing his gun and playing Russian roulette between her and himself. And, of course, it's been powerful since, but it was particularly powerful with Sean and Madonna up there doing it . . .

TOMTOM: I could be more beautiful than you. I could. I could make people stop on the street to look at me. I mean, you ain't so special as everyone thinks you are, Lorraine . . .

DAVID RABE: There was certainly something in the part that seemed made to order for her persona – the Material Girl, which was all I knew before we started working together: sexy and materialistic, that sort of cynical, provocative thing she has. She had lines like, 'I'm going to rule the world some day'; and she had probably been saying that all her life – as a child, even.

BARBARA LIGETI: Opening night, Madonna said to me, 'Hey, big sister, what the hell did you just do to me?' I looked out from the wings and there in the Mitzi Newhouse Theatre was Warren Beatty seated next to Cher seated next to Al Pacino. And for someone who was not a seasoned actress . . .

ART WOLFF: I know Sean has very strong feelings about Madonna's talent as an actor, and my memory of her performance is that it was quite good. I wish that she'd been able to grow with that. But I thought she dearly needed more of a framework to hang things on when she was acting. Sean, you don't ever want to say he was miscast, because he's such a character actor, but my feeling was that it didn't happen. I felt, actually, in that instance that she was probably better than he was. But that was fine by Sean, because that's part of the reason he did it, you know?

DAVID RABE: Sean has enormous technique as a stage actor, and he could handle the language and speak very fast and fill it with emotion and be heard and yet sound real.

And Madonna was the best Lorraine I ever saw. Truth is, I think if that had been the production she was first seen in, then everybody would have said she was a wonderful actress, instead of the shit she's received.

SEAN PENN: I'd go along with that. Rather than be condescending or presumptuous of our position, let's just say it was a new challenge for her. Because who was the audience for those weeks of rehearsal? And what do you feel about your audience? What makes you feel good about you in that company? I think that she's conquered new challenges by endurance in a lot of other ways at other times. But in this case, 'stretching' meant getting rid of that which came easy, and being uncomfortable – which is often a very productive thing. It's part of our lives, and it should be part of our work. She had a good time too. But that's the case for everybody involved with David: she's particular because – she's particular . . .

When she and Jamie Foley made the movie they made – I saw another version that I think would have been more encouraging to her as an actress at that time. But – and I don't know how much attention she pays to it – she's been wildly discouraged, externally. I don't know if she's *feeling* discouraged, but she's *been* discouraged. And I think there's a lot to be said for people having encouragement and rewards for their risks in some way. I don't know if there's anybody who doesn't require that.

What David wanted to do off of this was *Hurlyburly*: 'We had a good experience here, let's do *Hurlyburly*.' *Goose and Tomtom* – there were nights that worked and nights that didn't work. We didn't do it long enough, really. But if there's a play to explore, that one is it. I look at it again, and I get tempted . . .

DAVID RABE: During rehearsal there would be reports from Sean and Madonna of various encounters and harassment. I remember one of the co-producers had walked home with them one night, and he was pale when he came in the next day, shocked by what he'd seen. The paparazzi are always acting like they just walk around asking, 'May we take your picture?' Or even just sticking the camera in someone's face. But these photographers were really insulting them verbally, calling her this and that, asking Sean, 'Who do you think she was fucking last night?' I've never read *that* anywhere. There was a bounty, we were told: I can't swear to this, but if they could get a shot of Sean coming at them, it was guaranteed extra. That kind of stuff went on, really trying to provoke him. They didn't, at that point. But then they often did.

The remarkable Goose and Tomtom *was seen by barely a thousand people. The misbegotten* Shanghai Surprise *would need to draw that turnout many times over to make a hit, even though its presales ensured that Handmade Films would not be left holding the baby. In any event, it bowed on the coasts on 29 August 1986 and opened nationwide three weeks later, to the worst reviews of Penn's career and sorry takings.*

SEAN PENN: It's given fodder to my critics in a great way, if they need any more . . .

I remember I didn't want to see it. I was *scared* to see it. There was a version that could have worked, but we were not even within missile range of that. Then I had an idea . . . I said, 'Let's do a *What's Up, Tiger Lily?* on it.'[10] I mean, let's not think that we made what we set

10 This 1966 release was a Japanese exploitation thriller overdubbed with gags by Woody Allen.

out to make. And I wrote a script about trying to make a movie and having it go wrong, and doing a narration that, you know, made it something *funny*. Well, I tried to run this past Alan Ladd and George Harrison and Denis O'Brien – may he rot, and more, because he's a shyster – but I didn't get anywhere with anybody. And, almost as if to spite me for the battles we had, they released the picture. I had made a big mistake. And only Mike Medavoy paid no attention to it at that moment. Dawn Steel, too, down the line when it came to *Casualties of War*. But we had made *The Falcon and the Snowman* and *At Close Range* at Orion, and Mike had been involved. And now he said to me, 'You're one of my favourite guys, and I want you to come work with Orion.'

MIKE MEDAVOY: We were a very film-maker-oriented company. We brought people in as partners. United Artists had been that way: it had made deals with actors in the fifties – Burt Lancaster's company Hecht-Hill-Lancaster was there, Sinatra's company, John Wayne's for a little bit. So at Orion we chose those kinds of people who fit our mould. Sean, to me, was the best of the new group of actors coming up. I had met his father at Universal, first when I was working in the mailroom, then as a casting director on *Run for Your Life*. So we made a deal with Sean, and he fitted perfectly into the Orion system. He was an actor's actor, other actors wanted to be around him.

And I must say I feel towards Sean the same way as I feel towards my own son – protective. I want him to be all he wants to be and do all the things he wants to do. Because he's one of the good guys. As a person? He was taciturn, intense, dedicated. Sometimes I thought he slept in the office [*laughs*]. You kind of left him alone . . .

On 9 October 1986, Penn made an uncharacteristic appearance on The Tonight Show *with Johnny Carson, evidently designed to address the welter of negative publicity that had been deforming his career of late. He made clear that he considered his duty to the public was good work onscreen, and that he felt entitled to his privacy in other respects. Pressed, he conceded to a measure of immaturity.*

ANDREW DAULTON LEE: I was sitting in prison reading the *Wall Street Journal*, the *LA Times*, *New York Times*, *Newsweek*, and Sean was the 'bad boy' all over the news. I wrote and told him, 'You need to back off. You're very talented, and you're jeopardizing your future.' Of course, me being where I was, I didn't know what he had to deal with . . .

31 Penn on *The Tonight Show* with Johnny Carson, October 1986

SEAN PENN: You have to know that long before I was called 'the bad boy of cinema', I was – like the rest of us, probably – called a lot worse in schoolyards. And I guess I sort of lump it in with the rest of those sorts of comments, in that they never had anything to do with *anything* that I was experiencing. And when I was called that, I was never *nearly* as bad as I wanted to be at those moments.

HARRY DEAN STANTON: These photographers who come pushing in, jamming their cameras into your body – I understood why Sean punched a couple of 'em out. And other people have punched 'em out. They should.

JOSEPH VITARELLI: Some of it, where there were altercations or whatever, happened because it was so intrusive that *any* man, particularly if he's out with his wife and he's confronted, provoked in that manner, by fifty photographers with flashes . . . Granted, that was the bargain that she made. And he married into it. But it doesn't make it any less invasive.

JAMES FOLEY: Celebrities complain about being hounded by paparazzi, and you might think, 'Ah shut up, you're rich and famous. Who wouldn't want a bunch of photographers following you around like you're so important?' Well, the answer is, nobody would. The attention is not respectful. Quite the opposite: it's looking for and is desirous of friction. And that's true of print media too. What *People* magazine wanted was friction in Sean and Madonna's marriage, and, ultimately, divorce.

I think it took a toll, corrosive at some level, despite their best intentions to the contrary. It's one of those things bigger than any individual, you kind of have to ignore it and be above it. But Sean wanted to take it on and heat it up. And, of course, you can't. Not even the President of the United States can do that. So he was becoming so much more famous for something he didn't feel one *should* become famous for – his marriage. And it was overshadowing his intent as an actor.

In New York, Madonna began shooting Who's that Girl? *In LA, Penn was now developing something of his own that he hoped could sail as a Dennis Hopper project where their hopes for* Barfly *had previously foundered.*

DENNIS HOPPER: It was really a privilege directing Sean in *Colors*, a wonderful creative experience for me. And it was also a really wonderful thing that he did in hiring me to direct that movie, basically. It was an Orion picture, but it was Sean who put me in there. That's something that a guy like me never forgets.

SEAN PENN: *Colors* was the first one I did at Orion with Mike Medavoy, we were ground-floor together from that office. It was originally a script by Richard De Lillo, a Chicago story, and I was working with Richard and Robert Solo for a while on my own. It was based in Chicago, about fictional gangs who'd come up with a brand new drug. Have you seen *Showtime*?[11] There's a brand new dangerous gun on the street, and goddamn if they don't have to find it . . . This was like that.

DENNIS HOPPER: I read the script and we had a meeting at Orion, and I told them it was awful, terrible – that it wouldn't even make a bad

---

11 2002 action-comedy starring Robert De Niro and Eddie Murphy.

television show. It was about a white cop who had to bust a black gang that was selling cough syrup, and if this wasn't stopped then there was going to be a cough-syrup epidemic across the country . . . So, to me, it was bad news, and I told them we couldn't make it. Bob Solo told me I'd just rode in like a gunslinger from out of town and shot down a sure deal [*laughs*]. But then they asked me, 'What would make it good?' and I said, 'Well, you set it in Los Angeles, and you make it about an older cop and a younger cop. And make it about *real* gangs and *real* drugs.'

SEAN PENN: Dennis made it happen. I had thought about doing a gang movie in LA, but I didn't connect the dots, believe it or not. I was looking to do something that would have the excitement of a cop/crime drama, but not the kind I was seeing every day. It was, and still is, my contention that the subtext can be the plot, you just dress it up in a cop picture or whatever. What I wanted to do was a movie about religion – conflict with one's religion, policemen in conflict. Dennis looked at it a little cleaner than that – he just said, 'Have you read the fucking newspaper?' There was so much shit going on, but nobody was talking about it because it was all happening on the other side of the Harbor Freeway. And when Dennis talked about LA gangs, he talked about a particular culture, and it was a visual culture too.

DENNIS HOPPER: Basically Sean then got another writer in, Michael Schiffer, and presented me with a script, and that brought it up to speed. Then, as we were shooting, things got more interesting . . .

Colors *was then the tale of veteran South Central gang cop Mike Hodges and a newly assigned, younger gung-ho partner, Danny McGavin. Hodges has been working South Central for years, earning the gang-bangers' grudging respect for his low-key, quid pro quo demeanour. But for all Hodges' admonitions, McGavin wants to leap in among the action, make collars, 'get these assholes'. Making war all the time, ultimately McGavin is rejected as 'mean' by Louisa, a Hispanic girl he had previously charmed; and Hodges tells him he is a gangster, 'just like them'.*

DENNIS HOPPER: The LA Sheriff's team, Operation Safe Streets and the LAPD CRASH unit, which stood for Community Resource Against Street Hoodlums, they were responsible for handling all the gang crime in their areas. And so we did a lot of research on the street, went out on some cruises with CRASH, basically rode around with the cops and got to know them. And Sean is such an incredible researcher, man – I mean, he *really* gets into it.

SEAN PENN: The LAPD didn't have the reputation of the Sheriff's Office for busting ass or for being willing to expose themselves to certain risks, and there were several reasons for that. With the Sheriff's Office, Rodney King[12] was like an every-night affair – and all it took was a cross look. They wanted people on the street to know who was boss, and they fucken laid it down. It was a very enlightening and disturbing thing to see, because the feeling I got from them was: if you don't go out there assuming you're gonna be killed by anyone who looks at you cross, your chances of dying are enormously higher. Why? Because there's not enough of you. Because you're exhausted and you're not paid enough. Because you don't have the firepower, and your hands are tied legally on a lot of matters. And because you don't have perfect judgement in a crime zone, where there are a lot of drugs and a lot of heavy-duty weapons and real danger. So, the way the Sheriff dealt with it, I understood. But certainly, people's rights were violated, innocent people got beaten up. Meantime, the LAPD had a Police Commission with a lot of lefties on it, so their guys really were restricted, and the Sheriffs all had the reputation of 'Go get 'em.' With one exception . . . And I was with him.

DENNIS FANNING: I grew up in Chicago. I'm a fourth-generation cop. It's an Irish family so there's only three things you could be: a cop, a fireman or a priest. And when I was twelve, one of my best friend's dads got killed fighting a fire, so I figured being a fireman wasn't all that good. Priest wasn't going to work for me, because I liked women too much. So I took after the family trade. I ended up in Los Angeles because Chicago wasn't hiring. I was sent to the ghetto. PCP was big then: I used to make about twenty dealing arrests a month, and most of those guys were gangsters. 1982–3, I went to the CRASH bureau gang unit in South Central, responsible for handling all the gang crimes and homicides. Back then, if you worked a specialized unit you were the cream of the crop. The young guys, first five years, you walk round with your chest out like you're John Wayne: 'It's my fucken world and I'm just letting you be in it.'

12 See Chapter 9.

How I met Sean? I came to roll call, and I was late – I'm always late, been late my whole life. But I used to always open the door, sneak in, and sit down in the first seat of the back row before the sergeant called my name. This day, I open the door and some motherfucker is sitting in my seat: I gotta sit in front of him. The sergeant calls me, 'Hey, nice of you to show up, Fanning . . .' I deserved it. But I'm still pissed off. So I'm sitting there trying to listen to the information on the wire, vehicles, suspects, all that shit. I was on a plain-clothes assignment, so I'm wearing a .38 in a shoulder holster, but the holster was sideways so the gun was pointing straight back. I turn to talk to the guy next to me, and I can see whoever's sitting behind me ducking out of the way because my gun's pointing at him. He's distracting me. So I turn round and I say, 'Hey, look . . .' And now I recognize him. 'Ain't you that actor boy? Sean Penn?' He says, 'Yeah.' 'The fuck you doing here?' He goes, 'Uh, well, I'm here to learn about gangs.' I say, 'Yeah, good luck, pal. But if I don't put my finger on that trigger, this gun ain't going off. So quit doing a fucken dance back there.'

SEAN PENN: Dennis will tell you all day about how he don't give a shit who anybody is. And at a certain point, you say, 'Why do you keep *telling* me that . . .?' So we lied to each other and we became friends. I got tagged to ride with him because the sergeant wanted us to see some action. And Dennis was jacked – he was the guy.

I was in a position unique to my experience, in the sense that I was there sort of as a journalist. It was a strange and exciting time, occasionally a grotesque time. But I was with the good people.

DENNIS FANNING: When you get into a police car with a guy, the two of you could be the greatest cops in the world, but you might not have good karma together, so you're always ten seconds late – the bad guy just left, the shooting just went down. Other guys, other girls – you have instant karma [*snaps fingers*], the car becomes a shit-magnet. And that's what happened with Sean: as soon as he got in my car, we couldn't turn a corner without running into shootings, stolen cars, all kinds of shit. One night, we were in East LA; it was boring, nothing happening. I said, 'Ah fuck this, I'm gonna take him down to South Central, show him the Projects – Jordan Downs, Imperial Courts, Nickerson, all the baddest places in town.' So we're a block outside of Jordan Downs, and we hear gunshots. As soon as I take the corner, there's a guy, he's got a gun, he sees us, dumps the gun and tries to run.

I get out and chase, catch him, cuff him. While I'm cuffing him – fucken Sean goes and recovers the gun. I turn round and there he is, 'I got the gun!' So I say to him, 'Am I going to go to court and say, "I recovered the gun," when you recovered it? Or am I going to say, "Your honour, I handcuffed the suspect while the movie actor Sean Penn recovered the gun?"' 'No . . . Are *you* gonna come to court and testify? No . . . Well then, do me a fucken favour and go put the gun back where you found it . . .'

The kicker to the story is this: later on, we're shooting the movie in the Projects. There are kids hanging around the place while we're shooting. Sean notices this one guy in the background. And he says to me, 'That's the kid we arrested, right?' He goes over, talks to this kid, finds out he just got out of jail. So Sean gets him a job on the movie as an extra . . .

We rode around off and on for three months, so the more we rode around, the more shit we got into, the more Sean became the character. He stole a lot of my shit. Like the way he brushes his hair – that's all me, that's what I do.

SEAN PENN: When did I decide to model the character on Dennis? I saw his hair, that was probably it . . . I mean, it was pieces of behaviour more than personality. If Dennis spotted a suspect and he called in the number-plate, and it came back as a wanted felon with a warrant out, he'd stay behind him and not do anything until he got his hair brushed and a cigarette lit. Just in case he got killed. He'd smoke that cigarette in case it was his last . . . I mean, these are things that I was interested in: I don't know how much of these kinds of nuances play in the movie, the telling of the story. Dennis Hopper had his own thing to do. But it was a great experience.

DENNIS FANNING: Madonna pulled me aside in the beginning and said, 'Sean is very impressionable so I want you to *please* be very careful with what you're teaching my husband.' I liked Mo, got along with her fine. But she's like that, she gets along great with guys. She talked like a truck driver: 'Hey, how the fuck are you?' She wasn't all that friendly with my *wife*, but I think she has a tendency to be that way with women . . .

Sean invited me to New Year's Eve at Helena's. At this time, we weren't friends. My wife was like, 'Are you nuts?' I said, 'Hey, lookit, I'm doing this movie with the guy, he invited us, we'll go, we'll have fun, and some day you can tell your grandkids you spent New Year with Sean Penn and Madonna.' So we go to this A-list place right across the street from Ramparts police station. It's Sean and Mo, me and my wife, a chick who directs Madonna's videos, and a black gay guy, a choreographer, named Romeo. He tells me, 'I'm here so if she wants to dance, I dance with her.'

'What, you mean Sean don't fucken dance? Her own husband?'
'Yeah.'
'The fuck is that? Do you have a significant other?'
'Yeah.'
'How come you're not with him on this special night?'
'I am. He's outside. They won't let him in.'

And she's sitting right there, listening to me get this story. So I go out to the front, yell out the guy's name. He goes, 'Yeah, that's me!' I grab him by the wrist, pull him into the club. I say to security, 'He's with Sean and Madonna and me.' I sit his ass down next to his boyfriend, turn to her and go, 'C'mon, you want to dance with him? Dance. But why should his boyfriend be outside on New Year's Eve? The fuck is that all about?' She's looking at me like she hasn't been talked to like that in some years. We had a good time, left from there to On the Rox – they didn't end up too good . . .

DENNIS HOPPER: We were shooting in Watts, and nobody had shot a movie there since the Riots, so there was a curiosity around us. But nothing ever happened, until after we left the situations – then there would very often be some violence, because the gangs would come and watch us filming, and they would see each other on the other's turf. The day after we filmed a shooting in a church, a block away from that location there was a girl killed in a drive-by while she was singing in a choir. So it was strange. But they never interrupted the shooting. We had co-operation from both the Crips and the Bloods, just on the level that they were aware it was happening and that we were using real gang members as extras. I mean, my feeling from the start was that if you had real cops and real gang-bangers then you were probably going to get a pretty real picture . . .

Robert Duvall brought his own research and inspiration as Hodges, who seeks an easy nicknaming rapport with the gang-bangers rather than flat-out confrontation, and imparts some of that wisdom to

Penn's McGavin, nicknamed 'Pac-Man' for his voracious arresting tendencies. Hodges pays with his life, dying in a distraught McGavin's arms. But en route to this climax are several cop-on-cop confrontations.

DENNIS HOPPER: I remember Bob saying to Sean, 'I took this part because I get to kick your ass. Everybody in America wants to kick your ass . . .' And he said it a number of times [*laughs*]. But they were incredible together, man. Every morning they would come in, go to their separate trailers – they wouldn't run lines together. They would just meet on the set, and they would be line-perfect. But there was improvisation too, absolutely. Every night was another adventure . . .

DENNIS FANNING: I know we were making up dialogue every day as we went along. I was hired as a consultant. There were no plans for me to be in the movie, but then Sean pulled me into a scene, then Hop put me in a couple more. I would say, 'What do I do?' He says, 'You're a cop, it's a cop movie, do what cops do.' 'OK . . .'

DENNIS HOPPER: For the climax, where Duvall dies – the black social worker working the gangs, giving them advice and so on, he came and had a speech between the SWAT team and the gang members. Dramatically, it seemed really cool. But Sean said, 'That would never happen in a million years, man.' And he was absolutely correct. So we changed it right there. The poor actor, he was hurt. But Sean was right, the point was that it was totally unrealistic.

LINDA LEE BUKOWSKI: They shot a lot of *Colors* in San Pedro, so Hank and I went to the set one afternoon. Hank had to get to the track, so we didn't stay too long, but we said hello to Sean. And it was funny: every time Sean was doing a movie, he'd get into it, the character and the energy and the sensorial experience of it. And he was into this cop thing. There's a bar down in San Pedro where a lot of the cops hang out after hours, and evidently, after the shooting, he'd be hanging out with those guys down there. He'd come over and he'd be *packing*, man [*laughs*]. It was so cute.

DENNIS HOPPER: Sean became a cop, man. You could see it just in the way he searched people – he really did his homework. But then he was playing Dennis Fanning, so he had to be on his toes [*laughs*], he could have died at any moment . . .

32 On location for *Colors*: Penn and Dennis Hopper

33 'Sean became a cop, man': McGavin (Penn) makes a collar in *Colors*

DENNIS FANNING: Sean actually thought he *was* a fucking cop. Seriously. Swear to God. He was walking like one, he was talking like one, he was hanging out with us – I mean, he was *hanging out* – he'd get drunk and fucken party, man. He'd shoot off guns, go chase bad guys, pull up on a corner and just sit there, see how many different crimes he could spot: see who was dealing dope, who was stealing cars, who was doing what – just for the fun of it. Go to an ATM at two in the morning and count your money, see if anybody will try to rob you so you can kill 'em . . .

During the Colors *shoot, Penn, ever the music-lover, made a discovery that not only stimulated his imagination but would also transform his domestic arrangements.*

JOHN SYKES: Musically, Sean loves anything with a good, good edge. Just like with movies – he wants the tough substance. If he'd been older, an adult in the sixties, he'd have been hanging out with the protest singers, Bob Dylan, Phil Ochs, Joan Baez. Since he's younger, he's friends with Bruce Springsteen and Sinead O'Connor and Eddie Vedder and David Baerwald, because he wants artists who have passion and backbone and something to say. I also loved the music of David + David, out of which David Baerwald came.

DAVID BAERWALD: I had just put out a record called *Boomtown*. 'Welcome to the Boomtown' was the single, and it was on the radio.[13] And then I got a call from my manager saying, 'Sean Penn wants to talk to you'. I said, 'Oh really . . .?'

Obviously he was a fascinating character: to me, he seemed like a real rock 'n' roll movie star – in fact, he seemed *more* like a rock musician than a movie star. So, of course, I took the call. And he told me he wanted to meet me and talk about working on a screenplay. I thought, 'Oh, hey, what the fuck . . .'

So we fix to meet on a street corner. I drive down there. And what I see is a young man looking very much like a cop, driving a plain-clothes cop car, holding a big flashlight and shining a powerful beam into people's eyes as they're driving towards him. People are honking and swerving by. It's Sean. I get out and say, 'What the hell are you doing?' And he says, 'There's a big hole here.' And it was true – there was this gigantic

13 Twenty-four-year-old Baerwald had formed the duo David + David with David Ricketts.

hole in the road, and Sean was trying to warn people not to fall into it. He kept saying, 'I can't let them do that.' And, of course, most drivers just thought he was some maniac trying to blind them and kept going straight on into this fucking hole . . . So he was very misunderstood, just trying to help people who thought he was crazy. And that's kind of Sean in a nutshell. He's one of the more altruistic people I know, and yet people just think he's messing with them.

I had some flares in my car, and we put some of them in front of the hole, then we went off on our merry way to some steak joint. He told me how he had connected with my song. And it turned out we had a lot in common. We were basically the same age. We're both freaks. And we were probably one beach away from being surf buddies: as a kid I used to go camping right near where his parents lived.

So he wanted us to write this screenplay, and he figured it would be easier if we were in the same house: his and Madonna's place. I didn't move in immediately: it wasn't like love at first sight and bouquets by the bedside. But it so happened that I was going through a kind of a messy break-up with a girl, and she wanted to stay in the house we had and basically thought it would be a good idea if she did it without me. And Madonna was going to be on the road, touring, spending a lot of time in Asia. So Sean was kind enough to offer me his mansion. And thus began a wild odyssey.

HARRY DEAN STANTON: His getting in trouble with the cops, getting busted and all of his shenanigans . . . There was a line in a movie I did with Dustin Hoffman, *Straight Time*. Theresa Russell says, 'I'll stay with you as long as I can, but, you know, if it gets too out of hand, I'm gonna split.' In essence, I told Sean that. I said, 'I'll hang in with you as long as I can, but if you get too crazy, you're on your own.'

Throughout the Colors *shoot Penn was overshadowed by the legal repercussions of the altercation at Helena's with David Wolinski back in April 1986. In February 1987, he pleaded no contest to misdemeanour/assault and battery: he was fined and paid costs, and received twelve months' probation. But it was weeks, rather than months, before a further angry incident on the* Colors *set changed his plans for the year ahead.*

DENNIS FANNING: They were doing a rehearsal for a scene. A guy goes by on a skateboard, with a camera, taking pictures. The next thing I know is Sean's having words with the guy.

SEAN PENN: It's the middle of a scene, he's in my eye-line. So I go to berate him. He's bigger than me – he's like a shot-putter, thirty-five years old. I'm twenty-six.

DENNIS FANNING: I thought it was part of the movie. Then Sean's saying, 'Are you in the movie?' 'Yeah, I'm in the movie.' 'What you doing with the camera? Let me have the camera.' They 'Mother-fuck' each other, and the guy spits at Sean.

SEAN PENN: So I hit him. And I was so angry that I told my buddies pulling me away, 'I'm OK, I'm OK . . .' And I got free, and I ran back and I hit him again.

DENNIS HOPPER: I thought it was a stupid move, and I'm sure Sean thought it was a stupid move too, once he had time to reflect on it – because he was already on probation. Somewhere in there, there's got to be something that tells you what round it is, you know? And if it's the last round, you're better to take the dive. But Sean's a very sensitive guy, and if things are ticking him, you can't stop it.

SEAN PENN: We were gonna fight the case. I felt that the guy's spit, dripping down my face, was a progressive assault; that it would justify, emotionally, my second hit. But that's where it got a little tricky for the courts. I likely would have beat the case – certainly not done any time on it. Civilly, it might have been a problem, because the guy then took some pretty bad pictures of himself, bruised. Frankly, I don't remember that much happening; but I saw them and I thought, 'Uh-oh, this isn't good.' But I got a lawyer and we were going to deal with that. And I think I was just about to go into arraignment when I went down to Bukowski's one night. We went out, he and Linda and I, had some Thai food, and then went back to the house and stayed up all night. And I drank a lot of wine . . . I was heading back to Malibu, it was about two in the morning, and I knew this after-hours place in Crenshaw district, so I thought, 'Aw, I'll go over there.' I get off the freeway and I can see a set of lights and one car in the distance at this intersection. I don't want to get home too damn late, before daylight anyway. So I blow a red light. Well, that car I saw was a police car. I take off. Within a few minutes, it's like daylight – because of helicopters overhead. I pull over, get arrested for drunk-driving. I get locked up that night, but I'm OR-ed, 'Own Recognisance'.[14]

---

[14] Released from jail on the promise to appear in court to answer criminal charges.

What they didn't know was that I was facing a charge at the time. I call my lawyer, he says, 'It's a first offence, so I think I can get it reduced to a Reckless.' I tell him, 'Well, I'm going to jail – we both know that. Let's just do as little as possible.' Then we tried to figure out how to get it all in front of one judge.

Madonna's 'Who's That Girl? World Tour 1987' opened in Osaka on 14 June. But on 23 June, Penn, flanked by his lawyer Howard Weitzman, pleaded no contest before LA Municipal Court Commissioner Juelann Cathey, who ruled that he had violated his probation on two counts. He was sentenced to sixty days in jail but afforded two weeks' grace to sort out his business affairs. He was also fined for reckless driving, ordered for counselling, and had his probation extended to twenty-four months. The tabloid press practically soiled themselves in the delight of reporting Penn's apparent comeuppance: with husband and wife on separate continents, one facing lockdown, they now had at least one half of the story they most wanted.

SEVEN

1987–1989

I remember driving Sean somewhere in my car, and saying to him, 'I'm really sorry you had to go to jail.' And he said – one of my favourite Penn-isms, as I call them – 'A lot worse things have happened to a lot better people . . .'

Erin Dignam

SEAN PENN: So they gave me a sixty-day sentence. At that time, you got 'a good day for a good day', but I got into a couple of infractions that extended my time . . .

Ordinarily, I would have surrendered to the court straight after sentencing, but we pled the case no-contest, partly on the basis that they would give me until a certain day to surrender. So I was able to go to Germany, do *Judgement in Berlin* on furlough, then come back and surrender.

Penn joined Leo and Eileen in Berlin for a project dear to his father's heart, only his second feature film as director. 'I'm preoccupied by anything concerning injustice and the plight of the individual,' Leo told American Film.[1]

Judgement in Berlin, based on the book by Herbert J. Stern, relates how in 1978 an East German waiter had used a toy pistol to hijack a Polish airliner bound for East Berlin, forcing its pilots to head for the US airbase at Tempelhof in the West. The incident put both the US and West German governments in a quandary. No one had previously been tried in the West for escaping from behind the Iron Curtain; both governments wanted to commend the notion, but could they condone an act of terrorism? Remarkably, the hijacker was tried in a Special US courtroom set up in Berlin.

EILEEN RYAN PENN: Leo was always interested in what was going on in Germany. He went off and fought the war against Hitler after all. He got all the crew together at the start of the movie, a hundred people,

---

1 'Penn Pals', *American Film*, April 1988.

and said to them, 'OK, I just want to tell you all that I'm a Jew. And the last time I was over here I was up *there*' – and he pointed to the sky – '*bombing* you.' But he responded very positively to the young Germans working on the film, and they fell in love with him – they called him 'Poppa'.

34 On the set of *Judgement in Berlin*, 1987: Leo Penn and Sean Penn confer

SEAN PENN: My dad was getting older, into his late sixties. We went out in one of the public squares in West Berlin, where some of the landmarks were, and there was a lot of shelling damage on the buildings, clearly as it was from the war. But it was a beautiful Sunday afternoon, women and children walking in the park. And he saw that, and he really thought, 'This is what was here when we dropped bombs on this place. And there's the damage right there. And nobody who was around when that building got four hundred holes that size put in it is going to be around today . . .' And he got very emotional about that all of a sudden. It had nothing to do with the politics of it – it was just about his participation in life-taking.

My dad was not violent at all, not a temper-tantrum guy, very peaceful. But that night we went out to a bar, and about four people down the bar from us was a German guy about his age. We were having a drink, and all of a sudden he just leaned past me and said,

'Where the fuck were *you*?' And that was the other side of it: an American Jew, looking at a German guy, thinking, 'Were you a Nazi . . .?' I don't know what that tells. But I know I had to take a hold of him at that point . . .

Judgement in Berlin is photographed and assembled in an unflashy, economical, TV-movie manner, but its performances are top-drawer. The American judge, played with fire in the belly by Martin Sheen, is a Jew and a man of conscience, determined to stand up for the Constitution in properly trying the hijacker, Thiele (Heinz Hoenig), and his co-defendant (Jutta Speidel). Sean Penn is Guenther, another East Berliner who sat next to Thiele on the plane, and so, with his wife and child, reaped the unexpected benefit of his desperate act. At the last moment of the trial, he comes forward to testify on Thiele's behalf.

EILEEN RYAN PENN: Obviously, Leo wanted Sean to be in it very badly. And when the film came out, Sean got all the reviews. The German boys working on it thought his accent was unbelievable. He nailed that part – emotionally, and with the accent, the way he reaches for the right English words.

We came back from Berlin to LA, and that's when I had a horrendous first-hand experience of what Sean had been going through. We were trying to get into the elevators to the parking. And suddenly, the paparazzi were there at this little teeny elevator, right on top of us with their big equipment, pushing and pushing so that we were penned into this little elevator. I swear, I thought they were going to kill me – I couldn't breathe. And they didn't give a shit. They were treating me like a cockroach. Afterwards, I wanted to kill them. It was the first time I really understood how Sean could get that angry. He wasn't even *getting* that angry any more, he'd gone through so much of it. But I was in shock.

SEAN PENN: In the state of California at the time, anybody who wanted to could pay the money, $40 a day, and go to private jail. It's like if you want to pay to send your kids to a private school. So, if you want to get away from paparazzi and all the problems of Los Angeles . . . you just have to get a county sheriff to accept you in his jail, and then, unless the judge has a particular issue, you can go.

I started at Mono County, Bridgeport. Eight guys in a cell. We played backgammon. The trustee who was allowed to go out on the street, he'd go to a phone booth, pull open the change slot; somebody had left him a balloon with something to put you to sleep. He'd cram it up his keister, bring it in, and sell the pills. And that made time go a little faster . . .

Then Ken Hahn and his son – Jim Hahn, a city attorney now – who are Los Angeles staples and knew damn well how it worked: they just wanted to make some press for themselves, so they started in on 'preferential treatment'. They should have come and visited Mono County: me and Chris the murderer, a bunch of drug-dealers, a wife-beater. I just was pissed off, so I called my lawyer and said, 'Don't let them have any more press, let's go.' And I transferred.

DENNIS FANNING: The night before Sean went into LA County, I got some of the boys together and we decided to throw him a going-to-jail party: twenty-five cops, most of them Sean knew from *Colors*, and Sean and Jimmy Russo. Some of our guys worked off-duty security, so we got a comp room at the Bonaventura Hotel and a bathtub full of beer. But we had to get girls, right? I know how Hollywood works . . . There was a disco in the hotel, so we took Sean and walked him through the disco like he's a piece of chicken, then walked him out the door to the elevator. And about twenty girls followed us. 'Where you guys going?' 'We got a party upstairs.' We invited them all . . . In the end I sent everybody home, took Sean to The Pantry for breakfast. Then I drove him to County Jail, dropped him off, said, 'See you.' And I told him, 'No offence, but I don't think I should call you while you're inside. Those guys find out you got a pal who's a cop? It's bad enough you're an *actor* . . .'

SEAN PENN: Once again, they process me in. The drag was that LA County lock-up had just had an escape, so they were on maximum security the whole time: I couldn't leave my cell without a belly-chain and anklets. They put me in what's called '1700 Block', the protective custody unit where you're alone twenty-three-and-a-half hours a day, for the better part of a month in my case. All you have is your rack, a commode and a sink. You took a shower once a week, and they didn't have to get you out in the yard for exercise. You got one ten-minute phone call and one twenty-minute visit a day. So if you were out of your cell, it was a half an hour a day maximum, except for the time you'd have a shower or go to commissary. Three meals. That was it. Then the lights go halfway out. I never saw the sky for the whole time.

I had some books, but you read 'em fast when you've got nowhere else to go and no phone calls are coming, no TV. The amount of time I was in was so short, relatively, and the processing of new books took a while, because they worried about acid dips in the corner of pages. So I had Thurber, Raymond Carver – unfortunately, because it was very depressing – Willy Burroughs, and Montaigne.

DAVID BAERWALD: I brought Sean a copy of Montaigne's *Essays*: I'd always found there was an enormous amount of comfort in it, especially in such moments. Later on, I found Epictetus, which might have been better . . .

EILEEN RYAN PENN: I'm standing there in this long, long line to visit my kid, and I was the only white face among all these black and Hispanic ladies. They're all looking at this blonde white woman, dressed properly, like, 'The *fuck* is she doing in this line?' Oh, it was so sad – I felt so bad that he was in there. But he was doing pretty well, actually, and that helped me a lot. I'm sure some of it was terrible. You lose all your dignity. He told me about some policewoman who wanted to watch him on the toilet, because it's all open. But, you know, maybe he had to go through that to control some of the things that he would have liked to have done . . . I always thought that it maybe wasn't the worst thing that's ever happened to any human being on this planet. In Africa there are children starving with big bellies. So I wasn't feeling like, 'This is something my kid shouldn't go through.' I really felt, 'He's gonna learn from this too . . .' I think he was using it for another character he would do. I mean, come on – he did *Dead Man Walking*, didn't he?

DENNIS HOPPER: And he was in with Richard Ramirez, the serial killer, 'The Night Stalker'.[2] That was pretty interesting . . . Sean told me there was an incredible line of beautiful women who would come visit Ramirez and flash on him, propose to him – amazing. And I guess Ramirez was quite enamoured of Sean, because he kept sending him little notes, which Sean would tear up.

SEAN PENN: Ramirez was in the cell over the way. He had a couple of de-merits for contraband issues, marijuana, so there was a red taped

---

2 The loathsome Ramirez was apprehended by civilians in Boyle Heights on 31 August 1985. He initially faced fourteen counts of murder and twenty-two counts of sexual assault. In 1989, he was sentenced to death.

line that no one but authorized staff could cross to get to within reach of his lock-up. Other than that, people could get near your door – which was steel with a little wire-glass window in it. I've been in about two weeks when a face comes up to my window, middle of the day. This is part of how I end up doing a couple of extra days. It's a guy I knew from school. He'd heard I was inside. I'd played some practical jokes on him back then, because he was a bicycle thief. He still looked exactly the same – long blond hair – but he's wearing a trustee's outfit. I said, 'What can you get me?' He said, 'Anything from the mess.' 'Juice?' 'All right.' Then I realize there's a steel door between us. How's this gonna work? Well – this is fantastic – he took a big garbage bag, poured two gallons of apple juice in it, and lay it down on its side so the fluid lay in the bottom and flattened out. Then he slid it under the door, and, presto, I got a bagful of juice. I tie it round the back of my rack, out of sight – because anything unapproved is contraband. And I make a faucet by tying a knot in it that I can then undo so the juice pours out into my cup. So now I have the pleasure of serving myself . . . The next morning – boom! – door opens, three guards come in and start peeling my rack apart. Surprise inspection. Who tipped them off? That motherfucker. The bicycle thief . . .

In jail, you can get revenge if you want it – without moving. And I did want to extend his time a little bit. But I didn't. And he still makes me laugh . . .

*On 17 September, Penn was turned loose upon the bosom of commu-nity and family. His wife, he later told journalist Lynn Hirschberg, was 'not particularly' happy to see him: 'Going to jail is not good for any marriage.'*³ *He was also now in the fix of having to attend fairly futile counselling sessions for his supposed alcoholism and tendency towards violence, conditions which could have been usefully attribut-ed at least in part to force of circumstance.*

On 24 October, Penn hosted Saturday Night Live *in New York, introducing brother Michael's band The Pull and playing himself in the opening skit, 'Fatal Attraction II'. Spoofing the season's bunny-boiling stalker-thriller, Penn was harassed by rapper LL Cool J crash-ing into his dressing room. He protests. 'You were very nice to me in prison, you kept the bigger inmates away from me, I'm very grateful, but that's as far as it goes – I have a wife!'*

3 *New York Times Magazine*, 28 December 1998.

DAVID BAERWALD: Sean and Madonna had a lot of terrible fights and arguments. But even in that area they were unique, because most couples when they argue, you have an idea of what it might be that they're arguing *about*. Whereas the two of them developed this kind of code – key phrases and words that nobody else understood. I mean, I'm sure that the National Security Agency could have deciphered it. You would be in the car with them, and one would be going, 'Well, number three!', and the other would say, 'Yeah, but you number-foured my number two!' As for me, well . . . the expression 'Third wheel' often came to my mind . . .

ART WOLFF: A lot of couples relate to one another in that way, that acerbic kind of half insult. I mean, you surely saw the heat between them, you could understand why they were together, but . . .

LINDA LEE BUKOWSKI: You'd see things and sort of turn your head sometimes, and go, 'Oh God, here they go again . . .' or 'Why did this one say that to that one? *Why?*' Emotionally, they were two tigers, two volatile, dynamic personalities. I definitely feel there was a strong, strong caring attention and love. But they were knocking each other's egos too hard all the time, from what it seemed to me.

I don't think he really liked the particular lifestyle of her friends – I don't think they were compatible in terms of the people that he really wanted to surround himself with.

MATT PALMIERI: We were up at the house. Madonna was in a lawsuit and she had to go to court: at one of her concerts the security hadn't been done right – I *think* that was what it was. Anyhow, she had been working out like a madwoman, as she always did, and now she was in a rush to get in the shower and get presentable for court. But the water heater was broken, so she was really upset: 'I *have* to clean up, I *have* to have a shower.' Sean and I were sitting there, hanging out, like 'Yeah, whatever . . .' She kept yelling, and finally he said to her, 'We'll get you hot water, just chill out, will you?' So we went into the kitchen, put water in every pot and pan in the place, put 'em on the stove, heated the water and started filling the bathtub. After a half hour of this, finally, the tub's full, and Sean tells her, 'Get in and take your bath already.' She gets in and yells, 'It's too *hot*, damn it!' We look at each other and grin: 'Too hot, huh?' So we go and fill up the biggest container of them all with ass-cold water, heft it in there, and throw it onto her head in the tub. We trot off, laughing, very happy with ourselves . . . Madonna jumps up, screaming and yelling, and runs through the house after us. We look at each other – 'Oh shit!' – and run out of the house. We took off down that driveway like midgets fleeing a fire-breathing dragon, to escape any possible wrath of The Great Mo . . .

Now in 'straight time', his professional associations and his deal with Mike Medavoy intact, America's Finest Young Actor™ set about trying to generate and revive the kind of projects that had become his métier before he fell foul of the law.

DAVID BAERWALD: Sean and I wrote the screenplay together from 'Welcome to the Boomtown'. We took the characters from the song: Kevin is a not-overly-promising college baseball star who happens to be very handsome, Christina is a jaded woman running a modelling agency/high-end call-girl service, at the behest of Marlon Brando – who was going to play an elderly, ridiculously powerful Otis Chandler kind of figure. So there was a kind of traditional love story there, but what none of the characters notice is a sort of police state that is slowly encroaching around them: they're so hung up they don't see martial law coming to America.

SEAN PENN: There was a civil war going on in South Central, and a military build-up: they were starting to put in hydraulic steel walls in those neighbourhoods so you could lock them off and sector them. And nobody on the other side of the Harbor Freeway cares. So you have people paying no attention to Black Hawk helicopters flying by Gladstone's for Fish while they were discussing their résumés. And there was a *Bladerunner* aspect to it: we had billboards saying stuff like 'Schwarzenegger for President' – it was a bit ahead of its time in some ways – and 'Sex = Death. Don't Do It', this being the beginning of AIDS. I got very hyped to direct *Boomtown*, very attached to the imagery and how I wanted to shoot it, and I was extremely specific with Mike Medavoy. I believed on that basis that they would want to make it. And it didn't turn out to be that way . . . I remember going to Tom Cruise with it for the Kevin role: I never really got clear whether he read it or not.

DAVID BAERWALD: What I remember most about Brando is his laughing at me and Sean, saying, 'What's wrong with you two? You're so serious! When I was your age, I was interested in *sex*!'

Meantime, playing his strong acting suit, Penn had a dream project to hand, albeit one whose prospects were massively complicated by both the modus operandi and the personal health of its incomparable writer–director.

SEAN PENN: The actress Carol Kane had become a good friend of mine. I got to know her from the bars in New York when I was doing *Heartland*. One day, she told me that she had been talking to her friend 'John', and 'John' had seen me in a picture – I think it was *Bad Boys* – and compared me to Cagney. And I said, '"John" who?' She said, 'John *Cassavetes* . . .' I had seen *Killing of a Chinese Bookie*, *Minnie and Moskowitz*. Well, I kept telling Carol that I'd love to work with 'John'. And then eventually he called her and said, 'Have Sean Penn come up to my house. We're doing a reading . . .' So I showed up, a little late, and he and Ben Gazzara and a bunch of people were reading through a script. Then Ben stayed on afterwards, and I'd known Ben when I was a kid. John looks at me, then says to Ben: '*De-Lovely*!' And Ben said, 'Oh, *yeah*!' So we drank and talked, and then John and I started working on 'She's De-Lovely', as it then was.

The script was a Cassavetes original lying fallow from 1980, the story of a loving couple: love, as always in Cassavetes, compounded of innumerable dearly combustible elements. The project could not get off to a running start: prior even to first meeting Penn, Cassavetes had been diagnosed with cirrhosis of the liver and was gravely ill through much of 1986 and 1987. But the autumn of 1987 brought renewed impetus.

LOU PITT: John felt, after his treatment, that he was well enough to activate it. When I got a call to meet with him and Sean, Sean had already read it and was committed, and we talked about putting it together and arranging for the financing, and John wanted to direct. His feeling was that if Sean didn't do it then *nobody* was going to do it. This was Sean's project, he was the guy: 'If not him then I don't want it done.' The meeting lasted about forty-five minutes. John was up and about and energised, he was John in full flow, and we talked about how he wanted to make the movie. And he had a very captive audience – Sean was respectful and eager.

As 'She's De-Lovely' inched forward, Penn's interest in the original and unconventional also drew him to a script by an untested female writer–director for what was envisaged as a low-budget project. This one had a touch of kismet about it.

ERIN DIGNAM: I grew up on really good films and film-makers in the seventies: Wim Wenders, Fassbinder, Tarkovsky, Antonioni, Godard. I never saw *Breakfast at Tiffany's* and thought I wanted to be Audrey Hepburn; I saw *Picnic at Hanging Rock* and thought, 'I want to be *her*.' Let's say I was in the minority . . . So I wrote a script called *Loon*, and the inspiration was that I think relationships that happen between younger people oftentimes are very serious: it's not an adolescent fairytale like the commercial films say. The impact of one person on another is so huge when you're still young, picking and practising who you want to be; so *Loon* was about how a boy influences a girl when she's unformed.

It was a total fluke but the script went to CAA and then to Sean's assistant, Alison Dickey. She told Sean he needed to read it. He did, and he called me in for a meeting. It had never occurred to me that we'd be able to use someone like him – we were making the movie for $800,000. But true to form, as I later realized, anything that Sean reads that he connects to, he just celebrates that person so much. So we met in this little cubicle at Orion Pictures. I walk in, and really the first thing he says to me is, 'Didn't anybody tell you you're not sup-posed to write it that real?'

I think Sean related to the extent that Paul, the male character, *need-ed* to be involved with this girl, Loon. It wasn't just a superficial chase to get the girl: it was about trying, at a very young age, to be involved together in something that he needed her to make sacred. And I think Sean related to that intensity in the character, because he himself was very intense from a very early age.

Dignam's hugely intimate, closely observed, dramatically loose and allusive work required an exceptional young actress to make the lead role of Sara/'Loon' live.

ROBIN WRIGHT PENN: I was born in Dallas in 1966, and Texas was always home; it definitely felt like my roots. But my parents divorced and we moved to California, and then my brother and I travelled a lot with my mom because of her business: we had seen so much by the time we were twelve, thirteen years old.

I started dancing, and somebody at the studio said, 'If you want to make money, you could model . . .' So I went on calls, got an agent, did commercials, and then I was off to Europe on my own after I graduated high school. The work itself was a fucking nightmare – the beginning of why I'm in therapy today, I'm sure. Just humiliating; it destroys your self-esteem at that age.

Before I took off to Europe, my senior year in high school, I auditioned for all the John Hughes movies, got called back four or five times, lost them all to Molly Ringwald, who was *the* chick at the time. But I had a really persistent agent, Eileen Ferrell, who believed – she said, 'You've got it.' I didn't know what 'it' was, but I had a drive to maybe see if the ambition was existent outside her. I don't know that I had a real passion or desire, but acting filled me, in some way. And I didn't figure that out for a long time.

I got back from Europe and landed a one-off TV gig, *The Yellow Rose*. And then I got the soap, *Santa Barbara*.

ERIN DIGNAM: I had seen Robin on *Santa Barbara* and she was just entirely different on a soap opera than anyone had ever been. Then I saw her in a movie called *Hollywood Vice Squad* where she played a drug addict – and it was the same. What drew me in the beginning was her sense of truth: she cannot fake it to herself for a second. You believe she's thinking what she's saying. I think Robin felt at a young age that life was a serious thing: she was working by the time she was fifteen; she really is very stoic and capable and responsible. I'm ten years older, and she was absolutely on my level when I met her. And I am so happy that I met her.

ROBIN WRIGHT PENN: I had finished *The Princess Bride*. One of the actors on *Santa Barbara*, A. Martinez, was married to one of Erin's college mates, and he said, 'You've got to read Erin's script.' I went home and sat with it on the edge of my bed, didn't move, and read to the end, sobbing. Called her immediately, said, 'I have to meet you, I have to do your movie.' And hence, Mr Penn . . .

I didn't know who Sean *was* when I'd first met him. It wasn't official. I was nineteen or twenty, married to my first husband, who was in the soap with me. I was in New York for the Emmys, nominated for *Santa Barbara*. We were sitting in a restaurant, 2 o'clock in the morning, and my husband goes to the bathroom, so I'm sitting at the table alone. In walks this guy, he was with Tim Hutton – I don't know who Tim Hutton is either. And he stopped in his tracks, over by the wall, and we just looked at each other for about two minutes. One of those classic 'I know you . . .' looks. We were just lost. Then he sat down, and I was smoking, and he asked me for a cigarette, and we looked at each other again. About six months later, my husband and I saw *Racing with the Moon*. And I thought, 'That was the guy in the restaurant . . .'

I brought all this up when I met Sean with Erin, officially, and we had dinner. He was really vulnerable that day, only spoke when it was necessary. A different lad back then . . . I said, 'You know, I met you before,' and he said, 'I know.' 'Oh, you do?' He said, 'Yeah, I remember what you were wearing.' And he described everything, the colour dress I had on, and that it had flowers, right down to my ear-rings and the ring on my finger. I know, it's like one of those spiritual stories . . .

ERIN DIGNAM: Sean had said he would play Paul. Then it was in the news over Thanksgiving vacation that he and Madonna weren't spending it together. Then my father called and said, 'Isn't your lead actor Sean Penn? I was riding to work this morning and I heard he's getting divorced. Strange, isn't it? That it's on the news?'[4]

I was going up to the location in Northern California, and I called Sean and said, 'Is it true? Are you having problems in your marriage?' Which is an awkward, awful thing to ask anyone. He said, 'Yeah.' I didn't know him well enough to know how he was feeling but I asked him, 'Is this something you want?' And he said, 'No, I actually was surprised it came to a head this way.' But I could feel he was worried about *me*, he knew it would be hard to find somebody else for the part. I said, 'Well, thank you, I know you care about the movie and you've been so great since I met you, but I'm gonna tell you, you can't do this movie. It's just a movie. This is your life.'

Then I went into the shower and cried . . . But I knew it was the right thing to do.

Then he and Madonna got back together. He came up one day on

4 On 4 December 1987, Madonna filed for divorce in Los Angeles County Superior Court.

the set to see me and wish us well. And I said, 'Well, I'm glad you were able to save that situation.'⁵

LINDA LEE BUKOWSKI: Sean came over one day and he said, 'Madonna and I have split.' I said, 'Congratulations.' Because it *was* a relief; he showed a relief at that time. Then later on, he said, 'Well, we're back . . .' And we said, 'Congratulations . . .'

On 29 and 30 January 1988, Penn staged a showcase of a one act play he had begun in prison and subsequently completed, The Kindness of Women, *at a sixty-seat theatre in Santa Monica called The Pink. The action of the piece concerned a hard-drinking young man called Joe and his efforts to communicate with his wife, Sara. Scott Plank and Jill Schoelen played the roles. Harry Dean Stanton and Charles Bukowski were among the audience. John Cassavetes, in ever worsening health, nevertheless drove down to the theatre to assist Penn with rehearsals. Penn also received a helping hand with the set construction from Adam Nelson, a young actor whose work in a short called* Hotel November *had greatly impressed him.*

ADAM NELSON: It was about a guy who goes to Vietnam and leaves his girlfriend behind and what happens to him in the war – a poignant sort of story. It did well in festivals and was getting passed around town. Next thing I know, I got a call from the director Richard Sykes that Sean Penn wanted to meet me. I went to a restaurant in West LA. Sean stood up and shook my hand, said, 'You made me cry six times – that's how many times I watched your film.' We've been friends ever since [*laughs*].

Hal Ashby was also a fan of *Hotel November*. We went down to his house, and what a sweet guy. Those are the kinds of people Sean gravitates to: very talented, maybe on the fringe a little bit sometimes, people who the business forgets about.

DON PHILLIPS: There were a lot of people who were dying to meet Hal Ashby and held him in high esteem, because he really did flip off Hollywood. And Hollywood really did beat him down in the end. I remember him saying to me, 'What do I have to do?' He made eleven movies and nine of them are classics, and all of a sudden he couldn't

5 On 16 December 1987, Madonna withdrew the divorce papers.

get arrested. Hal was more of a recluse than anybody in town; the only time I was with someone else in his company was with Sean.

SEAN PENN: I first met Hal in the Colony with Tim Hutton. Later I got to know him much better – he started coming up to my house in Malibu. We spent a lot of time together in the period that was my first marriage, and quite separate from the marriage. When she was out of town, that house was Hal and I, playing pool.

ADAM NELSON: I used to live in Culver City and there was a street sign I'd pass by, Ashby Street. I said to Sean, 'Hey, man, it'd be cool if we could hand that to Hal as a present.' It was a blue sign, and I think I came up with the designation of 'Operation Blue Board' . . .

SEAN PENN: Adam and I went over to a hardware store and got metal-clippers. Adam was the lookout, and I climbed the pole and snipped the sign. We wrote on the back of it, 'You Are Now In Possession Of Stolen Property'. And then, quite late at night, we called Hal and said we had a present for him. We put it in the trunk of the car, an early 80s or '79 model Caprice, and met Hal at the Malibu shopping centre about two in the morning. The local police saw our two cars pull in together and wondered what the hell was going on. All we needed was them to ask us to open the trunk . . . but they recognized Hal as a long-term resident of the area and they took off. And we gave the sign to him right there.

Penn's capacity for larks was clearly related in part to the proximity of like-minded fellows and in part to the prolonged absences of his wife, who in February 1988 began rehearsal in New York for a role on Broadway in Speed-the-Plow, *David Mamet's sardonic assessment of the kind of Hollywood venality he had witnessed since starting an admittedly lucrative screenwriting career in the early eighties. But Madonna's absence by no means dispelled her shadow, as Penn found in the course of attending a week-long Cassavetes retrospective in Long Beach in March.*

DAVID BAERWALD: We were in a restaurant in Long Beach with Seymour Cassel and what looked like the entire USC football team. And some hulking linebacker comes up to our table and says to Sean, 'Hey! I just wanna shake your hand.' Sean just looks at him. The guy says, 'I do, man! I wanna shake the hand of the man who fucks

Madonna . . .' So Sean puts a cigarette out in the palm of the guy's hand. And all of a sudden we're in the middle of this forest of six-foot-eight, two-hundred-and-eighty-pound men, who want to stomp us into jelly. Seymour thought quickly and got us out of there – thank God. I think he learned a lot of interesting tricks in prison . . .

Come mid-April, Colors *was ready for US release. The combination of talents behind and before the camera had clearly produced something more complex than a police-procedural, and LA gang culture was sketched therein as rarely before, if not quite in the fullest likeness of life on the wrong side of the Harbor Freeway. Nevertheless, there was sufficient verisimilitude to inspire the* Los Angeles Herald, City *Attorney James Hahn and the self-styled 'Guardian Angels' vigilante group to protest the film's release for fear of it inspiring imitative violence.*

DENNIS HOPPER: The City Council did meet and try to stop it from being shown, and only by one vote was it not banned in Los Angeles, basically because the LAPD didn't want the names of the gangs, Bloods and Crips, publicized. They felt people didn't know those names already. That was their reasoning anyway . . .

DENNIS FANNING: There's a big uproar that there's gonna be shootings in the theatres. Chief Darryl Gates says, 'The cops who worked on the movie did it on their own time. They did not have departmental approval.' So if anything went down, he was gonna lay us out. Except I'm a fourth-generation cop, who's been known to tape-record shit myself and keep very good notes on meetings and places. So I let Darryl and the boys know that I wasn't going to be left holding the bag. By the next week, if you look at the *LA Times*, they were saying, 'Yes, we were involved in the movie, because we felt there is so much gang violence that it's about time the public was aware of what's going on. Hopefully, if we can save just one kid, then we've done our job.' Hypocritical motherfuckers, man . . .

DENNIS HOPPER: The protests didn't hurt the film. The notoriety it acquired really helped it economically, I believe. Medavoy and I would go from theatre to theatre and it was a huge success, lines around the block. There were a few incidents, but there wasn't really the violence that they had been projecting.

SEAN PENN: *Colors* made about $45 million in the United States while I was in Thailand, and I was really glad about that because Mike had taken a gamble on me. It wasn't as though he could go to the Palm Restaurant and proudly say, 'I'm making a movie with Sean Penn.' But he did it anyway, and without hesitation.

Penn's mission in Thailand come the late spring of 1988 was to play the role of Sergeant Meserve in Brian De Palma's Casualties of War, *scripted by David Rabe from a seminal article written by Daniel Lang for* The New Yorker *in 1969, then published as a book. It examined the true story of a five-man patrol of American soldiers in Vietnam, who kidnapped a young woman from her village, dragged her with them through a jungle mission, raped her repeatedly and finally killed her. One of the five refused to participate in the rape and abhorred the killing, and it was this soldier's testimony that eventually brought the others to a military court martial and subsequent prison sentences.*

DAVID RABE: The book is a wonderful read, and a quick read. The sergeant character, Meserve, was very haunting, because the guy was truly a leader and a hero in the combat situation, there's no question, with the skill, on one hand, of being instinctive and able to respond. On the other hand, if that gets twisted just slightly, it becomes a kind of outlaw mentality. Then you have the Eriksson character, who tries to stand up in those circumstances. The whole idea of not wanting to get laid in the army . . . I mean, you could really get yourself in trouble. You're out in the middle of nowhere, the only people who are going to help you out are the ones you're with, and you try to alienate them? So the whole thing was very complex and powerful and moving to me. What I'm saying of Meserve and Eriksson is as true as it was for Pavlo Hummel: you're trained for a set of circumstances that don't exist, for an orderly approach and a governed procedure of war. Then, when you get there, it's absolute chaos. And decency is co-opted or used, or abandoned or neglected.

I had approached Brian De Palma many years before about the material, and suddenly after *The Untouchables* he had enough clout that he came to me saying that he wanted to do it. Then he introduced me to Art Linson, and I went to work on a script. It didn't begin as a project with Sean involved, but frankly – though I'm very fond of

Michael Fox's performance – I was always thinking about Sean for Eriksson. I was thinking about the working-class quality Eriksson should have, and I felt having Sean there would be like Brando in *On the Waterfront*, that kind of presence at the core of the movie. Everyone was interested in the idea. But the people putting up the money weren't – because, I guess, of where Sean was at in that time. All the publicity he'd had was not that welcome in Hollywood . . .

SEAN PENN: If anything, there was a pariah aspect to what was going on between my private life and my work life. Paramount on *Casualties of War* said, 'First of all, we're not gonna spend this much money on a picture with Sean Penn in the lead, so he's going to have to play the Meserve character if he wants to do it.' I said, 'I'll do it, but here's my fee.' Dawn Steel had just come in to run Columbia. And Dawn Steel said to Art and Brian, 'If you guys can pull the movie away from Paramount, we'll do it, and we'll pay him.'

DAVID RABE: I talked to Sean as he was getting ready to go over there, and he was saying, 'I don't know how to *do* this guy.' I couldn't understand what he was worried about, but evidently when he got over there he *still* didn't know. And then suddenly – or so I was told – the voice came to him, then the rest of the character evolved.

SEAN PENN: I've had a conversation with Brian, about archness and the dramatization of villainy, which is not something, I think, that passes one dimension.

We rehearsed for a few weeks, but I only got the character the day before shooting. It was one where I leaned heavily on a specific person I knew: an aggressive guy who had a dark secret. There's something very pure about rowing a boat in a hurricane, being the captain of that boat and having to make sense of chaos where there's no sense to be made. And when I thought of those images, I thought of that person.

Does he talk like Meserve talks? I think, if you heard the two of us together on tape, they would sound pretty damn close . . .

Penn thoroughly assumed the armature of character and so made an agreement with Michael J. Fox from the outset that they would not fraternize during the show. Fox was not inclined to a similar immersion, which made for some lonely evenings.

Courtesy of Sean Penn. © Columbia Pictures

35 *Casualties of War*: Penn (Meserve) and Michael J. Fox (Eriksson)

ART LINSON: There was definitely a tension. Sean kept his distance from Michael – treated him like he was shit, in fact. I had dinner with Sean almost every night, so thankfully he didn't do it with me. But we were all living in the Amanpuri, a newly opened hotel in Phuket, with a big dining room that was essentially empty but for us, because nobody had heard of the place yet. So we'd go down to eat, but Sean would never sit at the same table with Michael. It would be Sean and me at one table, Michael on his own at another . . . I honestly think it was authentic, though, simply because Sean had to be a terrifying presence to Michael, and he didn't want to let Michael off the hook any more than he wanted to let *himself* off the hook. I don't think that he wanted to deep down *like* Michael and have any of that affection creep into the performance. And it could have been even more interesting than that, which is: he didn't want any of the fear that Michael might have had in him to not be in Michael's performance. I wouldn't put any of that past Sean . . .

SEAN PENN: I was surprised, myself, that Brian was interested in our working together. There's an operatic nature to the way that he makes films. And I knew, doing it, that it was going to be grandly stylized, to the point where you have a Viet Cong guy with a knife in his mouth crawling down a tunnel, and the fanciful shooting style, all that stuff. So it was just about trying to find synch with that, find something that was going to play throughout the picture. But once we started, Brian was primarily concerned with composition. There were a couple of times where he felt that I could liven things up a bit . . . but I was given freedom to do it.

ART LINSON: Brian allowed Sean to create the character that he wanted – just like Amy Heckerling let him create Spicoli. Just like De Niro created Capone for Brian in *The Untouchables*. De Palma's very appreciative of Sean's talent. He let Sean do what he wanted to do, and I think Sean let Brian do what Brian does as a director.

Among De Palma's unquestionable skills, one area where he has both excelled and courted opprobrium is in his finessed depiction of the murder of women. Casualties of War, half a world away from his brazenly Hitchcockian thrillers, was also that rarest of war movies, one with a female (Thuy Thu Le) at its dramatic core, albeit a female man- handled and raped and finally despatched. The viewer waits in trepi- dation for the men to fall upon her, but the sequence is finally presented from an enforced distance, mimicking Eriksson's own help- less point of view.

SEAN PENN: I often wonder about Thuy Thu Le. She had been flown out of Saigon in the baby exodus. Her parents got out too; they went to Paris and she went to school there. Then she came in for an audi- tion for this movie; and here's this traditional girl from a traditional Vietnamese culture, going back to Thailand to be raped. She seemed fine with it, seemed to make the separation quite well. But she did that movie in the knowledge that she was heading back to Paris afterwards for an arranged marriage . . .

Now, I can't have an objective view of the film, because of having a daughter. I started to see a piece of it on television once, and I just . . . found it ugly. Not the movie, just the dynamics of the character I was playing. I've participated in two on-screen rapes, where it was *very* disturbing to shoot. It's a harder thing, I think, than murder onscreen, for an actor and an actress, because of the gender matters. The gender you are matters, and what gender you're not matters. And the vulner- ability of women to this stuff . . . I mean, we don't know someone's history. And you figure you have one in four women – I think that's the statistic – who have experienced some level of molestation. You worry about that. And it can have a very ugly feeling to it in shooting it. I think, in both cases, there was a level of self-disgust involved that I was able to just give over to. But that's my least favourite thing to do in movies.

* * *

SEAN PENN: Then I came back from Thailand, and not long thereafter things fell apart, I think.

DAVID BAERWALD: I would always say to Sean, 'Why don't you play a nice poet? Some mellow guy, who'll give me a foot-rub?' But typecasting just took over . . . He'd been away in Thailand, and I didn't even know he was coming back. I got up one morning and there he was at the kitchen table. And he was that guy – the tobacco-chewing sarge. It's bad enough having a room-mate, but *that* guy?! [*laughs*] It was kind of inspiring, but in many ways, Meserve was not the guy I signed on to room with. He'd be going round the house, raging. And I'm like, 'For Christ's sake, man, I'm trying to eat my breakfast here. Don't rape and kill me, please . . .'

On 27 June 1988, the Penns were out on the town in Atlantic City, with tickets to a title-fight and the company of novelist Harry Crews.

The son of tenant farmers from Bacon County, Georgia, Crews was an ex-marine, connoisseur of drinking, fighting, writing and motorcyles and the author of Naked in Garden Hills, This Thing Don't Lead to Heaven *and* A Feast of Snakes. *Among his admirers was Madonna, who pressed Crews' latest,* The Knockout Artist, *upon her husband. This was the story of a young fighter with a singular glass jaw who makes a career from punching himself out cold for cash, before a perverse tycoon offers him a seemingly redemptive shot at training a new champ.*

Crews was at work in his lakeside cabin outside of Gainesville when Madonna's office called to invite him to the Mike Tyson/Michael Spinks fight at the Trump Plaza Hotel. Crews met the Penns at their New York residence on the appointed evening and found two polite book-loving souls. The scene in Atlantic City was an altogether different barrel of monkeys. Crews, no shrinking violet, was startled by the 'howling mob of photographers' and the appearance of 'a lynch mob'. Penn, still bearing the lean, crop-haired lineaments of Tony Meserve, made his displeasure plain. The real fight lasted ninety-one seconds . . .

Musically, Madonna's star was still in a phenomenal ascendant, but the reception of her acting in Speed-the-Plow *was barely more enthusiastic than that which met the release of the movie* Who's That Girl?. *Ever-attuned to the need to overhaul the brand, and practised in the pushing of a taboo button, Madonna now began to pop up on television and in public with bisexual actress/comedienne Sandra Bernhard.*

EILEEN RYAN PENN: Sean said to me once, 'You know, I made a mistake, I mistook a great first date for a marriage. I should have just taken her out.' Particularly Madonna then, she was really just into 'Everybody look at me, look at me!' I think she's grown a little bit since then, just as Sean has. She was fun, she was cute. I actually got to like her. But not as the wife of my son. I worried, because what she wanted out of life was not what Sean wanted. So they were . . . mismatched. Oh! Bad.

And then I thought also that she became so . . . vulgar, in certain ways. And I think she did it not because she was so vulgar in herself, but I think she wanted the world to *think* that: she wanted to shock. And she succeeded. But that was definitely not what I wanted for the mother of my grandchildren. It would have been a tragedy if they'd had a child. I think I would have had to be the parent . . .

Come the autumn of 1988, the 'She's De-Lovely' project, for all the powerful passions behind it, was no nearer a deal, much less a start date.

SEAN PENN: John, strangely enough, felt like we should all get paid: I don't know what was behind that. He may have been extending himself to me, but he thought that it had potential commercial value. And I didn't think that was going to happen with that material and that we should just try to get the movie made. We finally got Gary Hendler involved as a producer. Gary had run Tri-Star for a while. Then Gary got sick and later died. And then John felt he was too sick to make the movie, and he brought in Peter Bogdanovich. I didn't feel comfortable with Peter, so I suggested Hal Ashby. And John went for it. And then John and Hal both died . . . [6]

The last conversation I had with John, he was angry at me. They were still trying to get real money. Now it was getting more complicated, because it wasn't John directing any more: he didn't think he could make it through the working day. I said, 'This ain't going to

6 Cassavetes passed away on 3 February 1989.

happen now, so I'm going to go and do Brian De Palma's movie.' And John called me in Thailand: 'Are you gonna do this fucking movie or not?' I had never said anything *but* that I would do the movie, and that I would do it for nothing. But I figured I'd come back from Thailand and make a real plea for the thing. But then he was too sick by the time I got back and wasn't taking calls.

So Penn picked up pieces of work. He headed to his beloved Mojave Desert to direct a promo video for Madonna's brother-in-law, the gifted singer-songwriter Joe Henry. 'Here and Gone' was a cut from Henry's forthcoming Murder of Crows *album.*

DAVID BAERWALD: I've had a lot of hair-raising moments with Sean. I mean, he *is* a hair-raising moment, you know what I mean? We were up in the Mojave Desert, everybody was sort of sunburnt and happy at the end of the day. Juan Anchia was the cinematographer, and I was shooting pool with him. Dr Katz rushes in and says, 'Dudes! You gotta come out here! Sean's going nuts!' I go outside and I see a cop, standing over what looks like a dead dog – the guts are out there on the pavement. I go round the corner and I see Sean in the back of this flatbed truck, trying to get the clip into an M1 carbine rifle – he's going to go put the dog out of its misery. I say, 'Sean, there's a fucking *cop* right there. You can't go rushing around that corner with a machine gun, he's gonna shoot you.' And Sean goes [*Meserve voice*], 'Fuck you!' He keeps on trying to load this clip. It's a full moon, we're in the back of this truck, and we start wrestling over this semi-automatic carbine. It got pretty rough – I kicked him in the balls. But he was bound and determined to put this dog out of its misery. And now here's the funny part: they took it to the vet, and the dog lived. . .

SEAN PENN: Woody Harrelson was a friend of Michael J. Fox's. He came out to Thailand and I met him a second or third time there – I knew him first through Carol Kane when they were going out. And it was off of our bonding a bit that he asked me to do something with him.

WOODY HARRELSON: I remember one day we were playing basketball at his house in Malibu and his dog got loose. And he ran and jumped up on a wall and yelled for his dog at the top of his lungs – I mean, it was jolting, the passion and the power of it. I felt like it showed a lot of what he has in him. Just yelling for his dog was better than '*Stelllla!*' – or at least comparable . . .

So I asked him if he would do a little part in this little movie I did that I'm really embarrassed about, so I won't say the name of it . . .

Cool Blue *is a plainly misfired buddy picture/romance: Harrelson plays a Venice Beach artist searching for a woman who gave him one night in heaven and then vanished. Would-be quirky cameos fill out the picture, chief among them Penn as a kind of saloon angel with a white-blond pony-tail and a cod-Irish accent. Amidst the blarney, Penn quotes a stave from one of his Bukowski-esque poems ('Leather Girl') before urging Harrelson's character to – what else? – look inside himself to find love.*

WOODY HARRELSON: But Sean went so far above and beyond the call of duty in terms of all the cool little preparatory things he did for this little part. It cost him money, you know? And time. He didn't just walk through it, is my point. He had fake teeth made, he came up with the idea of the Irish accent. And it turns out at the end of the scene he's just a plumber. But he came in with these cards that said, 'Your pipes constipated? Call Phil.' Then we did the scene, and there was a moment where I turned and Sean kicked me in the ass. I was surprised. I'd been blocked to do such-and-such, so I kind of stifled my reaction to him. It was only after that I realized he did it in order to *get a reaction*. He could see I needed a kick in the ass as an actor [*laughs*]. So I'll never forget that lesson: if Sean Penn kicks me in the ass, I need to turn around and say, 'What the fuck?' Or whatever, depending on the rating . . .

Mike Nichols's Broadway staging of David Rabe's Hurlyburly *in 1984–85 had been exalted by the* New York Times *as 'a production of any playwright's dreams'. Rabe was not of that mind, and hence open to a remedial suggestion come the summer of 1988.*

BARBARA LIGETI: *Hurlyburly* in Los Angeles happened because Sean, David and Danny Aiello were sitting in a watering hole in New York called Columbus, another Pauly Herman[7] special, and they were talking about how David really wanted to direct his play because he felt Mike had ruined it . . . Sean and Danny wanted to do it. And Danny said to me, 'You gotta produce this.' So I said to David, 'Let me do some investigating . . .'

7 Host of Café Central and other celebrated night-spots, later the front man for the prestigious Ago restaurant in Los Angeles.

DON PHILLIPS: There is a little adjunct to Los Angeles airport where you can get small private planes, and one time I drove Randy Quaid out there for a flight to New York. Who comes off the plane but Sean and David Rabe? I have not seen or spoken with Mr Rabe for five years. He comes up and says, 'Don. I know. And that's what we're out here to do. Sean is going to play Eddie, and I'm going to direct it, my way.'

DAVID RABE: Mr Nichols is a brilliant director; he was great for me on *Streamers*. But figuring out what went wrong on *Hurlyburly* was like getting a PhD in directing, to learn how he had managed to make the play mean almost the opposite of what I thought it meant. The core element of my disagreement with Mike can be made very clear. The scene in the text at the end of Act One – Phil telling Eddie about his wife wanting a baby– was never performed. And it's dominoes: you take that scene out and the soul of Phil, any sense of decency in him, is unavailable. He's just this guy who yells and beats people up. You don't have a sense of his struggle with himself. The next domino that falls is that Eddie's valuing of Phil becomes ridiculous. Why does he like the guy? Then you're free to make it seem that what Mickey says about the two of them is correct. So my guess is that I was trying to direct it from the point of view that Eddie was the main and sympathetic character: not to soft-pedal the bad and corrupt things he does, but to find a way in which he's wrestling with that stuff.

Sean was really a champion of Scott Plank for the role of Mickey. As a human being Scott was much more an Eddie, much more heart-on-his-sleeve and impulsive a person. But when we worked, he did it, and did it beautifully. Given the talent he had and the looks, I expected him to be a big star. But he clearly had demons.[8]

We ended up in the Westwood Playhouse: a nice space, but like a large off-Broadway house. It all happened fairly quickly, but by the time we opened, it flowed, it was funny, it had clarity and momentum. And quite moving, in its own way. It doesn't really want to be all that moving, that play, but it was, in a backwards way.

BARBARA LIGETI: David put back in the scene Mike had cut, and the play still ran shorter than it ever ran on Broadway, because David directed it in this exuberant, I would say 'sloppy-dog', fashion – all

---

8 Scott Plank was found dead on 24 October 2002 at his LA home. He was forty-three.

Courtesy of Sean Penn

36 *Hurlyburly* on stage, 1988: Scott Plank (Mickey), Penn (Eddie)

these wounded men onstage. It had great vitality. And Sean unlocked the secrets of Eddie. No one ever inhabited that character better.

SEAN PENN: It wasn't unhappy, doing that play: the journey of it, my god, what an organic theatrical experience. And David is the best director I've worked with in the theatre. But I think I was beginning to experience a disenchantment with the audience.

BARBARA LIGETI: We took a calculated risk, because the play is a scathing indictment of Hollywood – but Hollywood loves to see that, they've got armour, they can laugh about it. And we sold tickets. But people weren't coming to the performance; they were just buying tickets for the 'event', or leaving after the first or second act. I'd call them up and say, 'Why the hell did you leave?' 'We love the play, but we saw it in New York, and Sean was doing it beautifully, but we had to play tennis at seven . . .'

DAVID RABE: Madonna was around during *Hurlyburly*. All during the period I knew them as a couple, that stretch from *Goose and Tomtom*, they would be stormy and then calm and happy. I remember we had a party up at their house. Madonna played her first tapes of *Like a Prayer*, and we listened, and it was very exciting. Everything seemed OK at that point; there was a lot that seemed to me like they were very happy and very much in love. And then, well . . . the tensions, the pressure of love isn't always so good. I remember one rehearsal Sean came in a little ragged; his hair was all crooked and he said something funny, attributed it to something: 'The way you look when your wife screams at you in the morning,' or something . . . Then we opened the play, I stayed a few days and left. And I never went back.

LINDA LEE BUKOWSKI: Hank and I were invited to opening night in Westwood.[9] So we went in a limousine, and the place was completely packed with well-known people and celebrities. Madonna was there. And the play was just a knockout – Sean's performance was a *tour de force*. He became a man, when I saw him in that play.

Afterwards there was going to be a party at a big club. Hank and I didn't go out much, but we figured if we were gonna do it, we'd go for the whole dip – go to the silly party, see the stars, come home and fight . . .

So we met up, the four of us, in a hotel lounge and ordered some drinks. And the lady was a little bit edgy. Sean says, 'What are we gonna do?' I said, 'Well, there's this party you mentioned.' 'Yeah, you wanna go?' Hank says, 'We're here, we got the limo. Might as well.' And Madonna was not happy about that at all. Sean asks her, 'Well, what do *you* want to do?' 'I don't know . . .' Sean looked at me. I said, 'Let's go to the party.' And I looked at her and said, 'Sean, this is your night, baby. You were incredible, and you deserve every bit of appreciation you get tonight.' So they got in their limo, we got in ours, and we went to the party. And Madonna was just sitting there, really pissed off that nobody was talking to her.

I think that's when I realized that it was going to be really hard for them to make it. She should have been overjoyed for her husband and the brilliance of his work, happy that he was getting this attention. And Sean was so sweet, trying to be nice to her, because he loved her. But she just wasn't used to not being the centre of attention.

I empathize with their situation only because I know what it's like to be really, really loving somebody and just having difficult times. And if you're emotionally expressive and you let it out, it's going to

9 16 November 1988.

cause problems. In *their* positions it's just going to be exacerbated to the highest degree of theatrics.

So, well, the night went on. They probably went home and fought too. I don't think Hank and I fought that night. It made us grateful . . .

On 28 December 1988, the couple had an argument over breakfast that culminated in Penn asking his wife to leave. She intended to return for personal effects, but, Penn would later tell Rolling Stone, *'I had made a threat that I would literally cut her hair off. She took it quite seriously.' So seriously, in fact, that Madonna advised the local authorities of the same, also alerting them to the presence of guns on the Carbon Canyon premises; and so a SWAT team attended the scene. The tabloid papers went into ecstasies of imagining what form of lurid violence could have precipitated the role of law enforcement in the end of the affair. In such reports, Penn was unflaggingly cast as the bully, and his now ex-wife did not deign to refute them. As Penn later told* Premiere's *Christopher Connelly, 'Yeah, well, that was confusing to me. I've always wondered, and I guess I'll never know, how aware she was of the effect of her passiveness in those areas . . . '*

BARBARA LIGETI: *Hurlyburly* was still running, and the *National Enquirer* called me up one day and they asked me if there was any truth to the rumour that Sean had tied Madonna up and force-fed her dog food. My response, unpremeditated, was, 'She's a vegetarian.' The guy said, 'You're not taking me seriously.' I said, 'Look in the mirror . . .'

DAVID BAERWALD: I was living there all through that whole period when he supposedly tied her up like a turkey. In fact, I think I was there that day. The reason I say 'I think' is because there was no turkey-trussing going on, of course. Utter hogwash. It had absolutely no foundation in reality. I was there in the morning when she left. I had to go some place, and I left Sean at the kitchen table. I wasn't there when the SWAT team showed up . . . An over-reaction? I think that would be one of the understatements of the decade, really. It was extremely uncalled-for. And really irresponsible – because she could have got him hurt, no question.

On 5 January 1989, Madonna filed for divorce, citing 'irreconcilable differences', in Los Angeles County Superior Court. The settlement was theoretically complex, given the absence, at Penn's insistence, of a pre-nuptial agreement, and the legal phalanx now surrounding the corporation that was Madonna. But each took away what they had brought separately to the union; as to the two properties for which they both put up cash, Madonna took the New York apartment, Penn the Malibu house. Madonna quickly acquired an estate in the Hollywood Hills, and, in early February, began work on Warren Beatty's Dick Tracy. *The successful* Like a Prayer *album and an abortive deal with Pepsi-Cola that nonetheless netted her $5 million followed hard upon the Decree Absolute.*

In dolorous synchronicity, the end of the Penn union coincided, on 27 December 1988, with the passing of Hal Ashby from pancreatic cancer.

DON PHILLIPS: I saw Sean over at Hal's house while he was dying, that three-month ordeal that just got worse and worse. In life, Hal was a recluse. But in death, he wanted everybody around him. And, any given night, you might see Jon Voight, Jack Nicholson, Warren Beatty, Shirley MacLaine, Jane Fonda, Sean . . . Nobody in Hollywood would believe this, but they loved him and they were there to comfort him. Everybody would take a body part, his arms, his legs – six or seven or eight people rubbing him, caressing the skin, just to ease his terrible pain. And he loved having everybody around. That's not the way he was in life.

SEAN PENN: When I went to Hal's memorial service, there it was – the Ashby Street sign. They had put it up there on the podium.

After the demands of Hurlyburly, *the grim terminus of his marriage, a taste of the director's chair . . . Penn was of a mind to have done with acting. But he had already committed to a project with Art Linson and Robert De Niro. Penn's and De Niro's mutual regard was some years old. Several prior efforts to collaborate had foundered before 1987, when De Niro contacted Linson, who had for some years owned the remake rights to* We're No Angels *(1955), a comedy in which Humphrey Bogart leads a prison break-out from Devil's Island and finds his softer side in the doing.*

ART LINSON: We're No Angels came about because Bob and Sean wanted to work together. I went to David Mamet and told him this. Mamet said he'd write a script, and it all fell together. I was coming off having made a lot of money for Paramount with The Untouchables, so they supported the investment. And it did seem like a pedigree situation: that cast and Mamet and Neil.

NEIL JORDAN: I was working on *High Spirits* and having a very hard time with American producers, when I was sent David Mamet's script. I love David's writing: he has a simplicity that you obviously don't find a lot in the movie world, and his dialogue is very smart. But this was a different kind of territory for him.

Mamet reupholstered the original scenario to make a tale of two unassuming convicts, Ned and Jim, who get hitched into a break-out by the psychotic Bobby and make their way to a northern border town, where their best refuge from the pursuing prison warden is to masquerade as a pair of scholarly priests expected as guests of the local monastery, and then wait for the right moment to skip across a bridge into Canada. The pretence, however, brings with it taxing chores – prayer, confession, vespers and suchlike – while crazy Bobby remains threateningly at large . . .

NEIL JORDAN: I suppose it reminded me of movies like *I Am a Fugitive from a Chain Gang*, where you have guys escaping from prison, tumbling down hills and breaking off chains. What I liked about the script, really, was that it was like an interesting, acerbic little fable about religion and the ridiculous nature of belief. I liked the irony that these two characters escape from a prison and end up in another kind of prison. Also, it was very sweet: I think Mamet, being from a Jewish–American background, let himself be far kinder to the Catholic Church than I would have been . . .

They asked me to go for a meeting with De Niro and Sean in New York; flew me over on Concorde. So I was being courted, I suppose. I'd admired Sean, absolutely; he was a thrilling young actor, and Robert De Niro was a legend. But it was a strange situation for me, because I'd never been a director-for-hire before, and I'd never experienced 'Hollywood'. I had just done movies in Ireland and England where I'd done what I wanted, really. I didn't realize that if you haven't written the screenplay then your opinion as a director is only as valid as everybody else's. And so the job of directing a movie becomes as much an act of diplomacy as anything else.

The thing about Mamet is his rhythms, isn't it? It's a kind of dialogue that only exists in Mamet World, the kind of staccato rhythmic stop–start nature of it. I didn't have the licence to change it, and it's not the kind of thing you can improvise.

ART LINSON: We did have a couple of bad meetings about it with Mamet, where Neil tried to talk in his Neil way of 'I'd like it if you could do this and that,' and Mamet basically said in his Mamet way, 'I've been paid. I'm not helping.'

NEIL JORDAN: De Niro was anxious to do big, broad, mainstream comedy. He'd just done *Midnight Run* with Charles Grodin. I have to say, though, that if one were to cast three individuals to do a light comedy, I really wouldn't have chosen myself and Robert De Niro and Sean Penn. Would you?

And basically it's not shot like a comedy. It's shot like a fable, two guys finding themselves in different ways. I wanted the opening in the prison to be kind of Dante-esque in a way: 'Thou art in hell,' or at least between heaven and hell. And I found this wonderful location, an old mine, so I was able to give almost a kind of Fritz Langian hugeness to it. Maybe it threw a shadow over the rest of the movie, Jimmy Russo breaking out and shooting the guys. Very graphic, isn't it? But then again, that was the way it was written. Well . . . [*sighs*] maybe I'm not a comedy director . . .

JAMES RUSSO: Sean and Madonna were finished, but I think there was a lot of pain there for Sean: not so much missing her but just the disruption in his life. So for him to do a comedic performance, something that light – it could have been a good distraction, but I think it was difficult.

NEIL JORDAN: We were having dinner in a restaurant, and some Italian mobster guy at another table said something about Madonna to the girl he was with. And Sean got very angry and it resulted in a bit of a scrap, kind of a shoving match went on. So obviously there was some kind of stress there. Sean and De Niro kind of railed a bit with each other, head-to-head. There was tremendous respect, of the older actor and the up-and-coming talent, they obviously wanted to work together very much, but there was kind of a *jousting* aspect to their relationship is how I'd describe it: a bit of one-upmanship. It was quite a tense set, let me put it that way.

37 *We're No Angels*: Bruno Kirby (Deputy), Penn (Jim), Hoyt Axton
(Father Levesque), Robert De Niro (Ned)

ART LINSON: Neil and Sean, they didn't get on that well. They had a definite problem with regard to artistic differences over how things should be done.

NEIL JORDAN: Sean was renowned for giving directors a hard time. I think he regarded that as part of his job description in a way [*laughs*]. So we had a kind of tempestuous time, really. He approached the part from totally within the character: where he would stand, how he would be. And from within the skin of the actor, there's always a falsity to film-making, the whole procedure of following marks and all that. I was making this expensive film on quite a scale, so I was kind of immersed in the broader visual picture, and sometimes I'd need my actor to move from here to there, just in order to tell a visual story. And Sean's character would . . . want to do different things. Sometimes we clashed over that sort of thing.

Bob is a very specific kind of actor. There's a remarkable simplicity and honesty to what he does, but if the script has him reacting to two thousand people running towards him, you almost have to *get* those two thousand people running at him.

Whereas Sean went through the entire thing with a simplicity: he would always do it one way. It was just sometimes there'd be a struggle to *find* that one way, you know? But then he would hit it, with a great sense of the inarticulacy of the character he was playing. I can't think of anyone who's better at playing those kinds of guys who don't have language to express their feelings. There are certain things Sean does that no other actor can do just in making the inarticulate speak. And I loved his performance, I think it's spot-on. It's the sidekick role, but it's lovely.

The film's chief love interest sees De Niro pursuing prostitute and single mother Demi Moore. Yet perhaps the more affecting romance is that of Penn's Jim with a young monastic novice played by John C. Reilly, a bashful fan of 'Father Brown's' theological writing, whose eyes, full of shy emotion, betray warmer feelings. De Niro's 'Father Riley' is openly resentful of these efforts to 'shine on his pal'.

NEIL JORDAN: I know, I know . . . [*laughs*] It was what Mamet had written, and I tried to bring it as alive as best as I possibly could. 'Puppy love' is maybe what it is. Obviously, a guy who's a monk and wears a skirt and has sworn himself to celibacy, then finds himself deeply attracted to this criminal who's on the run . . . well, maybe there are overtones to it. He just wants to save him, doesn't he? He sees a soul there, a similarly innocent soul. He wants to save this beautiful soul that's beating like a butterfly inside this cagey human being. It was kind of wonderful, that.

JAMES RUSSO: The weather was crazy, the location was two hours from the hotel – it wasn't a pleasant shoot. But we laughed like hell up there. I remember one funny incident – this is the kind of imbecilic stuff you do on a set just to break the monotony . . . We were hanging out in Sean's trailer, sitting there bored, late in the afternoon, might even have had a couple of beers. Sean had a very proper assistant, and she went into the bathroom at one point. Sean was in his priest's outfit, and I was in the woman's dress I wore in the movie, and underneath I had on this Union suit, long johns. So I ran and got talcum powder, and I pulled down my pants, and we put the talcum powder all over my ass, and then Sean pulled down *his* pants, and we put the talcum powder all over his balls and his cock . . . So Sean's standing over me, and I've got my long johns pulled down round my ankles, I'm going, 'Uh! Uh! Uhh!!' And this girl comes out and turns white. White as the talcum powder . . .

ART LINSON: Sean was using his time, though, he was writing every morning, so that was probably his major form of therapy . . .

SEAN PENN: I was so taken with 'Highway Patrolman', the story had stayed in my head and germinated over the years in such a way that I filled it in from a three-minute song to a two-hour movie. I had tried to get different writers interested in doing a script, with the idea that I might act in it. Then I was making *We're No Angels* and I would go back to my trailer and work on the script. And as soon as I'd started typing, I knew it was something I wanted to direct myself. It came very quickly, out of pictures in my head more than words or characters. In terms of the confidence to do it – the easiest route was going out and seeing how little there was that I responded to in what others were doing. I knew I could do something that could make me more interested than what I was seeing.

NEIL JORDAN: What did strike me at the time about Sean, actually, was that he was a tremendously vital actor who felt somehow . . . *humiliated*, by acting. Or at least found acting not entirely satisfying. You often find the more intelligent actors feel that: that they're not in charge of their gift, really. And they want to be, and it's frustrating for them. Now, that's probably because he wanted very strongly to direct.

We're No Angels was meant to be the last hurrah, and yet Penn, dissatisfied, felt there was a better note on which to bow out. At Orion, Mike Medavoy was cultivating a project entitled Hell's Kitchen, *derived from a* New York Times *article about 'The Westies', a savage band of Irish mobsters whose boss, Jimmy Coonan, formed a lethal alliance with the Gambino crime family in the seventies. The Westies had since been driven out of business and into jail thanks to a public crusade by then-US Attorney Rudolph Giuliani, and their New York neighbourhood, 'Hell's Kitchen', was morphing into a gentrified area called Clinton where yuppie apartments might flourish.*

Medavoy developed a script and attached Phil Joanou, a director somewhat akin to James Foley: a confident stylist, keenly attuned to music. Penn's role was that of Terry Noonan, a neighbourhood kid who returns unheralded to the Kitchen and falls in with old friend Jackie Flannery, chief attack-dog for the Irish mob marshalled by his own brother, Frankie. Noonan is in fact an undercover cop, charged with infiltrating the Flannery gang. But in the process, Noonan dis-

covers he is still enamoured of his childhood sweetheart, fair Flannery sister Kathleen. Like At Close Range, *the film – eventually titled* State of Grace *– would treat family ties as a moveable feast, subject to the vying claims of business.*

SEAN PENN: Mike Medavoy was the one who called. Phil Joanou was involved. And there was a script by Dennis McIntyre,[10] and I asked for revisions by David Rabe. I wanted him to take out the predictable, replace it with the unpredictable and the lifelike – Rabe-ify it . . .

DAVID RABE: I look back and maybe I'm being kind to myself when I say that, if I'd known Dennis McIntyre was ill, I might have had second thoughts.[11] But I didn't know that, and I got involved. I didn't change the storyline much, but I did change a lot in the relationships between characters and a lot of dialogue. And it's a different feeling writing a script you know will definitely get made [*laughs*]. You know that because they're already scouting locations . . .

Gary Oldman – somewhat of an English counterpart to Penn in his fastidious career choices and exertions, and now taking American roles – was the speedy, psychotic Jackie, who thinks himself the prince of the neighbourhood, mourning the good old days as he wields his axe and issues stitches to the ill-favoured. 'He's the real Irishman of the piece, you know?' Oldman told Rolling Stone, *having perhaps crossed the line between script and reality. Ed Harris replaced Bill Pullman as Frankie. R. D. Call came on board as Frankie's grim henchman Pat Nicholson. And Robin Wright was cast as Kathleen.*

ROBIN WRIGHT PENN: I was on the phone with Sean, sort of perfunctory: 'Isn't it great that we're gonna work together?' Then I said a really stupid thing: 'But let me tell you something' – because I knew there was nudity in the film, and I'd never done it, and wasn't going to – I said, 'Listen, I'm not gonna do this.' And he said, 'Look, I'll take my top off if you take yours off.' I said, 'OK!' I wasn't even thinking [*laughs*]. And of course, once we were on the set, it was, 'We made the deal, remember . . .?'

But I was scared out of my brain making that movie, because it was my first one with real actors. *Princess Bride* was comedy; Christopher

---

10 Playwright, his major works including *Modigliani*, *Split Second*, and *National Anthems*.
11 McIntyre developed cancer and would die in 1990.

Guest and all those people were great. But this was serious shit – Gary Oldman and Ed Harris and Sean. And I felt very babe-in-the-woods, just trying to fit in and not show that I was petrified.

Another key role in the picture proved harder to fill: Borelli, the Italian capo, who compels Frankie to whack his brother Jackie in the name of good commercial relations ('For the sake of family and blood I'm gonna give you this opportunity').

JOSEPH VITARELLI: I was in LA and Sean called me. He said, 'I'm working with this young guy and I think you'll like him, and I'd like you to meet him. Maybe you should do the music.' Ultimately I didn't. Morricone scored it. That competition was probably a little too stiff, shall we say? Particularly given I was twenty-eight at the time.

So I went to New York, and we went out to dinner – me, Sean, Phil and Gary Oldman – at the West Bank Cafe. And Phil, for the first part of the evening, has his head in his hands. I said, 'Look, Phil, you haven't even started shooting and here we're talking about the music – I feel like I'm imposing.' He said, 'No, absolutely not, that's not the problem. We're going to start shooting in two weeks. And so much of the film pivots on this character, Borelli, who we haven't even cast yet.' He felt that everyone he was seeing had done this part before. And he described him – a guy from the streets who's risen up and become all powerful, doesn't have to say much, just walks into a room and he's likeable, but yet you're afraid of him at the same time.

The more detail Phil adds to it, the more I'm having these thoughts. And I look at Sean, who's laughing. He says, 'You thinking what I'm thinking?' Phil says, 'What the hell are you guys talking about?' Sean says, 'Joe's father.'

When I was a kid, my father was very charismatic, a people person, unlike me. Any group, he'd be in the middle of it, telling stories from his old neighbourhood, Mulberry Street, Mott Street, the Lower East Side.

So Phil says to me, 'I didn't know your father was an actor.' I say, 'He's not.' Phil says, 'C'mon, guys, forget it. If it were a cameo, fine. But we're gonna take somebody who never acted before and give him a starring role with Sean and Gary and Ed Harris?' Sean said to Phil, 'He *is* the guy. He's not a gangster, but he *is* that guy. He's got a face that you'll never forget. And he's charming. Just meet him.' Phil says, 'I'll meet him, sure, but Orion is never gonna go for this.'

Well, my father walked in, and they cast him immediately. Nobody had ever seen anything like him. He was just . . . good. And of course, that face![12]

BONO: I know Sean found this guy, a genuine goodfella. There's a scene in the film that says everything about an Irish guy trying to be Italian. Ed Harris, he's got his Armani suit on, he's sitting there doing his thing. Except he doesn't know how to eat. Crumbs all over the place. The Italian boss goes, 'Frankie. Don't make a mess. You kids from the West Side . . . '

38 *State of Grace*: Robin Wright (Kathleen Flannery),
Penn (Terry Noonan)

Perhaps the most subtle work in the film was by Robin Wright, who made Kathleen into an enigma, frankly desirous of moving uptown and leaving her rotten family behind, but drawn back into Terry's arms as much in pique over how he could ever have abandoned her. Once she has learned of his own exquisite spot, his personal/professional guilt ('I'm a fucken Judas cop'), she coldly achieves closure.

ROBIN WRIGHT PENN: You want mystery there, instead of the pat 'Oh, I've always been in love with you, I could never live without you . . .' The film needed it. From what I was reading, there was this sensibility of resentment in Kathleen, it was, 'You fucken crossed the line, you involved yourself, you infiltrated. Then you left.' And I guess I was

---

12 Joe Vitarelli Sr subsequently became a bona fide movie face in *Analyse This* (1999). He passed away in January 2004.

lumping it into the Irish thing of loyalty: 'And now you come *back*?' It's unheard of. Sacrilege, you know?

DAVID RABE: For what it's worth, I urged Phil to let the audience know early on that Sean's character was a cop. The whole front end became very random: you have a scene like Frankie interrogating Terry while they're playing pool, trying to feel out whether he should take him on: well, it has no tension. Whereas, if you know he's undercover . . . But really, more important is the story of this guy going in there and getting drawn, slowly, slowly, back into an old way of being, finding his personal relationships with these people overtaking his ability to keep the separation and prove to himself that he's left all this by being a cop. That story gets muddled.

State of Grace wound up as a piece of polished surface: it has a look and a mood. But for all the five-star acting talent, its characters appear drawn as much from well-remembered movies as the Hudson River docks. The film's finale sees Terry take out Frankie and his goons in a slo-mo shoot-out set against the backdrop of a St Patrick's Day parade: like Peckinpah remaking The Godfather. *Unfortunately, the material can't be elevated so.*

SEAN PENN: It was a similar situation to *At Close Range*, with me not as involved. But similar sensibilities involved. Again, I would go back to 'versions', from script to film. And when I say that, I'm starting with me and working backwards . . .

R. D. CALL: Some people may disagree with me but I think Sean was as good as he's ever been in that film. He brought a lot of himself to it – there's a lot of him in *all* of his work, but there are moments and scenes where . . . he was there.

Penn's Terry is conscientious but inwardly conflicted, brave to the point of feckless, a professional at an evening's carousing but a man unable to hide his finer feelings. In the movie, his best friend is killed and his beloved deserts him. Real life was kinder.

ROBIN WRIGHT PENN: Sean and I kind of tried to sneak around a little bit together during the film, but it was never an official anything. We made a date for dinner one night. He had a suite; I showed up there, the door was ajar, no lock. I hear, 'Come in, come in!' I could tell he was in the bedroom. 'Go ahead, have a seat . . .' So I go into the living room and sit down. He comes out wearing a pith helmet, a bola tie, a jockstrap and cowboy boots. And I busted a gut laughing. I thought that was the funniest fucking thing. I found out later that was the real test – to see if I could take it [*laughs*]. And I guess once we got back to LA, we started hanging out more . . .

Among the first of Penn's friends to observe this burgeoning new relationship was John Sykes, head of programming at MTV, who had been introduced to Penn through Madonna in 1985 and remained a fast friend after the marital break-up.

JOHN SYKES: November 1989, I was doing some MTV International business in Tokyo when Sean called and said, 'I'm in Bangkok, come and join me. I'm going on to Phuket and we can spend a few days together before we go back to the States.' I got there, knocked on Sean's door and Robin opened it. She said, 'What are you doing here?' And Sean says, 'Oh, I forgot . . . I invited John along for the weekend.' What he also forgot was that this was the first get-away weekend he was going to spend together with Robin . . . So I end up as the third wheel on a long romantic trip to the Oriental Hotel in Bangkok and the Amanpuri in Phuket. There I was, 9.30 every morning, knocking on the door asking, 'So where we going today?' And they're two such sweet people, they'd just say, 'Well, we'll take this tour, or go to that beach . . .' And I don't think they had one dinner alone together that whole vacation.

One day we went to a place where they train cobras, then grab them and squeeze the venom out and bottle and sell it as an aphrodisiac or something. There was one guy whose job it was to step into the pit and taunt the cobra, and I was terrified just watching this. Suddenly something grabbed onto my ankle, as hard as it could, and I was *sure* I'd just got bit by a snake. I looked down behind me, and there was Sean on his hands and knees, crawling around. The prankster . . .

Casualties of War *was released in August 1989, a peculiar time for this gruelling piece to vie in the marketplace with* Honey, I Shrunk the Kids. *It was very well-received, perhaps most conspicuously by De Palma's long-term advocate Pauline Kael, even though its makers had reached disparate conclusions on its final merits.*

DAVID RABE: My problem with the movie, for what it's worth, is that

Eriksson has a speech that comes after everything, where he says, 'Everybody says we could get killed tomorrow so we don't have to care about anything, and in fact that's why we *should* care about every little thing.' It was meant to emerge out of someone who was very conflicted, even about what he had witnessed, and his own loyalties about the fact that Meserve had saved his life. And now it finally dawned on this guy that he had to *do* something. But the way it was done, it sounded like an expression of what Eriksson had clearly known all along – when he arrived, even. It wasn't Michael J. Fox's problem; it was just that Brian wanted to separate good and bad more cleanly than I thought it should be.

Also I felt the ending as done was just a kind of mockery. I had set it much as it is in the book, Eriksson seeing a Vietnamese girl on a bus in the Midwest in winter. He hands her something she forgot, she turns to leave, and he says, '*Chau co*' – 'Hello, Miss' in Vietnamese. They look at one another, she says, '*Chau ong*' – 'Sir' – and leaves. And to have her walk off into a blizzard would have been really powerful. That dialogue she has in the film, 'You had a bad dream' – I did write it, under duress. But they had basically said, 'You'll write it better than we will.' And the Morricone music . . . I begged Brian to change it. Vietnam was so important to me, and I felt it should be done the way I wanted. I still think the movie's got some wonderfully powerful sequences and performances. And if the end had been somewhere in the middle where you could forget about it . . .

But Sean brought that sense of being the leader and the hero, that inherent quality of a young man taking on the responsibility of these other young men. Plus he brought the craziness and the sense that once you step over the line, you're over.

ART LINSON: I think Sean's performance made it clear that Meserve was just as much a victim of Vietnam as a man of intrinsic menace. He never begs to tell you that, but that's what he does. It's one of Sean's best pieces of work – unheralded, I think. And also one of Brian's best movies.

Christmas 1989 then saw the unveiling of We're No Angels, *Neil Jordan having spent the post-production period grappling with the issue of precisely what kind of tone this light comedy born of dark sensibilities should possess onscreen.*

NEIL JORDAN: Bob had tended to give a lot of different line readings. It was almost like he gave four different performances, and the later takes were always broader. When I first cut the movie together, my instinct was to eliminate all the big comic broadness . . . and I feel in the end we let too much of it back in, because his performance was much too broad in the cut that went out. But we tested it and got remarkably high results [*laughs*], way up in the eighties and nineties, the best I've ever had. I said to the head of the studio, 'This would probably be a good film to bring out around Christmas?' And the guy very seriously said, 'This would be a good film to bring out *any* time . . .' But, for whatever reason, it didn't set the box office on fire.

SEAN PENN: I thought it was much better than they all said, but there's a lack of balance in it. We could have done better. And I get along with Neil great now.

NEIL JORDAN: Sean always says to me now, whenever I send him a script, 'How come you only send me your big American movies? How come you do all these little ones and I never get them?' Maybe I'll find something for him one day – if he's still acting . . .

By late 1989, Penn was undoubtedly conscious that he had achieved some exceptionally fine work in a series of partially successful movies. The solitary, sovereign expression of writing and the craft of directing – which he had, after all, observed and practised since his youth – were now calling to him.

DON PHILLIPS: I went over to see Sean about a project I had, and he said, 'Don, I'm sorry to tell you this, but I'm not acting anymore' I said, 'You what?' He said, 'I hate it, I don't want to do it, I'm not taking a job. I'm going to be a director, and nothing's gonna stand in my way.' Now we had touched on those conversations before, but never so serious. I said, 'You know what? I would love to be the man who produces the first movie you direct.' He said, 'You would? OK, come to my house tomorrow morning at 9 o'clock. I'll give you something.' So next morning I drove out to Carbon Canyon, and he handed me a script, called 'A Slow Coming Dark', by J. Claude McBee. He said to me, 'This guy's on death row in San Quentin. I've had it a while. I find it very intriguing. I think I'd like to make it. Do me a favour: read it and tell me what you think.' I read it, and I think, 'Oh my god in heaven, this is genius, this is modern day Cain-and-Abel.' I call Sean and tell him I have to see him. And I say, 'What did he do, kill twenty-seven people? I don't give a shit if they *electrocute* this guy – this mother-fucker can *write*.' Sean says, 'You really love it, huh?' I said, 'Sure do.' He said, 'Well, I wrote it.'

SEAN PENN: 'It's a slow coming dark, a slow coming dawn' – *An American Tragedy*, Theodore Dreiser. It was a line that stuck out when I read the book, and then I found out it had other connotations: some death row inmates had adopted it as a slogan at one point. Or maybe I made it up . . .

DAVID RABE: Was directing Sean's vocation? I knew he felt that himself – he would talk about it. I didn't understand how you could be frus-trated with acting and be that *good*. But it made sense, because Sean does have a dimension of abstract intelligence. A lot of actors are smart people, but they don't theorize a lot, they're more instinctive; whereas Sean, in my experience, has this combination of both. An actor is just in one part of the story, and they're kind of stuck in that. But you saw that Sean had the tools and almost the *need* to be in that other relationship to a story. And when he talked about it, I kind of wished he wouldn't . . . Selfishly, I think, as a writer, I in some ways didn't want to hear it. I wanted him to be an actor . . . [*laughs*].

WOODY ALLEN: A friend of mine said to me, 'Sean Penn wants to meet you and ask you some questions about directing.' This was some years before I worked with Sean. And I said, 'Sure.' So he came over to my editing suite, and we chatted. And he was, you know, tortured . . . But I could see right away that he was someone who was interested in the artistic side of film-making, no bullshit. He was not trying to self-aggrandise, he was not trying to be commercially successful at the expense of anything else: he wanted to take the tough route and try to make really good, interesting films. Of course, nothing I told him was of any help at *all* . . .

Intermission

LINDA LEE BUKOWSKI: The only time I ever saw Hank and Sean have a discrepancy that was, to me as an observer, potentially volatile – and thank God it didn't go into anything – we'd been sitting around for a long time, and we got into 'blood prejudice': meaning blood relatives, intimate family members, having such an attachment to each other and such a possessive sense of security among themselves that, even if one of them had done something horrible, they would stand up for them.

Hank didn't believe there should be a deception there. I think he felt that sort of mentality extended hugely through the world and is a reason why there are great discrepancies between cultures and tribes and so on – because of blood prejudice, 'us and them', the duality that makes people judgemental. So you stick to your own, and even if you're wrong, you're gonna stand up for them.

SEAN PENN: Sometimes when these discussions get a bit passionate over some wine it's hard to remember the exact tale of the tape . . . I think some hypothetical could have come up. I have a lot of examples, and they might have come out in trying to get to the heart of the matter with Hank. Your brother goes and tunnels into a bank vault, he steals money – that's one thing. He tells you about it? I don't turn him in. On the other hand: he goes and puts a fake gun in the face of a young bank teller, and traumatises her for life? He's got a problem with me. And I don't think Hank and I would have huge difference on that point.

My best recollection of it is that it really had to do with the culturally demanded idea of obligatory love for blood relatives: 'He's my father, I love him'. Which Hank took enormous exception to; and found it offensive that we would all subscribe to that notion.

LINDA LEE BUKOWSKI: Hank had a horrible life: his father hated him and beat him all his childhood; he had scars all over his body. And his mother was a submissive little woman who stood by the father for fear of what might happen if she didn't. Then there's Sean's family: close, caring, creative, making each other be part of each other. In that situation it's easy to see how that feeling could develop to protect the family members. Look at *At Close Range, The Indian Runner*. The family. Blood prejudice. So that was an edgy one.

SEAN PENN: Both sides are right in this argument. I think there's a place in love for absolutism. So there's a place in lovelessness for absolutism too; you have to accept one if the other. The area in which I had a place of absolute belief and love had to do with family. And where Hank didn't had specifically to do with family.

And, by the way, I entirely embrace the theory of that kind of faith as being 'blood prejudice': I think that is a legitimate criticism of a lot of status quo thinking.

I think that family comes before country or, I guess, anything else; and particularly the love in family. And family has an extension – a wife, say. It's an innocence that you protect. But there's also a chaos to which we are responsible to maintain a balance, by saying, for example, 'I hate that my father did this, but I love my father.' I didn't have anything to hate that my father did, so I just loved my father. The counterpoint is totally legitimate, which is that Hank was beaten and abused and diminished and disrespected by his father. But you fight the point as a point of faith, not as a point of literal dissent. I did feel that I wanted to push the button in that conversation with Hank, partly because of Hal Ashby's death. Hal's father had committed suicide, I believe, in front of Hal, who then left the house and hitch-hiked to Los Angeles at fourteen and raised himself. And Jon Voight said to Hal, days before he died – he was in and out of consciousness – he said, 'Hal, you gotta forgive your father.' And Hal said, 'It's just so hard . . .' And I saw that in Hank. And far be it from me to presume that everybody is looking for the same forgiveness. But I never saw forgiveness hurt anybody. So I thought it was an argument worth having.

EIGHT

1990–1991

You must leave the spectator free. And at the same time you must make yourself loved by him. You must make him love the way in which you render things. That is to say: show him things in the order and in the way that you love to see them and to feel them . . .

Robert Bresson, *Cahiers du Cinema*, January 1965

JOE ROBERTS: I went home that night. Watered my garden. Kissed my baby. And held my wife until morning. Life is good. My brother Frank. . .

From *The Indian Runner*, screenplay by Sean Penn, 1991

Set in Omaha in 1968, The Indian Runner *tells of Sergeant Joe Roberts, a sheriff's deputy since the loss of his farm to creditors, who awaits the return from Vietnam of his unruly younger brother Frank. Having shot a man dead in self-defence, Joe is physically and emotionally discomfited, and seeks succour from his Mexican wife, Maria, and his ailing parents. The sibling reunion, alas, is less than Joe had hoped. Frank arrives in town detached and distant, makes his excuses and leaves. When their mother dies, Joe seeks Frank out and finds him with a tattoo-etched torso, a virulent mean streak and an adoring waif-like girlfriend, Dorothy. Their father's subsequent suicide and Dorothy's pregnancy make possible a rapprochement and a fresh start for Frank. But Joe becomes haunted by the possibility that he and his brother are doomed to be temperamental opposites – that they have nothing in common but blood.*

SEAN PENN: There was a theme that came into the second draft of the script. The first title I had was 'A Slow Coming Dark', then 'Greetings from the Wasteland'. Then I came to *The Indian Runner*. I stumbled on a book by Peter Nabokov, a Berkeley anthropology professor, nephew of Vladimir. It was a chronicle of Native American running, its history in that culture. I read it, and there was something in it. So I spent some time with Nabokov, drew some inspiration from him, and put it into the movie.

I've been asked many times, 'Where did Frank's anger come from?' Springsteen wanted to know that too. And I referred him to his own lyrics from another song on *Nebraska*: 'Sir, I guess there's just a meanness in this world.' That was answer enough for me, because I don't always think there's an explanation for these things. But there are our ancestral sins: the criminal past of the settlers in the United States, this hustled land. It inhabits some part of our subconscious, because it got passed on by our fathers, and their fathers, and those before. I viewed that as a sort of shared disease in the culture, and – it's a leap – but I wanted to see if that had anything to do, if not literally then politically, with the damaged spirit of people like Frank.

DON PHILLIPS: I gave Sean's script to two producers, and they said, 'This is pretty damn good, but who's ever going to see a movie about a guy who murders somebody and gets away with it? No one will ever give you the money with that ending, never.' So Sean put the script away, until I happened to know that my friend Thom Mount, who now had his own company, was closing in on Japanese money to make a slate of films. I knew Thom was a big fan of Sean's. And Bruce was now more huge than ever, and here you had a Springsteen song visualized by Sean Penn. Thom thought we might be able to attract a Tom Cruise, a Robert De Niro. So Thom said yes, and Sean and I were in business. Then, of course, there was no Tom Cruise in this movie . . .

Over at his place Sean had a really interesting book of photographs from the sixties by Dennis Hopper, just plain ordinary folks across the country. There was a picture of a guy at a diner, with his hair up in the air, wearing a white shirt with the cigarettes rolled up in the sleeve and a tattoo on his arm. And Sean said, '*That's* Frankie!'

Then Sean calls me and says, 'I got the television on here, it's HBO, and there's a movie on called *Fresh Horses*, and there's this actor in it . . .'

SEAN PENN: I was over at Robin's little house in Santa Monica Canyon, waiting for her to get dressed for a date. The television was on, sound off, and I saw a face: he was only a cameo in a movie, but I saw the face that I'd had in my head when I wrote *Indian Runner*. He had something, an angularity, a severity to his handsomeness that I perceived as being like Frank. So I watched the movie through, and I called Don and said, 'Find out who he is.'

DON PHILLIPS: It was Viggo Mortensen. We sent the script to Viggo, who was playing the seventh or eighth lead in *Young Guns 2*. We flew to Tucson, Arizona, and bam! He was our man, and we were off and running.

SEAN PENN: David Morse was somebody I had in my mind for a long time and wanted to work with. I didn't know him, but I had heard from directors who had tried to use him in parts in movies I had acted in and it didn't work out for one reason or another. I had seen him in a movie called *Inside Moves* several years earlier.[1] There was just a kind of soulful dignity about him that I responded to. I asked to meet with him and decided I wanted him to play Joe.

DAVID MORSE: Leo Penn had directed me in an episode of *St. Elsewhere*, and one day between shots, he waved me over from his chair and told me that Sean had asked him to send his regards to me, that he'd written me a letter once, after seeing *Inside Moves* – which I never got.

Now I was having a terrible time – nobody would give me a break in terms of any kind of significant work in films. So I couldn't believe I was being asked to go meet Sean for the lead in this film he had written. I got a copy of his script, and I think I probably had the same response that a lot of people had: which is that I couldn't believe that Sean Penn had written it. Just because it was so beautifully written. Why you wouldn't associate that with him, I don't know, because he was obviously such a talented actor. But until I actually sat and talked with him and reconciled the script with who he was, I couldn't quite do it.

Our first meeting was up at his house in Malibu. I remember driving through the gates and up that long driveway, sitting on his oversized furniture, looking at his oversized stereo system and out over the Pacific Ocean. Sean was dressed in a black suit with a white shirt, his business look . . . But what really struck me was this enthusiasm for what he was about to do with *The Indian Runner*, his first directing, and the *love* that he had for that story and what he invested in it. He was so excited. It was like meeting a boy, in some ways. Which is not what I expected . . .

DON PHILLIPS: The funny thing is that I didn't want David Morse. I just didn't believe in him and Viggo as brothers. So Sean and I banged

---

1 Directed by Richard Donner in 1980, a drama about disabled people meeting and finding common ground in the unlikely setting of a seedy LA bar.

heads there a little. But Sean believed in David so much that, with his own stinkin' money, he set up a screen test. We tested a few actors, including Liam Neeson. Sean directed it, and Viggo was there. And Sean wrote David a special scene that wasn't in the movie, where he had to get angry, cry and laugh, all in the same scene. Only an actor could do something like that to a fellow actor – say, 'OK, buddy, hit this note and that note and *that* one.' And boy, after David was done, I was totally convinced. I fell in love and knew it was the right choice. Then Sean rented a beautiful suite at the Chateau Marmont and we cast the rest of the picture.

ADAM NELSON: Sean hired me to read with the actors; he didn't want a casting director doing it. He would spend a half hour or longer with each person; he wanted to delve in, see what you could bring out. But I have to say, when Patricia Arquette came in . . . You could take another equally capable actress and put them side by side, but you couldn't duplicate what Patricia was doing as Dorothy, just based on who she was as a person. She had an innocent quirkiness, it was unique: she wasn't acting, she was just being involved with this guy and loving him. When she came in, that was it.

Valeria Golino would play the role of Joe's wife, Maria. Her partner at the time, a young Puerto Rican-born actor who had studied at the Stella Adler Conservatory in New York before striking out for LA, would also contribute a madcap cameo to the picture as an amiable Spanish-speaking pothead.

BENICIO DEL TORO: I remember the first time I met Sean, clear as day – because I was paying attention [*laughs*]. It was a dinner, a woman introduced me to him and said I was terrific in this miniseries[2] and he had to see it, blah-blah-blah. I said, 'Listen, I can't take a compliment in front of this guy, I really can't.' Sean turned to me and said, 'You know, compliments are like shit. They're better when they come out . . .' And that locked in. I thought that was completely right.

Then I hung out with Sean a couple of times, but I wasn't going to have conversations with him, I just wanted to sit and listen to everything he had to say – to learn, really. He'd talk about John Cassavetes, and I didn't know who that was. So I took a mental note and went straight to

2 *Drug Wars: The Camarena Story* (1990)

a video store: I remember asking, 'Uh, do you have any Cassavetes films?' And the kid saying, 'Who?'

Then Sean called me to do a little cameo in *The Indian Runner* and I came in and decided, 'Okay, I'm gonna play here.' And it was really silly of me; but Sean just let me run with the ball. He doesn't expect an actor just to fulfil what he has in his mind, like a lot of directors do. He likes people who take chances, fall on their faces . . . he's right there by their side.

DON PHILLIPS: Our production designer was Michael Haller, who had been Hal Ashby's designer. I made Hal a promise just before he died. He told me, 'Next movie you make, the first person you hire is Michael, because he is the artist who has the keys to the black box.' I introduced Michael to Sean and they hit it off instantly: boy oh boy, totally in synch. Sean drew on a big piece of paper the outline of his town, the buildings, the people, the cars. He'd already visualized in advance where he'd want the camera. And Haller found that town, and that's why we ended up in Omaha.

With principal photography slated to begin in late August 1990, Penn drove his Ford pick-up from Los Angeles to the location.

SEAN PENN: We were going to do a movie on Dr Katz one time. I talked to Sam Kinison about playing him. It was going to be called '8 5 1/2'. Because he was almost eighty-sixed out of every place in New York . . .

DR KATZ: I had to retire, get out of what I was doing. And when Sean was making *State of Grace* I went to him about a job, asked him if he had anything. I wound up being his right-hand/left-hand man, whatever you want to call it. I called myself 'a gentleman's gentleman'. Did you see the movie *Arthur*? I was John Gielgud. Whatever had to be done, I did. On *Indian Runner*, I was Sean's assistant, I did craft service, and I played 'Guy on Commode'. Sean would introduce me just as Dr Katz: I had a PhD from some mail-order university. Sometimes I even wore a minister's collar . . . He looked after himself mostly, except certain situations. And those arose.

HELENA KATZ: We rented a great house in Omaha for Sean to live in, like a Tudor mansion, told them it was for a movie. Then we said to the lady at the realtor, 'Actually, it's for Sean Penn, but we'd appreciate it if you didn't tell anybody.' And she was so honest, she didn't even tell her teenage children for two weeks.

39 On location for *The Indian Runner*: 'gentleman's gentleman' Dr Katz and Penn

DR KATZ: Then someone wrote in the local newspaper that Sean Penn was here, so now people are driving by. Now Sean had personally shaved my head for my part in the movie. And I'd been a sergeant in infantry, I had the loudest voice. One day, three kids knock on the door. The front door had a peephole. I look out, with my shaved head and bulging eyes . . .

'Is Sean Penn here . . .?'

'DO I LOOK LIKE FUCKEN SEAN PENN?!?'

The expectation had been that Penn and Robin Wright would be forced into a little professional time apart, as she was awaited on the set of Kevin Costner's Robin Hood *in England. But, as it happened, an enormous change of schedule was afoot.*

DAVID MORSE: We were driving around on a scout – we hadn't started shooting yet – and Sean was sitting in the car beside me. But I could see that he had this *thing* going on inside him – he was clearly so excited about something. And with all these other people in the car, he leaned over to me and said, 'I have to say this.' I said, 'What?' And he told me that he and Robin were going to have a child. Such a great thing. He was so thrilled. And I felt like I had been given a gift, that I was someone he wanted to share that with.

40 *The Indian Runner*: Penn directs David Morse (Joe)

ROBIN WRIGHT PENN: So I was in Omaha for most of it, pregnant and very tired. The place was, I'd say, bleak at best. K-Mart was the highlight of the week . . .

DR KATZ: The day before Sean left for Omaha – and after going through all the pains to get the money, all the deals, this and that – he sat down and asked his father, 'How do I direct?'

DAVID MORSE: During the rehearsal period, Sean really encouraged Viggo and myself, and Valeria and Patricia, to spend as much time together as we could, to really blur the lines of our professional relationships and make them more intimate. So we'd go to the county fair as a foursome and so on. We all wanted this authenticity to what we were doing, and the lead was coming from Sean: he really wanted to get this real truthful feeling of being out there in Omaha. He had worked so hard: all the studios having turned the film down, all that he had fought for in getting each of us to be playing these roles. It's just a monumental effort to get to that first day of shooting, and so exciting when you get there. And then, when we saw the first dailies – I can remember how disappointed Sean was, because of the way it looked. And Sean, who had grown up in movies, had never had to crystallize so quickly and decisively what he felt his vision for the style and the imagery of the film should be.

SEAN PENN: A lot of the imagery had been in my head to begin with, sort of a young boy's memories of that period in the sixties: the model and colour car that Patricia Arquette drove was exactly that of the girl across my street in Los Angeles. And I had written the script largely with the lenses in mind, and the movements – subject to change with the actors, but there was a graphic I had pictured. I hired Tony Richmond as DP because I'd spent some time with Nic Roeg, and Nic was very supportive of Tony.3 Also I felt that the sensibility of the movie was rooted in the period during which Tony had shot most of his stuff. But he'd moved on into what, in my view, was a slicker look, from doing a lot of commercials. And when the streets were wet and it hadn't rained . . . I didn't like it. There was a kind of technical demand that I felt was so arbitrary that you had to fight fire with fire. So we sent half the lighting package home, arbitrarily, and said, 'OK, so now what?' We went out with a B-unit and shot some stuff without any light, at very high speeds, then looked at it in dailies, and I was thrilled with it. It made for a muddier, grainier look, which didn't bother me at all – I wanted something a little bit distressed . . .

DAVID MORSE: And you saw over the course of a week that Sean, in a certain way, became the DP on the show. People look at that film and talk about how beautiful it is, the winter images and all that. And I don't want to take anything away from the DP, he was going through a hard time, but Sean really took over what that film was going to be: it was almost a muscular thing in getting in there and trying to turn another person's vision around so it fitted the way he saw it.

---

3 Richmond had shot several pictures for Roeg including *Don't Look Now* (1973), *The Man Who Fell to Earth* (1975), and *Bad Timing* (1980).

DON PHILLIPS: It's a common thing with crews to say, 'First-time director, he don't know what the hell he's doing . . .' And I think, initially,
the crew were a little taken aback that Sean would take his time. Once
he locked in on something, he knew exactly where he wanted the camera, but usually it wasn't where they thought a 'standard' director
would place it. So there was a little bit of animosity between Sean and
the crew on that score. Well, Seanie fucken straightened their asses out
one time. He said, 'Look, boys, it's my movie, I wrote it, I'm directing
it, and if I want to put the camera where I want it, or change my mind
about that later, then I have every right. I have your tickets here,
Southwest Airlines, back to Los Angeles. Anybody who doesn't like
this job and what I'm doing here, I have no hard feelings.' Nobody left.

For the car chase at the end of the movie, Sean decided he wanted to
be on top of the car while it was travelling. So Sean gets up on that
freaking hood, and they strap him in and he's shooting. When a crew
sees that, you know that henceforward they will *die* for him. Sean ended
up buying fifty pigs' ears so that he could practise being a tattoo artist,
and everybody in the crew wanted to get a tattoo on their arm from Sean:
you wouldn't believe the number of electricians, gaffers, grips . . .

DR KATZ: I was the first person he tested on. He gave me a couple . . .

DENNIS HOPPER: Very honestly, if Sean said to me, 'We're all going to
go to Alaska now, and we're just taking T-shirts,' I would go. Simple as
that. So to act in his first movie that he directed was really an honour and
a privilege. And Sean knew exactly what he was doing – he was *there*.

*Where Penn's expertise was taken somewhat more for granted was in
the acting department, where actors might be expected to trust not
only his faith in the characters he had written but also his conviction
about what they themselves could achieve. But Penn had cast boldly,
not only in his largely unfamiliar leads but in the two very different
screen veterans whom he had cast as Mr and Mrs Roberts.*

DAVID MORSE: Gene Hackman was originally going to do it, and then
there was talk of Jon Voight doing it, and it was so exciting to think
about the prospect of those guys: they seemed so right for that story.
Then I remember when Sean told me he was casting Charles Bronson, I
felt like, 'You really want that guy to be playing our father in this movie?'

DON PHILLIPS: Charlie had lost his wife Jill Ireland to cancer; of course,
the father loses his wife to cancer in the movie. And Charlie had lost a

son to a drug overdose, he had a bad seed; and Viggo was playing Frankie, the bad seed.

DAVID MORSE: And I was so . . . *glad*, that this man did this movie. His own experiences, his wife and the son he had lost . . . there was a real *meaning* to him in this movie that some of these other actors might not have found. And he's so touching to me in it.

DON PHILLIPS: When he revisits the little home movies that he made when his sons were boys and starts crying – the world had never seen old tough guy Charlie Bronson cry. And for twenty-five years, Charlie hadn't made a movie without his moustache. Of course, Sean's first phone call to him began, 'Charlie, I've got something very important to ask you –' Charlie said, 'You want me to cut my moustache . . .'

Sandy Dennis was Sean's inspiration for the mother. I said, 'She's always been one of my favourites too, but I understand she's dying of cancer.' He said, 'Well, let me go talk to her.' And that's what he did; he flew to New York, and she agreed. And here she was playing a woman who was dying of cancer. So both she and Charlie had something very similar in their lives if they wanted to expose that. She was a native of Nebraska, so it was like returning and doing her final work at home.

DAVID MORSE: You could see a fragility about her, she obviously wasn't well. But Sandy Dennis was not a fragile presence. She just had a great core to her, the kind I think you only develop after a lifetime of suffering different things. And she and Viggo especially, I loved watching the two of them together – he wrote some poems about her that were beautiful, and they had a relationship that was very nice to watch.

The Indian Runner *unquestionably contained some debt to the kind of American film-making Penn had loved since his days frequenting the Beverly Cinema and the Fox in Venice. But his writing and scene-making were fired with the unmistakable originality that can only be drawn from life. An early scene called for Joe to be confronted by the distraught parents of the young man he has shot and killed. Penn cast his mother and Harry Crews. As Eileen weeps and curses, Crews locks Morse in a baleful gaze – and breaks into an old West Virginian standard, 'The Ballad of John Henry': 'Captain said to John Henry / Gonna bring that steam drill 'round / Bring that steam drill out on the job / Gonna whup that steel on down, Lord, Lord! . . .'*

DON PHILLIPS: Now where does that come from? Your son has just been killed . . . It's genius. And inspired casting.

SEAN PENN: Earlier that year I'd had a sort of musical evening at my house. I'd had a movie idea for Levon Helm and Harry Dean Stanton, a brother story for these guys to play two musicians. And I wanted Harry Crews to get involved, so he flew in and we had a fairly drunken night to see what Levon and Harry were like together. At some point that night, Harry spontaneously broke into 'John Henry'. That was it, it was going to be in *The Indian Runner* . . .

DAVID MORSE: Sean really tried to find the unusual. He was telling a very difficult story in some ways; we were trying to find areas to lighten it up. Life just isn't linear; there are these quirky things that happen in our lives. And I think that's what Sean wanted in the story, these moments that come out of no place.

SEAN PENN: I had always experienced directors for whom their right hand was usually the director of photography. I found myself more inclined to the actors, but Michael Haller was also somebody I deferred a lot to: he deepened what I was after by what he'd put in frame or the questions he would ask of me. Mike wasn't a moviegoer, so his look wasn't based on other movies. He just knew the way he read your story. And it was great to have him really pull the clothes off of ideas I had sometimes.

I grew up in a range of lower-middle class to upper-middle class homes. I think Michael, when he read the script, caught me in a certain resentment for wealthy people that I didn't know was there. I had written that Frank steals a car and intentionally goes into a wealthier neighbourhood to steal it from a rich kid who's having a party; then he uses it to rob a gas station and abandons it by the side of a road. Mike asked me, 'Why does he go to a rich neighbourhood?' I said, '*You* know . . .' And he said, 'Well, if it's resentment towards the rich, why let the rich kids get their car back? Just burn the fucker.' I said, 'Yeah!' And that happened to come at an important time for such a visual in the movie.

JAY CASSIDY: Sean had written a lot of specific songs into the script. And, boy, the Jefferson Airplane song, 'Coming Back to Me' . . . It was scripted, not cut-to-cut, but all the events were there – the car theft, the robbery at the gas station, David Morse awake in bed, Bronson watching his old movies. So we just listened to the song and figured out how to fit its structure to those events. Sean's a poet in terms of his approach to telling stories. And he's not interested in telling the same old story. I mean, *The Indian Runner* is a ballad, really – it's based on a song, right?

The Indian Runner *comes down to a fork in the road: Dorothy is birthing Frank's child, but he sits brooding in the tavern bar owned by Caesar (Dennis Hopper), a joint he has already cleared once before in a bloody punch-up. Joe arrives, tightly coiled and hot, to take him back to bedside; but Frank is too mired in a funk. The world, he's conclud-ed, is like a school math class, where the brightest kid, 'the clown in the front row', forces everyone else to keep up at his pace, regardless of what they have or have not grasped from the lesson. Here as much as anywhere, Penn the reluctant schoolboy was declaring one half of his loyalties in this sibling dispute.*

DAVID MORSE: Do I think Frank and Joe are the two sides of Sean? Just from having known Sean, I would say, yes, I do. And I think there's more than two sides to that coin – if that's possible. Because you've got the edge as well, and then all those little grooves in it . . . When people first meet Sean, what people expect is the Viggo side. What they don't expect is a man who is really compassionate and enthusiastic about the things that he does and his family.

Sean had decided that Viggo and I were going to rehearse for two weeks, but we were only going to rehearse our big scene in the bar. So he had a bar set up in a gymnasium where we could shoot baskets but also really do our work. And during those two weeks, I have a feeling it was harder for Viggo because Sean identified more with that role, and he would really try to push him to do certain things. But Viggo just kept holding back. He never really did the scene in those two weeks.

SEAN PENN: Viggo is, by nature, a very poetic character: he *is* a poet, and a painter. And some of his poetic nature was very good for the part, in the moments of tenderness with Patricia. But I did find that when he was photographed head-to-toe, some of the danger of Frank would go out the door: Viggo's inherent kindness as a guy showed in a sort of languid movement. And that was a lesson for me about what parts of people express themselves without trying. So he did some work with a friend of mine on a certain physicality to try to overcome

41 On location for *The Indian Runner*: Dennis Hopper (Caesar),
Penn, Viggo Mortensen (Frank)

that, so that when I needed an edge in that space from head-to-toe,
there was clear and present danger.

DAVID MORSE: I think Sean was still a little nervous going into the bar
scene. Then I remember a real struggle for what was going to happen,
what the moments were going to be between the two of them. And
something happened, it crystallized, and suddenly Viggo was on fire.

SEAN PENN: I think I stimulated Viggo's temper. And, as I remember, I
think I got a little bit personal. But I think he was professionally
responsive, he knew where to go for what I was looking for. When
you're abusive to an actor, it's one thing – when you're abusive to a
character, it's another. And I think I found it was helpful to both of us
to raise my own tempo a little bit, get in the same place as him, share
the vibe . . .

DAVID MORSE: I felt like there was a real violence also in Joe, a violence
he shared with his brother, but he was able to deal with it in a way that
Frank wasn't. It frustrated me a little bit that Sean didn't want to let it
be seen. But it's probably better for the scene that you don't see it until
Joe cuts his hand open with the broken bottle.

Joe's parting gesture is one of 'blood prejudice', meant to instruct Frank on which side his heart should be beating. It leaves him chastened, but not so much as to make him abandon his bar stool: at least, not before he has beaten Caesar to death with a chair.

DENNIS HOPPER: If you play a small part, it's nice to have a beginning, a middle and an end: that one had a middle and an end, and the end comes very quickly [*laughs*]. I remember rubbing the bar a lot. 'OK, yeah, better get this bar cleaned, man.' And I give a little speech to Viggo's character. And then he kills me.

DAVID MORSE: It was the scene after Frank has killed Dennis Hopper's character, and Joe gets the phone call at their place. Sean had the camera outside the house, shooting me through the window. And right up to that phone call, I was resisting something in the material: I kept fighting the idea that my brother had actually killed somebody, and I'm going to let him go, and he's a murderer. Even saying that *now*, I struggle with it. Because Joe then has some complicity in that murder – and that's quite something to say of someone. You can say it's love, or weakness, whatever; but you don't just let somebody walk away from killing somebody. So I didn't know what to do with that phone call, and I thought, 'If I just do something internal here, you can read whatever you want into it.' Sean didn't want that. Finally he came indoors and said, 'This is bullshit, what you're doing. You've got to *do* something.' So I just had to go with, 'This is terrible information Joe's hearing, and it's killing him.' Finally I had to give over to how Sean felt the story should be. So I look out the window and see Frank in his car, and the car chase begins. But then the last image of Joe seeing Frank as a boy, before he drives away: that was just . . . genius, I thought.

DON PHILLIPS: Sean knew he needed snow for the opening scene, so we had to shut down at Christmas and come back to Omaha two months later. It was a wonderful thing for Sean, because it meant he could edit in the meantime and see what worked and what didn't. And a couple of things didn't work – in fact, they were terrible. So we were able to reshoot certain scenes, and it changed the dynamic of the movie.

JAY CASSIDY: Sean rewrote some stuff to take advantage of what he knew, and it made for a much more efficient first act of the movie. The original script, and what we shot, had a lot more conflict when Frank arrives back and visits his parents. In fact, it was more to the point to have a scene of Frank telling his brother his parents would be relieved if he didn't stop in . . .

Photo by Michael Tighe
Courtesy of Sean Penn

42 *The Indian Runner*: Penn takes charge of make-up for seven-year-old Frank (Brandon Fleck)

Penn would comment upon the film's American release, 'The movie deals with issues that I've been trying to work through and resolve in my own life. One is the question of responsibility. A mature life means responsibility. That in turn means compromise. I've come to recognize compromise as an interesting option.'

DON PHILLIPS: Sean was going to get married to Robin in the shut-down period. They had set the date. But it wasn't the right time. Then one week before, it was like, 'I don't think so . . . We've still got work to do.' And they had to send all the gifts back.

For the purposes of his movie, Penn had persuaded an Omaha couple to admit him to the delivery room at Clarkson Hospital and film the birth of their third child, an obstetrically frank set of images that would stand for Dorothy's labours in the final act. As dumbfounding as this vision must have been for Penn, he had his own share of life's finest moment when, in Los Angeles on 13 April 1991, Robin Wright gave birth to a daughter, Dylan Frances, delivered by Dr William Dignam.

ROBIN WRIGHT PENN: I was very close with Erin and her family right from the get-go, and her dad was really like a surrogate father to me. When it was decided – 'My dad should deliver', 'Of course!' – it was a little bit awkward: 'I know you so well, isn't that weird?' But I wouldn't have had it any other way. He's a saint.

MATT PALMIERI: We were all up at the hospital, and Robin went through a twenty-one-hour ordeal: because she's a very slim, slight girl, and they wanted to do a natural childbirth, without the big needle. We were waiting for ever – ordering pizzas, yakking, sleeping. Finally, they decided they needed to do a C-section. At a certain point, Sean came out, looking a little pale, and whispered to me, 'You wouldn't believe what just happened. Robin looked up at me and asked, "Have they cut me yet?"' And Sean had looked down, and the doctor had his arm all the way inside of her – and he was just speechless. All he could do was nod his head at her and smile weakly . . . It was very sweet of them then that they asked me to be Dylan's godfather. Sean was my best buddy, and I couldn't have been happier to say yes.

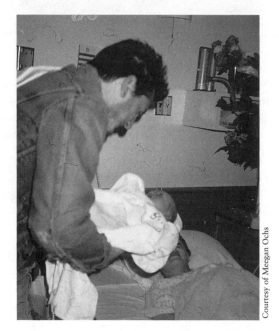

43 April 13 1991: Penn cradles newborn Dylan Frances,
mother in repose

MEEGAN OCHS: Sean called me at 11 o'clock at night and he said, 'She's born, and she's amazing. I really want you to come see her.' I went in the next day. The wild thing about Dylan is that, the day she was born, her mouth was *exactly* Sean's. I just looked at her, thinking, 'My god, here's this little person and she's got your mouth . . .'

JAY CASSIDY: 13 April, we were still on the mixing stage with *Indian Runner*. We had to get it ready for the Cannes Film Festival, so not only did we have to get a finished print, we had to get it subtitled. Sean showed up at the studio the day after Dylan was born, having lived through one of life's great events. And he was ecstatic.

SEAN PENN: I wanted on *The Indian Runner* the billing Writer/ Director, because that's how I was lining up all the credits – Editor: Jay Cassidy, instead of 'Edited By' and so on. I just liked it for the picture. But the Director's Guild would not permit me to *not* use the word 'By'. In the DGA you are guaranteed 'A Film By' if you want it. They told me it's not 'auteurial' enough without the 'By'. I take issue with all this talk. It's like 'Independent Film' – you give me an independent direc- tor, and I don't care how much money he's got or who the distributor is, you get an independent film. But Gene Reynolds said at the arbi- tration, 'Sean, you have to understand, we remember the day when the director was stuck on the same card with the composer.' And I remem- ber some films where the composer should have been up there without the fucken director . . .

JAY CASSIDY: We temped in a lot of blues songs as score for *Indian Runner*, and the composer Jack Nitzsche was just so thrilled when he came in and heard them. 'That's the stuff I grew up on!' So his score came from the same palette. Then David Lindley – fantastic musician – arrived with ten guitars and sat there and played. Springsteen had allowed Sean to make *The Indian Runner*, and the deal was such that if he didn't like the final film, it couldn't have the 'Inspired by . . .' credit. So there came the moment when we finished the film and showed it to him. And he liked it . . .

DON PHILLIPS: We took *Indian Runner* to Cannes and had a great time, Sean and Charlie Bronson and I. The film got an unbelievable recep- tion – the ovation was maybe seven or eight minutes, the French audi- ence just clapping and pounding their feet on the floor. Then Sean got up on the stage and said, 'Now I know what it feels like to be Jerry Lewis . . .'

Madonna was at Cannes with *Truth or Dare*, in which she says that Sean is the love of her life . . . She had already had her première, but she had stayed on. One night there was a big party – typical Cannes, everybody was there: De Niro, Stevie Wonder, Mick Jagger. We had a section roped off, we're sitting on a couch – me, Sean, Thom Mount, Charlie. All of a sudden, out of nowhere, the bodyguards stand aside, and *she* comes bursting through the ropes. She's in a silk dress, and she tries to jump onto Sean's lap. Sean kind of jumped away. But everything in that place stopped. Of course, the papers the next day are all, 'They met! They danced all night! They were in each other's arms!' And it was brutally wrong.

Indian Runner didn't do a lot of business: it did a hell of a lot more in Europe than it did in America. But it got rediscovered on cable. And Cannes even brought it back in 2001 for a special screening on its tenth anniversary.

DAVID RABE: I was very taken by *The Indian Runner*, the boldness of it and the lack of convention – some of which I guess I felt was slightly more than workable. But it has great scenes, and it was raw and daring – and lyrical at the same time.

DENNIS HOPPER: That movie's just really, truly wonderful. I feel *Indian Runner* is a masterpiece. I just think it's one of the great movies.

JOHN BYRNE: I went to see it in Glasgow and I was expecting it to be good, but I wasn't expecting *that*. It was shockingly good. I thought it was the most intelligent film I'd seen in years. For a début, a first feature, sure – but then for somebody to come up with that at *any* time in their career . . .

Come the summer of 1991, Robin Wright returned to work from her pregnancy for Gillies Mackinnon's The Playboys, *playing a headstrong single mother in rural fifties Ireland. Husband and infant were also in attendance on location.*

ROBIN WRIGHT PENN: Dylan was only about six weeks old and we took off, and that was really rough – your first child, it's a whole new life, you're just unsure. You're thinking, 'A *nanny* . . .?' So it was a difficult time and a great experience at the same time. We shot in Redhill, near the Irish border, County Cavan, stayed at the Slieve Russell. But Sean's always doing something, he can't stay in one place too long without being productive or doing his own work – he wouldn't be a good housewife, you know what I'm saying? He is pedal-to-the-metal in the brain, all the time.

SEAN PENN: I was working on *The Knockout Artist* – not fruitfully. It was a *bear* of a time adapting someone else's novel, especially one that I loved; I wanted it *all*. And to get 120 pages, I wrote 800. Harry Crews is a tall-tale teller, and what on his page has the sleight of hand to avoid archness in, say, a villain – every moment I wrote was like a sting on the score. And I just couldn't beat it.

MATT PALMIERI: I had quit my job at MGM at the same time and went to visit my girlfriend in Paris, but I would regularly escape to Dublin to meet up with Sean where he was spending a lot of time while Robin worked. We'd hang with Jim Sheridan and his brother Peter, and Bono and The Edge. We'd have dinner with them and great parties at Bono's house in Dalkey.

BONO: This was one of the smaller of the big nights. Guinness and whiskey . . . I think we might have been talking about *Iron John*, Robert Bly: certainly, intellectually, we were running up and down Killiney Hill in the nude, but all in the safe confines of my gaff. Sean started reciting poems. And when men start reciting poetry to each other, there can only be two things going on . . . this one was definitely drink. But he had some pretty good poems up his sleeve. And he knew I loved Bukowski's work: I'd always been a patron of the City Lights bookstore, and I'd discovered Bukowski from those shelves. Then Sean asked to use the phone.

SEAN PENN: I called Hank, said, 'You know who Bono is?' And I hear Hank: '*Linda?* You know somebody called *Bone-o?*'

BONO: Sean came back, said, 'There's somebody on the phone for you.' I said, 'It's five in the morning, who'd be calling me?' I pick up the phone. 'Heyyyy, Bono. Hank Bukowski here. I just want to put you on to my wife Linda here, I think she wants to, ah, *fuck* you.' Turns out, far from anything untoward, she's a very elegant woman, used to her husband's ways, and she had been to every U2 show in Los Angeles. We talked and had a laugh, agreed to meet up at some point in the future . . .

MATT PALMIERI: Sean and I took some trips, one to Amsterdam with Peter Sheridan. They'd been talking about doing a Brendan Behan film together. We got a penthouse in a great old hotel right on the canal and ventured out into the city for some fun. We very quickly found it at

The Ritz, a huge, cavernous rock 'n' roll/performance-art club. It's filled with every walk of life in every conceivable form of unusual dress. The music's blasting, we're partying it up – when all of a sudden a full-on stage act starts. A transsexual, dressed and made-up like Madonna, comes onstage with dancers, starts singing 'Like a Virgin' at the top of his/her lungs, and commences to go at it with a big black dildo – and I mean *go at it*. And we're looking at each other like, 'Who set this up? Did *you* do this . . .?'

But Peter was fascinated, and he went and talked with them afterwards. And we end up going back to the Madonna impersonator's tiny, grubby little flat in a tenement on the outskirts of Amsterdam, sitting on grungy couches with nine transvestites, drinking and smoking pot. And Sean proceeded – as only Sean can – to get them to discuss sexual politics and Reaganomics, while I sat in the corner, drunk and dumbfounded, shaking my head . . .

For all his nocturnal enthusiasms, Penn had felt the great shift wrought by parenthood: as he told Playboy, *'You find out you don't want the night so much. . .'*

MATT PALMIERI: I saw in Sean the classic change, which is that his priorities became that child, and that child only. All of a sudden, there was somebody in the world who was far more important to him than he was to himself.

MEEGAN OCHS: Dylan was, I guess, about seven or eight months old, and just getting to the point where she was pulling herself up on her feet. Now, when I worked for him, Sean used to be the cootie freak of the world: incredibly concerned about germs. At a party, he wouldn't eat dips – he was cootie-phobic. I was over at the house in Malibu, and it had a courtyard in the middle. Dylan was inside and pulling herself up against the glass of the window. She had her mouth up against it. And Sean sees her and goes running up to the other side, where his dogs and the elements have been – we're talking a dirty, dirty window. And he pressed his hands up against her tiny little hands, and kissed the glass where her mouth was – and this glass is so filthy that most anybody would be grossed out, never mind Sean the Extreme Cootie Man. But he was just kissing and kissing, totally oblivious to it, because he was kissing Dylan through the glass. And I'm thinking, 'OK, the man has *changed* . . . '

NINE

1992–1994

I'll have to use a strange term here . . . 'good'. I don't know where it comes from, but I feel that there's an ultimate strain of goodness born in each of us. I don't believe in God, but I believe in this 'goodness' like a tube running through our bodies. It can be nurtured. It's always magic, when on a freeway packed with traffic, a stranger makes room for you to change lanes . . . it gives you hope.

Charles Bukowski interviewed by Sean Penn, *Interview*, September 1987

The new father and former actor had spent two years in the role of 'director of The Indian Runner'. *His creative energies were now devoted to finding a follow-up. But in March 1992, he permitted himself a near-surreptitious furlough from his self-imposed acting ban, albeit two days in service to his oldest friend.*

MATT PALMIERI: I decided to direct a short film, a total labour-of-love project. I asked Sean to act in it, and he said, 'Sure.' It's a little parable about the eighties: Ed Begley Jr plays a junior bank executive from LA – basically a thoughtless, self-involved bastard – who has to go out and foreclose on some poor family's house way out in the desert. As he's driving, he sees an armadillo crawling across the highway and runs it over, at which point his car breaks down. He's picked up by this wacky tow-truck driver, Max Perlich, and they motor off to a dirty, broken-down service station manned by Harry Dean and Sean, the grungiest car mechanics in the history of the American desert . . .

We were going to shoot out past Lancaster, so we all drove to a hotel the night before. It just happened the first day of shooting was going to be my birthday: 7 March 1992. So I say, 'We all ought to hit the hay, we've got a 6 a.m. call.' Sean says, 'Fuck that – it's your birthday. You're staying up *allll* night . . . Bartender? Drinks!' And we proceeded to down shots 'til the sun came up. At 5.30 a.m., we get into our separate cars and race each other through the desert at a hundred-plus miles an hour, the sun rising in front of us. We come screeching

Courtesy of Matt Palmieri

44 *Cruise Control*: Matt Palmieri (writer/director), Harry Dean Stanton,
Penn, Max Perlich

into location all at once, power-sliding our various cars, with the crew all shaking their heads, saying, 'Boy, this is gonna be an interesting one . . .'

And it was. We shot for two very full days and, somehow, we got great stuff. It cut together nicely, people liked it and it got nominated for an Academy Award. It might seem irresponsible to some that Sean would get me trashed the night before shooting, but I think he had a plan: he kind of knew that I was really nervous about my first directing, and that if he made me party all night, I would lose that and be open and ready. And working with my old pal, seeing him do what he does up close, was a great experience. He had fake teeth and he contorted his face . . . The night we premièred the film, Eileen came, and at a certain point into it, she turned to me, annoyed, and said, 'Matt, I thought Seanie was in this movie, that's why I came!' I pointed at the funny-looking guy on the screen and said to her, 'That's your boy Seanie right there, Eileen, standing next to Harry Dean, holding the dead armadillo . . .'

Penn and Robin Wright had made home in Carbon Canyon, though neither was in regular residence. In the spring, Wright reported to the set of Barry Levinson's Toys. *Penn would presently take out a second address.*

JOSEPH VITARELLI: Robin and Sean were living in the Malibu house for a while, but that probably wasn't such a good idea. It wasn't going to work, Robin was not going to live in that house. And who could blame her? Sean and Madonna had lived there . . .

ROBIN WRIGHT PENN: I had it blessed: California spiritual cleansing or whatever. I don't know if that shit works [*laughs*] but I did it anyway. They told me, 'Oh, you can rid the spirits with sage . . .' I said, 'OK, fucken rid 'em . . .'

After the euphoria and wonder of fatherhood, the inevitable onset of new and equally profound anxieties: such was the germ of the project Penn settled upon as his next assignment.

DAVID BAERWALD: It was that parental fear: it became apparent once he was a parent that he had parental fear – to go all Cole Porter on you for a second . . . It's especially so for many men: you grow up and you try to create an invulnerability in your life, and in Sean's case, he became rather successful at it – which is not to say he's immune to suffering. But then when a child enters the picture, it opens this whole universe of unbelievable dread.

SEAN PENN: It so happened that around that time Eric Clapton's child had died.[1] And it was in all the newspapers. And it sort of clicked with me that I wanted to write about that, as sort of an exorcism of my own newfound concerns. The *Crossing Guard* script took no time: thirty days. Robin and I were in a split. I was writing in a little apartment by the beach in Malibu and also a room at the Bel Age hotel. And I think I probably put fifteen days in at each location. I then worked on it after that, but I was ready to go at that point.

The Crossing Guard *opens up on Freddy Gale, a divorced middle-aged jeweller, sodden with booze and bad company, bent upon avenging the accidental death of his little daughter Emily five years previously. John Booth, the drunken driver responsible, is due to be released into the community, and Freddy is nursing a pistol and counting the days.*

---

1 On 20 March 1991, at 11 a.m., four-and-a-half-year-old Conor Clapton died when he fell from a fifty-third-storey window in a New York City apartment.

Freddy's ex-wife Mary, remarried and prospering, is angered and sad-dened to hear him threaten Booth's life. Nevertheless, on the night Booth returns to a trailer parked in his parents' suburban driveway, Freddy bursts in and is twice taken aback: first by the want of a clip in his gun, second by Booth's calm and penitent request that his life be spared. Freddy, disconcerted, issues a warning that he will return in three days.

SEAN PENN: I originally ended the piece with Freddy getting arrested for drunk-driving. It was laziness, really – I got to page sixty and thought, 'Wow, what a great ironic end if this guy is after the other guy for drunk-driving, then he's drunk-driving on his way to kill him and gets pulled over. Leave 'em with that . . .' Then I thought, 'But it's only sixty pages long . . .' So I kept going.

DAVID MORSE: Sean had no problem writing Freddy, but he was much less sure of who Booth was. So he'd keep sending it to me and asking for my ideas. My feeling was this is a guy who had to survive in prison having committed a crime that every guy in there would want to kill him for. And it either broke him or he got stronger for it. I figured it was more interesting if it was the latter. He still can't forgive himself for what he's done. Unfortunately, he was drunk; but I know I've had experiences in my life where I'm fortunate a similar thing didn't hap-pen. So I felt a real sympathy for Booth. And Sean's word for that film was 'compassion'.

DAVID RABE: I remember reading the script, feeling for sure as I read it that the hammer was going to fall on somebody. And so the final rec-onciliation between the two men was so powerful, really remarkable stuff: I felt such a pleasure in Sean's decision not to have them kill one another at the moment. That felt like a maturing, in terms of how he could view the human complexities: that these two guys could be on this course but then end up unable to play out that simple violence, which is so easy – most movies, that's *all* they want to do.

SEAN PENN: I'm a sort of anti-psychiatry person – I've never known anybody to get *better*. There's a natural tendency to deal with things in ways that are active. Rage is active, but that doesn't help. New-age spirituality is active, and full of crap. So where's the balance? When we made the film, we dealt with a group, Mothers Against Drunk Driving, people who had lost children that way. And one thing they told me was that denial had a bad rap. That struck me. If you say that a piece of lead between the eyes can kill you, but something like the loss of your child can't . . .? I think you would literally die if there wasn't any denial. So denial is part of the camp of survival instincts, as is fear – fear is a necessary thing. But does fear stop you from entering doorways, or does it make you conscious of the need to enter that doorway?

If Penn's new project was conspicuously the vision of a new parent, it was not the only product of these new and taxing circumstances. Not previously a full-blown political animal, he had begun to appreciate the truth in the maxim, 'If you don't do politics, politics will do you . . .'

SEAN PENN: Shortly after my daughter was born, I found I was looking at the world in a new way: you start looking beyond your own life time. I started sponsoring some political lectures in Los Angeles, and one of the guys I ended up with was Craig Hulet. He anticipated the riots that would follow the verdict in the Rodney King case.

DAVID BAERWALD: Sean and I made a trip to San Francisco to hear him speak, and he made the hairs stand up on the back of your neck: a very effective fear-monger and rabble-rouser. He had a lot of shocking information about this or that. The stuff that got me scared most was about the breadth and extent of the Emergency War Powers Act, and how easy that would be to reimplement. I had a natural concern about the increasing police state in the US, and this seemed like a road-map for that. And some of that data fed into *Triage*.[2]

The world had seen the eighty-one-second video recording, made by a concerned citizen on 3 March 1991, of LAPD officers beating intoxicated black motorist Rodney King with batons. A Simi Valley jury of eleven Caucasians and one Filipino found those officers not guilty of excessive force. By early evening of 30 April 1992, Southeast and South Central Los Angeles were convulsed by rioting, arson, looting and shooting.

ERIN DIGNAM: When the riots happened, I saw on the news that all the markets had been looted and burned down there – people couldn't

2 Baerwald's brilliant second solo album, released in 1993.

even get stuff for their kids. I was with my five-year-old niece and I said, 'Let's go down to the market and ask people to give Pampers.' We put 'em in a truck, drove down to South Central – and there was nobody white to be seen, but who did I run into . . .?

SEAN PENN: I was living out at the little apartment in Malibu, didn't have a television, but I got a phone call from a friend telling me that riots had started. So I got in my car and I went down to South Central – and got a shopping cart thrown through my windshield . . .

I had the radio on, and on my way into 'the ghetto', as it were, I could see about twenty different fires, including one in a shopping centre. It looked a *lot* worse than what was being reported. And I didn't see a lot of outsiders around, so this was clearly going to be implosive to the people who lived in these communities.

I could feel things were getting too heavy, and I turned the car around. I stopped at a red light; there were three cars in front of me and a guy with a shopping cart going across. Then the guy just lifted up the cart and whacked the hood of the first car: he looked like he was just enjoying the chaos. The light changed, and the second car starts honking, so the guy with the cart comes back and hits *his* car too. The guy in front of me drives around and away. I'm still sitting there, and now the guy is coming towards me with his cart. I had a gun in the car, under my thigh. When he lifted the cart, I pointed the gun through the windshield at him. He had no reaction whatever: just threw the shopping cart through my windshield at me. It smashed the glass and bounced back off my hood: broken glass everywhere. He started coming round to the passenger-side door. I followed him with the gun, and the whole time he was looking at me with no concern whatsoever that this white guy was – even in fear – gonna shoot him. He's looking at me out of curiosity, almost. So I drove off, back into town. And my car was a kind of trophy from what was going on ten miles behind . . .

I immediately called Craig Hulet, said, 'Get down here.' Because there was unquestionably going to be a lot of live television going on, and I thought it would be very interesting to get his views expressed. He agreed to get on a plane right away. I wasn't interested in being another actor with a political viewpoint, but I did think I could help get this guy interviewed, because these riots could have been anticipated for all kinds of reasons. The next day, he and I headquartered at the Dufy Hotel. And we would go each day to wherever there were fires, wherever it was happening, and try to get him on news shows and so on: we were mildly successful – he did speak on the *Arsenio* show, the same one that Mayor Bradley went on.

Then a funny thing happened: Jerry Brown came to town, campaigning for President. Oliver Stone called and invited me to a function for him. I went with Hulet to Jerry Brown's campaign headquarters, introduced them, and they had a conversation about the riots.3 And then Mikhail Gorbachev came to town, representing his Gorbachev Foundation. He was going to speak and try to raise funds for medicine. Oliver invited me to come along with a bunch of, let's say, more successful Hollywood people than me, who had a history of leftist beliefs, who were going to meet at the Downtown Biltmore with Gorbachev and his wife and his translator. And me . . .

I asked Gorbachev a question that wasn't answered. In the former Soviet Union, he had taken the progressive ideal for all it was worth, with the least amount of violence. And he had sort of insinuated that what we needed in this country was a relative *perestroika*. I said, 'You had those agendas. But in the United States, we have a human and sovereign ideal at one end, the progressive; and a human and sovereign ideal at the other end, the conservative. But at their core they're divided by a corporate ideal that seems to have no regard for humanity *or* sovereignty, in most cases. How did that affect your dealings with Reagan and the United States?' He didn't answer the question and turned, I think, to Barbra Streisand and continued to answer her question about his favourite Hollywood musicals, or something like that. So I remember leaving there feeling it had been very interesting, but very disappointing that he didn't even acknowledge my question. I went back to the Dufy, and as I passed the desk, they told me I had a message: 'Mr Gorbachev called . . .'

So I called back, and got an A&R guy at Capitol Records who I had worked with on the soundtrack for *The Indian Runner*: they were the local corporate sponsor of the Gorbachev Foundation event. I said, 'Hi, I was calling for Mr Gorbachev.'

'Oh, Sean, you just missed him. And he was so impressed with your spirit, and he didn't feel that he'd fully answered your question. And

3 Brown, the most left-leaning Democrat in the 1992 field, would later address the riots in terms of the socio-economic contexts of increasing 'globalization' and falling working-class wages.

he'd love to see your movies.'

Well, it did strike me that nobody thought the movies I'd made could be translated into Russian, and he wasn't going to watch me in English. And he hadn't only 'not fully answered my question', he hadn't answered it at all.

So I said, 'Well, where's he going next?'

'He's going to San Francisco.'

'How's he getting there?' It wasn't long after he'd left office, and I couldn't picture him getting on United Airlines.

'He's taking a private jet.'

I'm thinking that's pretty expensive – and he's out here trying to raise money.

'Whose jet?'

'Exxon's.'

Well, I don't know what that story tells, except that you use their money if you can get medicine for your people; and it doesn't do you any good to spit in their eye by informing some leather-jacket-wearing actor in Hollywood of your own true feelings about some of the ways in which Corporate America and global banking affects a lot of choices made. Nonetheless, it was probably a boot in the butt for me to get up and pay attention. And then, down the road, there would be certain times when I just felt I had to do or say something . . .

In the autumn of 1992, U2, riding a return to creative and commercial splendour with the Achtung Baby *album, rolled out their hi-tech 'Zoo TV' tour through the US. As they reached Los Angeles in October 1992, the moment came to make good on a pledge.*

SEAN PENN: Bono called me: 'We're playing Dodger Stadium. Will you bring the Bukowskis?' 'Absolutely.' Robin and I got a limousine, picked up Harry Dean, went down to San Pedro, picked up Hank and Linda, drove to the stadium. And we were on the sound desk in the middle of the place, able to drink and smoke, whatever we wanted. Hank had never been to a rock concert in his life. But the *size* of it, and the devotion of all these people to the performers onstage . . . and all of a sudden Bono comes out to a spotlight and says, 'This is for Charles and Linda Bukowski.'

BONO: And I got Larry Mullen to sing 'Dirty Old Town' for him, the Ewan McColl song. And Bukowski, I think he would have *liked* to have scoffed at rock, you know . . . but he couldn't get the grin off his face. Afterwards, he robbed Helena Christensen's seat and there was a bit of a row: she didn't know who he was – and she had a copy of one of his books in her bag at the table. And there was another accident with Axl Rose, one of those nights . . . but he was loving it. And Sean was enjoying how things had worked out, and I was very pleased to be introduced to him. I owe Sean for that.

SEAN PENN: So we drank and talked and stayed until about 3 o'clock in the morning. Then we told Hank it was time to go, said goodnight to Bono and the guys, got in the car. Then, as we're on our way home:

'Sean Penn – *faggot*. You *faggot*. I always *knew* you were a faggot . . .'

Basically, whatever it took not to say, 'Thank you for the night . . .'

We get to the house in San Pedro, open the car door: Hank can't get out. So Harry and I grab an arm each. He's *drrrunk*. We go to the front door, he screams, 'Look, Linda, what he's doing! They're touching me. Harry, you should know better!'

I looked at Linda. 'Should we let him go?'

'Guess so.'

'You all right, old timer?'

Harry and I let loose his arms, we turn to walk back to the car. And we hear this 'pop!' behind us. He'd gone right down on his head, deep red blood coming out. I run back, pick him up. We carry him in to the couch, I run to the kitchen, get a wet rag, run back. His eyes are closed. I straddle him and press the rag to his head. His eyes open. He sees me straddling him . . .

'He's a *faggot*! Goddamn it, get off of me! Linda!'

Now he's conscious. He should have gone to the emergency room, but Linda got him upstairs, we left, dropped Harry Dean on Mulholland Drive, and got back at dawn. There was a message showing on the phone. I pressed the button.

'*Heyyyyy*, kid. *Great* night . . .'

* * *

SEAN PENN: I was going to do *The Crossing Guard* originally with Harvey Keitel and David Morse. The idea was to shoot it 16mm, handheld. Then things changed. Harvey was going through a very difficult time; the film wasn't going to be his primary focus, and it had to be, so we parted ways. I soon thereafter went to Jack Nicholson, and he gave me an answer really fast. You know, in so many ways, if there's been an angel on my shoulder in the movie business, it's been Jack. I was at the Bel Age, and I got a call from him saying, 'I'm in.'

JACK NICHOLSON: Sean had mentioned that he was writing, and then he gave me the script, and that's all it took.

People tend to look at Sean's movies as darker than they're intended. This was a story about forgiveness, in a kind of *extreme* way, and I liked that – I liked the relenting of vengeance in this extreme man; and then the counter-story, the man who's trying to save his own life and doesn't know if he has a right to: the way that John Booth kind of accepts the situation, and looks Freddy in the eye, and eventually leads him to a catharsis. It's a terribly powerful, poignant story, a very human situation, and a lot of scenes dealt with awkward, unusual juxtapositions of characters. And one of the things about Sean's scripts is that they're not overly plotted: there's room for air and interesting direction for behaviour. You know that you're going to get to do some *acting* – the kind of acting that you like to do . . .

Plus, I wanted to work with Sean. He hadn't acted for a long time. I knew he was very dedicated to getting another chance to direct, and I thought I was possibly in a position to give him a leg-up. I liked *The Indian Runner*. And this was a very unusual story – probably not destined to be a commercial success. But I was in a moment when I didn't think that was important. Having maybe dropped the ball myself on my own directing aspirations, I always felt as an actor that I would be helpful to directors – because pretty much anything off-centre needs support to get it going.

SEAN PENN: It then took a long time to get financed even after that, because we were talking about difficult subject matter and the complexities of Jack's deal, despite his willingness to make things easier on us. One of the studios wanted to try to take advantage by setting a new precedent on a back end: 'OK, now Jack's committed to a smaller movie, maybe we can reduce Jack's deal in the future . . .' And that wasn't going to get by Jack. He only wanted what was fair, and what was fair with Jack is a *lot*, because of what the movie then means to their video collection and so on. So we danced a lot with the studio before we finally came back to Harvey Weinstein. It took us a year. And part of that was also waiting for Jack to fulfil a commitment to

Mike Nichols. For a while Jack had a slot that was either gonna be *Crossing Guard* or *Wolf*. Once it was *Wolf*, we had to wait.

In the course of the wait came glad and unexpected tidings: Robin Wright was once again pregnant. For all his efforts to plough a clear creative furrow behind the camera, Penn was now facing a set of personal and professional circumstances suggestive of the need for a return to his principal mode of gainful employment.

SEAN PENN: I hadn't worked as an actor for four years. And that was entirely intentional. But I ran out of dough – I had a kid now and bills to pay. Then I get a late-night call from Brian De Palma. There was money. I certainly was interested in working with Al Pacino. And I'd had a very good relationship with Brian on *Casualties of War*.

Carlito's Way was based on a pair of novels by New York judge Edwin Torres and concerned the efforts of Puerto Rican ex-convict Carlito Brigante (Pacino) to get out and fly straight in New York, those efforts rendered nigh impossible by the dangerous shenanigans of his defence lawyer Dave Kleinfeld, a stupendously coked-out shyster who has placed himself in deep water with the Mafiosi goons he previously and lucratively defended. Kleinfeld draws Brigante first into co-ownership and management of a nightclub, then into the foolhardy killing of an imprisoned Don. This was the kind of frankly unsympathetic character part Penn could eat alive.

DR KATZ: I asked Sean, 'Did you like the script? You're not whoring yourself out?' He said, 'No, it's a good script.' And Al Pacino had just won the Academy Award, and it was going to be a year before he directed Jack Nicholson. I said, 'This is great, it'll get rid of your bad-boy image: you act with Pacino, then you direct Nicholson.'

SEAN PENN: And I thought I could do something with the character. I was worried, in this case, about the operatic, because we were on more familiar territory to me here than *Casualties of War*, in terms of the story and the environment. I had long talks with Brian about it. I think he's a bold film-maker, and I really had an extraordinary time with him the first time round. But what I can say is that when we sat down for *Carlito's Way*, it seemed to me – I say respectfully – that he was looking to make a raw picture: to make one really raw picture. Then I remember stepping into the set of the nightclub that Carlito owns a gigantic chunk of. Well, these characters were based on real guys, and I had gone around New York with them, and I had seen the real place – which was about the size of my den, in a shitty part of town, with a beat-up parquet dance floor with sawdust on it. And what I walked into was a place *twenty-two times* the size of my den, flashing lights through a glass floor, high ceilings, probably a $5-million set. Carlito just got out of prison and he's supposed to own two thirds of this – how'd he pull that one off?

And that maintained: very difficult, very complex moving shots through twelve hundred extras before the camera arrives at you – so, God knows, when we got it, we *got* it, don't ask for another take. The emphasis was in those areas. And I felt a little duped. And that created tension.

ART WOLFF: Sean's choices for that role – how he dressed, and the red curly hair and the glasses he wore – those were more than just props to add a finishing touch . . .

SEAN PENN: I was looking through period stuff, articles on lawyers, just going to the library and researching. I looked and looked for something that struck right with the words. And then I saw it. It was a still photograph of a young law student from *Life* magazine. And I said to myself, 'Aw fuck. I'm gonna go round New York like *this* for four months? OK, here we go . . .' I wore a baseball cap every day after work. Looked like Bozo the Clown, though, fucken frizzy red hair sticking out all sides . . .

Photo by Louis Goldman. Courtesy of Sean Penn
© Universal Studios

45 *Carlito's Way*: Al Pacino (Carlito Brigante), Penn (David Kleinfeld)

DR KATZ: That bothered him when he looked in the mirror: he'd whine about his fucking hair. I had to give him his reality checks every now and again. I said, 'Sean, there are guys married with two children who drive two hours to work every day, two hours home; they hate their job, their wife's probably fucking the garbage man, and they have hair like that all their lives. You have it for ten weeks; and you're gonna make more in ten weeks than they're going to make in a lifetime. So I think you can live with the receding hairline, don't you?' And he agreed.

SEAN PENN: Alan Dershowitz threatened a defamation case against us. I'd never thought of him. What was funny was that I had in my script, the whole time I was shooting, the still photograph of the law student that I took the look from. And I couldn't *wait* to get to court and show this photo and call all the witnesses who knew I'd had it since the first rehearsal: because, other than that, Dershowitz is looking at that character's corruption and saying, 'That looks just like *me* . . .'

I had a tremendous time with Al. He's like the least dependent actor. There's nothing you're gonna do that's gonna fuck him up: he'll just go with it . . .

DR KATZ: Sean likes his pranks . . . Al Pacino had an affair with Penelope Ann Miller, and she went public. Sean sent me to Barnes and Noble, said, 'Find me a coffee-table book about Spencer Tracy and Katharine Hepburn.' And he had me put it in Al Pacino's trailer, with a note: 'Do you think this could be us one day . . .?'

Sean would later tell a festival audience that he never saw the completed Carlito's Way. *From its self-conscious set pieces to its hope-dashing finale, it was unmistakably* un film de De Palma, *if not the one Penn had first imagined. But his performance was roundly hailed, and he would receive a Golden Globe nomination for Best Supporting Actor in January 1994.*

SEAN PENN: While I was shooting *Carlito's*, I was called by an agent at CAA. He said, 'We're representing this girl, Shania Twain. We'd like you to do a video for her.' I watched the first video she'd done. She was a star, I saw that – that was easy. It was an opportunity to go to Nashville and sit with a quote unquote 'country artist'. And I had always wondered what was up with country music . . . So I committed to do it as soon as I wrapped. And I didn't come away with enormous answers, but I liked her very much: a nice person who had gone through a lot in life. She clearly had all the goods professionally, as a performer, though it still took some years after that for her to break. And, no, I had no romantic relationship with her: I was very much with Robin at the time. And Shania had no attraction whatsoever to me. None. I'd like to think that was in part because I still had the red muff from *Carlito's* . . . Sweet woman. . .

On 6 August 1993 Robin Wright gave birth to her and Penn's second child, a boy. Dr William Dignam once again delivered the baby.

DENNIS HOPPER: Sean was going to name his first child Hopper, and then he had a girl. And so he told me his first *son*, he was going to name Hopper. But by then he was working with Jack on *The Crossing Guard*. So he named the boy Hopper Jack.

ROBIN WRIGHT PENN: Hopper was our second happy accident . . . And then I went off to do *Forrest Gump*. I was so anxious to work after almost a year, I was chomping at the bit come my ninth month. My mother said, 'How can you up and go right after you have a kid?' But I needed to. And we worked it out, but that was a rough time, with two little kids. I worked all over the place with that movie, a long shoot. And Sean was scouting for *Crossing Guard* and needing to be home.

DON PHILLIPS: We starting casting *The Crossing Guard* in a lovely office out in Malibu, and we had been going for maybe a month. It was November 1993. And then the fires came.

JOSEPH VITARELLI: Some idiot in Calabasas dropped a cigarette or something – there was a rumour of arson. But you get that dry brush, and it's lethal.

SEAN PENN: I was on the Santa Ana Freeway, coming back from scouting Chino Prison. I could see smoke from the freeway and I just had a feeling – my house was burning: I turned on the radio and yes, indeed, Malibu was on fire. Knowing where I lived, I knew our place would likely end up in the route. So I got out there, and it was a mess. The flames were just coming over the top of my hill. But I'd been in fires in Malibu before that, and I thought I had a sense of things. So I put the dogs in the truck, and some other stuff, and then I thought I had some time. I was in the kitchen on the phone to Robin in Washington: 'It looks bad, this thing's gonna go. What should I get?' All the things on her list I got. And then I could see the dogs through the kitchen window, I saw they were getting smoked out, and *that* made me run out to the truck: 'Gotta get these dogs out of here.' And had I not done that then, I'd have been in big trouble – because, literally, as I pulled down the hill, what looked like a lot of smoke then turned into a lot of fire, twice the height of the house. Normally, fires don't burn very fast downhill – this one *screamed* downhill at about 40 miles an hour. A fire truck was destroyed on my driveway within ten minutes of my leaving.

I screeched down to the bottom of the hill and all my neighbours were there. They asked me, 'How does it look?' And my feeling was that everybody's house was gonna go. We all went onto the Highway and made the left, and it was like newsreel of the exodus from Saigon: horns blaring, nobody moving. And cars were catching fire, because the flames were jumping the highway. But there was some organization, though we didn't know it, in that firemen were watching from the sky and holding traffic where they thought they could get away with it, so as to get people out of hot zones ahead of us. And it seemed like enough of an open-air place that we'd be alright. But it was heavy, really heavy . . .

I came into town, and it was on the news that my house was gone. But still, you never knew: they were also saying Charlie Bronson's house was gone, and that was not true. Malibu was now an emergency zone, and they weren't going to let anybody back in there who had left, but we came back up that night. Dennis Fanning badged our way in. And the only thing up there was flames shooting out of bent metal pipes from gas lines that hadn't been shut off. I had a stucco house, and there was nothing left. Nothing. It had really burned hot . . .

I went over the grounds that night with a flashlight. My daughter's bedroom was the last room I had spent any time in 'cause I went in there to get her drawings from nursery school. I'd taken one last look at her bed, which was brass, with little animals on the four corners. And now I was thinking, 'Where did *that* go?' I swept the dust away on the terracotta-tile flooring of the house, and there were these splash marks, like silver paint. And that's what was left of that bed. Metal, plastic, wood, concrete – everything was dust. It was over.

If I had not got the videotapes of the kids out of there, it would have

been heartbreaking. But I did. I got a box of Robin's early photographs, which was pretty much the only one she had. There were
paintings of George Yepes, the first painter I ever collected – I was his
museum at that point: beautiful stuff, including an original that
became a Los Lobos record cover, tango-dancing skeletons with hearts
inside.4 And I couldn't get those. So I feel terrible for George that that
stuff went. But that aside . . . I mean, there's something nice that I
don't get in that conversation of, 'Sean, you really have to get your
archives together. You know that picture that's yellowing? You need to
put that in a frame . . .' I don't have any of that stuff to worry about.
The kids weren't attached to the place, so I wasn't worried about
them. They were so young, by the time they'd spent two days in
Washington, the hotel was like their new house. And Robin never
liked the place, so I wasn't worried about her.

ROBIN WRIGHT PENN: It was always a running joke, 'Oh, how devastating that the house burned down . . .' And what I truly felt was: it
was a terrible floor plan anyway, really bass-ackward. This incredible
view of the Pacific Coast with canyon surrounding you, and there was
one room you could see the ocean from . . . That house never worked.
But I never felt it was my house anyway.

DON PHILLIPS: I swear to you, the next day, Sean had to go out and buy
underwear and socks and shirts. He had nothing. And he took it like
a man.

   We moved the offices from Malibu to Culver City and finished casting there. Nicholson was in place. Sean said to me, 'What about
Anjelica for his ex-wife?' I said, 'Boy, she'd be perfect. But given their
history, do you think she'd do it?' Sean said, 'Well, I'll ask Jack.' Jack
has a nickname for everybody; he calls Anjelica 'Toots'. And he said,
'If Toots wants to do it, I have no problems.' And she was now married to Robert Graham and very happy in her life.

ANGELICA HUSTON: Jack and I had split up some two or three years
previous. So for me, it was . . . well, it was a choice [*laughs*]. There are
a couple of things you can do with bad endings: you can try to remake
them a little or you can put them away. But one of the blessings of
what I do for a living is that it can be very cathartic: it can give you a
new way to look at things. I thought it was an audacious idea, and

4 *La Pistola y El Corazón.*

that Sean would be a trustworthy person to do it with. Plus, the part contained sufficient vitriol on my character's part – and Jack's – for it to be playable, and resonant. It was a passionate part, someone who'd been abandoned – by her daughter, by her husband. And I knew about that, on several levels. So I thought, 'Yeah . . .'

SEAN PENN: We were just getting ready to shoot. Robin got back from Washington. Things were not so good with she and I at the time. Then she got back and things didn't get better. We rented a house in Santa Monica and made it through the picture.

The start of shooting in mid-January 1994 was designed to gather disparate material for the opening reel: Nicholson's Freddy, soused and lost in the dark world of a strip-joint and boorish drinking buddies, Huston's Mary silently in the midst of an exquisitely painful meeting of a bereaved Mothers Against Drunk Driving group.

ANGELICA HUSTON: It was a real MADD meeting. These people agreed to conduct it as such and allow us to shoot. Very upsetting. But then my mother was killed in a car accident, so I didn't feel entirely bogus being in that room – not that she was killed by a drunk driver, but I could relate. Sean just shot it as you would a documentary, very simply, very quietly; one barely noticed the camera and yet it was moving around as people were speaking. And it was solemn, quiet, intense . . .

DAVID MORSE: I had gone out on a scout with Sean and Vilmos Zsigmond, the DP. And Vilmos was going to quit the film because Sean kept saying, 'I don't really want to do anything fancy with cameras, I just want to get the actors.' And Vilmos said, 'Well, then why did you hire me?' But Sean sort of talked him into staying. Then, as soon as he started seeing dailies, he changed. He really started to get Sean and see what this film would be. Then he was constantly finding little things between each take – 'Let me try this'. And it was really wonderful to watch him work, the moments that were his instinct, his ability to sense them coming and find them with a camera.

HELENA KATZ: Monday morning, they're due to start shooting the bar scene, an early call. Eddie's going to be in it with Jack and Bobby Cooper. We wake up at 4.30 to an earthquake. Eddie calls Sean and Robin, and they're freaking out because Dylan is staying at Robin's mom's in Hollywood Hills and they can't get through. We jumped in a car because

Sean said, 'I can't stay here. I have to go see that Dylan's OK . . .'

DAVID MORSE: We lost our house in the earthquake. I've never really experienced terror in my life until that. The house came off its foundation, and my wife Susan barely made it through. And one of the things that was going through my head was *The Crossing Guard*. Four years of trying to get this thing made, and then just as we start filming, to have the world seemingly come to an end . . . That night we had to sleep on the floor of my agent's house. We had a child with pneumonia, and we didn't know what we were going to do for a home. We had to get my wife and the kids out of Los Angeles. I couldn't do the film and be worrying about them. So I didn't see my family for five months, which was hard on all of us.

Whatever omens were there to impute, The Crossing Guard *was the first show to resume shooting in LA after the 17 January earthquake. Penn set to gathering the sequence of Freddy in a strip-joint redolent of the red-lit dive run by Cosmo (Ben Gazzara) in Cassavetes'* The Killing of a Chinese Bookie.

JON SCHEIDE: We built the club downtown, and we were in it for nights and nights. Actors and real strippers, and real drinkers [*laughs*]. Adding character and flavour and *seasoning* . . .

JACK NICHOLSON: It's the dark part of Sean's character. He is attracted to that downtown quality, there's no doubt about it. I mean, he's been getting out of it as he gets older, 'matures', or whatever you want to call it. But he shares that with Bukowski – this feeling for lost souls and the kind of green-tinted, late-at-night quality: 'Where is everybody? What's everybody doing . . .?'

BOBBY COOPER: Sean made a list of guys he knew who he felt could be just like low-life characters whaling on Jack, not impressed by him. And then he surrounded him with us.

DR KATZ: I told Jack, 'If it wasn't for that one eyebrow you got, you'd be a fucken plumber' . . . One time a magazine wrote that I was Sean's 'id' – I had to look it up in a dictionary. Then I tried to find out who knew us that well.

Sean threw a party at the Monkey Bar halfway through the shoot, for morale. In the movie he was using girls who worked at a strip place and did routines to songs like burlesque. So now one of the strippers gets up on the bar, does a strip. Then Sean has *me* do a strip. Then he's had a couple of drinks, so he gets up on the table and puts his tushy in my face. I said to myself, in a matter of seconds, 'If I kiss his ass, it's a story for a day; if I put my tongue up his ass, it's a story for a lifetime.' What do you think I did? Sean turned ninety shades of red. But – we got engaged that night . . .

JOSEPH VITARELLI: I visited the set of *The Crossing Guard* and Sean was shooting a big scene with Jack. Sean comes over to me and says, 'This ain't Samohi.' I said, 'Bet your ass it isn't. And by the way, that's Jack Nicholson you're directing . . .'

JACK NICHOLSON: Sean's a *very* good director. He'll tell you very sharp things to work for, or what a situation is like, or another way of going about it. He doesn't have to say that much, but it's always useful. He's very specific in his work, very helpful – more helpful than most. And I've worked with great directors.

So much of The Crossing Guard *would hinge on the conviction of a pair of mighty scenes Penn had scripted for Nicholson and Huston, the first being Freddy's unexpected call to Mary's new home to declare his murderous intentions for Booth.*

SEAN PENN: I always thought of it as a kind of ridiculous scene. You have this marriage that collapsed on the basis of the two parties dealing with their shared loss in different ways – not because the love had ended, but they're torn apart by this horror. Now she's gone her way, she's established her group therapy sessions and she's married a very calm guy. Meantime her ex-husband is a maniac who's counting off the days to when he's going to kill the man who did this thing. He's never been able to get her to share his rage. She was scared by it, initially. So he comes in and he wants to be recognized on one level, but she's away on another.

JACK NICHOLSON: It's one of those scenes where everybody feels they're in the right and yet there's no way to resolve it for any of them. You know that the bomb is in the house, and that he's obviously 'misbehaved' a lot before this. And there's a kind of craziness that makes you *want* these confrontations. He's very reasonable, then he just loses it. And she pretty much tells him what she thinks too.

ANGELICA HUSTON: It was really well written, and Jack at this point was very comfortable to work with, because he's just . . . true. He goes straight to the point, and I go straight to the point. So it was actually exciting: we got to trade punches.

SEAN PENN: And between them is this passive new husband, in a head-lock, offering to make everybody coffee . . .

DON PHILLIPS: Robbie Robertson had done a terrific job in a movie called *Carny*, but he hadn't been on a screen since. And he was nervous. This is a guy who's played before thousands and thousands of people with Bob Dylan. But Sean had a way of sensing that and giving confidence: 'Relax, you're the man, you can do this.'

SEAN PENN: I just looked at it and thought it would be much too embarrassing a scene to direct. So I said to the actors, 'I'm going out-side, you guys do it.' I was gone for three hours – it took 'em about that long – and once they had it together, I came in and shot it.

ANGELICA HUSTON: I liked the way Sean worked, the same dynamic as my father, really: 'All right, see where you get with it, then show me what you've done.' It may be that actors who turn to directing can be a little mooshier about letting their actors take over, because they know actors know more about what they're doing than anybody else – they're the ones getting shot doing it. So we found our own block-ing, shot it in pieces. And it wound up funny and ridiculous and hor-rible . . .

The fine line that Penn was toeing in his conception of the piece, between tragedy and a form of bitter absurdist comedy, is augured by that first Freddy/Mary showdown but entirely declared in the subse-quent scene where Freddy makes his pilgrimage to Booth's trailer in order to shoot him, realizing too late that his gun is unloaded.

JACK NICHOLSON: That was probably the hardest scene for me, where he's in the trailer with Booth. It's hard – to come to shoot somebody, and then you don't shoot them. You just want to make some kind of believable chaos, I think. I tried to do a couple of things that fore-shadowed it, but the fact of the matter is that he went with an empty gun. And that's a Freudian slip of a huge kind. Then he's in this small area, pointing an empty gun at a guy he's just threatened to shoot, who's a *huge* man.

DAVID MORSE: If I was surprised by anything . . . it was the authority that John Booth took in that scene: a kind of physical authority that he had, and an authority born of the experience he'd had, which Jack's character didn't.

JAY CASSIDY: What Booth asks is to allow the fact that Freddy's probably justified in wanting to kill him, but then makes a perfectly reasonable request: 'Just give me a couple of days . . .' Freddy's acceptance is also face-saving. He can't say, 'I'm not gonna shoot you because I don't have the bullet – even though I spent the last five years of my life stewing about it.' So human behaviour is never not ironic. And Sean's ability to get those characters in a room with that idea is wonderful.

Penn's personal stake in his movie was mirrored and affirmed in the casting of many of his nearest and dearest in scenes that were often semi-improvised. Katz and Cooper traded jibes with Jack. As Booth's best buddy, Penn cast David Baerwald and shot a party scene in his Venice apartment, with Erin Dignam throwing in a cameo as an argumentative guest. Dennis Fanning is the traffic cop who apprehends Freddy. In a single shot, we see Leo Penn at the wheel of a fishing boat. And then there is a vinegary customer in Freddy's jewellery store, who gets a taste of the seething Nicholson so familiar from the roadside diner of Five Easy Pieces *or* The Shining's *Overlook Hotel. Here, Penn unleashed Nicholson on his mother.*

EILEEN RYAN PENN: I did an awful pushy New York lady, very insensitive. I have this whole thing about my ring being the wrong size and how I have a very important thing to go to, and the ring doesn't fit my finger. So Jack takes my finger, sucks it, slips on the ring and says, 'You're right, you're a perfect size seven.'

SEAN PENN: My mother had gone out and bought this anti-bacterial stuff that gets rid of any germs on your hands, and she's in the trailer scrubbing, 'cause Jack's gonna have to put her finger in his mouth. She goes up to him before the scene and says, 'Jack, I just want you to know, I have thoroughly sterilized my hands.' He says, 'That's good, Ma. You're on your own with my mouth . . .'

The vocational title of The Crossing Guard *drives home its thematic notion of our perennial need for guidance through the thicket of life towards some safe haven. Penn made the theme explicit in the briefest*

Courtesy of Sean Penn

46 *The Crossing Guard*: 'A perfect f*cking seven . . .' Eileen Ryan (Customer), Ryo Ishibashi (Jefferey), Jack Nicholson (Freddy)

of early scenes, Freddy driving past a school crossing and locking gazes – a slow-motion point of view – with its elderly attendant. The casting, here as everywhere else, was meaningful.

ERIN DIGNAM: Sean called me and said, 'The crossing guard, the face I want for that man, that otherworldliness – you know who it is? It's your father.' Who, of course, delivered both Dylan and Hopper . . . 'Do you think your father would be in the movie?' 'Ask him.' He called my dad, who thought this was hilarious, and said, 'Thank you, Sean, but I'm sure there are *actors* who will want that part.' Sean was like, 'I think your father turned me down . . .' So I told him, 'Dad, Sean really needs you.' So my dad called Sean back and said, 'I'm available' – this for a scene with Nicholson – 'between 12 and 1 on Wednesday.' And he did it, in his hour off from the hospital. He said, 'All Sean did was tell me to look in the camera.' But my dad's got this very Zen, wise-owl thing; he was always that way. Sean gave my dad a still of himself in the movie; it says, 'To the deliverer of angels.' He has it on his desk still.

The counterpart to the embittered relations of Freddy and Mary is the budding relationship of Booth and JoJo, an abstract artist he meets at Baerwald's apartment. She is a kind of female ur-figure who stands for life, but cannot quite wrest Booth from his passive pit of guilt. The role was earmarked for Robin Wright, one she executed beautifully, albeit at a less than placid moment in her and Penn's shared life.

ROBIN WRIGHT PENN: I think it's a beautiful distorted view of what we are – 'women', if you want to put us together – or what our female response would be. And I beg to differ, frequently, on that. Sean's women, they're ideals instead of actual beings sometimes. They sort of transcend human nature. And yet it's what we aspire to be, kind of, in the purest sense. And it's also the beauty of Sean's writing.

DON PHILLIPS: Their dark times pervaded the make-up and the mood of the movie. I know Sean was going through his own little personal hell. At the same time he had to deal with Robin being in the film, to work with her in quite a difficult situation. But they were very professional, they didn't take their problems out on the picture. And there were some tough scenes; I mean, he had to direct a love scene between David and the mother of his children.

DAVID MORSE: It was difficult . . . I love Sean, and I love Robin. And it was clearly not a good time for the two of them. There was also the thing that, in a certain way, I had to fall in love with Robin, with JoJo. And Sean knew that – if he were doing the role, he would have to do the same. But that kind of feeling, even between characters – it's a very awkward thing . . .

The scene where JoJo and John sleep together for the first time, there was a lot of discussion between Sean and I as to what this should be. I had different ideas about the way Booth would approach her. My sense was this was a man who barely feels that he deserves to be alive, much less making love with this woman in that intimacy. And Sean was always . . . not comfortable talking about any of it. Then the day finally came when we had to do it. And it didn't happen the way I wanted, and I don't think it was how Robin wanted it either. What happened was a more traditional love scene, movie-ish, with candles and so on. It was fine. But we had a lot of time set aside for it, and usually you'd do it once in a master shot, 'OK, that worked and that didn't, let's try it a different way.' But we did one master and Sean said,

'OK, print! That's it, move on.' It was like he could handle watching it for exactly one take. Then we got into the coverage and he could barely come into the room to give direction; just stayed back at the monitor, very distant. And, you know, usually he's right there with you. But it was so uncomfortable for him, and hard not to feel self-conscious.

The low ebb of male/female enmity caught in the film is a climactic scene in a diner where Freddy, in mounting distress, convinces Mary to meet with him in a last effort at reparation or even reconciliation. Shot in two takes, constructed largely from one, it is a surpassingly brilliant dramatic passage. The cleft couple first unexpectedly find some rapport in shared memories of the past.

ANGELICA HUSTON: This was one of those instances where the timing, the information, what the characters had to say to each other really correlated. And also the receptive atmosphere of a good director in Sean, who's quiet and appreciative and knows what to give you in order for you to do your work.

JACK NICHOLSON: I loved the speech that Anjelica had about how the two of them were survivors. I might have told Sean that story before he included it . . .

47 *The Crossing Guard*: Jack Nicholson (Freddy) and Anjelica Huston (Mary)

ANGELICA HUSTON: When you have a repertoire from knowing some-one for a long time, you can also more easily imagine those times, or remember those times – be they on a plane from Vegas or a hotel room in Des Moines, you know?

JACK NICHOLSON: And I loved that particular part of it – *why* she had loved him, what the guy was like when he was on his feet, you know? So you see what he's lost, and still he can't reconcile. The death of a child, you know, it's a hellish idea. I know why he reached out for her, I know all those back-and-forth real things that people go through. Then she tells him she pities him. 'You *pity* me? OK . . .' He really gets furious at that point. I don't think he wanted to hear *that* from her. And I understood that guy: I *know* that kind of 'OK, I really am on my own here . . .' feeling.

ANGELICA HUSTON: I had to accept his last line in that scene – 'I hope you die. I hope you fucking die' – which is fine, in terms of the scene. If it were me? – and this is the one area in which I think maybe Sean's males characters can go but the females can't – I would have attacked him with a fucking kitchen knife at that point. But the movie wasn't about me. This guy, I think, was set on his course. In some way, to me, thinking about it now, it's a little bit of an easy ending there between them. But in a way I think that's where Sean's fascination lies – with heroic male figures.

JACK NICHOLSON: You can see his behaviour's irrational. And you've seen guns. And hopefully, the audience is in suspense throughout about what this man's going to do and how it's going to end.

SEAN PENN: I don't know anybody who can resolve the idea of losing a child. But when these characters have closed minds and are clashing the whole time, there's a comic aspect to that. I had circus music in my head the whole time making this movie. So what I did was put Freddy and Booth in a chase, leading up to the cemetery. And as I was writ-ing, all by myself in a room, I was laughing. 'So, they chase. And then – they chase some more. And then they get on a bus and they're stuck with a bunch of people between them.' Freddy's got the gun, but they can't do anything in this public situation. And there's a moment when the two of them kind of look at each other, and it's like, 'What do we do now?'

JACK NICHOLSON: Of course, in the final chase, after he *does* shoot at Booth and thinks that he's killed the guy, that's probably the first second when he realizes that all this has been *very* wrong, what he's been up to. And he immediately puts up his hands, like 'Whoah . . .' Then after Booth gets back up, he's following the guy like he's the White Whale, you know? No more guns. And where's he going?

DAVID MORSE: I remember reading the ending and thinking it was . . . awful. So sentimental. In my terribly logical mind, I was thinking, 'Is it complete coincidence? Or am I bringing him there to the cemetery?' And I just kept struggling. I felt like it was working too hard: the pink marble of the stone and his daughter's name there, and the two of them holding hands at the end. But sometimes logic doesn't help you. Sean had a very strong feeling, and you can't fight it after a while. At a certain point, I just had to give myself over to it: 'This is his story, and I have to help him make it.' And in the end, yes, I found it moving.

JACK NICHOLSON: I had no misgivings: I felt it was pretty logical, actually. There's a certain style to it in that it's a long chase where John Booth is actually, unbeknownst to him, leading Freddy to forgiveness. And I looked at that as a very affirmative statement to make. I mean, the guy's life is ruined, *whatever* happens. But at least you feel like, after this, maybe he'll go on.

The resonance of The Crossing Guard's *mournful conclusion was underscored in Penn's own life by the loss of a friend, one who would inspire a closing dedication to the finished film. Charles Bukowski was diagnosed with leukaemia in 1993 and underwent chemotherapy and hospital treatment that put the cancer in remission. He bade farewell to alcohol and tobacco, adopted a healthy diet and developed an interest in transcendental meditation. But the reprieve was not made to last.*

SEAN PENN: It wasn't unexpected. It was terminal. Linda was taking him to a Zen centre on Sunset Boulevard. He had got into some spiritual healing that turned out to be very good for his head at the time. They called me one day saying they were in the Malibu area, and I went down there and we had a late lunch at Gladstone's for Fish. That was the last time that I saw him. Things went south. I would check in and he wouldn't be available. He didn't want to see anybody in hospital, and then he went home. Then we were shooting up at the cemetery

OUR LITTLE LAMBS

Courtesy of Sean Penn

48 *The Crossing Guard*: journey's end for Freddy (Nicholson)
and Booth (David Morse)

in San Pedro, right around the corner from their house, and I called him up. He answered the phone, which he never did – usually he'd let the machine screen the call. And he told me he was sitting on the floor of the bathroom, in terrible shape. He said, 'Visitors aren't doing me any good, but I've got Linda here.' And he basically sent her a love letter down the line: that was all he wanted to talk about that morning, just how lucky he was that he had her. That was the last time I talked to him. He died within a week or two. And I shut down shooting that day early enough to go down to the service.

LINDA LEE BUKOWSKI: After Hank died, Sean was a gem. What he did was like what a loving son would do: he took me *on*. He came over, visited, hung out. Or he would invite me to openings of movies. He even had me do a little part in *The Crossing Guard* – which got cut [*laughs*]. But a whole half a day was spent shooting this scene with David Morse. It was just totally from his loving heart. And he never let up.

It's odd, because there are certain people I've known over the years that I was with Hank who I'd hang out with occasionally and get to know; and after Hank died, they were *gone* – out of the picture. And here's Sean who has a million things he's juggling in his life, and he takes the time, checking in, being there . . .

SEAN PENN: Robin and I made our way through *The Crossing Guard* and then pretty much split up, for over a year. And so what I did, because I was then leaving the rented house in Santa Monica, was to buy an Airstream trailer and put it up on the Malibu property, and I started living up there.

ERIN DIGNAM: It's not like something happened at that juncture in their relationship that split them apart; it was really like something that was there from the very beginning that wasn't resolved and just grew. They were familiar with the tension between them from the day they met: it was inherent, because they're very different as people, their temperaments are very different. But they got together so fast in the beginning, then they were having Dylan, and their lives just got going and they were working. But there were unresolved things, and those built.

And because they're so different, they had different solutions to how they were going to deal with this incompatibility, how they were going to actually live together and continue together. Robin is so silent that she needed her space alone, almost – within the relationship or without. That's not how Sean would have resolved it. But he wasn't able to put it back together by *his* means, talking it out, maybe convincing her to be different than she is.

49 Penn plays horsey for daughter Dylan's third birthday

50 Penn and two-year-old Hopper Jack

JOSEPH VITARELLI: Once Sean and Robin separated, the trailer seemed the logical place to go. It's as if you go through some difficulty in your life and you own a little hunting lodge somewhere or a cabin, up in Big Bear or the Sierra Nevada. It was serene, sort of like Walden Pond, a bit of a Thoreau experience for him, to some degree. Except that he had a television and telephones and gas and electric. He actually had them run the power lines up to the trailer . . .

The trailer sat squarely in the middle of this stellar mountain-top property, looking down on where the main house had been. It was fundamental, but good. Big *Easy Rider* poster on the wall. A couple of little bunk beds on either side. Certainly none of the accoutrements of staying at the Peninsula. But, Lord knows, that option was always there. All he needs when he's working is a typewriter, and he had that. His dogs had their own area. He wrote a lot up there, and read a lot. The kids were at the trailer, many, many times, and they loved it. Everybody loved it, we all went up at one time or another. Jack was up there, De Niro was up there, Nic Cage. And we'd have barbecues and sit out, like the ultimate camp ground. Sean had one of those shitty little $20 barbecue grills outside. But his barbecues started getting better after a while, because of doing it night in and night out. Some nights we'd take the guns out and shoot at things. Very rarely, but that did happen a few times.

Matt Palmieri was then in the terrible position of having seen his mother, his father and a brother all diagnosed with cancer in the space of a mere two years.

MATT PALMIERI: Sean wasn't seeing his kids as much as he wanted. And so he was in his own hell, and I was in my hell with half my family dying on me. I think we tried to be there for each other, at least subconsciously. There ended up being a lot of high jinks involving booze and gasoline and guns and cars . . .

We used to take gasoline and set rings of fire on the dirt pad next to the trailer late at night. One time we realized we were stuck in the middle of the ring and couldn't get out. Then we realized we had left a huge gas can open . . . we both dove through the fire, capped it and ran off with it before it blew us and the whole mountainside to kingdom come.

A majorly annoying habit of Sean's is he loves to watch live surgery shows on cable at all hours, which drives me crazy. I would pick at him, 'Hey, at least let's watch a ball game.' He'd say, 'No , man, this

Photo by Willy Rizzo. Courtesy of Sean Penn

51 'His barbecues started getting better . . . ': Penn cooks out at the Airstream
trailer for guests including Jack Nicholson (right) and Art Linson (centre)

is good stuff, check it out.' I finally said to him, 'You know, you're a
fuckin' kook. Anyone ever tell you that?' And he says, 'Oh yeah?' and
goes to his gun closet, grabs his Glock 17, walks over to my car and
taps two shots through the front window. 'How do you like that?' he
says. Such an idiot – I yelled at him for a while, then we laughed our
asses off. Then I went and turned the channel to a ball game . . .

JOSEPH VITARELLI: All of this couched in the grief he was going
through with Robin, which was pretty extreme for him. Despite whatever distractions they may have brought into their life in that period,
it was still, I think, a difficult and lonely period for him. A transition
period; or perhaps, more accurately, a waiting period.

JAY CASSIDY: Sean finished principal photography on *The Crossing
Guard* at the beginning of May 1994. We began cutting the negative
version number 1 the following February, 1995. So we spent a lot of time
editing . . .

I think the first cut of the movie was four hours. But it's a reductive
process. You're finding the essence of what it is you have to do; you
have to explore every avenue. We got through the actual editing of the
scenes, in most cases the way they should have been cut. But at the end

of the first act, Freddy tells Booth, 'You've got three days . . .' and then you have parallel stories over three days, so you have to inter-cut them in a way that builds and advances and doesn't get boring. That's a hard structure. By nature the audience get very impatient, because they know the end point, in time if not as an event. We had a cut and showed it to Miramax: the scenes and performances were good, but nobody was quite happy with it.

SEAN PENN: We'd started cutting on film, and the Avid was just becoming an industry tool then. And for some of us, that was a little bit like electric invading acoustic. But we got about halfway through *The Crossing Guard* and then we started digitizing stuff. No question, we would have been up shit creek without it. I was having a lot of difficulty finding the kind of concentration you need for cutting on film. This became more a cutting process of manifesting inspired moments than holding onto anything more concentrated, because I was in so much of a personal struggle at the time. So the Avid saved me from too much time spent with myself, waiting on splice and tape or for the dissolve to come back from the lab two weeks later.

JAY CASSIDY: To their credit, Miramax said, 'Here's some more time and money.' And over the next three months the film found its final form. *Now* the structural thing was easy, because that's where the Avid shines. Now you could do the kind of experimenting with dissolves and transitions that Sean liked to do.

SEAN PENN: But I was finding it difficult to let go of that movie. Warren Beatty either said it or repeated it: 'You don't finish a film, you abandon it.' I believe that. And I did some more shooting, about five days of it.

DAVID MORSE: We shot a scene where John kind of flips out on the bus, and then a scene where he goes from there to visit JoJo. That was improvised, and a whole experience all in itself. I didn't think the scene should even be there – his coming back to her at that point. But Sean had fought to have these extra days, and Miramax had come up with the money. So Sean, Robin and I met and talked for days before about what the scene should be. But he and Robin were again having a bad time, so those meetings together were awkward. We came up with stuff, and Sean was supposed to go and write it. Then the next day he wouldn't have anything, but he was gonna write it, he was gonna write it . . .

Then it turned out we would be shooting all night; for some reason that's what Sean wanted. So we got there at 5 p.m., and he was supposed to have pages for the scene, and there was nothing. The set's built, the crew's there, one of the big Miramax guys is there to oversee this thing, and we don't even know what we're gonna be doing.

And Sean . . . he's not somebody who hides his feelings in any way, sees no point in doing that, and saw no point that night. And his feelings for what was going on between him and Robin were just about as low as I had seen. They weren't communicating. Finally he told the DP to light the set – for something, didn't know what – and kind of sat there brooding in his chair, nobody talking. And then it came time, and he said, 'All right, just – go do something. David, go knock on the door and come in. Robin'll dance for you. She's got this cool dance that she does.' I'm thinking, 'Oh shit . . .' So we got music there, Robin and I got stuff in our heads. I knocked on the door and came in, collapsed on the floor, and the scene went on for about ten minutes. And Sean came over and did his version of yelling: 'This is taking forever and it's bullshit. You've got to do something more. And it's got to be faster, whatever you do.' And this was so unlike anything I'd heard from Sean before. But it was like he just wanted to get out of there and have this over with.

So we went the whole night doing this, and it was excruciating: just an ugly evening. The Miramax guy went away tearing his hair, thinking, 'We just wasted $150,000.' And out of it came a scene that I think is [*laughs*] one of the best in the movie. I don't think you could tell this movie without it. A lot of people talk about the moment where I try to give Robin a hug, and she won't let me, and I wind up grabbing her round the neck. That never would have happened if we'd done the scene in any kind of conventional way. It came out of all the turmoil that Sean was feeling and Robin was feeling, and that I felt because of them – these two people, and they're struggling to express something, some kind of connection. That struggle to find something was exactly what that scene was.

JAY CASSIDY: We had the film cut, and because Sean and Springsteen are mutually respectful friends, Springsteen came to a screening, probably November or December 1994. And a few days later, he sent us a song, 'Missing' – a great song, too. So we used it as the title song. It came late, but we were happy to get it. And then we had some delays with the composer, so we didn't finish everything until the end of February 1995.

JOSEPH VITARELLI: Originally I was going to co-score the film with Jack Nitzsche, but he was really sick, his life was just falling apart, God bless him, rest in peace. Drugs killed him, but I think he died of a broken heart.[6] He was a beautiful composer. He was beginning to fail during *The Indian Runner* but there is still music there that's so specific and peculiarly Nitzsche. He actually told Sean, in my presence, that he was going upstairs and getting his gun to shoot me. Subsequently, he produced a bunch of cues, and I just backed away, then came in near the end.

JAY CASSIDY: And then Sean was off on *Dead Man Walking* as an actor, so *The Crossing Guard* basically sat for three months. He probably didn't look at it . . .

DENNIS FANNING: Friends for me are like family, like blood – they're somebody you die for. That's the bond we had growing up in Chicago. In LA? I've been very close with partners. I have a thousand acquaintances. Friends, I can count maybe on one hand. Sean ended up being of those. You know what? I don't agree with his politics a lot of times; I don't agree with some of the shit he does sometimes. But if I had to, I'd go to the wall for him.

The Tuesday before Christmas 1994, my wife got diagnosed with a brain tumour. We got a second opinion on Wednesday. Thursday, I had her and my kids on a plane to the Mayo Clinic in Minnesota. My son was fourteen months old, my daughter was two and a half. My wife had a 5.6-sonogram oligodendroglioma to the left temporal lobe. They gave us the weekend off for Christmas. Monday morning they started her operation. It was ten hours, and they didn't think she was going to live through it. When she came out, she could talk, but she'd lost her memory. After a couple of days, I drove her and the kids down to Chicago to convalesce at her mother's. Then we had to get back out to California. I couldn't take care of two babies and my wife on a plane alone. Everybody I know has kids, families; they couldn't drop what they were doing, and I couldn't afford to buy a ticket for 'em.

When the hospital thing started, Sean had said, 'You need anything?

6 Nitzsche died of a heart attack on 25 August 2000, *The Crossing Guard* his final screen credit.

Call.' So I did. But because of what you do for a living, you don't really know how tight you are. I think Sean was in Hawaii. He dropped everything and flew to Chicago, spent the night at my in-laws. The next day he put my kids on the plane. Because it was Sean, they upgraded my wife's seat to first class, and I took care of my wife while Sean walked my son around for three hours. His name's Sean too, he was just a baby, and you know how it is for babies flying, he was crying all the time. But Sean carried my boy around that plane . . .

That was the one. We were tight before, but at that moment? That was the final nail.

TEN

1994–1996

> I've learned in the last couple years about forgiving myself, but you might as well be speaking Greek if you tell me you have no regrets. I have very serious regrets. I've got regrets that don't have statutes of limitations on them . . .
>
> Sean Penn, *Rolling Stone*, April 1996

In 1995, from the midst of chaotic and heartsick circumstances, came perhaps Penn's most brilliant screen performance, forged out of true-life material as authentic and painful as one would expect for such creative galvanism to happen.

Sister Helen Prejean of Baton Rouge settled in New Orleans in 1981 to work among the impoverished. In 1982, she began a correspondence with Patrick Sonnier, a French-speaking Cajun on Death Row in Louisiana for having, with his younger brother, murdered teenagers Loretta Bourque and David LeBlanc in November 1977. Loretta Bourque had also been raped. In 1984, Sister Helen witnessed Sonnier's death by electrocution. She further wrote to and witnessed the killing of Robert Lee Willie who, in May 1980, with a friend named Joe Vaccaro, had picked up Faith Hathaway as she walked home alone from a bar, took her to a remote place, and raped and killed her. This was not even Willie's first such outrage. But from these experiences came Sister Helen's written ruminations on the process of ministering to the condemned perpetrators of despicable crimes, entitled Dead Man Walking.

SEAN PENN: Susan found that book and gave it to Tim. She really marched it through, she drove that train, no question. And you could feel that it was . . . quite a loving thing for Tim to give her that movie, in a way. There were things around that movie and those two people that were very positive to be around at that time: what they were doing, and why they were doing it.

SUSAN SARANDON: I had read Sister Helen's book when I was in Memphis working on *The Client*. Then the last week of filming was in

New Orleans, Lousiana, and I found Sister Helen and arranged a meeting with her while I was there. She wasn't sure which of the two gals from *Thelma and Louise* I was . . . but she did know that I came highly recommended by some people in Amnesty International. So we met, had a great evening together, and she basically gave me the book to work with.

Then I spent the next year or so trying to get Tim interested in it: he was really more focused on *Cradle Will Rock*, but he hadn't quite got the money or the script ready to shoot yet. Meanwhile, Sister Helen visited with us, staying in our house, so both of us got to know her quite well. Then Tim was carrying around both scripts and working on them that summer of 1994, and it was *Dead Man Walking* that kind of got its fingers into his imagination and he decided, for a limited budget, to try to do it. Everything in the script he wrote was based in fact. It was an assimilation of the two men at the centre of the book.

In Tim Robbins' script, Sister Helen visits with Matt Poncelet, sentenced to death for his part in the rape and murder of a young couple, so leaving two sets of parents bereaved. Poncelet, scaled with fascistic tattoos, casually racist and occasionally admiring of Hitler, is a virtual poster-boy for capital punishment. Nevertheless, he asserts his innocence: that, wasted on hallucinogenic drugs, he had only assisted as his associate Vitello carried out the vile crimes. The journey of the film, then, is that of Sister Helen's efforts to have him accept guilt and suffering and so be redeemed by it. Robbins, an actor associated with the political left, might have been expected to take aim at miscarriage of justice, the most conspicuous flaw in the state's case for killing killers. But he wished the audience to grapple with harder choices.

SUSAN SARANDON: The question was to take the most loathsome person and threaten to kill them in the most quote, unquote 'humane' way. In the beginning, when we were trying to get the funding, there were people who said, 'Well, Poncelet has to be innocent.' Or, 'He and Sister Helen have to *consummate* their love somehow.' So nobody – even these supposedly independent sources of money – really wanted to do the script the way it was. Until people saw it, they just thought it was a movie about the death penalty. I don't know that we *sold* it as a love story, but for me that was the aspect that was really important. How do you unconditionally love someone who isn't your child? I don't know if that's even a concept that's supposed to exist for adults.

But if you're religious, that's what you attempt to do. This woman is struggling with the bond, the attempt to love this really despicable person, this Nazi racist – that's the task she's set for herself, despite the terrible crime that he's committed. For me, that was what led to the redemptive aspect of it, and what made it more than just a polemic about the death penalty. The fact that she just makes one mistake after another was also really important, because I didn't want to play a saint: I wanted somebody who was a human being trying to learn compassion, trying to remove hatred from her heart in a very, very difficult situation. Because that's what these remarkable people do. They don't ask if you're guilty, they don't say, 'I'm withholding from you unless you're innocent.' They try to help you die with dignity.

It was important to cast the right guy. And I just couldn't imagine anybody who could be both as seductive and as scary in that role as Sean. Sometimes you can find an actor who's really good at getting angry, being threatening. And then you can find actors who you believe could love. But you very rarely find them in the same guy. And it was totally coincidental that he bore such a striking resemblance to one of the men in Sister Helen's book . . .

TIM ROBBINS: I had a cordial relationship with Sean. I'd been a huge fan of his – Spicoli, you know? Then I did a movie called *Five Corners*, and I met him and he told me he had loved it. And he'd seen *Bob Roberts*, and I would run into him from time to time. But I don't live in LA. Then he had announced he was quitting acting. And I knew exactly what he was talking about, because I had quit acting too, only in my head – I hadn't announced it. You get to a level of frustration with the kinds of scripts you're reading, it's a stagnation that can be very mind-numbing. But when I was thinking about who would be in *Dead Man Walking* – I obviously wanted the best actor in America, as I thought. And that was him.

SEAN PENN: I was in the office of the cutting room on *Crossing Guard* when I got a call from Tim Robbins' assistant, saying, 'Tim's on a plane, he wants to see you – today.' I wasn't being asked [*laughs*]. And I didn't know Tim very well at that point at all. But he came with the book *Dead Man Walking*, and said he was working on a script for it. I read the book and told him, 'Sounds interesting,' and then he gave me a script. And I thought, yeah, it was probably time to be called upon . . .

SUSAN SARANDON: We had a couple of meetings in which Sean was incredibly humble and sweet, and all of the things that everybody at that time said that he wasn't. But he was a little dodgy with his scheduling. So we waited.

SEAN PENN: I kind of hedged for a bit: I was a little worried. It was a great script, and I responded very strongly to it – but that was part of what I was worried about. I was in such a difficult place; I was not sure where my family was going to end up, and so I felt that the kind of commitment and concentration that this movie was going to take, and the time away, was really going to be . . . rough. Then I didn't end up having an awful lot to say about time anyway – because we *needed* time. So I took the job. And certainly was glad that I did. But it was very difficult – it would have been difficult under *any* circumstances.

TIM ROBBINS: I had absolute trust in Sean creating the character, I knew it was going to come. I wanted him to go down to Angola[1] with Sister Helen; that was important to me that he meet her and see that prison, just so he could be in that environment which is so specific. We weren't going to be able to film there except for a couple of exteriors – all the interiors would be shot in New York. So I needed all of us to have that sensory feeling of what it was like to be in Angola. We had to carry that up to New York with us, or the movie wasn't going to work.

SEAN PENN: Where as a director I've been able to offer more to actors is because I've written the script – I mean, it's rare that one actor's process to get to things is the same as mine. And *Dead Man Walking* was so well written that a lot more of my work than usual came straight out of what Tim wrote. But I arranged to go out to Angola with Sister Helen and visit on Death Row. I drove down to New Orleans, about eight hundred miles. On my way down I stopped in Charlotte. Don Henley of the Eagles was down there, and I ended up having a big night. I had my deadline to be in New Orleans: Sister Helen was gonna pick me up at 7 a.m. Anyway, I got dosed with seven hits of acid in a bar that night and went fucken *crazy* for thirty-five straight hours. That was a thirty-five-hour trip to hell. I somehow got the word out to her that I wasn't going to be able to make it, and I came back to California. And I had to recover: that took me about five days just to

1 Louisiana State Penitentiary, which houses the state's death row and execution chamber.

get over the fatigue and the flu-ish feeling I had from beating myself up all those hours. Then I ended up driving all the way back to New Orleans . . .

Sister Helen was obviously very directly helpful to Susan, but for me it was just nice having her involved. There may have been some keys that she gave me to some things, but what I remember more is just the exposure that she gave me. My approach to that sort of stuff is 'Let's see what gets in.' Interrogating someone on Death Row for information about their feelings is not where I'm going to get my information. I just throw myself in there: 'Hey, how you doing?' And let's see what they say. I trust what I'm not comfortable with, sometimes, as being what I'm comfortable with . . .

Then I got together with a fella named Bradley, who was part of the Bandidos Motorcycle Club, and he had a tattoo parlour out on the West Bank, Marrero, the other side of Lake Ponchartrain. I went out there and I told him about this acid experience I'd had. And that's when I got *that* [*taps right forearm*]. This caged spirit, a sort of commemoration of that day, the feeling that I had there. And it says, 'NOLA – Deliver Me', NOLA being New Orleans, Louisiana. Knowing that I was going to do the picture and my arms were going to be seen, I figured, 'Well, we'll just include this. It hasn't been seen elsewhere, and it'll fit in just fine . . .'

52 Penn with 'NOLA' tattoo newly acquired for *Dead Man Walking*, and Bradley of the Bandidos Motorcycle Club

TIM ROBBINS: Sean showed up with that tattoo, and to me it was just an extension of Poncelet, you know? And that's some dark shit you have to go through to be there. I don't know how much of it was the drug or just Sean allowing this character to . . . enter. But that, I'm sure, was very difficult – to carry that particular character, with all the demons and the darkness, and the violence and the denial, and the hatred and racism.

EILEEN RYAN PENN: He made himself look exactly like the real guy.[2] He had pictures of that guy, and when you looked at Sean, honestly, it was just amazing – the whole look, the little beard, the pompadour hair.

TIM ROBBINS: I think it all has to do with the hair-do . . . It's Sean's finest hair-do on film, no question. But I'll tell you, if you really do the research in that real situation – hair-dos mean a *lot* to those guys, some of them have fantastic hair-dos, because it's all they have when they've got so much time on their hands.

SUSAN SARANDON: There wasn't really any discussion of the death penalty or politics while we were working. When we were in Angola, they actually did execute a guy from New York, and some people went and stood outside the prison. But then other people were at the hotel, partying . . . So it wasn't a situation where people got together to do a movie because they all felt the same way about the issue. But we did see *The Crossing Guard* right before we started shooting, and that film was like a preliminary to *Dead Man Walking*: obviously these were themes that Sean was already mulling over.

SEAN PENN: *The Crossing Guard* is a sort of anti-thriller, an anti-revenge story. In the United States, what we offer people, if they've had a loved one killed, is the idea that their peace is based on taking another life, and that gives them what they call 'closure'. And so it restricts or cuts off any other possibility, even the Christian ethic that supposedly promotes forgiveness. Hypocrisy is the primary experience of American life and it's encouraged at every turn. Movies encourage it. And so I guess I try to make the movies about the effect that has on people.

TIM ROBBINS: I remember the night in the swamp in Louisiana where

2 Robert Lee Willie

we filmed the rape and murder. That was a disturbing night, horrendous: because even though we weren't going to be filming any close-ups, we still had to shoot it in two different versions – Poncelet's version, and the truth. And we also had to do it from a few different distances and angles. So what I would have liked to be a very short night simply wasn't possible. And being with these two kids who were being thrashed around and having to act as if they were being raped and murdered . . . it was really tough. I'd talked to everyone beforehand about propriety and not wanting anything inappropriate to happen, nothing sexual, or any kind of 'Oh, in the moment I really felt like I had to hit him . . .' That we all had to be safe with each other. There are actors who can only be 'spontaneous' and 'real' if they just do erratic things: 'It don't matter if I hit that person, or if I pull my dick out – it's a film and it's important.' That shit happens. The excuse for it is 'art', and that's bullshit. It's abuse.

And I was impressed with Sean . . . because he was fucking *nuts* in that scene. I mean, drugged-out nuts, acting; but at the same time, completely controlled and disciplined as an actor as far as respecting

Courtesy of Sean Penn

53 On location for *Dead Man Walking* in Louisiana: Penn, Susan Sarandon, Sister Helen Prejean, Tim Robbins

those two kids. And at the end of the night, horrible as it was, he'd done everything he could to make it okay for them.

SUSAN SARANDON: We didn't shoot too much with Sean in Louisiana, but once we came to New York, we shot almost all of our stuff together in sequence, just the two of us. So it became almost a second movie. This was really a pretty quick, low-budget sort of experience; we didn't have time for a lot of takes, and there were a lot of scenes cutting to the outside, because we had initially assumed it might be a little bit boring, just these two talking heads. But it ended up that it held together quite well, actually . . .

It was helpful to shoot in sequence, but also pretty crippling. When you don't have anything between you but a cigarette and a hair-do, and you're pretty stationary, you become just completely locked in to the other actor and completely dependent on them. And Sean used all of his energy to help make me better and to connect – there were none of the assassination attempts that sometimes happen between actors on sets. He didn't waste any energy in any attention-seeking dramatics; he was completely there for me, so I tried to be there for him. So I couldn't help but fall in love with him for that and respect his commitment. All along, I was drawn to the material because I felt it really was a love story that examined unconditional love. And once we got to New York, guys on the crew would come up to me and say, 'Ah, now I understand what you were talking about . . .'

SEAN PENN: And I felt *infinitely* connected with Susan in that stuff.

TIM ROBBINS: While we were shooting, Susan made a joke one time about what the Sister Helen Doll would say, you know? Like if you pulled a string on her back, she'd go, 'I'm *sorry* . . .' So she was a little concerned that she was *listening* a lot. But I think that's part of the power of her performance, she's one of those actresses who's able to listen, and yet be saying something in her silence. That's not easy: that's why it's an extraordinary performance. That, matched with Sean saying a lot but not really saying *anything* – the kind of person who's full of shit half the time. But he's saying a lot in the subtext. It's just that bravado in Sean's performance – the false sense of self and what it is to be a man; and you can *see* it's false. And that is ultimately what makes him so vulnerable, and why you feel for him.

Poncelet's forlorn efforts at federal appeal, gubernatorial pardon and even lie-detector vindication are twin-tracked with Sister Helen's endeavours to both succour him and penetrate his shield of denial, dismissing his would-be suavity ('I like being alone with you') and his stubborn vainglory ('I ain't no victim'). In what is a strikingly physical performance, Penn's incremental descent into Poncelet's mortal fear and vulnerability is perhaps most keenly evident around his close-set eyes, once memorably evoked by Harry Crews as 'flat, the way a nail-head might be described', but which become as pools in the film's distressing last half hour.

SUSAN SARANDON: I felt that the moment when Poncelet asks the guard, 'Can Sister Helen touch me?' was just so heartbreaking. Or when he's not allowed to be with his mother and to have her touch him.

ART WOLFF: I think one of the greatest scenes ever put on film is Poncelet's farewell scene to his family in *Dead Man Walking*. It's extraordinary, the sweetness in it . . .

Several such strokes were drawn from the last hours of Robert Lee Willie. His mother's wish to hug him, denied for 'security reasons'; his subsequent tears in a last telephone call with her ('I just let it flow'); and the realization Sister Helen pressed upon him in considering what ought to be his last words ('I really hope my death gives them some peace, the victims').

SUSAN SARANDON: It was an odd and really fabulous but painful situation when you're counting down to the demise of your co-star . . . And so as it progressed, and we got into that last week of shooting, once Sean got strapped down to the gurney he wouldn't even get up – I would just stand with him the whole time, talk to him, help him smoke a cigarette or whatever.

Robbins was unsure that Poncelet's silent death by lethal injection would be sufficiently dynamic. He filmed an alternate version in which the condemned man suffered a horrendous allergic reaction to the first shot, causing convulsions. Penn played it both ways and many times, exhausting himself. But finally, the chillingly sedate version was Robbins' preference.

TIM ROBBINS: Sean was a champ that day – boy, that was hard. But particularly psychically gruelling for him: because you're acting your death. And it's not like a war picture where you're shot and you fall down. This is a planned death, one that the character's had to live with and think about for years and years. And then it gets to the day and it becomes about hours, and then it becomes about minutes, and then seconds. And then comes that moment of premeditation: here you are in front of all these people who are there to *watch* you die. Guys on Death Row have to deal with that. So as an actor Sean had to deal with it, in the ten weeks we had leading up to that moment in the film. And on the day, he's got to do it several times, and in two different ways . . . [*laughs*]. Now, the 'serene' version was just as hard psychically, I'm sure. But when you combine the two, it's hardcore.

54 *Dead Man Walking*: Penn (Matthew Poncelet)
and Susan Sarandon (Sister Helen)

SUSAN SARANDON: At the start we had just jumped in, but I know by the time we finished filming, my *skin* hurt. I hadn't understood how intense it had been, because it went fairly smoothly compared to most movies. But the very last day of shooting, Sean finished a little before I did, and I was still doing some little pieces of scenes. Meanwhile, he went away and shaved, and cut his hair. And then when he came down to the set – it was one of the most jarring things that I've seen. For me, it had been like watching one of those animal specials on TV where you fall in love with a manatee after an hour and a half: I had so come to accept him with this weird hair-do and goatee, the whole business. Now that he'd shaved, it was almost scary to me. You know, you just eventually trick yourself into thinking this is your reality, and it does become very intense. I'm sure that Sean had to disengage also to a certain extent. He drove across country after that, and I can't speak for him but I don't know how he could have gone through the part and not been pretty deeply affected.

SEAN PENN: I'm in a world of a character that basically is saying, 'The most you can be, the most you can evolve in terms of your choices, is on the last page of this picture.' *Dead Man Walking* was shot reasonably in sequence. Unfortunately it wasn't an open-ended book in terms of where my character goes next . . . That one, quite simply, was just an oppressive set of circumstances in the sense that the character and the story was just . . . sad. Disturbing, all the time disturbing.

But the other thing is, so much of being an actor in movies – especially if you're a leading character in a piece – is that all-day, every-day thing of catching a light here, hitting a mark there, waiting on measurements . . . as well as connecting with another person in the scene, creative choices, all of those things. The concentration, in one area or another, is all-consuming. You start to dream about it. Even if you're out drinking the night after the day, finally you let it own you in a certain way, and you have to. So it's a *big* fucken school's-out-for-summer feeling when you're done. The second that thing is over, man, the whole world opens up, and you're predatory towards it. It's not so much cutting off what's just past – it's moving *forward*. You're starting life again, you can just be free. Give me a car and a country I can zig-zag through if I want – and I can stop, and go to sleep? I don't have to be anywhere on somebody else's time? – and I'm a bird. It's like *Easy Rider* . . .

DR KATZ: *Dead Man Walking* Sean didn't have me work on: he said, 'Doc, you'll take me out of character . . .' But we drove Sean's car from

LA and met him the day they wrapped. This was the 1987 Buick Grand National. They only made so many. It belonged to a construction guy; guy didn't want to sell, but Sean kept offering . . .

SEAN PENN: So I had my Buick. And Peter Sheridan, Jim's brother, flew out. We were friends, and we were talking about doing the Brendan Behan story, *The Bells of Hell*, and we drove back across country. But things were still rough at home, and so I was coming back to all of that, and that lasted still for a while after *Dead Man Walking*. And then it found its way out, and we got to start anew. We got . . . married.

Through the summer of 1995, Penn was back in the Airstream but routinely checking into the Shangri-La Hotel in Santa Monica for weekends with his children. These domestic arrangements were acquiring a permanency. 'Robin Wright isn't really a part of my family, except she is the mother of my kids,' Penn told Paris Match.[3] *'The war between their mother and I is over. We have separate lives and we're trying to do what's best for the kids.' With* The Crossing Guard *finally in shape, he took it to the Venice Festival in September for a gala unveiling prior to its autumn US release. There, he was conspicuously flanked by twenty-one-year-old singer-songwriter Jewel Kilcher. Penn had heard her demo tape during the making of* The Crossing Guard, *commissioned a song – 'Emily' – for the soundtrack, and they were now an item.*

JOHN SYKES: We had just begun to play Jewel on VH-1, and Sean had called me when he was making *The Crossing Guard* and raved about her, said, 'I'm gonna do her video, help her whatever way I can.' I had to say, 'I beat you to the punch, Sean. We love her already. But this surely does help.' And he *did* do whatever he could . . . We hung out a lot in that time, and I love Jewel, she's a friend too, although it was a bit awkward because my wife and I are so close with Robin and love her so much. But because Sean is one of my best friends, I would always be his friend.

ADAM NELSON: I get a call from Sean saying that Jewel is opening for The Beach Boys, and do I want to meet him there? So we go, and after the show we all head back to the trailer – Sean, me, Jewel, and one of her friends. A lovely California evening, we're surrounded by fifty

3 12 October 1995, interview by Yves Averous.

acres of rugged hills, we're kickin' back – and Sean asks Jewel if she can play a couple of tunes? So she does, and it's pretty cool, because these songs were about to make her famous. Then Sean spots a rat that's been bugging him for a week now, sneaking in and out of his trailer. He lets us know he's spotted it and that, next time, if he can, he'll do something . . . About a half-hour later, we'd forgotten about it, we're all just sitting there in the middle of a sugary-sweet Jewel ballad, and *blam*! A shot goes off – loud and startling. And the rat's lying there in two pieces. Sean had shot it in half with a laser-sighted 9mm Glock.

Afterward, I think Sean felt a little bad, but he knew it had to be done . . . and after we'd disposed of it, I think Jewel just picked up where she left off . . .

SEAN PENN: I like the Venice Film Festival, it's a great festival in a lot of ways. But I was devastated by the *Crossing Guard* screening. It seemed to go OK, but not for me. That screening room, and the amount of reflective ambient light off of any light image on the screen – it looked like daylight in there. I could see the colour of the collar of somebody's shirt from twenty yards. So I felt the movie, which was hyper-intimate and really needed you to go into it and stay into it, was shown with great distraction. That was much worse to me than a bad reaction in the press conference. But, in any case, we got a hammering. Generally, they had a big problem with the ending. The strange thing is that the Italians, for all of their Christian forgiveness, were quite upset. The word 'vendetta' is, I believe, an Italian word. And they didn't like seeing that incomplete.

JAY CASSIDY: And to top it, the Italian press were saying, 'And this from *Sean Penn*?', meaning the personality that they knew about only from reading the newspapers.

SEAN PENN: We took a lashing and we gave a lashing. And it caused a stir. I don't remember the other specific criticisms. But I do remember Jack straightening them out on my writing and where it was coming from. And that was really nice.

JACK NICHOLSON: The press conference wasn't to me an impressive occasion. I thought Sean was very good, very astute. But there were a lot of very low-credential newspaper people who just said a lot of crazy stuff. A guy in a camouflage suit gets up, asks me did I think it was weird that I wore my *hair* the same way all the time in the movies? Normally I would say, 'Well, I don't . . .' But as I remember, this was the point at which I thought, 'Well, OK. Let's see what we can do here to make this have some *seriousness*, you know?'

When The Crossing Guard *then opened in the US in November, a measure of that Venetian disquiet was replicated in the press reviews, though Penn's ambition and Nicholson's performance were both widely admired.*

BOB RAFELSON: I think Sean might have shown me a review for *The Crossing Guard* – saying, 'The best performance Jack Nicholson has given since *Five Easy Pieces*' – and said, 'See? Look at that!'

JACK NICHOLSON: I really think it's a fine movie. I always got the impression it was very well received. But, you know, it's one of my best acting jobs, so therefore . . . I'm glad if people like it, but there are plenty of things they've loved of mine that I'm a little bit softer on than they are. Whereas I still look at *The Crossing Guard* as one of the most satisfying things I ever got to do.

AMY HECKERLING: I loved *The Crossing Guard*. I cried. And I was *really* surprised that it wasn't like Oscar-time for everybody. When you think about what movies people get excited about, and that one was overlooked, it's crazy . . . I thought Sean accomplished there what he had touched on in a lot of his acting performances, and in *The Indian Runner*. It seems like a very big theme for Sean is redemption, people finding their souls. I don't want to be analyzing anybody, but . . . certainly something in him makes him interested in people wanting to be good.

ERIN DIGNAM: I never thought that Robin and Sean would split for ever. But it did get dark. It was scary, that time period. I was worried as they were. It overlapped into the making of *Loved*, and I think both *Loved* and *The Crossing Guard* shared some of the darkness of what was going on.

Dignam shot her second feature as writer–director in the winter of 1995–96, with Penn's Clyde Is Hungry as co-producers. Returning to her family home in Los Angeles for Christmas week, Hedda Amerson (Robin Wright) is subpoenaed to testify at a hearing about the physical abuse she received at the hands of an ex-boyfriend now charged in another abuse case that led to a woman's death. Prosecutor K. D. Dietrickson (William Hurt) is on a kind of mission: 'The defendant', he asserts, 'has a habit of disabling women.' But the hearing becomes a kind of psychodrama in which Hedda fails to vilify the man, speaking only of the motives she herself attributed to his violence: 'I knew he was trying to get past my skin, to me . . .'

ERIN DIGNAM: I think *Loved* came out of my experience of having made *Loon*: I didn't condemn the male character in that film, and because of that I felt I was almost put on trial for some of my points of view. So, very simple, huh . . .? 'You think I didn't condemn him that time? Look at me now . . .' I said to Robin, 'I want to put a character in a position where everybody else in the world is stupid about the subject except for her.' And I wanted to see Robin perform that, because of that honesty. Also I wanted it to be clearer that people fall in love and they're in Plato's cave: they don't know what those shadows are, how anybody else fell in love or what it meant to them.

ROBIN WRIGHT PENN: I so get it in Erin, I understand it completely and love it in her. I always said, 'You've always been an inspiration to me because you have such a beautiful faith in people and what they can be.' But trying to play it? There were mixed feelings, I was angry. Why can't I love in this way? If someone treated me like that, that kind of rage and abuse, I would fucking want to kill them. She didn't see it like that. Does it make it right? No. Is it still abusive? Totally. But it does not negate that the love is there. And I found that very hard to play.

ERIN DIGNAM: We basically had finished *Loved,* but one of the producers, I would say, was afraid of the movie. Sean saw me struggling with the cut issue, and he said, 'Will it help if I do a scene in the movie?'

SEAN PENN: I came in and I traded my participation in order to get Erin the power that wasn't in her contract originally. My deal goes into play when final cut becomes a sideliner to the director; so she now has final cut if I'm in the movie. That was my producing contribution . . .

ERIN DIGNAM: I felt something was missing off the top, an introduction for William Hurt's character that was stronger. Sean suggested I add something with him in the office as William's boss. But I felt that if I ever directed Sean I would want to use his talent and see it at play, not just get information into a story. I wanted him to be an *extreme* character. I had lived in New York next to a street person, and one day I came home and he was knocking on my neighbour's door – his mother actually lived next door. That was shocking to me, disturbing: why didn't she take him off the street, when he's obviously mentally handicapped? That was inspiration for this character. I told Sean the story. And he worked so hard to put that character there for this one scene on one day. We had a costume meeting. Sean said, 'I know somebody who lives on the street, or barely off it, someone I kind of grew up with. And when I see him, he's always wearing a suit as if he's just come from a job interview. I want to be in a suit, but barefoot or in socks.' And he wanted a suit that was a little too small for him . . . He took the bed-head hair from someone else, another eccentricity. And then the way he waved is the way Hopper waves: when I saw him do that in rehearsal, I was like, 'Ohhh . . .'

Penn would make his appearance at the very start of the picture, a clearly stricken neurotic who encounters William Hurt's Dietrickson at the end of his morning jog in the hills. Hands rigidly on hips, his gaze pained, walking stiff-legged, 'The Man on the Hill' approaches Dietrickson by his car and asks, 'Can you help me?'

© Crosslight / MDP Worldwide

55 *Loved*: Penn ('Man on the Hill') and William Hurt (Dietrickson)

ERIN DIGNAM: I think Sean saw this man as very childlike, frozen at whatever age he had progressed to: like a lost child who could walk up to a stranger and hold his hand. And at the very end he says, 'Could you, would you hold *me?*', like he's unworthy of being touched. One of the deepest issues of the movie is what your worthiness is. And that completely blew me away.

People said to me afterwards, 'How did you ever think of Sean playing someone like that?' But basically how I see Sean as a person is in that character: extremely sensitive, a vibrating string, where the air moving in the room could affect his chemistry. It's interesting that he and I have remained so close for many years. Because , , , I'm female And I'm so close to Robin. But that character in *Loved*, that's maybe more what a female sees in Sean: that really vulnerable, intimate man.

ROBIN WRIGHT PENN: It's pretty close. An exaggerated verbalization of it. But the tone? Sean's big on love, big on love . . . I am too, in a different way, I think. Maybe it's execution where we differ. But where it comes from, the need for it, is the same.

Was Sean Penn then an actor once again? Dead Man Walking *had opened on the coasts in the last week of December 1995 and gone wide a fortnight later to the best critical notices of his career. And whilst the film's treatment of capital punishment ensured disparate responses among audiences, it had, as a piece of art bearing upon a grave issue of public interest, clearly done its work.*

TIM ROBBINS: Sister Helen, who is out there in the field, travelling around and talking to groups – she believes that the film had something to do with a sea-change in thinking about the death penalty. Certainly she thinks the support for it has gone down a few points since the movie. I think it fed a debate. And I think that was because of the humanity that was brought to the film by the actors, the nature of how it was presented, and the dignity given to the victims' families. It allowed people to feel that they were not being manipulated, and so it allowed them to have real discussions about the death penalty afterward.

Evidently, if Penn saw irresistible virtues in a piece of material then he could be swayed back into costume. And anything that came with David Rabe's imprimatur was to some extent pre-approved – though 'Hurlyburly: The Movie' was, at this juncture as at any before, a wildly improbable proposition.

DAVID RABE: There was always a recognition that *Hurlyburly* was a really difficult piece of material and that Hollywood was very unlikely to be interested in doing it. But I'd turned down any number of offers where people came to me. I remember one: we talked, and they were offering a decent amount of money and blah-blah, and I thought, 'This is pretty good.' Then at a certain point they said – one of the great lines – 'But, you know, nobody does drugs in Hollywood any more. So you probably should eliminate that stuff.' That was the end of that. This was when they were being very clean out there in terms of their image. And it *is* different now. But still . . .

In the end, the movie came about because of Tony Drazan. He wrote to me expressing his interest in adapting it and sent me the two films he'd made. And it wasn't so much the approach to the material as much as it was the personal nature of those films of his. I thought it was worth the risk.

TONY DRAZAN: In December of 1995, I asked David to put me in touch with Sean, because he was my first choice to play Eddie. That was really a no-brainer. So I called up Sean, and he said, 'What are you doing in twenty minutes?' And we met over lunch. I did most of the talking and still finished my meal, and Sean did most of the listening and didn't seem to touch his food. He said, 'Well, I don't see how you're gonna do it. But if and when you do, I'd like to read it . . .' So it was a quick lunch. But I sort of got the impression Sean had unfinished business with the play.

I moved to Connecticut for four or five weeks in February 1996, rented a house near David's, and commuted every day in the snow to his home, where we would tackle the text. We finished it on a Friday, the first weekend of March 1996, and got it out Fed-Ex to Sean. Monday, he called us and said he was in. No strings attached. The only question mark was how he was going to fit it in.

During my first week or two back, Sean and I hooked up, had some sushi in Chaya Venice. And he was talking like I knew a lot of the history of *Hurlyburly*: the history of the history . . . I didn't know any of it. So Sean at some point goes, 'Who you thinking about for Artie? Because you've met Linson, haven't you?' I say, 'No, why?' Artie is not *based* on Linson, but there was some suggestion of an Art 'element' . . .

ART LINSON: I knew David Rabe when he was out in Los Angeles. They say one of the characters is named 'Artie' because of me. I don't know if it's true. None of it looks like me when *I* look at the damn thing . . .

TONY DRAZAN: So Sean picks up his cell phone, calls, says, 'Art? I'm with Drazan. We're doing *Hurlyburly*. We're coming over.' We go to Linson's house, in a very beautiful section of Santa Monica, and I remember, clearly, Linson was sitting at his dining table, he had a glass of white wine, and his wife was serving up this beautiful repast – poached salmon and steamed vegetables. Sean stands by the fireplace, sucking on a cigarette at a safe distance from Art, who doesn't want the smoke wafting in his direction. And I'm smoking with Sean, because . . . I want to be smoking with Sean.

There was a lot of buzz on Sean at this point because of *Dead Man Walking*. Linson doesn't know me at all, and I don't think he was a terrific fan of *Zebrahead*, though it was a nice little picture. He looks at me and he says, 'You know, every time I get *him* to a place where he can break out, an asshole like you has gotta come along and pull him right back down. I get him to the mountain top, then you drag his ass back into the valley, and I gotta start this fucking climb all over again . . .' And I thought that was wonderful. This was a guy I really wanted to know.

Then Art says to Sean, 'Has he met Phillips?' I go, 'Who's Phillips?' Sean says, 'You haven't met Don? That's Eddie, man! You don't know any of this stuff, do you?' 'No.' 'Well, you're in for a treat.' 'Oh yeah . . .', says Art. Then Sean got on the phone to Dr Katz to get Don, no matter where he was, and bring him over to where Sean was living. So we go over to Sean's place. He calls Michael Keaton, and Michael comes over. Then the door bursts open, I hear, 'Here comes the dog and pony show!' And it's Don. He says to me, 'Why the fuck are you doing this piece of shit?' And Sean's just sitting across the room, smoking his cigarettes, watching this thing unfold. He had opened a door, and I walked right through. And I loved it.

We basically cast a version of the movie in that time. There were commitments from Sean and Robin and Kevin Spacey.

KEVIN SPACEY: I did *Hurlyburly* in New York in 1985. I had auditioned for a national tour of *The Real Thing* and met Mike Nichols then. Mike decided on that basis to ask me to audition for *Hurlyburly* and I got the understudy – which turned into an eight-month job. I started out doing Phil, and Mike would come and say. 'That was great! How soon could you learn Mickey?' And then: 'Great! How soon could you learn Eddie . . .?' We used to joke that I was like the pinch-hitter warming up in the bull-pen, because I ended up playing all of the male roles. And I really just fell in love with the play.

I saw Sean play Eddie in Los Angeles. Sean and I had talked about how much we loved the play, and at this point my film career was just taking off, so we thought, 'Hey, maybe we could pull this off and make this movie.' And we joined forces. I think it's an entirely unique circumstance where the understudy actually gets to play the role in the movie version, so I hope I gave a sense of hope to understudies everywhere . . .

TONY DRAZAN: Now we were going to go out and do the movie. But it wasn't that simple. In fact, it was a good year and a half before we could finance it. I think everyone in this town who read the script took it way too personally. All the indie big dogs said, 'We don't love what this is about. But, putting that aside, there are so many *words*, you can't sell this overseas.' It was Sean who anchored it. He never wavered: even over the next eighteen months, as the budget dropped from twelve to eight to four, and his money went from an appropriate amount to scale, he remained steadfast. I think he became even *more* committed . . .

The dog-and-pony show of Oscar nominations in February 1996 yielded Penn his first such nod for Best Performance by an Actor in a Leading Role, Dead Man Walking. In the social whirl that trailed Hollywood's Biggest Night of the Year™, and after months of reported disaffection, Penn and Robin Wright re-emerged as a couple. Once again, there were enormous changes at the last minute.

SEAN PENN: *The Bells of Hell* came just at the time when there was a possibility of putting this family back together, and I had to bow out of it so I could be there and do that. Robin and I started spending time again, sleeping over at each other's houses.

ROBIN WRIGHT PENN: And he asked me if I would go with him to the Academy Awards. He was bringing his parents.

SEAN PENN: The Academy Awards, it's just . . . I'd watched them enough years to know I wouldn't be comfortable sitting there. But I *was* gonna go: my mother and father wanted to go, it was their one time to go; Robin wanted to go, and she thought I was being selfish not to participate in that. And an awfully good case could be made for that. And then she got sick that night.

ROBIN WRIGHT PENN: Just as I was about to get ready, and the woman was coming with the dress, and the make-up and hair people were on their way – I collapsed. Nobody could figure out what it was. They thought it was gallstones. I'd had an ectopic pregnancy, a pregnancy in the tube instead of the uterus. The egg went up a fallopian tube and burst the tube, so you're bleeding internally and they have to tie the tube off and cauterize it. By the time they had done all the tests, it had run into the time that Sean had to be dressed and ready to go. I wanted him to go, and he said, 'No way, I'm staying.' And he was there at the bedside, sort of like a pretty picture . . .

Then when I went in for surgery and I was going to be out for nine hours anyway, he went off to the after-party.

And after that, we got back together. You go [*looks to heavens*], 'Were you on to something? Did it have to be that fucking dramatic?' I do think it was something up there, something higher, just sort of doing it for us. But it's always been drama in my life with Sean, always. It's pronounced: that's the word I would use for him, in every way – presence, emotional life – 'pronounced'. I think it's in his blood. He's always at the heart of something. Never a dull moment . . .

JOSEPH VITARELLI: When they were separated, there was no doubt in my mind – and I told Sean repeatedly – that they would get back together. Particularly with the kids, but . . . because no matter how tumultuous their relationship is, you'll catch moments if you're around them long enough where you see how much they love one another. And this is not interview bullshit – it's a real, powerful thing.

Now it *was* a complete surprise to me that, having got back together, they were then married, suddenly, literally within days. I was in London with Patty Clarkson when I got the call. Sean said, 'We're getting married.' I was thinking, 'OK, in a month or two if they want to do it quickly.' Sean says, 'No, this Saturday.'

I think Robin was the one who decided they should get back together and that they should be married. And I think Sean's response was, 'Yes. Thank you . . .' [*laughs*].

ROBIN WRIGHT PENN: As I remember it, it was almost like it was out of our hands in a way, the words just came out. Shall we do this? Yeah, we should do it.

This rekindling, I think a lot of it was, 'What are we doing?' In a way, you kind of accept: we're going to be volatile, this is not going to be easy. It's *never* been easy. But why are we waiting for it to become easy? And also this theory behind it of, 'Are you *ever* ready? Did we plan to have these kids? No. Can we imagine life without them? Never.' At a certain point, you do kind of just throw it up in the air – with abandon. 'Why don't we just –?' Sean likes the phrase, and it's so true: there are no plans – life is what happens to you when you're making other plans.

ART LINSON: Sean and Robin came over, sat down with Fiona[8] and I, and he said, 'Look, we're going to get married in ten days. And, god, you know . . . we're thinking maybe we're gonna have it in Santa Monica . . .?' I said, 'You mean – you want to have it *here*?' He said, 'Well, god, you know . . . Would you want to do that?' I said, 'Oh yeah. We've got, like, ten days to pull it off. But I'll do it.' And we did. And so they got married in my house, right out in the backyard.

DON PHILLIPS: Just before Sean got married to Robin, we had a teeny-weenie bachelor party: Timmy Hutton was living next door to me at the beach. Tim had a poem that he pulled out and read to Sean, kind of a famous poem about love and commitment. Then I got out a piece of paper from my pocket, all wrinkled – fourteen, fifteen years I've had it. It's a very famous poem called 'Footprints'.[9] I read it to Sean and he said, 'Let me look at it.' Then he said, 'Can I have this, Don?' I said, 'Yeah, sure, call it one of my gifts to you.'

Boy, that wedding was one of the happiest times. That was the moment for it. Really a hip, cool, joyous wedding. Art did his lawn up and made dance floors over the swimming pool. Everybody was dressed to the nines. Robin was beaming. The kids were there.

MEEGAN OCHS: But again, miraculously, there were freaking helicopters . . .

DR KATZ: Would have been better off letting one person in, just to get

---

8 Fiona Lewis, English-born writer and film actress, wife of Art Linson.
9 Many have claimed to be its author: the two most frequently named candidates are Margaret Fishback Powers and Mary Stevenson. Until 1987 it was attributed only to 'Anonymous'.

them off your back, but Sean wouldn't do that. What he had me do before the service was go down to Third Street Promenade and get a thousand balloons and a tank of gas, so I'm sending up all these balloons as a distraction . . .

DON PHILLIPS: And lo and behold – it was a total surprise – that poem was part of the vows. Sean just translated it for himself.

MEEGAN OCHS: It was just Sean and Robin sitting there looking at each other. When they exchanged their vows, she was miraculously calm, and he was shaking, weeping – it was beautiful, incredibly moving. And Sean told that incredible poem, where you imagine yourself walking on the beach, and in the hardest times of your life you can only see your own footprints, and you're thinking, 'Where were you in those times when I needed you most?' And it's in those times that she was carrying him – the footprints were hers.

Then the rest of it ends up being just a fun party with all these icons of American film speaking: Jack Nicholson, Marlon Brando, Warren Beatty reading Rainer Maria Rilke . . . They have such tremendous love and respect for him, and they were there to celebrate his marriage, passing this cigar between them as each one got up to speak.

JACK NICHOLSON: I remember feeling, 'Uh-oh, I'm gonna have to say something here . . .' Which I don't, usually. I wish I was more graceful in that way but I'm not a good public speaker. But it was one of those cases where I think it sort of fell to me to get Marlon off. Once he gets rolling, he can roll . . . [grins]. So as I was sitting there, I wrote some sort of a poem about the day, which I got up and started to say. And then Marlon came up and started fooling around . . .

DON PHILLIPS: Marlon kneels and begins, very methodically, to take Jack's pants off: undoes his belt and his top button and his zipper. Jack acts like nothing's happening. It couldn't have been better rehearsed. Finally Marlon pulls Jack's pants down. There's Jack in his beautiful suit, talking very seriously about his friendship with Sean and how much he loves Robin and how glad he is that they're together – pants down round his ankles, in his shorts, perfectly unbothered.

JACK NICHOLSON: It went nice . . . Marlon and I will always work well together. And the big fella's pretty funny. We all had a good time. The evening continued on, I remember that much. It was rousing. A good Irish wedding . . .

JOHN SYKES: At my wedding back in 1991, I'd been having the first dance with my wife when Sean cut in, and I backed off to let him dance with my wife. He said, 'No, I'm dancing with *you*.' And this wasn't a slow dance – we had Buckwheat Zydeco playing, they busted into a wild tune, and Sean had a freshly-lit cigarette in his mouth, about an inch from my nose . . .

So, when the dancing started at Sean's and Robin's wedding, I basically broke in and danced with Sean. And Marlon Brando became intrigued by that: I guess he thought, 'Okay, it's time for the men to start dancing.' So he grabbed me and began to dance, then got me in a bear-hug that was so hard I felt the air stop. I said, 'Marlon, Sean danced with me at my wedding, this is a *joke* . . .' And he looked at me and said, 'This is no joke.'

ART LINSON: Brando danced with my Guatemalan maid, which I don't think she's ever recovered from. Bob De Niro was in the back, looking at the whole thing, very quiet. When you have all of those people in a Santa Monica bungalow – it created a bit of havoc in the neighbourhood. But I didn't let it concern me. I just drank heavily and let it happen . . .

HARRY DEAN STANTON: Robin is great, by the way. She's a great comedienne and a great dramatic actress. She's gorgeous. And she didn't take any crap from him: I think that's one reason he stayed with her too. I love her. You can write that – I'm in love with Sean's wife. She's my favourite wife.

ELEVEN

1996–1998

I've always admired Sean's ability to discern what's going to be an interesting role and an interesting film. And even when he's been in a film that hasn't ultimately worked out in its totality – I've always understood why he did it.

Kevin Spacey

Sean has done a lot of movies for little or no money, certainly for someone in his sphere. And he's turned down *colossal* amounts. Do you know how many buddy-movies this guy's been offered? It's one thing to say, 'I'm gonna turn down $10 million', and another thing to *do* it.

Joseph Vitarelli

SEAN PENN: *Hugo Pool* was sort of a favour. And it was a lark.

BARBARA LIGETI: Robert Downey Senior is an oddball creative artist: *Putney Swope, Greaser's Palace* – he was one of the pure true independents. *Hugo Pool* was a mission-piece. It was really made to illuminate ALS, Lou Gehrig's Disease. It was written by Robert and his second wife, Laura Ernst, who was dying of Lou Gehrig's Disease. The money couldn't be raised in her lifetime. Then we went full throttle. I was inviting everybody and the kitchen sink who had some viability. But Sean's participation, practically speaking, made it happen, because the people who put up the $2 million for a very special-interest movie wanted some star power. Sean knew that. He told me, 'I'll be there.' And he stepped up to the plate beautifully.

Penn, as an angelic hitch-hiker in azure-blue shoes, was one of many chipping in cameos to a sweet piece about a lissom pool cleaner (Alyssa Milano) and her budding love for an ALS sufferer (Patrick Dempsey). Also cast was the director's son, the mercurial Robert Downey Jr, another alumnus of Santa Monica High School, now labouring under the substance addiction which had long beleaguered his career. Penn had appeared in his documentary of the 1992 presi-

dential election, The Last Party, *and had taken more than a casual interest in how he managed his talents. As Downey Jr later recalled for* Playboy *magazine, 'I remember him saying three or four years ago, "You have two reputations. I think you know what both of them are, and I think you'd do well to get rid of one of those reputations. If you don't, it will get rid of the other one . . ."' These concerns came to a sharp head in mid-June 1996.*

MATT PALMIERI: Robert had locked himself inside a spare bedroom in his house. He was at one of his lowest points. His wife called Sean and I, and we went there to see what we could do. Eventually, after much failed negotiation yelling through the door, Sean kicked it down. I tackled Robert and carried him out of the house, kicking and screaming. We jammed him into a car, drove him to the airport, put him into a rented jet and flew him to Arizona and put him into Sierra Tucson, one of those rehab clinics – from which, of course, he broke out of two days later, walked out into the desert, and hitched a ride back home. Eventually, we both realized that there's really nothing you can do for someone in that situation: they have to do it for themselves – which is what Robert is trying his best to do as we speak . . .

What next for the newlyweds? Their honeymoon picture, so to speak, was a project that Penn had lived with for a decade or so. After John Cassavetes' death in February 1989, he had taken an option from the estate to direct 'She's De-Lovely', but that aspiration went on ice once The Indian Runner *became a reality.*

SEAN PENN: Then I was going to do it with Gary Oldman. But Miramax, who wanted to make the picture, wouldn't give me the $8 million that I wanted to make it in black and white. And that was the movie I saw, so I walked away from it. And then, a couple of years later, I got a call from Nick.

Nick Cassavetes had made his directorial début in 1995 with Unhook the Stars, *part-financed by the French outfit Hachette Première, whom he then sold on the notion of 'She's De-Lovely'. Miramax came aboard too. Cassavetes approached the more-than-ready Penn for the lead role of Eddie, and he in turn proposed the mother of his children for the part of Eddie's beloved Maureen. The newly–minted* She's So Lovely *(the Cole Porter Estate protected its title) rolled in mid-July*

Photo by Joyce Rudolph. © Miramax. Courtesy of Sean Penn

56 *She's So Lovely*: Penn (Eddie Quinn) and Robin Wright Penn (Maureen)

1996. This story of tempestuous lovers reunited had all the parallels in film history and tabloid column inches that the newlyweds could possibly stomach, but more important was the chance for Penn to repay a debt of love to Cassavetes as the barfly/grifter Eddie, and for Wright to efface her looks and long-standing screen persona.

ROBIN WRIGHT PENN: *She's So Lovely* was a huge marker for me, because I had an opportunity to play a character nobody had ever given me, a camp character. Before, it was like, 'OK, could you just play the soulful wife? Could you bring it down, please? We just want to see your eyes . . .' Then I was in New York with Erin, and she said to me, 'You've got to meet this girl from Brooklyn. She *is* Maureen.' She was my size, slim and petite, beautiful, piercing eyes – and a bouncer in a nightclub. Just loud and fucken ballsy, *right* out there, everything *in your face*: 'What are you *saying*?' So the satisfaction was that I was able to go for it and bust out, let myself have colour. And to work with Sean – and we had such a great time. Hated each other in life, but had a great time on the set . . .

JOSEPH VITARELLI: The idea behind that whole film was, 'Let's not take this too seriously, and these are not nice people.' And those, I think, were Sean's very words. Because, really, the scenario is just dreadful. This woman has got a life with a steady, stable guy – and he's John Travolta, for chrissakes – and he's got a nice house, he's a contractor. Then along comes Sean, and, God almighty, he's just out of a mental institution, having near killed a guy in a drunken rage. And he's sitting outside their home guzzling wine out of a broken bottle. With Debi Mazar, sitting in the back of the car, telling him 'You look great, honey.' Then he goes in there saying, 'I'm here to take her back.' And she leaves!

ROBIN WRIGHT PENN: She leaves because it's the right thing to do. That's Cassavetes. Maybe that's why we accept it, because it's him. But he always wrote crazy love – just fucken crazy, there's no explanation for it, and there doesn't have to be. That's the beauty of his message, I think. Look at *Woman Under the Influence*. It's a departure from our reality maybe, but it's out there, believe me. And he paints it true to life, I think. Or maybe it's what goes on inside people, whether they do it or not . . .

DON PHILLIPS: Sean and Robin were living up in the Palisades, and they were making *She's So Lovely*. And I was casting *The Game* for David Fincher. The original leads were Jodie Foster and Michael Douglas. Michael had signed on the understanding that Jodie was going to play his sister; Jodie and David decided that the film would have a greater impact if Michael played Jodie's father. Michael disagreed. So Jodie decided not to do it, even though they had signed contracts, and there had been foreign sales on the strengths of these two names. Jodie ended up suing the company, and she got paid off. So, there we were, left without the other lead. The story, originally, had been about two brothers, and they now decided they might as well go back to that original. And it was put to me: 'Don, can you get Sean into this movie?'

Sean was back to acting, but they were always giving him some frigging excuse not to pay him the kind of money he should have been getting. He was always being soft-soaped. I knew this, and I told Sean, 'Look, if you do me and Fincher a favour for three and a half weeks of shooting, I'll pay you a lot of money.' Sean doesn't like me to say how much he made, but it was a nice chunk of change . . .

Sean dug Fincher, and I think he eventually found something to bite on in *The Game*. I think he dug the fact that his character instigates an enormous change in his brother by making him crazy with the idea that he really set him up. Fincher came up with the idea that Sean's character was constantly smoking where you weren't allowed to in public. In the movie, it's a very private club that Michael's character belongs to, and Sean lights up a cigarette. Michael says, 'It's illegal to smoke in restaurants in California,' and Sean says, 'Fuck California!' Now *that's* a Sean Penn moment . . .

SEAN PENN: I wanted to get out of Los Angeles. I'd been trying to get Robin to move out before we ever broke up. I looked at a lot of places I was dreaming of when I was driving back from *Dead Man Walking*. And then I spent a little bit of time at Bruce Weber's ranch out in Montana, which was great, and made me think about it more.

ERIN DIGNAM: They had been talking for a while, I think, about where they wanted their kids educated, what kind of environment, and they'd always been interested in their not growing up in Hollywood. And then Robin got car-jacked.

ROBIN WRIGHT PENN: I was in the truck in the driveway. Hopper was in a car-seat in the back, Dylan had jumped out already. This kid came up. He had a coat on and there was something in his pocket, and when he pressed it up against my ribs, it felt like a gun. He was threatening to take my truck, and I told him I couldn't give him my keys until I'd got my kid out of the back seat. I offered him my back-pack that had a lot of cash in it, but he didn't want that: he wanted the car. I said, 'I'm sorry, I can't.' And just as the guy was moving in on me to take my keys – 'I don't care about your kid' – Hopper jumped into the front seat with me. It had never happened before that Dylan had the strength to push the little button that released the belt on his car-seat: this was the first time she did. And it was a blessing.

DON PHILLIPS: Robin called the police after they left, and they caught those guys. Thank God Sean wasn't around – he'd have shot 'em . . .

ROBIN WRIGHT PENN: And, yeah, that was the last straw. I hated the city; it was destroyed for me, the whole vibe, the trust. I wanted out. Again, though, it always feels like there's something up there that gives you a nudge to wake you up – 'Stop pontificating, just do it.'

DON PHILLIPS: While we were shooting *The Game* up in San Francisco, all of a sudden the money was coming, and Sean and Robin bought a home up in Ross in Marin County, coincidentally where David Fincher grew up. And we call it 'The House that *The Game* Bought' . . .

SEAN PENN: One of the reasons I wanted to move to Marin was because Lynn Milner was on Death Row in San Quentin and I thought I'd see a lot more of him. I felt this incredible shame that I hadn't spent more time around him. And that continues today. One of the difficulties I had in Los Angeles was you'd come up to visit, go through the whole process, and suddenly there'd be a stabbing on the tier and they would shut the whole prison down, and you'd have flown in for nothing. They don't make it easy – the corrections department or the fraternity mates.

Lynn's since had his sentence commuted to Life Without. Now he's all the way down in Salinas Valley, which is three hours each way, plus the waiting and the processing – it's very difficult to visit. So it's not a thing where I feel I've been a particularly consistent friend. But I got two kids, and it's hard.

In October 1996, Penn's Clyde Is Hungry Films pacted with Mike Medavoy's newly formed Phoenix Pictures, in a throwback to their fruitful arrangement at Orion in the late eighties. The business, though, had not got any more receptive.

SEAN PENN: Mike and I had had a long, good history – and we still have a good relationship. But that moment at Phoenix was a difficult one. Mike had had the courage to do *The People vs. Larry Flynt*; and then, out of a history with Barbra Streisand, he put an enormous amount of money into *The Mirror Has Two Faces*. Those two movies came out as I made my deal, and they didn't perform. And there were people involved there who were very bottom-line business guys, who had a very simplistic view of what worked and what didn't work. And when Mike didn't have enormous support from the people he worked with, then he tended to be working from the back of the line. So I felt we were sort of putting some Band-Aids on past wounds, which were legitimate wounds – because I liked *Larry Flynt* a lot. And that wasn't the time to be in business at Phoenix, not for us.

There was, however, an exceptional Medavoy/Phoenix project to which Penn was wholly committed as an actor: the directorial return of Terrence Malick, translator of Heidegger, Rhodes scholar, MIT instructor, alumnus of the AFI's first-ever class, and cinematic avatar ever since Badlands *closed the 1973 New York Film Festival amid raptures. Malick had begun to live between Paris and Austin, cultivating ambitious projects. One was an adaptation of James Jones's 1962 novel* The Thin Red Line, *a sort of sequel to his hugely successful* From Here to Eternity *that offered a grimly detailed anatomy of the members of a US rifle company, C-For-Charlie, in their desperate effort to secure superiority on Guadalcanal Island. By 1995, Malick, in tandem with Medavoy, his agent back in the seventies, was ready to make a leap.*

SEAN PENN: Before I went to *Dead Man Walking,* I was over at Phoenix, and Mike Medavoy said to me, 'Terry's in town and would love to meet you. Maybe you'd like to come at the end of our meeting and you guys can hang out?' Well, I went, and we had a coffee together near Book Soup, and we expressed a mutual interest in working together. I said, 'You know, if ever there's something . . .? Any time.' Many months later, I was driving around some other places, rambling a little bit. I stopped in at Austin and called a number he'd given me to track him down at that first meeting. We got together for lunch, and that was the first time he mentioned *The Thin Red Line.* I said, 'Whatever you're doing, I'm in.'

As Malick cogitated, Penn took another Phoenix job, albeit impromptu, with another writer–director he considered worth the candle. Oliver Stone had adapted U-Turn, *a twisty, back-stabbing western-noir B-picture about a gambler whose car breaks down near a desert town, so luring him into a heaving snake pit of lust, money and deceit.*

SEAN PENN: I had been asked to do the movie when it was called *Stray Dogs*; and then there was a problem with Kurosawa, who owned that title. But I wasn't considering working at that moment, so I turned it down, and Oliver hired Bill Paxton. It took them longer than they thought, and Paxton had had some problems, and Oliver called and said, 'Would you do this?' Nick Nolte was already committed. I was committed to *The Thin Red Line* but I checked with Terry; and Mike was making both movies, so that was easy. So I just jumped in. And I don't know that I had any more than a week before I started shooting . . .

MIKE MEDAVOY: Bill Paxton couldn't have pulled off that part. Bill and I just laugh about it nowadays: he kind of dodged a bullet, in a way . . .

In early November 1996, Penn drove his 1967 Chevy El Camino all night from California to Superior, Arizona. The shoot would be six six-day weeks: tough material on a tight schedule. The experience by no means belied the expectation.

SEAN PENN: I don't know if Oliver – at least at that time – knew where the actor's voice comes from. And so he seemed to have a need to drown everybody else's voice in order to channel his own through them. Not only was I not interested in that, I'm not *capable* of it. So it was like loggerheads. And there was such a kind of glibness towards everybody, a kind of general arrogance and megalomania that just . . . bugged me and didn't respect my participation or anybody else's. It was like, 'Let's just make a miserable situation more miserable, because I don't trust that the actors can make it more miserable on their own.' We're talking about that environment that's created when somebody's just *yelling* at people all the time, telling them that they're doing shit work over here or there. And for one thing, it takes *all* the fucken fun out of it. So where I thought people could be encouraged to do their best work, I thought they were being scared into making the least mistakes.

Oliver gets good people in, and they collect footage, and then he gets in three different editing rooms with three different editors. And it's bold. It was just, basically, that every day was an irritation. But I think there was, in our own way, some mutual respect for what each other had to offer the piece. And I came out of it feeling that we'd made a good movie. But it wasn't a warm and fuzzy experience . . .

In the spring of 1997, Penn put his shoulder behind Democrat state senator Tom Hayden's ultimately unsuccessful run for Mayor of Los Angeles against Republican incumbent Richard Riordan. Hayden was talking about revamping public transport, cleaning up the environment, increasing drug-treatment programs and creating inner-city jobs; borrowing the contemporary lingo of centre-left social democrats across the Atlantic, he vowed to be 'tough on crime, but equally tough on dealing with the causes of crime', and called for 'a peace process within the inner city'.

Courtesy of Meegan Ochs

57 April 1997: a fundraising evening for Tom Hayden,
with Meegan Ochs, Penn

SEAN PENN: I believe in Tom Hayden, and he's maintained a certain idealism and he's very bright and tough about it. He was anxious for me to get involved, and I didn't have a lot of preparation for it, but sometimes you just take a stab. I don't know if it was helpful: he was running a tough race anyway.

Penn spoke up for Hayden on the UCLA campus and fronted a fundraising evening for him. At the same moment, complications arose over the completion of She's So Lovely.

JOSEPH VITARELLI: I wrote the score for *She's So Lovely* in less than two weeks – by necessity. There was a lot going on about the cut. What happened was a decision to spend a lot more money in a short period. They decided to re-edit the film substantially, and they knew they were running out of time because they had committed it to screen in Cannes.

ROBIN WRIGHT PENN: It wasn't a pleasant vibe between Sean and Nick, I don't think. But in the end it bettered the film. I think the editing maybe lost the rhythm that is so important to John Cassavetes' stuff, and Sean was trying to modify it, to salvage that.

SEAN PENN: Nick was a great director to work with. We had such a good time, and I knew he'd made a good movie. I didn't feel that his editor was necessarily serving him best. There was an agreement that had been made in my getting involved in it that there would be a certain sort of participation if necessary. And it turned out in my view to be necessary. He and I both know now that *he* made the movie; there was a period where he wondered if he was being usurped. There was certainly a contest of wills, which he was going to lose 'cause he was up against the economics at the time and the original commitments, which exceeded what he was sharing. But that's part of what you like about him: he's a cowboy. Nick has spent so much of his life talking about other people, his father and his mother. And he's so unique himself: a big, tall, totally fearless person. He will tell you exactly what he thinks when he thinks it, and he'd tell it to Louis B. Mayer too. I find him enormously bright, entertaining and talented. We're friends. He would not be my friend if there were any legitimacy to his position at that time, in any aspect of it – because Nick Cassavetes is a tough motherfucker. There's no forgiving a robbery; there *is* acknowledging the due partnership. And that was understood, after a little time to digest.

JOSEPH VITARELLI: So I was brought in at the eleventh hour to write this whole orchestral score. They totally supported me. But it was like, 'You *have* to tell us that this will be done on this date.' There was only one way to do it. Sean had the idea, and it was a smart one. I had a little house in Santa Monica, so me and Sean camped out there, moved a whole Avid system into my den, and they started to re-cut the movie and would pass the reels out, one at a time, and I'd score them. So Sean and I were basically living and working at my place twenty-four hours a day. My neighbours started sending me letters. 'What's all the cursing and yelling about?'

The music is like a twisted homage to Mancini, but there are other parts, like the big brooding orchestral dirge after Sean shoots the guy. A lot of timpani. Sean and I wound up on the stage at Paramount with a symphony orchestra, screaming at each other: 'I want more fucking timpani!' 'Fuck your timpani, we got enough . . .'

And the quote at the beginning of the film is complete fabrication, attributed to someone who never existed. With a date, no less . . . [1]

1 'Love is that kindness, so rarely kind, and never at all proper.' B. R. Dignin, 1892.

SEAN PENN: It says 'B. R. Dignin', right? That's *Bottle Rocket* – the character that Owen Wilson plays. I had just seen *Bottle Rocket*, and I thought he was the new philosopher of our age, so I made up a quote that I thought led us into the picture. I told Wes Anderson before Cannes – didn't tell anybody else . . .

JOSEPH VITARELLI: The reception at Cannes was great. Those performances, the three of them . . . Sean, brilliant, as always. Robin was breathtaking. I've never seen Travolta better. I don't know why the *film* didn't do better. Maybe it was too dark.

SEAN PENN: How do I feel about it? It's Robin! [*laughs*] I love it. I loved it when I first read it. I love the way it portrays love – the mess of it, the blinding hysteria of the females of our species, the startling rage in the males. And it's funny too. Robin's stunning in it. But for too many women on the jury that year who would have liked to play the part, I think she would have walked away with the Cannes award . . .

Wright was recognized with the female performance prize at Seattle the following month, but for Erin Dignam's much-delayed Loved. *The public reception of the film was nevertheless something of a lion's-den experience for the director and her lead, with Penn as an interested observer.*

ERIN DIGNAM: Seattle was the first place *Loved* played to an audience, in a huge Landmark Theatre. We were going to do a Q&A, and I got a call saying, 'We're considering having security in the audience, in case there's trouble.' They weren't sure if factions of the audience would feel I was condoning violence against women. We walked onstage, the entire audience had stayed, and the energy was intense.

ROBIN WRIGHT PENN: It was two sides of a coin. They either loved it and sobbed, 'Oh my god, I *was* that woman.' Or there were people who were just vitriolic: 'How can you fucking make a movie like *that*? Are you out of your mind? That's not love, that's sick.' So poor Erin was being bombarded with both. I was thinking, 'It doesn't have to be one or the other. Why can't it be one person's vision or experience?' But again, I was judging it. I was probably judging it while I was making it.

ERIN DIGNAM: I was in shock. A typical girl, I kind of cried on the stage. But there was so much focus on Robin. Sean was up there too, but eventually he sat down at the edge of the stage and smoked and watched us talk. I was talking about how it was important to de-glamorize Robin in the part – she wore no make-up – and I said, 'It's just hard to make her look bad.' Sean raised his hand. 'I see her in the *morning . . .*'

In summer 1997, the Penns prepared their move to Marin County and the renovation of a Spanish stucco house to their exact specifications.

JOSEPH VITARELLI: They bought a substantial piece of property with a relatively small house and built it up. They've lived in places a fraction of that size in the past, so it was somewhat unlike them. But I think they realized that in order to maximize the value of the whole property they should build this truly magnificent house.

ROBIN WRIGHT PENN: We thought it would take a year and a half from the time we purchased the property. It took three years . . .

ERIN DIGNAM: We all kind of moved to Marin together. Then Sean and Robin went to the coral reef in Australia for *The Thin Red Line* for the next five months.

Phoenix Pictures alone couldn't get The Thin Red Line *before the cameras, so Laura Ziskin's Fox 2000 stepped up to service the $52-million budget, contingent upon Malick securing an adequate roster of marquee talent. In fact, the film's final cast list would boast Penn, George Clooney, John Travolta, Nick Nolte, John Cusack, Woody Harrelson and a sheaf of talented others, some of them onscreen for mere minutes.*

MIKE MEDAVOY: Sean was the first actor in. He was the first one to say, 'Hey, just let me know when you want me to be there and I'll be there.' And he was helpful also in trying to put the movie together.

WOODY HARRELSON: Sean was the one who suggested *The Thin Red Line* to me, said, 'You got to do it, this guy is one of the greatest directors ever.' I liked Terry. I'd seen his films, but I didn't really see it that way until later . . . Now, having worked with him, I admire the hell out of him; he's just an amazing guy. But I'm sure Sean talked to Terry about me. And then it was kind of cool, because I'd just done a bunch of movies and I was real tired of working, but Terry basically let me pick a part. And I said, 'OK, I want to be this guy who dies on page 73 . . .'

SEAN PENN: It was a *large* project, you know, and not the kind that I wrapped my head around all that well, because I was committed just on the basis of Terry. I read it, and I *got* it; and I read the book. But I still felt, 'Well, once this is a go-movie then I'll figure out what my place is in it.' I didn't get into a lot of script conversations until later, relative to my part.

Penn's role was Sergeant Welsh, leader of C-For-Charlie, the thin battalion trying to take Guadalcanal from the Japanese. In Jones's novel, Welsh is seen by the grunts as a kind of madman, his eccentricities (an alarming grin, a concealed flask of gin, a tendency to insist loudly that the war is solely about 'Property!') considered barely tolerable even in wartime. James Jones knew of what he wrote, having fought and killed at Guadalcanal in 1943. His own career hit the skids when he went AWOL after being denied leave and a limited-duty assignment, leading in turn to a humiliating demotion. As such, the near-insolently ungovernable figure of Private Witt in The Thin Red Line *has shades of self-portrait, and Malick unsurprisingly made Witt (Jim Caviezel) his protagonist, albeit translating him into a kind of enigmatic warrior/pantheist.*

SEAN PENN: Originally, Welsh had something really going against him, in terms of James Jones's book and in the life of James Jones, which is Jones was prejudiced. He was looking at it as a private talking to a sergeant, the guy who's telling you what to do, every day. Not a good chance that's going to be objective. It carried over to Terry's script, originally. And I didn't think it was dramatically fair to my character to take on the biased storytelling owned in prose by a writer who is, fair enough, speaking from his own point of view. I thought we had to be a little bit more like detectives into the psychology of why it was viewed this way, otherwise it doesn't play as natural.

We shot a lot of improvisations, and there was no *question* that Terry was going to be juxtaposing elements radically. When you work for Terry, it's a palette, and you're a colour, and you've got to let him form you. And, in a way, I felt most effective the more neutral a colour I was. Or I wanted to be the water on the palette, and he could portray me as visibly or invisibly as he wanted, depending on how he wanted to touch it in the cutting room. I really wanted to just say a speech or behave in such a way that – and I'm exaggerating here – depending on a piece of music Terry played over the scene, it could be clear that Welsh was lying about everything he was saying; or, with *no* music, there was no question I was speaking the truth, and I believed it, and you ought to believe it too. And I think it kind of worked out that way.

The Thin Red Line rolled in June 1997 in the Daintree rain forest near the small town of Port Douglas, Australia.

58 On location for *The Thin Red Line*: Adrien Brody (Corporal Fife), Woody Harrelson (Sgt. Keck), Penn (Sgt. Welsh)

© Twentieth Century Fox. Photo by Merie W. Wallace

WOODY HARRELSON: It was kind of an idyllic time out there in Australia. We were all in the same little area: I was there with my kids, Seaner had his kids, Jack Fisk, the designer, and Sissy Spacek had their kids – there was a real festive family thing going on in that little enclave. But Seaner was wanting to get on top form: as with everything, when he focuses on something, you know about it. He'd put on a little gut, so he was modifying his diet and he'd done his research and realized he needed to raise his metabolism. So he decided the best thing to do was two-a-day workouts, long runs in the morning and in the evening. He even had an idea about what pace he needed to run at – he was *scientific*. And he talked me into doing it too. My place was only a short walk from his, and I'd be sitting there at the end of the day, so tired, just wanting to lay down for a while. But I'd sense when the time was coming. And I'd be dreading it. 'Please, Sean, just let me just sleep . . .' Then I'd hear the rat-tat-tat: 'C'mon, buddy! Let's go.' 'Ah, Jesus . . .'

It was a real pleasure working with Terry. Genius manifests in so many different forms, I guess. With Sean, it's easy – you hang out with him for an hour and you know the guy's a certified genius, without question. But Terry Malick . . . he's so unassuming and so humble: keep in mind, he's a guy who hadn't worked for twenty years. He just looked at the business as a fraud, I think, and backed off of it. But when you think of *Badlands*, the beauty of that simple story . . . boy, did he take a huge, huge jump back into directing [*laughs*]. You couldn't imagine a much bigger project: creating a war, basically, with so many people, so many props, artillery, weaponry, everybody's got their own rifle. And then all the cranes and the big shots. I remember asking him, 'Why did you take off such a bite?' He has a way of talking, almost like a savant. And he said [*high Texan accent*]: 'Oh . . . I never really thought it would be such a big thing. I guess, if I were to do it again – I'd do it different . . .'

But I love his style, you know? He'd come out in the morning and he'd really *look* – at the way the grass was blowing in the wind on the hill and the way the sunlight was slipping across the grass. And he'd say, 'Hmm . . . let's set the cameras up *here*. Facing *that* way.' You couldn't always tell what he was after, no. But everybody had faith in him: it wasn't like people thought, 'What the –? This guy doesn't know what he's doing.' No, this is Terry Malick – it's not just your average Joe. So you just believed. 'You just *believed*, brother!'

A company of actors bivouacked in close proximity naturally created the potential for high jinks, perhaps because rather than in spite of the gravity of the project. And so a low-intensity war of pranks began between Penn and Harrelson.

WOODY HARRELSON: It started with little stuff . . . One time I got this plaster-of-Paris snake from props that looked exactly – I mean *exactly* – like a real snake, coiled and lifted up ready to strike. You couldn't imagine a more daunting image. And I set it on the steps of Sean's trailer so he would come off of a scene and see this thing. I walk ahead of him and make like I'm peeing. He goes to his trailer, opens the door, sees this frickin' dangerous poisonous snake, ready to strike, steps back on his heels a split second – and in the next, reaches and grabs the thing by the throat, yanks and rips the head clean off it. He's standing there, staring at this snake head in his hand, adrenaline pumping through his body . . . and I'm thinking, 'Oh my god, that is the most fearless act I ever saw . . .'

Then it was just slow, sure escalation, because you've got to outdo the thing before. And Seaner did, well, probably the best practical joke that has ever been played on me.

He hadn't been working a particular day, so he'd had many hours to do this: he got some picture of me and made up a poster that read something like: 'WOODY HARRELSON DAY! Come meet the star of film and TV in person! He will sign pictures – $12 apiece!' And there was a time and a place where this was going to happen. Anybody who knows us would know it's a joke, but anyone who *didn't* . . . And he put up, I think, two thousand of these things around town: you couldn't pass a telephone pole in any direction but you'd see at least four of them. Again, the focus of this guy . . . I tried to pull a few down, but it was just too huge a project to undo. The real genius of it was I had to actually *go* there on the day to the place, in case anybody showed. And I think there were two or three poor unfortunates there, and a few others who Sean had told, 'Be there so you can see this.' He got me good. He raised the bar way, way high. So I had to think of something to top that.

I got Nick Nolte to call him one night from a police station, saying he'd got caught driving drunk and he didn't have his licence and could Sean please come down and help him? So Sean hurried down there. And we had it all set up. Seaner comes in, there's a cop who starts dealing with him, and then to one side there's another cop dealing with a prisoner, a bad-lookin' dude with handcuffs on – who's really a cop. I had been rehearsing earlier in the day with these guys. So this guy's all grumbling and upset as Sean comes in: 'Take these cuffs off me so I can pee.' The cop uncuffs him, tells him to relax, takes him back where the bathroom is. Then all you hear is some tussle taking place, shouting and banging, then what sounds like a gunshot, and the prisoner comes out holding a gun – which couldn't shoot if you wanted it to, it's just a prop. But Sean sees this maniac guy with a shaved head screaming, 'Everybody get on the floor!' Sean gets on the floor with everybody else – everybody's in on it except him, Nick's trying hard as hell not to laugh. Then the guy says to Sean, 'You! Gimme your car keys. We gotta go get your car.' Sean's like, 'OK.' He opens the door. And on the either side is me. 'Gotcha, buddy . . .'

Long story short: things kind of got out of hand after that, and me and Sean had a falling out that lasted for several months. There are certain things I did that I regret. And it just got to the point where we nearly came to blows. Eventually, I was in the San Fran area and I got in touch with him, said something to the effect of, 'I love you too much to hate you.' We got together. There was still a lot of tension, but it was really good to talk. And now it's better than ever. Maybe sometimes you've gotta sink to that in order to move to another level . . .

* * *

BOBBY COOPER: In Hollywood, you go to rehab, you come out and get a sitcom. With Sean, it's like you go to jail, come out and get a great job. Maybe I should go in jail, then come out and he'll give *me* a job. You hear that, Seanie?

Penn had long been of a mind that friendship ought to be inviolable. Given that his world of acquaintance had been one of ever-widening circles, this principle required considerable exertion and vigilance, and made for a few surprises. In the early summer of 1997, an old associate contacted him with a special request.

ANDREW DAULTON LEE: I was getting ready to get released and I wrote Sean a letter, talked to him, and said, 'Look, I'm not quite sure what the hell I'm gonna be doing. I need a place to park and I need a job to deal with my parole situation.' So I went to work with Sean's company at Mike Medavoy's place in Culver City.

I was a fish out of water. Most people there had this encyclopaedic background in the business. They'd say, 'Get a hold of so-and-so.' I'd say, 'Who?' So it was kind of a slow process. And, oh God, Sean was great, because I didn't have a clue. I hadn't made a phone call in years. Now I'm in an office with a phone that has buttons all over it. One time I punched one of them and disconnected a conference call between Sean and Gabriel García Márquez . . . four different countries all tied in and I made them all disappear.

But his sense of humour is something. We were driving in Hollywood on the way to the office one day, not long after I got out. Sean says, 'I got an idea.' Pulls out his phone. 'Let's call Hutton up!' So he calls and says, 'Hey. I got somebody wants to talk to you.' Hands me the phone. I say, 'So you got any more microfilm or what?' There's a pregnant pause, and Hutton says, 'Who is this? Oh shit . . .'

Twelve, thirteen years previous – how life can be funny – Sean took my mother to dinner. Now I'm out of prison, working for Sean, having dinner with his parents and driving them back and forth while they're doing the play *Remembrance*. I sat there thinking, 'Man, this is strange. You can't write film scripts like that.'

Remembrance was a really noble thing Sean did for his parents. They hadn't acted together in forty years. And it was the last hurrah.

Leo Penn had furthered his directing career in television – three hundred hours of prime-time drama, an Emmy along the way – until, in his early seventies, he found the work no longer forthcoming. His health then worsened, heart trouble prompting a triple bypass operation; and after this recovery came the blight of lung cancer.

But four decades after The Iceman Cometh, *he and Eileen were reunited onstage in Graham Reid's* Remembrance, *a bittersweet Belfast drama about the romance between a Protestant man and a Catholic woman tending the graves of sons killed in 'The Troubles'. Their closeness is threatened by Bert's hard-drinking policeman son Victor and Theresa's fiery daughter Deirdre, wife of an incarcerated IRA man.*

'It's like getting married again, renewing your vows,' Leo Penn affably told the LA Times. *'It's misleading to say it's a geriatric* Romeo and Juliet *– but it is.'*[2]

EILEEN RYAN PENN: Veronica Brady, who lives on Point Dume, was the director. The two producers live out here too, and they asked Sean to put his name to it. That meant a lot. Sean put money up and backed us, all the way, to be able to do it. Leo was very, very brave: he did the play with me while he was going through chemo. It was very hard, but it meant a lot to him. And he loved the part.

JOSEPH VITARELLI: Sinead O'Connor and I assembled a lot of Irish

2 'Their Son, the Producer', *LA Times*, Diane Haithman, 21 September 1997.

music and did a couple of original things. And it was 'A Clyde Is Hungry Production'.

ANDREW DAULTON LEE: I loved Leo. We're both from Lithuania, so that was kind of a kick. He was funny, always wearing his ball cap and shorts. And he was one of the most fundamentally decent people I've ever met. He had a kind word for everybody. God, I would have done anything for him. He would say, 'You gotta get out of that halfway house. Tell 'em you got to pick me up in Malibu at eleven in the morning so you can come up to the beach below the house.' So I'm sitting out there on Paradise Cove, calling my brother on my cell phone . . .

EILEEN RYAN PENN: Jimmy Gandolfini played Leo's son. How about that? He hadn't done much of anything before. I went to a surprise party for him in New York in 2000, and he said to me, 'Eileen, remember when I told you I couldn't make a rehearsal one day because I had to go get seen for a part in a dumb little TV show . . .?'

ART WOLFF: Opening night, I'm standing in the lobby, it's five minutes to seven, and Sean is particularly nervous. I'm thinking, 'Why wouldn't he be, his mother and father?' I go over, put my arm around him, 'It's gonna be fine.' He goes, 'Says you. Gandolfini isn't here.' I said, 'You know the lines?' He looked at me like, 'Are you crazy?' 'Just kidding, he'll be here.' 'He'd better be.' The play went up a little late that night . . .

EILEEN RYAN PENN: Leo had neuropathy from the chemo – he couldn't feel his feet. Can you imagine being onstage and not knowing half the time if your feet are on the stage? And, oh, I just wanted to take him home with me and take care of him. But he begged me to do it, and I think it made him live another year. And he was charming and funny and wonderful in it. One night we had an Irish theatre group in; they filled the theatre. And I thought, 'Oh my god, they're going to be really honest about our northern Irish accents . . .' But they loved it, they were screaming 'Bravo!' at the end.

ANDREW DAULTON LEE: There would be parties afterwards, sometimes out in the parking lot behind the theatre. People would show up who Leo hadn't seen for years and years. I think most of them knew he was dying. But they came out of respect for Leo and all his years in the industry. I tell you what: I don't think any son could have given his parents a better gift than Sean putting that play together.

Oliver Stone's U-Turn *appeared at Telluride in late August 1997 and was readied for an October release. But something of the film's ill-mannered production wouldn't die, and reared its head once more in a* Premiere *magazine set report wherein producer Clayton Townsend murmured something about Penn's supposed discomfort around the 'powerful' Stone; and an anecdote was shared of the actor expressing annoyance over 'a producer's son' who had slighted his assistant.*

SEAN PENN: There's the old idea of professional courtesy, 'What happens in the field stays in the field.' I didn't say anything. But then they mouthed off, and only their view of what happened appeared – which was not accurate and not honest, but a nice little convenient way to dismiss the contribution of others to the great god Oliver's piece.

There are a lot of people round Oliver who worked like spies; and a producer who's worked with him a bunch of times, who's really such a punk, his knee pads are worn out. At that time he was boning Manuel Noriega's daughter on the set, so 'Manny' would call collect to the production office a lot. I ran into him in Marin and I couldn't let him know how I felt, 'cause he was with his daughter at the time.

And they had this little wrapped-round-their-little-finger journalist from *Premiere* magazine, and they sort of slagged me off publicly; and it was a bias having to do with one of the incompetents they had hired, based on his being the son of one of Oliver's sycophants. He was incompetent at his job and, additionally, in my way. If there was any slagging to be done, it was the other way round. And I felt *really* double-crossed. I didn't need any more of that crap at that time, these guys making a spin on their own irresponsibility, having had so many people gunning for me. Then Mike Medavoy was concerned about a public war developing by the time the movie came out. So I kind of let it go for a while, exercised some restraint, because of Mike. But then, after it came out, I took the bars off, let a few things fly.[3]

MIKE MEDAVOY: I'm glad I made that movie: it's not like I feel it was a waste of my money and time. I still think it's an interesting film. I just think Oliver went overboard, and once you do that, you start to alienate people. It worked for him once on *Natural Born Killers*, but it didn't work twice.

---

3 'You could have called *U-Turn* "Dr Dolittle", because being able to communicate with the director was like talking to a pig . . .' *New York Times*, 28 December 1998.

SEAN PENN: I thought it should have been much more violent – which it was at one point – because I thought that would have been a lot funnier. In a movie, if you hit a person twice with an axe, it's violent. If you hit 'em four times with an axe, it's hyper-indulgent violence. If you hit 'em *eighty* times with an axe, it's hysterical. And that's what *U-Turn* was, originally. I think Oliver was sort of arbitrarily pushed to cut it down, and it became a little too real in its violence at times, when it should have been camp. Nonetheless – I still think it's a fun movie to watch.

Meanwhile, I've since sort of buried the hatchet with Oliver. I ran into him at Sundance, and we had a great conversation. But, you know, working with someone and talking to them in a hallway are two different things sometimes . . . We just have very different personalities. He was very piggish in our situation. What he's like now, I don't know. But I'm all for him.

In November 1997, Hurlyburly *was finally ready to roll, albeit financed by foreign pre-sales and a leveraged bank loan. The core cast were still in place, though Meg Ryan replaced Holly Hunter and Chazz Palmintieri came in for Tom Sizemore. Penn and family had returned from Australia to a rented place in San Anselmo, as construction on the family home was under way. The kids started new schools. Los Angeles, site of* Hurlyburly's *dissipation, was now, to some degree, behind him.*

TONY DRAZAN: Sean's caveat was that he asked us to shoot the movie up north so he could be close to home where he had just moved: he wanted to wake up in the morning and get his kids to school, and that seemed totally reasonable. But, in the wonderful world of Sean, what ended up happening was we were shooting nights, and he would basically crash where we were anyway. He had his weekends at home, but the kids only came to the set once or twice – it didn't seem entirely appropriate . . .

Once the cast was assembled, we managed a day and a half rehearsing in LA. Within about forty-five minutes, Garry Shandling suggested we just go to the Ivy for lunch, and that *was* the rehearsal, really. We spent hours there listening to Sean's provocative taunting, and Garry feeding off of Kevin's acerbic comebacks. In fact, the target of everyone's aggressions was Garry, who deflected it all masterfully.

GARRY SHANDLING: Artie is trying to be one of the guys and fit into their world. Certainly I was right for the character, because he wasn't quite as toughened up as the others. I didn't have drug issues. I had mother issues . . . I was doing *Larry Sanders* at the same time, but I couldn't imagine not taking the opportunity to work with that ensemble. I remember sitting in the living room set in-between takes with Sean and Kevin and Chazz, and realizing everyone sitting there had either won or been nominated for an Academy Award. At that juncture, I had, I think, a Cable Ace Award, now obselete. But I brought it up . . .

TONY DRAZAN: I convinced Mike Haller to do the production design on the movie. We started doing our scouts, and then he got sick, and it was the second bout. He said, 'Aw, I don't wanna slow you guys down.' But he designed the whole show, found a house for us up in Berkeley Hills. We flew up there. Kevin and Sean wandered around talking bullshit, I got a sense of how they would move in the space, Mike was making notes. But on the flight home, we could tell Mike was in a great deal of pain. So he kind of phoned it in from LA and did some work so we were ready when we came down there for a few days, and he was brilliant, to the end. He came to the screenings, and the greatest compliment I got on the movie was from Mike a short time before he died. He said, 'Well . . . it ain't for sissies.'

ROBIN WRIGHT PENN: *Hurlyburly* is just verbosity genius. I love it. I loved it when I saw it onstage with Sean. A lot of people are disgusted by it or feel it's all semantics: 'What is the purpose exactly?' Which is what it's about. What are you striving to achieve by talking something to death, analyzing to the point of vomiting? How do you get to a real honest relationship? Does it ever *really* have anything to do with what you're actually fighting about, ever? The genius of it is that all those inner thoughts we have are verbally expressed in the piece. It's like cocaine. And Eddie is sort of the apex of that; he's just diarrhoea of the mouth, no thought or feeling left unsaid. It's all out there. And he transports everyone else into that, too.

Sean knew the material inside out. He'd done it before for a month, been tortured by it for a month already. And between the intellects of Sean and Kevin, you really need smart actors to be able to do that kind of material.

KEVIN SPACEY: I always thought while I was doing the play that although Mickey ends up as the one whom the audience maybe enjoys the most, because he's quite, to use Eddie's term, 'flip' – which is one of my favourite terms *ever* – there's a part of Mickey that's dead. Yet he's created this veneer that's actually quite engaging. And, god knows, we know a lot of people like that . . .

TONY DRAZAN: I did sneak a peek at Sean's script as we approached shooting, and the margins were filled with notes and questions. His process seemed to be annotated in the text, and that was the surprise to me, because everything Sean does seems to happen right there. He looked at me smugly two days before we started and said, 'All you have to do is shoot it . . .' But Kevin was technically amazing and gave Sean a kind of foundation that allowed him to get out on the limb, as Eddie does. Some nights, after twelve, thirteen takes, Sean would start struggling with the lines, and Kevin was always there to anchor him. Kevin's sharp, he shoots bullets. And he never missed.

We didn't have any of the usual wagons, so the living room of that house was where the actors would be when we weren't shooting, and there was a lot of just hanging out: a very nice perverse community. We'd have a little drink at three or four in the morning. A little tequila by the camera kind of gets you through the rest of the night. But I'm pretty certain the only things those guys were snorting was Vitamin B and stuff that relieves constipation. So there was an enormous amount of flatulence on set.

ROBIN WRIGHT PENN: All the boys, they were shooting at night, sitting around, tired and waiting for the set-up. They decided they were going to write suicide notes and put 'em in a hat, and just pick them out and read them and guess whose each one was. Everybody knew Garry Shandling's was his.

GARRY SHANDLING: I had two – one that seems to be the, uh, winner, which Sean always repeats back to me when he sees me. It read, 'I'm not mad at anyone. This is just something I'm doing for me . . .'

We laughed a lot during *Hurlyburly*, which is, of course, an extraordinarily dark movie. I was so scared about just keeping up that in-between takes I would be funny, like a defence mechanism, and that would start the ball rolling. But Sean joins right in. A lot of the joking we would do would be sexual – somewhat dirty, somewhat *penis-oriented* types of joke, if I can put it that way. But I think of Sean as someone I can say that kind of thing to. In fact, he inspires it. And yet it's done with a great sense of fun and camaraderie, and that's a lot of what Sean brings – the best kind of male bonding. I don't know if anyone else would express it that way. But then I'm probably the most sensitive of anyone you'll interview. Other than Sean . . .

The midway crux of Hurlyburly *is a bear-pit masculine gathering in which Eddie, attempting to go clean and sober in his so-called 'meaningful relationship' with the absent Darlene, allows himself to be drawn into Mickey's exuberant retelling of how the two of them once introduced dancer Bonnie to an out-of-town actor, and watched her fellate him happily in the car ride back from the airport. A pall is cast in Eddie by his delayed remembrance that Bonnie's six-year-old daughter was also in the vehicle, something Mickey professes not to recall.*

59 *Hurlyburly*: Kevin Spacey (Mickey), Anna Paquin (Donna), Penn (Eddie)

SEAN PENN: The story about the kid in the car . . . there is a celebration of the wild time going on, with this dark, dark thing underneath it. There had been a lot of exploration of that when I did the play with David. It's the implosion of Eddie, at that certain point, against these indulgences. The soul was gonna rise up, you know . . .

DAVID RABE: On some level it has to be, 'Yes, they are evil companions, they did this together.' But Mickey can blithely leave out any sense of culpability about the little girl. Eddie says, 'No, that's part of the story. You can't just pretend it was this pure lark. We weren't 'blotto'. It's important you know we did this rather horrendous thing.'

TONY DRAZAN: The scene was shot very early, the third night. And I loved that Eddie was calling Mickey out, that Sean was piercing Kevin with these arrows. I'm sitting watching, thinking, 'This is great. Just squeeze his fucken balls, take his breath away, whatever it takes . . .' Because if you're Mickey, who the fuck is Eddie to put that on the table? We then ended up with a problem in the cutting, though, because, halfway through the picture, it seems that Eddie has become extraordinarily conscious of the irredeemable nature of their friendship. But that gives you a sense of how strong Sean was in that scene, his sense of betrayal in that living room.

GARRY SHANDLING: I think what's great about Sean in that role is his bringing this kind of frightened, desperate, needy, compulsive–obsessive personality to full bear. It was miraculous to watch on the set – even occasionally being in the scene with him – watching all his different explorations . . . Then it stops, and he's a guy checking the camera angles and talking to Tony.

DAVID RABE: The place where Sean took the performance to a level much further than I'd ever imagined is the sequence out on the deck with Bonnie. When I first saw it, I was agog. But I love it now, it's the highlight, in some sense, of the entire film to me.

> EDDIE: She doesn't love me . . .
> BONNIE: Who?
> EDDIE: My girlfriend doesn't want me . . . Bonnie? I'm a real person. You know? I'm not some goddamn TV image here, OK? I'm a real person. Now, you know that, right? Now you know that? I just . . . Suck my dick . . .

TONY DRAZAN: It was four or five in the morning, very cold, teeth-chattering weather, and we were running out of time. The second take was very strong. Sean came up to me after and he was lit, saying, 'Man, that was it!' I wasn't sure. Just as Sean pushes himself and those around him, sometimes I think it takes someone else to remind you that you've got further to go. I didn't know how to direct him there, except to lay down the challenge to him to try one more.

SEAN PENN: Where I sort of let it go in that scene was just . . . not even trying to be anything other than just being with words what you are inside. Naked, in some way . . .

DAVID RABE: Previously I guess he'd always had it a little more under his control, a little more manipulating, a little more defensive – not as absolutely raw, with his hand in his flies, on his dick, and really the infant, the little baby he becomes there.

TONY DRAZAN: 'She doesn't love me!' – that was gut-wrenching to me. But it's fucking funny, too. It's like, oh my god, somebody help this guy. The crew broke into applause afterwards. And that's the take in the movie.

By the spring of 1998, Penn was settled in Marin and Clyde Is Hungry Films installed in Francis Coppola's building on Kearney Street, San Francisco, a fertile environment for directors as disparate as Werner Herzog and Wayne Wang. Of course, his usual companions of an evening were now two hundred miles away.

LARS ULRICH: Sean and I live in the same zip-code, and that zip-code is a small place. I'd been living in Marin for eight years or so: one day I'm in the local takeout deli and I turn around and there's Sean Penn . . . I didn't have a lot of friends in Marin, certainly not outside of the Metallica thing. And I guess we were both looking for someone to hang out with in that part of the world. I think Marin represented a kind of sanctuary for both of us, away from what we do for a living. But at the same time, in a bedroom community, it was kind of nice to have a friend who shared some of the same life experiences . . .

If you move around Marin in anything but a low key you're gonna stick out. But Sean's low-profile: he's as much at ease sitting at the local watering hole on 4th Street, San Rafael, as he is hobnobbing in Hollywood or New York with the famous of the famous. Maybe *more* at ease . . .

San Rafael-based singer-songwriter Jerry Hannan had, after a long sojourn, cut a CD with brother Sean in the name of The Mad Hannans and was playing one-nighters in the area, showcasing songs of a wry, sardonic, somewhat troubadour sensibility.

JERRY HANNAN: There's a club in Fairfax called Café Amsterdam, tiny, but a real charming place, and I was playing there in early 1998. Sean Penn comes and sits right up front, two feet away from me, while we're playing. I got down off the stage – which is a foot high – and he shook my hand, said, 'Hey, I think your music's great, let's go get a drink.' I never met anybody famous before in my whole life. Except for Huey Lewis. But he's a local dude . . .

Sometimes you meet somebody and you click, like, 'I'm gonna know this person.' And I felt right away, if Sean had been just a regular Joe like me – and I was detailing cars when I met him – but if he was an auto-detailer, I'd be hanging out with him. On the other hand, him being a movie star, I didn't know if I'd ever hear from him again – he's got things to do and people to see, right? But we hooked up in a couple of days and just sat around his office in Francis Coppola's building, listening to records. I heard him asked once what he'd like to be if he wasn't an actor, and he said, 'A songwriter.' And we have similar tastes. The music he likes, I like. I mean, I like my music and apparently he does too [*laughs*].

After the long drought, there had been a deluge of acting in the past two-year spell; but Penn remained committed to searching out directorial possibilities through the first-look deal at Phoenix, usually of a heroically challenging variety.

MIKE MEDAVOY: They were all difficult projects – there's a reason why they didn't get made. I think *Autumn of the Patriarch* was the one that came closest. We tried to do it with Marlon. We talked about various people to direct, Bertolucci, Pontecorvo – Gillo did, in Marlon's own words, one of the best movies Marlon ever made, *Queimada!*

SEAN PENN: Michael Fitzgerald4 and I went down to Mexico to meet with Gabriel García Márquez. But Márquez had had a terrible experience with Hollywood over *Love in the Time of Cholera*, and the legal case surrounding that had cost him money to get the rights back, so he didn't want to get in bed with any of us. I came back and told Marlon, and he said, 'Well, let's go down there . . .' And we had a great time in

---

4 Producer of several John Huston pictures, including *Wiseblood* (1979).

Mexico. But it didn't work out, just because of the state of the business relative to the elements involved . . .

So, in the interim, Penn was unable to resist the enticement of a Woody Allen picture to begin shooting late summer/early autumn 1998. Sweet and Lowdown *was to be a bittersweet mock biopic set in Allen's beloved thirties, charting the sorry life of Emmet Ray, the second finest jazz guitarist of his day. The comedy of Emmet arises from his almost impenetrable self-regard: he drinks like a newt, spends money like an overgrown kid, and blithely extols his own complex genius, expecting women to love him for it. But he plays guitar like a dream, and so wins – without earning – the love of a mute, innocent laundress named Hattie.*

WOODY ALLEN: The script originated many years ago, in the sixties, it was called 'The Jazz Baby', and I thought that I might act in it at that time. But it was all very vague, and I didn't know if I could play it anyway, so I put it away. *Much* later, I happened to be looking at it, and I thought that, with a rewrite, it would be an interesting project. I made a few changes, knowing I wasn't going to play it. The original had more outright comedy, *comedian's* comedy, and more of my kind of dialogue. So I took out the kind of thing I was doing at that time, a jokier approach, and it became more character comedy.

I'd only seen a few of Sean's movies, but there was a vast range of characters he had played. I had seen him play quite a likeable character for Dick Benjamin and the fascinating lawyer drug-addict in *Carlito's Way*. And he was always wonderful. So he was someone I felt could play the dramatic, temperamental scenes very effectively, as well as the comic scenes. There are great dramatic actors who can be wonderfully funny: Robert De Niro for one. And Sean is another. Because what is comedy, really, except being real in a situation, having some kind of intellectual grasp of where the humour is and behaving accordingly?

ART WOLFF: I was as annoyed as everybody who loved Sean's work, hearing him constantly talk of how he hated acting and didn't want to do it any more. I remember saying to him, 'It's because you're always playing these incredibly heavy-duty guys. Why don't you do some *light* stuff? Not light in terms of substance but in terms of style, stuff where you can be *funny*.' Sean as a human being is one of the funniest people in the world. Knowing his integrity, he wasn't going to do yesterday's romantic comedy with whatever starlet of the moment. But *Sweet and Lowdown*, I thought, was a great opportunity for him . . .

And then, another job arose. Director Philip Haas, known for his literary bent, was now essaying one of Somerset Maugham's lesser works, Up *at the Villa: Kristin Scott-Thomas playing an English widow in Mussolini's Italy, contemplating marriage to a colonial administrator until she stumbles into a foolhardy scrape and is bailed out by roguish social gadfly Rowley Flint. This was perhaps queer casting for Penn, but a challenge, one that would allow him to bank-roll some development costs, work with the splendid Scott-Thomas, and pass an agreeable six weeks in sunlit Siena.*

ANDREW DAULTON LEE: Sean tells me, 'Get a passport. We're going to Italy.' Here I am, out of prison not quite a year . . . The agreement Sean made was that he wanted to be home by 4 August for Hopper's birthday. He said, 'I don't care how many hours we end up shooting a day, you figure on getting this film in the can by then.' So we're shooting on Saturdays. The producer David Brown would come to me and say, 'We're running over today, we got another hour and a half to shoot if we can, could you talk Sean into doing it?' I said, 'I'll try, David . . .'

One night Massimo Ghini, the Italian lead, talked us into going out to dinner at a new French restaurant. He didn't tell us it was the grand opening . . . We get there, they sat Sean at the end of a table where there was no escape, and all of a sudden all these Italian woman are arrayed around him and there's paparazzi putting cameras in his face. Sean says, 'Someone's probably getting this live by satellite. I'm out of here.' We had a great driver, a Serb, twenty-eight years old. Sean says, 'Lose these people.' So the driver starts zig-zagging down the streets in Florence, and it was getting hairy. Finally Sean looks at me and says, 'You want to be Dodi or Princess Di?' Then as we're getting near the Hotel Medici, he says to me and the driver, 'Let's make a pact. If they follow us into the lobby? Let's beat the shit out of them . . .'

However unconventional the role of Flint might appear, there was something to Penn playing a character whom Maugham extols for 'a sort of gentleness behind the roughness of his manner, a thrilling warmth behind his mockery, some instinctive understanding of woman as a different creature from man'. 'It's much like what I see in the mirror,' Penn would tell a journalist.5 But he didn't come away feeling that he had quite nailed it.

SEAN PENN: I wanted to approach it in a much different way, actually. But when you're working with people you like and have respect for, as I was – and it paid quite well, and I wasn't the whole movie – I didn't want to be disruptive. See, another part of it was that I was preparing for another movie at the time, and there's an infidelity in that which I think, probably, takes you off your game. I maybe wasn't giving the commitment that I otherwise would have liked to. So there was a bit of a lesson for me in that movie. I was extremely engaged in the preparation for *Sweet and Lowdown*, and that meant guitar lessons all day – in the trailer, in bed, everywhere.

WOODY ALLEN: We felt Sean had to take lessons. I wanted him to look comfortable and be able to finger it and appear to be playing it, to have some sense of reality about that. So we sent him a teacher and he worked with the guy. I never thought he would actually *learn* the guitar. But I was amazed – he showed up on the set and he could actually do some things with it. Nothing I could imagine myself doing . . .

The prize temptation for some actors assigned the male lead in an Allen picture – most recently, Kenneth Branagh in Celebrity *(1998) – was to essay an imitation of the writer-director's own celebrated screen persona.*

SEAN PENN: Never occurred to me. I read the script, and about halfway through I just felt like I could hear the guy. And then, you know, I went about building the blocks to be able to find an endurance to it. But there was a music to the guy that I could hear right away: for better or for worse – I felt I knew where it would go.

In the role of Hattie, Allen cast a very young English actress fresh from a brilliant feature début in a BFI production written and directed by Caryn Adler.

SAMANTHA MORTON: I was nineteen. Woody had seen me in *Under the Skin* and brought me in. It wasn't a reading, I was playing a mute . . . so we just had a chat. And Woody wanted me to be like Harpo

5 Haas and Penn quotes from 'The Burden of Integrity', Juan Morales, *Detour*, May 2000.

Marx, so I just got on with it. I was playing somebody who was so in love with Sean's character – not obsessed, not infatuated, it wasn't even about *fancying* – she just unconditionally loved this man, in the purest, kindest sense. So they're a quirky couple.

I knew Sean's name and I'd seen various things of his. But I don't get nervous about people. What I *did* find interesting, working in America for the first time, was how much he was respected – it was almost like people were more excited about working with Sean than with doing a Woody Allen film . . .

DR KATZ: Sean told me, 'Now, Eddie, this is a very grown-up movie, so don't violate Woody Allen's space. If he comes over to you, talk to him. But don't go over to him.'

The first day, Sean's in hair and make-up. I come in and say, 'Hey, I just saw Woody. He introduced himself, he was with a woman, and I said, "Is that your wife, your daughter or your sister?"' Now, I *didn't* say that. But I'm *capable* of saying it. And Sean just gave me a look . . . But Woody Allen and I became fast friends.

Sweet and Lowdown *commenced principal photography in late August 1998. As is his wont, Allen shot the entire picture, even some Hollywood-set sequences, within forty-five minutes of his Manhattan home. Barely were they underway, however, before Penn had to confront his father's gravely worsening health.*

EILEEN RYAN PENN: Leo was so ill with the cancer and the chemo. Myron McNamara, his pilot in the war, was still healthy as could be, still playing tennis, and he would come visit Leo at home and at the hospital. And then Myron went. His wife said he was looking at a newspaper, and he just bent his head over . . . Leo gave the eulogy; he insisted on going for Myron. He was so ill, I was afraid of his doing it, but Myron's wife was thrilled, and Leo gave a beautiful speech about all the wonderful things Myron did, how he had saved them all on that plane. Then it was only a couple of months later . . .

SEAN PENN: It wasn't very long into the Woody picture. I was on the set in Brooklyn, over one of the bridges, and Michael called and said, 'It's not going to get better from here . . .' So I flew to Los Angeles. And we were all there with him, until about an hour before. Then we left my mother with him. I went back to the hotel for an hour or two. And I got the call in the room that he was gone.

EILEEN RYAN PENN: I think it was very painful for all the boys, but they all reacted very differently, very differently. I saw pain in all of them. But I think they were also grateful for having had whatever time they had had with a great dad. I think, I hope, that's what they were focusing on. Their dad would want them to keep functioning and doing the things they do best and staying healthy.

CHRISTOPHER PENN: I think both Sean and Michael realized that I was possibly more vulnerable, because I didn't really know my dad as closely as they did, just because of age difference. My dad and I were very close; and still are, even after his passing. But they knew more basics, and I think they were more cognisant of my sensitivity to it. So I don't think Sean really let all of his emotions show, specifically to me.

MATT PALMIERI: It was very interesting and somewhat revelatory for me to watch Sean go through his own experience of great loss, because I had not handled either my mother's or my brother's death very well. I watched Sean deal with it much more gracefully than I did. And I would say part of that was because he was blessed with the fact that, on a day-to-day basis, he had those wonderful kids to think about and take care of, and he had their love and his wife's love coming at him all the time. I think that was a real source of strength to him. It's hard to get too down about anything, even the loss of a parent, when you have that in front of you every day.

SEAN PENN: The service was set for about a week later, so I went back to New York, and was shooting, and then I came back for the service.

JOSEPH VITARELLI: Leo died of lung cancer. And Sean and I were smoking at his funeral, outside, round a corner. I mean, we really needed a cigarette that day . . .

ART WOLFF: I remember Sean announcing, 'We just want everybody to know that Dad is in the casket, and he's in his shorts and his sandals and his baseball cap and his Hawaiian shirt . . .' And there were people who came from Leo's army outfit in the war, talking about how he was one of their most decorated and flew all those missions.

EILEEN RYAN PENN: Christopher was the one who was so into his father being a hero in World War II. At the funeral they came and did the whole thing of honouring him with the flag that they handed to me as the widow. Christopher arranged all of that . . .

SEAN PENN ('Kilroy Was Here', May 2003): *September 12th, 1998, I sat upon a wooden church pew as a military honour guard reached across my lap to place a precisely folded American flag into the stoic hands of my father's widow . . .*

. . . it was this cloth of Stars and Stripes and all it had meant to him, and had come to mean to me, that brought unexpected and unrestrained emotion. The soldier, in his fine dress uniform, began to speak to my mother 'In the name of the President of the United States and in gratitude for your husband's heroic . . .' And that was it, I was gone. I thought, where the hell did this flood of emotion come from?

But, the answer came quickly. My father loved this country so deeply, and he had passed that love and patriotism on to his three sons . . .

Courtesy of Sean Penn

60   April 27 1996: Penn on his wedding day with father Leo

EILEEN RYAN PENN: When Leo died, I got so many letters from people who had worked with Leo and became successful, and they were so grateful to him because he had been so generous with his time for them. The boys, I'm sure they all privately miss him every day, as I do. There's nothing worse than losing a spouse of so many years. But it's not productive to wallow in it. That's why I force myself to stay as active as I do, doing plays, painting, reading, going to Europe. Every night when I pray, I pray for all his friends who have passed away. I say, 'I hope you're all together talking about old times . . .'

61 On location for *Sweet and Lowdown*: Penn and Woody Allen

WOODY ALLEN: You know, I was amazed. Sean had walked on the set and I knew nothing of his father's illness. His father passed away, and he was back on the set right on schedule two or three days later, and he was as brilliant as ever. And it was not something where you have a morbid, lachrymose actor wandering around the set in a daze for a week, nothing of that at all. I couldn't believe how professional Sean was about it. At the same time, I didn't doubt for a second his real feelings about his father, because when he talked about it, he displayed those feelings.

SEAN PENN: One would have preferred not to be involved in anything, at that time. Because it just hits you, and you reel from it – and then where do you go? You use your emotional system as an actor, and your emotional system's all taken up elsewhere. So the humour that was there was very strange for a couple of days – until you find a way to turn around. I mean, Woody Allen's comedy is very rooted in real stuff. I think if I'd been out there doing Keystone Cops, I would have had a much more difficult time. But ultimately there was stuff there to relate about how I felt.

WOODY ALLEN: When you're with Sean, you see that he's very sensitive and that he suffers all the time. So, obviously, the suffering of his father's death, it was nothing new to him in a certain sense. He's wounded by the appropriately tragic and awful mess that everybody's in in life, the difficulty of that. He's not a light-hearted, happy-go-lucky individual who just bounces along. He thinks about the world, and it causes him a correct amount of suffering: suffering that you see in great artists who find the world a very difficult place to make excuses for.

SAMANTHA MORTON: It's funny, the way our scenes were written – at the time I remember thinking, 'There's something here.' Maybe we brought some of our own little things . . . I'm not like Hattie at all, but in some ways I felt very like her. I'd arrived in New York and was given an apartment, and I sat in it on standby for weeks because Woody was waiting for clouds . . . And I just felt a little bit naive. I was used to everybody having a chat on set about how they're going to approach this today. But Woody would be quite monosyllabic at times about what he required, and you just have to not take any of the stuff personally. I just had my lip buttoned the whole time, anyway, playing Hattie . . . but Sean handled him really well.

62 *Sweet and Lowdown*: Samantha Morton (Hattie) and Penn (Emmet Ray)

SEAN PENN: One day Woody calls, 'Cut,' and says to me, 'Sean, do you know what was wrong with that take?' Long pause. '*Everything* . . . '

WOODY ALLEN: I always speak quite frankly, so if Sean gets the whole scene wrong, I have no compunction in telling him as much. I always am rough with actors that way, but they don't get upset because they know it's within the context of accepting them as great actors. And I have no problem at all if the actor says, 'I can't say these lines' or 'This joke isn't funny.' In fact, I almost never had to give Sean direction in the whole picture. There may have been two or three times when I said, 'Can you be a little more intense in the scene?' or 'A little lighter?' Or 'Can you go a little faster? You're dragging it out.' But 98 per cent of it was just hiring Sean and getting out of his way. Sean Penn certainly doesn't have to worry about me. I mean, he was a genius actor long before we met. He's no ham, he doesn't overdo anything: for all his changes of costume and changes of affect for different characters, he's always a subtle actor.

ART WOLFF: It's a Sean hallmark – he works internally but the physicalization of what he does is so acute. I mean, just the moment he comes onscreen in *Sweet and Lowdown* and you see that *walk* he does. Then he's capable of such extraordinary sweetness, as when he runs into Hattie again at the end.

Emmet, having once abandoned Hattie for a vacuous slumming socialite, returns some years later to surprise her in a break from her laundry work. Standing over her, he launches once more – if strangely more nervous than before – into a tale of the great times they will have if she ups and leaves with him. Hattie, with her earnest mien, scribbles a note that cuts him dead: 'Oh . . .? Happily . . .? Kids . . .?'

SAMANTHA MORTON: Hattie, she's very simple, but she's not stupid. She's very innocent, and with the love she had for him, she would have died for him. But when he finds her again, she's moved on. And it's not that she doesn't love him any more and that she would never love him again. But she has her children now. And it's so tragic . . . [*laughs*].

WOODY ALLEN: Sean did it the first take, and I said, 'It's silly to do this again. That was brilliant, you'll never do it better than you just did.' Because it was just of those moments when he made it sing, the whole situation was so expressively reflected in his face. I put one or two cuts of Samantha in because I thought that was effective just as punctuation. But he did it in one take, and it was really only one print – if the negative cutter had put a scratch on it, I would have been in trouble . . .

SAMANTHA MORTON: We were so in our characters. In that sense, I don't look at my fellow performers, I just kind of be with them and react. But ultimately I watched the film and was mind-blown by what Sean did. I remember really, really laughing.

And working with him then was so good, because I was very impressionable, I think. And the way he approached his work, there just seemed to be no bollocks around him – he didn't need pampering, he came in the morning and got on with it, shared the make-up trailer with everybody else, always professional, always polite and respectful and decent. I tell you what, I've worked with such monsters since – men with such confused egos because of how everybody treats them. I didn't realize how different Sean was. It's difficult to articulate how much bollocks some people come out with, and how much they need to be adored in order to perform, or how they're so afraid of looking a twat that they won't *do* something. And Sean's been acting for years, but I found him still really refreshing . . .

Hurlyburly *had its Los Angeles première on 14 December 1998. Penn was back in town with a mission for the following morning.*

DENNIS FANNING: Sean says to me, 'Hey, I need a favour. Can you pick me up tomorrow at the Peninsula Hotel at 9 o'clock and bring me downtown?' 'Yeah, sure.' 'But you gotta wear a suit . . .' So I get there, late as usual. Sean's pacing out in the parking lot, he's frantic. 'Give the valet your key, you're driving my car.' It's a big Daimler. Cool. I ask him, 'Who are the guys in the white van following us?' 'That's *Sixty Minutes*. They're doing a thing on me.' 'OK. Where we going?' 'Just hurry up, we gotta go pick up Marlon.' 'Listen, what have you guys got going on?' 'I'll tell you when we get there . . .'

So we get Marlon. I take them downtown, and when we get there I'm like, 'OK, what the fuck are we doing at the Ronald Reagan State Building?'

'We're here to get Geronimo Pratt out of jail. He was wrongly convicted for that murder in Santa Monica. He was set up by the FBI and the LAPD.'

'Are you guys *nuts*? I can't even be near you on this. Get the fuck out of the car . . .'

Sean thinks this is funny, ha-ha-ha. I could be fired for this shit . . .

Geronimo Pratt served with the 82nd Airborne in Vietnam, then with the Black Panthers as 'Defence Minister'. In 1972, he was found guilty of the 1968 murder of schoolteacher Caroline Olsen in Santa Monica. Pratt was then unaware of evidence that the FBI had him under surveillance at a Panther meeting 333 miles away at the time of the killing. Pratt was sentenced to life in prison, and ultimately spent twenty-seven years, eight of them in solitary confinement, with appeals rejected at every level, before Orange County Superior Court Judge Everett Dickey freed him.

SEAN PENN: I was aware of Geronimo's case: it was Marlon who focused me on it at that particular time.

History is the one subject in school that made some sense to me, because you can see it repeat itself in your own life – in your home and out of it. And you either believe that we can make changes or you don't. And if you're involved in movies, you can believe we can make changes . . . and that we have to. So getting involved there was a no-brainer to me, simply on the basis of the way Geronimo had been framed.

I had an interest in COINTELPRO.[6] It's not a piece of American history that the average American, even people my age in the United States, is aware of. But there's just no question about it at all but that Geronimo was subject to those deceptions and illegal manoeuvrings – and in fact the FBI has admitted it and, I think, paid approximately $2 million in restitution, for twenty-seven years of a life. And then later, once Geronimo was out and I got to know him, he got me focused on some things also . . . [7]

TONY DRAZAN: We had taken *Hurlyburly* to Venice and it was a great success. Sean came away with the Best Actor award. And the early press was very good, and we actually believed for a brief time that audiences everywhere would just love the movie. When Don saw the

---

6 Acronym for a series of FBI counter-intelligence programs, 1956–71, intended to 'neutralize' political dissidents.
7 See Chapter 12.

dailies and the various cuts, he was like, 'You're gonna get the Academy Award, you pricks! That performance of Sean's . . .' Don's view now is like, 'I don't care for the piece; it's lacking in redemptive qualities.'

DON PHILLIPS: *Hurlyburly* is for me like a bastard son, and Sean knows that. It was so dark for me – I saw no light. At the end of the movie, when Anna Paquin says to Sean, 'You want to fuck me?' and Sean says, 'No, I'm tired,' whatever – that's redemptive? Turning down a blow job from a fifteen-year-old? Give me a break.

TONY DRAZAN: Eddie, in a moment of . . . consideration, for himself as well as for her, opts not to. 99.99 per cent of us would say that's hardly a redemptive moment. But that's where we stood. We did shoot a take where I had Sean leave the frame – one, two beats on sleeping Donna – then he re-enters the frame and says, 'Donna? I changed my mind . . .' Couldn't do that to the audience. Couldn't do it to David. Can you imagine? 'Oh, David, we did a quick rewrite on the end. What do you think?'

DON PHILLIPS: Sean keeps kidding everybody by saying that he was doing me. I don't think he's quite doing me, do you? But he likes to say that. I have no malice in my heart about it. I'm not angry. It's just like Sean says – 'It ain't one of Don's favourites . . .'

SEAN PENN: I'll use the medium for whatever it will do, even if you're compromised in some way or other. That's why we did *Hurlyburly*. I just wanted to get that unique language out there, you know? I mean, I saw the first production of the play that David *loathed*, and fell in love with his writing right there, and it provoked so many things in my own work. So I can't feel like I'm alone in this. And if somebody goes to a film and comes away with that language, that's a valuable thing.

Hard on Hurlyburly*'s heels, Terrence Malick's* The Thin Red Line *bowed in the US on Christmas Day 1998, twenty years after* Days of Heaven. *The picture went on to earn seven Academy Award nominations and claim the Golden Bear at the Berlinale in February 1999. Upon its first announcement one of the most eagerly awaited films in history, its initial audiences nevertheless needed more than a moment to digest what the maestro had done.*

MIKE MEDAVOY: Terry's Terry – he lives in his own world. I think Terry loved Sean and felt indebted to Sean for being the first guy to stand up for him. I think the process of making it got to everybody. But I think the movie will outlast us.

SEAN PENN: Was there a more formal script at a certain point? I guess so. But, see . . . a script is a guideline for a director: it can be a complete notion, but it's also a way to express the spirit of it, and the economy of it, to those who are financing it. And the movie is *ten times* what the script was.

DENNIS HOPPER: I thought *The Thin Red Line* was the most pretentious thing I ever saw; nothing that I could get involved with on any level. I think *Badlands* is a great film, and Sissy Spacek's narration in *Badlands* is wonderful, but he didn't shoot the movie with that in mind. He put the narration in afterwards – which is fine, whatever it takes. But I think narration is not a way to tell a movie. So I look at *The Thin Red Line* . . . War is not poetry to me, man. And this is not storytelling.

WOODY HARRELSON: I heard someone describe it as like an epic poem, which I thought was an apt description. And I guess it came out around the same time as Spielberg's movie,[8] which I thought ultimately – though it did show some grim details of war – was a bit of a glorification of what war accomplished. Whereas Terry's movie I thought was a wonderful, more anti-war sentiment, and that I was really proud of. I thought it was a beautiful, beautiful movie – I still do. Though I do think he could lose a little time out of the middle . . .

* * *

DAVID BAERWALD: I'd say Sean and I both kind of suffer from the incongruity of our lives, in terms of the businesses we're in and what we want to do. Both of us are 75 per cent of the time at war with everyone around us.

WOODY ALLEN: Sean's a literate and sensitive person; he knows who the other good actors are and who the good people are, and he knows what's junk and what gets fobbed off as great on the public but is *really* junk.

---

8 *Saving Private Ryan* (1998).

ANDREW DAULTON LEE: Sean told me they'd tried to get him to do *Con Air* and he told 'em, 'Nope'. But he said, joking, about how all the guys who did it must have got together and laughed and said, 'Yeah, let's just prostitute ourselves for this one . . .'

BOBBY COOPER: I remember Sean had just got back from *Thin Red Line*, and late one night we were driving up to Marin County. He's telling me he just turned down $10 million. I'm going, 'How could you do that?' So we pull up to this diner about 4.30 in the morning. And the waitress says, 'I know you, you're a big movie star.' She points to me. Sean's getting a big kick out of this. The bill comes and he does one of these, 'I don't have any money. Can you loan me a hundred . . .?' You turn down $10 fucking million and borrow money from *me*? Something's *wrong* here . . .

In late 1998, with a pair of movies to promote of which he was well pleased, Penn submitted politely to publicity rounds, but nevertheless let more than a few things fly. John Cassavetes had once lamented that, since money had became the be-all and end-all of film-making, he was surprised film-makers didn't simply stack up dollar bills and point their cameras at them. Penn was channelling some of the same ire.

When Fox didn't deign to subsidise a private plane to Houston for a screening of The Thin Red Line *arranged by Malick, Penn published an acerbic letter in the* Daily Variety, *contending that this was a poor return on his personal commitment. 'Has anyone at 20th Century Fox considered', he wrote, 'that it might not be my policy to do 7-figure favours for multinational corporate interests as I did when I took the salary you paid me on* The Thin Red Line?'

The barb was directed also in respect of Fox proprietor Rupert Murdoch, whose British and American tabloids had spent over a decade pelting Penn with all manner of calumny. Penn tallied the sums and figured Fox were penny-pinching him on $6,000, 'which, against the price cut I offered in my deal to act in this movie, seemed equivalent to the fair market share of one hair on Mr Murdoch's formidable ass'.

This was the sort of fighting talk that made headlines at a time when Hollywood leads were beginning to earn $20 million a picture and were expected to mind their manners in return. But then Penn had never accepted an invitation from Jerry Bruckheimer. He clearly understood the pitfall of diluting his own brand: 'By necessity I've *gravitated to other things. Some of them don't work as well as some of the commercial movies that other people do. Sometimes you fail at the things you believe in, too.'9*

Still, he wasn't shy in letting his peers know what he felt were the acceptable standards. A remark to journalist Lynn Hirschberg about Nicolas Cage's recent career choices caused a public rift between the two. The designer violence of the Silver/Bruckheimer white-vest, squib-hit action pictures was a particular bugbear. Penn, for all his authentic machismo, had no desire to cavort in schoolboyish imitation of the same on a cinema screen. In the light of Operation Desert Fox, the Clinton administration's bombing of Iraq prior to Christmas 1998, Penn felt such showboating took on a uniquely crass appearance: 'What do you do', he rhetorically asked one interviewer, 'if you're making one of those movies, you're off on location, away from your family, and suddenly we attack Baghdad and children are getting killed? Who are you in the world then?' This preoccupation would recur.

She's So Lovely, The Thin Red Line and Hurlyburly had in one sense represented Penn making good on debts of love to Cassavetes, Malick and Rabe. It wasn't that he was madly keen on acting again. He wanted to direct; and he had material in the works. For a long time he had struggled with the sense that being an actor was not a job for a grown man; being a writer–director, clearly, passed muster. But something else might be needed too: an engagement with politics, the exercise of a voice.

ERIN DIGNAM: Everybody was asking Sean why he was making statements again that he was going to quit acting. 'What was *that* all about? He wanted to quit before, then he started acting again and gave these great performances.' I knew how excited and touched he gets by watching other performers, and I'd heard him say, 'I just die to direct, to see those kinds of performances in front of me as a director.' But we were sitting in his house one day, in their breakfast alcove, and I said to him, 'I'd like the answer. *Really*. Why you're quitting acting. Because I don't think it's good for those of us who need to see stories.' I was giving him the whole guilt thing. And he said, 'You know what it is? When you give yourself to a performance, when you have to get into the mind of somebody else, if you do it right, you do have to leave

9 Interview by Paul Sherman, salon.com, 14 January 1999.

yourself behind for that time period – whatever it is, March-to-May 1996. You don't live your own life. You are gonna lose chunks of it.' And I got that. It's like the poem Bukowski wrote about poetry: basically, 'If you don't *have* to do it, *don't* do it, man.'[10] Because it should cost you to do it. And you have to give on that level if you're Sean. And at that particular moment, I think he honestly was spent.

10 If it doesn't come bursting out of you / in spite of everything, / don't do it. / unless it comes unasked out of your / heart and your mind and your mouth / and your gut, / don't do it. (Charles Bukowski, 'So You Want to Be a Writer?')

TWELVE

1999–2001

Sean, even when I first met him at twenty, loved the idea of just getting in a
car and driving, disappearing – just checking out places. He was attracted
to a certain kind of . . . what detractors call 'low life', what Sean would say
are interesting people. And if you look at the three films he's made as
director, they are about these people.

Art Wolff

MIKE MEDAVOY: Sean always comes up with interesting material – he's
always out there. It's not always the most commercial material; and in
the world we're in, it's harder and harder to do interesting material.
But he sits down in front of the canvas and thinks, 'OK, now how am
I going to do this so that somebody will go look at it?' The problem
with the movie business is it's such a damn expensive canvas.

He spent a couple of years at Phoenix: out of that, so far as I know,
came *The Pledge*, which we developed for him. There was a script for
As I Lay Dying, but it never got beyond that.

SEAN PENN: The Kromolowskys entered my orbit originally with the
Faulkner adaptation, which Michael Fitzgerald brought to me. It
wasn't for me, but then Michael and I became partners and I agreed
that we could try to produce the movie. There weren't a lot of actors
who were interested in doing it. But through that relationship, I got
the script for *Autumn of the Patriarch*, and that was a wonderful job.
And then, when I was looking for something else to do with Jack, I
came across, through Michael, *The Pledge*.

DON PHILLIPS: Jack loves to read detective novels – Sean noticed that
when they were making *The Crossing Guard*. And they had a conversation to the effect of 'We should make one of those one day.' Because
if you have Jack on board, that usually gets you the money and green-
lights your movie . . .

JACK NICHOLSON: I've read so many thrillers I don't know *what* I've read: all of MacDonald, all of Ellroy; I like the Tom Clancys and all the legal thrillers. I'm very nocturnal, and it keeps me from watching the same movies all night long. It's a kind of recreational reading. And because I'd directed three movies and hadn't had any commercial success with them, I always thought, 'One day I'll do a thriller . . .' Plus you get great information about one thing and another; there are always peripheries to it, like the woman from Richmond who writes Kay Scarpetta. So I liked the genre.

Friedrich Dürrenmatt's sequence of slender, existential detective novels, such as The Judge and His Hangman *(1952), and* The Pledge *(1958), are fables that toy with the genre in order to indulge the author's pet themes: the helplessness of man against insatiable evil, and the impossibility of avoiding moral contamination in the act of revenge. In* The Pledge, *Dürrenmatt's narrative is encased within a sly framing device, his narrator (a lugubrious crime writer) sharing a brandy with an old police chief (Dr H) who instructs him as to why true crime is so much more infernally complex than fiction. His example is a debacle suffered by his 'most capable man', Inspector Matthai, who made a vow to a pious bereaved mother to catch the killer of her child, but whose patiently wrought if diabolical plan to snare the villain with 'live bait' was undone by a simple twist of fate, the killer himself killed in a road accident en route to the scene of the sting, leaving Matthai humiliated, discredited and crazed.*

SEAN PENN: I always said it's a 'No-good-deed-goes-unpunished' story. And I would find enormous comfort in that as an audience. I wanted everybody who's ever been punished for doing something good to see that it happens to other people too. I can identify with that, because I'm a saint . . . So I thought, 'Yeah, that would be great, but here's the things I'd like changed.' Jerzy Kromolowsky read it and had a position on how to do it, and he and his wife wrote a draft that was very well-structured.

JACK NICHOLSON: When Sean brought me the Dürrenmatt book, I read it and I told him, 'I don't see any *movie* in this, Sean.' Because I had read so many. And the novel's a flashback: we know the cop is now a derelict. That's an easy adjustment to make in a film – you just don't make it a flashback, end of problem. But because of the flashback, there isn't a lot of suspense in the novel.

Then when I read the script, I felt there were a lot of strange things in it that could have gone a lot of ways, and if I feel that reading something, then I always kind of think that's the way an audience will see it. So I thought, 'Oh, all right, I see that there's a *difficult* movie here. But there *is* a movie . . .'

And then I read an essay that Dürrenmatt had written about writing the novel. He wrote it in reaction because he was furious with the form – the way the good man follows the clues and inevitably catches the bad man. Given the tough existentialist that Dürrenmatt is, he was aesthetically offended by this completely dominant aspect of the form and wrote the book in rebellion, really. So this is the one where the good guy follows the clues, he's right; and then he doesn't get the guy, and he's the one who is punished. So that in itself gives it a certain literary uniqueness. Because, after all, in most detective pictures since *Oedipus Rex*, the question is 'Whodunnit?' And then they find him, and that's who. So this was a unique formal departure, and I liked it for that reason. And I knew Sean had the credentials to do those departures. You know it's not going to be a crowd-pleaser, otherwise [*grins*] they wouldn't do every one the same way. But nonetheless, sometimes it's worth it . . .

ANDREW DAULTON LEE: The deal with Phoenix came to an end, then we got a new deal with October Films and we were working in an office building off Sunset and Doheny. Sean was trying to put *The Pledge* together. But he still had the office in San Francisco, and he was rarely down. I was going to the office every day but there was really nothing for me to do. I get real uncomfortable to sit and take a cheque when nothing's going on. But that's Sean loyalty. I finally told him, 'This has been nice but I've got to go do something.' That Christmas, I gave him a letter thanking him for everything he'd done since I got out. If I'd hired a team of psychiatrists to put together a release vehicle to help me reintegrate with society, they couldn't have done better than my going to work with him. The guy treated me swell and he didn't have to. Didn't owe me a thing. So I don't have anything grisly or nasty on Sean; I didn't catch that side of him. Maybe he just didn't think he could top *my* bad-boy image . . .

In February 1999, a coalition of blacklisted screenwriters and actors and interested leftists formed a committee to protest against a Lifetime Achievement Oscar for Elia Kazan that had been successfully pro-

posed to the Academy board by Karl Malden. Full-page ads were taken in the trade papers of 19 March, condemning Kazan's actions and the Academy's wilful blindness during the blacklist era, and asking attendees of the Academy Awards to sit on their hands when Kazan mounted the stage. There were 350 signatories to the advertisement, including Penn.

SEAN PENN: I supported a silent protest – not to disrupt, but 'In memory of . . .' It wasn't in the name of the father. My dad would have believed Elia Kazan deserved that award as much as anybody. And I'm all for Pete Rose getting in the Hall of Fame . . . My only feeling had to do with the way in which not only the Academy, but the Screen Actors Guild, anybody, had acknowledged what really went on: it's the problem of guys who don't even get acknowledged in death, much less their own time. At a certain point I had a conversation with Karl Malden about my dad, and he sort of belittled the situation: 'I know your father, I know he was blacklisted a little bit . . .' This like 'A little bit dead', or whatever . . . And I think people were most upset with Elia Kazan because he was a god at that time, and he could have turned the blacklist around largely. He was also an immigrant who came here and got the fruits of this place. Now here was something that *is* so political, the Academy Awards, taking a position. And I felt there should be some acknowledgement. Amid the loud voice of all that stuff, the pat-on-the-back-ness of the business and the advertising quotient, it was an opportunity for this business, whose participants once paid such a price. And to acknowledge, in some official way, those people who paid that price might have been a better way of approaching the question of what were the just rewards of Elia Kazan.

The latter half of 1999 saw Penn venture supporting roles in a pair of unusual pictures. Over the summer, he shot a cameo for Julian Schnabel's Before Night Falls, *and that autumn he was in Halifax, Nova Scotia, for Kathryn Bigelow's* The Weight of Water, *playing a poet whose wife (Catherine McCormack), while boating in the vicinity of Smuttynose Island, becomes immersed in an infamous murder case of the 1870s hinging around a repressed young Norwegian immigrant (Sara Polley).*

SEAN PENN: *Before Night Falls*, I wanted to help Julian out, because I know what it's like to have to hustle to finance a film. But my feeling about it – well, for me, it's a bit of a miss on my part. I was so happy to be *any* part of the movie. I thought it was a beautiful movie: Javier Bardem is a great actor, and Julian did a bang-up job on it. I just would have liked to have been better in the picture. But it was really doing it with no preparation, just jumping in in-between other things, family or professional – really sneaking it in to help him get that done.

The Weight of Water, I was there only three weeks. Kathryn Bigelow I had a very good time with. It was a very different picture than most of her movies. And to meet her, that's what you'd think she's doing all the time – she's got incredibly deep literary interests and photographic interests, a very bright and cultured person. So – I don't get all the genres she's into [*laughs*]. I mean, she does it like a *guy*. And I think that's interesting. But she knows that I'm not that interested in those kinds of pictures. Nonetheless, she's a pretty formidable, brave woman, and I like her very much. And I thought Sarah Polley was great in that movie. But I don't think many people saw it . . .

MEEGAN OCHS: When Sean and Robin's house was finally done, I said, 'It's so beautiful! Why would you ever want to leave it?' And Sean said, 'That's the point . . .'

JOSEPH VITARELLI: Mercifully, Robin's got great taste. I think she once said to me that her ideal house for the two of them would be an adjoining kitchen and separate houses. And perhaps she has that now. Sean's got a spectacular room, replete with bar and lounge and a pool table, big cushy couches, a great stereo and a plasma television up on the wall for screenings. That's his little spot, and it's the best hang-out place on the planet. If you could afford it, every man – *every man* – would want to live like this. My guess is it was Sean's idea and Robin's execution: that Robin took Sean's idea of bordello-red walls and made it in deep burgundy, with good material. So he's got this fantastically elegant place that still feels like it ought to have 'Club House' written on the outside door. It may have been Sean who designed all of it, but I don't think so. I spent too many nights in the trailer . . .

Plus he's got a complete Avid editing bay there, telephones and computers – it's the dream director's suite.

Finally, in the winter of 1999–2000, The Pledge *dropped into the frame. Elie Samaha's Franchise Pictures financed, with Warner Bros as distributor.*

SEAN PENN: The Kromolowsky version was set in a *Fargo*-esque landscape: flat, white lakes. It lacked religion to me. I wanted a much more vertical landscape. And I was trying to locate it in a real place to me, which would be the Sierras, where you had flatlands and mountains. For economic reasons we scouted Canada, and I found places that looked right. I did a rewrite on the script that made me feel like I owned it by the time I was going – I'd convinced myself of that, anyway. There were some themes that I'd brought into it and focused on that were not in the novel or the first drafts that were kind of my secret path through it.

ART WOLFF: Sean really wanted to make that film about retirement: you're getting old, what do you do with your life? When he told me that's what the film was about, I said, 'Great, just keep it to yourself! Don't tell Elie Samaha. He ain't gonna be so happy.' Franchise Pictures was not interested in making a film about retirement [*laughs*]. But that's why you have the great scene of displacement between Jack Nicholson and Aaron Eckhart – Jack in the office where he lived for all those years, looking for a place to stub his cigarette. He's being told, 'What are you doing here? We don't need you any more. The case is closed, you're done – finished.'

But Nicholson's detective-protagonist Jerry Black is morally skewered by his pledge to the pious mother (Patricia Clarkson) of murdered Ginny Larsen. While his colleagues readily accept a barely coherent confession extracted from a retarded Indian man, Black pursues other ominous clues, such as Ginny's crayon sketch of the 'porcupine giant', a tall dark man bearing prickly little gifts.

JACK NICHOLSON: So he goes and starts looking around, probably just to put his mind at rest, and then he sees things that make him address a certain pattern. He's a good cop, after all. But this could be the story of a man who's having separation anxiety for all the audience know at that point . . .

DON PHILLIPS: Sean and I cast *The Pledge* together, and we agreed on everything. Jack got his full price this time, and by the time we paid Jack, we didn't have a lot of money for the other actors. Plus they were going to have to fly into Vancouver. But you get to work with Sean Penn and do a scene one-on-one with Jack. So Sean and I made dream lists of who we could put in. The Indian was a short list: 'Let's get Benicio.'

BENICIO DEL TORO: You know what? Let's face it – I'm a little crazy, Sean's crazy too, so I can say this. He called me up from his car, said, 'I got a part for you in my movie! I need you to do it! Check it out!' 'Sean, whatever you say . . .' He sends me the script, I read it, and it's like an epic in three minutes: I have to be a retarded guy, be accused of a rape and a murder I didn't do, not believe it, then *believe* it, and to an extent that I have to shoot myself. How am I gonna do *that*? He goes, 'Don't worry! We're gonna give you this really long *hair*.' 'Okay.' So I sit down to get my hair done, and it takes twelve hours . . . Then I get there to do the film, out in the middle of nowhere, and the first scene he wants me to do is a long shot where I run about half a mile in snow up to my waist . . . But it was great. I thought, 'The only way I can do this and believe it is if I do *Rain Man*.' And Sean really encouraged that. He just respects the process, he's like, 'Do unto others as you would have them do unto you'. He also has good taste. In his movies, all of them, he's had actors who can hold their own, from the smallest parts to the largest.

DON PHILLIPS: We wanted Jack's boss to be a guy who could stand up to Jack: I suggested Sam Shepard. Aaron Eckhart was Seanie's idea. So we started to get some momentum. '*He's* in it? *She's* in it? *I'd* like to do this.' I said to Sean, 'How about Vanessa Redgrave to play the grandmother?' Jerry's psychiatrist was written as a man, but after some readings Sean felt it would be interesting if the role was played by a woman, to put that sexual tension into what she was asking him: 'Do you masturbate?' and so forth. We both thought of Helen Mirren. And we got Harry Dean, fighting and scratching all the way. We wanted Lori to be young, thirty-five or thirty-six, and to have a young daughter. We must have read thirty or forty candidates – damn good actresses, some very famous ones too. And in all my interviews with them, they would say, 'Yeah, Don, sure. Robin will end up getting this part, so what am I doing here?' And I would say, 'No! Not this time!' Finally it came to the point where both Jack and myself raised the matter with Sean: 'Well, what about your wife?'

ROBIN WRIGHT PENN: It was like, 'Well, do you want to do it?' 'Not really . . .' 'You're gonna be there anyway with the kids . . .' 'All right.' Not even a month before shooting, we tried it out on a soundstage, and Sean wanted to see a look. American trailer trash – like the chicks you see in bars when you're driving to Bishop, California. 'How about

changing the hair colour?' 'Let me just go that dirty mousey brown
. . .' I ran out to the drug store, got a bottle of Clairol and went to the
bathroom. So we did the hair, padded the tits, padded the ass, and it
was like, 'Let's do it.'

ANGELICA HUSTON: Oh God, I don't want to psychoanalyze him, but
. . . I'd say in Sean's movies, there's generally a small blonde girl who
tears his heartstrings by getting run over or murdered. And maybe
that's his mantra for his own daughter – his fear mantra.

DON PHILLIPS: I went up to Vancouver and looked at every little girl,
and I met a kid called Pauline Roberts, seven years old. I knew that
Sean does not like precocious little children, and for her to be so beautiful too . . . So Pauline came back a second time, and this time she
wore her glasses. We talked, eventually we looked at each other, and
Sean said, 'You got the part.' And she said, '*I* knew I'd get it . . .'

SEAN PENN: It's tricky working with young actors, especially in such
dark territory. I can say flat out I would never ever allow my child to
work in that kind of a role. But I have the excuse of being an American
hypocrite. And she was Canadian . . . She was a talented young girl,
and you go in there and try to make it as private and gentle an experience as possible.

*Penn asked Art Wolff to act as an on-set coach to Pauline Roberts, given
his considerable experience in directing child performers in television.*

ART WOLFF: I saw Sean on *The Pledge* under incredible pressures, and
I thought he behaved brilliantly. He sent me the script, and I read it
and said, 'You have a four-season movie here. How many days do you
have to shoot this?' He said, 'Fifty-five, including some bits in Reno.'
I said, 'You'll never make it.' He said, 'I have to: it's the only way to
get it made.' But it was all predicated on everything going right, every
possible thing. The weather made for pressure – that, and a lousy line
producer. On Sean's first two movies he had David Hamburger, whom
he would love to have used on this one. But Elie Samaha said, 'No, I
have my guy.' And it seemed more to the point to Sean to give in on
that than it would be to give in on the other thing that everyone was
pressing for, which was to change the ending. I think Jack even coun-
selled him to try not to say, 'What? Are you out of your fucking mind?'
but 'Well, we'll think about that . . .'

JACK NICHOLSON: Sean wanted to shoot places where they hadn't shot before, so we were way the hell out in the middle of nowhere plenty of times. Jerry's gas station was on an Indian reservation, four or five hours' driving from Vancouver. I put something like eight thousand miles on my work car on that movie: that's like back and forth across the country. I slept in the car a lot . . . It was frightening, those huge lumber trucks that you see throughout the picture – and rain, and night, and curling mountainous roads. I mean, Canada is very much wilder than I thought once you get up north there.

SEAN PENN: Jack had to shoot a brutal schedule, totally out of sequence: I was sending him back and forth to his trailer changing clothes twelve times a day. Freezing temperatures. And now it's supposed to be freezing in the film, now it's not, 'I'm gonna CGI the snow in later, guys, but trust me, it's snowing now, let's shoot.' It was tough. But, man, it was like working with some kid who just got his first job, he was so hungry. Nobody else could have done what Jack did, because of his positive attitude and his skill. You really got a taste of the world champion . . .

Jack is so able, in his make-up, to throw a match in a box of fireworks, and at the same time he can work on a level of subtlety and give you fireworks that are entirely about a cumulative effect. On *The Pledge*, we had a constant checking back-and-forth about, 'Did we dramatize this nuance of character yet?' And Jack has a very professional etiquette: he gathers index cards that graph the entire performance and what are the little tiny things that have to somehow find their way in. And if he doesn't get them in in this scene, this card, then something has to transfer to another. He's constantly re-reading his script start to finish. So it doesn't take a lot of directing with him, it's more . . . partnering.

JACK NICHOLSON: Sean's very patient as a director. He's confident in me. I've worked with a lot of great people, a lot of them great friends, and I don't have quite the same sense that what I'm doing is satisfying to what it is they're after as I do with Sean. See, with Sean, I never have to worry about 'How much do I have to show?' I understand his aesthetic going in. When you play the detective for Sean, you get to behave the way they would behave, and it's a non-dramatic way where you don't have to heighten it. Now, there *is* a very specific line over which it goes dead if you play it too quietly, so you gotta have something going. But you're free, while dealing with the most hideous things, to not necessarily register it emotionally. And this is a great luxury. It's beyond relaxing – it instils a confidence in myself as an actor that I don't always have. I've been acting for a long time, and working with Sean is very good for my acting. Because you do get pushed sometimes when you're working – just to explore, for the most part. But, you know, I'm easily pushed . . . [*laughs*]

Also, Sean has a brilliant eye – he's photographically very brilliant in terms of how he wants to see it, what the shot is. He's very inventive with the camera too. His movies are *his* movies – I mean, there are no mistakes in Sean's movies.

No scene in The Pledge *better exemplifies Penn's picture-making capacities than the moment when Jerry Black takes it upon himself to carry the dire news of Ginny Larsen's killing to her parents at their turkey farm, and finds them among their fowl in a vaulting, hangar-like barn.*

© Franchise Pictures. Courtesy of Sean Penn. Photo by Douglas

63 On location for *The Pledge*: Penn and Jack Nicholson (Jerry Black)

JAY CASSIDY: That scene was shot with the intention that you wouldn't hear anything but the birds. And you knew what was coming, so distancing from the experience was more than OK – you didn't need to pull that heartstring. But it's bad to shoot around turkeys because they're so skittish, they kind of go nuts and kill one another. So it ended up mostly shot from one direction, because when Sean turned the cameras around, they suddenly had a turkey revolt on their hands. Much more coverage was just impossible, and then the production manager had to pay for fifty dead turkeys . . .

Among the many cameos that adorn the picture, perhaps none is more resonant than that of Mickey Rourke, an intermittent screen actor in the previous decade, in the role of Jim Olstad, the broken, institutionalized father of a long-lost girl, from whom Jerry seeks information in support of his serial-murder theory.

64 On location for *The Pledge*: Penn, Mickey Rourke (Jim Olstad); behind them with viewfinder, Chris Menges (DP)

DON PHILLIPS: Mickey wasn't on the right track in terms of his career. He had been dearly, deeply considered for *Hurlyburly*. He just rips your heart out in *The Pledge*.

SEAN PENN: I'd always admired Mickey's talent. It always struck me, in any generation of this stuff, there's really only one or two guys that you get excited about, and Mickey certainly had always been one of them. And nobody has documented his ability to punch himself in the head better than he has. He had burned a lot of bridges for a long time. We had been friends on and off because, certainly, our bridges had been burned also. But I was always a fan of his. And I just felt we needed him. He and I ran into each other. He seemed in a better way than he'd been in a long time. I asked him if he'd do it, and he said yes. He came up, I shot two takes with him, said, 'See you in LA . . .'

His tenuous evidence collected, Black then attempts to convince his ex-colleagues Eric Pollack (Shepard) and Stan Krolak (Eckhart) of the integrity of his theory.

JAY CASSIDY: A simple scene – Jerry gets an audience because of who he was, and then he basically blows it. They think retirement has caused him to lose a screw. Jerry has to go too far, cross a line in that scene that he's never crossed before, and you have to see it. Sean worked very hard on that scene, shot a lot of takes to find those moments. And Jack did a number of different performances . . .

JACK NICHOLSON: We even darkened a Band-Aid on Jerry's hand so it looked like it was an increment of disintegration. It's like – he *knows* how they're reading him. He *knows* that they're not seeing this. And I'm very proud of the last line in that scene where he says, 'I made a promise, Eric. You're old enough to remember when that meant something.' That's me speaking out to my times, you know?

Penn steers us unfussily towards the unhappy realization that Jerry's best intentions are leading him into evil, once he befriends roadhouse waitress Lori and draws her bonny, blithe daughter Chrissy into his design to catch the killer. Worse, and contra Dürrenmatt, there is real feeling in the fondness Jerry lavishes on Chrissy and the fledgling intimacy he shares with her mother.

JACK NICHOLSON: I told Sean, 'Let's emphasize the fisherman in him, picking the good spot where the fish go.' And then Lori's situation prompts him, and he's sort of surprised. I don't think he ever thought she would be attracted to him. Then he's very careful about it: he wants to make sure the little girl's always in sight, and he really feels that no harm could possibly come to her – he's self-deluded to that degree. But he knows the guy is out there, he can feel it. And he's right. And he's punished for being right. Still waiting . . . To me, that's what makes the movie great.

In the end, Jerry is still chasing phantoms at the riverside site of his carefully laid snare operation when his true nemesis, the barely glimpsed 'Wizard', crashes and burns in a road accident miles away. So, while Jerry's ex-colleagues and surrogate family desert him in mingled pity and revulsion, Penn's camera zeroes in on the Wizard's roasted, blackened corpse at the wheel of his flaming sedan . . .

JAY CASSIDY: At the very end of May 2000, we were filming the scene of the face-off by the river. And we had rain . . . Jack loves the LA Lakers, and we were starting to get into the play-offs at the beginning of May – you don't want to be asking Jack to work when the Lakers are in the play-offs. As a worker, Jack's wonderful, he's right there every morning. But at the same time his deal was that there were only so many days he could work on the movie. And we were using them up just getting the whole company out there on the rocks and then having to light close-ups under big 20-by-20s, because it was raining. So we said, 'We'll come back in a month and a half.'

We were stopping principal photography without some major pieces, which made the company crazy. We left without the scene of Jack crossing the river and having a little face-off with Aaron Eckhart. And the whole wreck scene, the burning car, the burning face. But you can't fight the rain. It just meant we had to catch up.

Sean wanted me to come up to his house and edit the picture there. I went to Robin and I said, 'Robin, is this *really* OK?' and she said, 'Yes, it's *really* OK, it's why we built it this way . . .' For Sean it's great, because it just allowed him to be with his family, and his kids were at the age where he really wanted to be there. And it helps me, too. No commute, right? Just walk up the stone path from the guest house . . . And since you're stuck there with nothing to do, except for his movie, we'd work on weekends, in the evening, at weird times. Sean's quite a night person. And when you're really deep in a movie, you're not quite fit for normal life – your head's in a particular space, you have trouble with normal interactions. Then Jack came up and spent a lot of time with the cut before we went out the second time.

SEAN PENN: Jack stayed in the house for five days, and for the better part of those days I'd take a walk: my version, as it were, was intact in the memory of the computer. And he and Jay just re-cut the things that he had ideas about and attacked a lot of stuff. The last couple of evenings, we'd review that stuff and either I would like it, not like it, or it would provoke something beyond itself. But Jack's got a great editing mind; he's not a guy who comes in to just look at himself: he's looking at the storytelling, and he has an avant-garde sense of it too. There were certain sequences that were very affected by him – here as on *The Crossing Guard*.

Penn completed his cut by depositing us back where we began in the film's opening moments: Jerry, sun-baked and rotten with booze, rocking on his heels outside his lonely gas station, conducting an angry dispute with himself. The main musical theme, glacial and shivery when first heard over the opening credits, now grows percussive and exultant, and the camera ascends to leave Jerry stranded, a natural fool of fortune.

JACK NICHOLSON: You know, it's funny, because you can't win with Dürrenmatt. Even the people who like *The Pledge* – many of them still wanted Jerry to catch the killer and get together with Lori. But you couldn't make this movie and defy what Dürrenmatt did – it would be unfair, it would be karmically unjust . . .

HARRY DEAN STANTON: Everybody got into discussing the ending on that one. My strongest feeling was, the name of the movie was *The Pledge*. He pledged to this woman that he would find the killer. I think he and the woman, they should both know the guy who got killed in the wreck was the one who did it. And let him end up out on a lake fishing, instead of sitting there going crazy about it. But you bring that up to Jack or Sean and they would say, 'Oh god, I don't want to talk about it . . .'

SEAN PENN: I had a final-cut deal on all my movies since *Indian Runner*, and I got the final cut on that one with some struggle. So I'm not gonna release something that's not a director's cut without you knowing it – oh, there would have been a gun battle in the streets on any of my movies if that weren't the case.

DON PHILLIPS: Sean is the happiest, most joyous, upbeat person to be around when he's directing. He's absolutely in his own nirvana. And that is transmitted to his wife and his children and his friends.

65 On location for *The Pledge*: Penn directs Nicholson for the much-debated ending sequence

ROBIN WRIGHT PENN: As a person, Sean's very influential: he will push and push until you go the place that he feels you need to go – he's very present, very aggressive, in his energy. But as a director he sits back; he has so much faith and trust in what will come if you just let it be. Not like the directors who are just in your face with stupid blanket statements: 'More energy! Can you be angrier? Be funny!' Sean just feeds you bait, and it's so beautifully, subtly done. And, on that note – we get along great when we work, he's so easy. He *allows*, you know what I mean? And he doesn't allow as a person a lot of the time. He's getting better, but . . . he's so driven, Sean's so far ahead, as a personality. He's ten steps ahead of us right now. . .

MEEGAN OCHS: He's an infinite pixie, that Sean, he always wants to get you at the moment you're not expecting it. He loves that – that little smirk on his face, like he's gonna surprise you. Which is why it was such fun that Robin was really able to surprise him at his fortieth birthday.

ROBIN WRIGHT PENN: It was really tough, keeping it a secret, 'cause he's so snoopy. Always, 'What are you doing?' I'm hiding shit in the guest house, saying, 'I'm making you something, you can't look.' And I'm bringing tents, umbrellas, tables, all the booze, stuffing them in there . . . Then everybody flies up from Los Angeles.

Courtesy of Meegan Ochs

66 Surprise! Penn with Lars Ulrich on his 40th birthday, August 17 2000

LARS ULRICH: Sean had been fearing the day. Robin called me and asked if I'd be the facilitator, and I'm always quite happy to facilitate . . . We all wallow in thinking that we can play tennis, and I had set up a match at Brad Gilbert's place nearby. We talked about the possibility of maybe getting together that night and having a drink. Then, four o'clock, Sean and I jump in his car and go up to Gilbert's, and play doubles for an hour-and-a-half. Brad, of course, is in on it, acting the very gracious host, refusing to let us leave until we've drunk a couple of specially-made margaritas, which Sean meekly sips his way through. Then on the way back to the house I'm still trying to drag out time, when Sean suddenly decides to stop by a barbecue store. And that bought Robin the extra fifteen minutes she needed . . .

JOSEPH VITARELLI: And it was, as far as I can tell, a *complete* surprise: I think Robin actually pulled it off. Because Sean came home in his tennis shorts – and that's a dead giveaway right there . . . Robin put up a big banner over the pool, 'Happy 40th Sean.' And the two of us just stood there, thinking, 'It's not possible, is it . . .?'

MEEGAN OCHS: That day you saw around you, yes, some friends who are new, and friends of the last ten years. But really it was like Old Home Week: friends from high school, from the very early days of his career – Joe Vitarelli, Art Linson, John Sykes, David Baerwald.

Sean had a very interesting idea about friendship that he told me within the first few months of our knowing each other. When he met someone who he thought could become a friend, there were lines established – he called them 'Chinese lines'. And he'd say, 'Between those lines is the area in which you can remain friends. There's certain behaviour you can do whereupon you cross out of those lines, and you can't ever cross back in: that person can be in your life, but they can't be your friend any more. But as you grow to know and love somebody, those lines get further and further apart, until finally they're so far apart that it's impossible for that person to cross out of them.'

And I loved looking round that party and seeing people from Sean's whole life: the true friends, the ones who didn't pass through the lines . . .

On 12 September 2000, the citizens of Selma, Alabama, went to the polls for a run-off mayoral election between long-time incumbent Joe Smitherman and black businessman James Perkins Jr. Selma is known the world over, albeit in infamy, for the violent repression of protestors at the outset of the famous march to Montgomery, 7 March 1965, in the name of the black franchise. Peaceful marchers were beaten bloody that day by troopers on the Edmund Pettus Bridge.

SEAN PENN: I went to Selma with Geronimo Pratt and I spoke at a church. Some associates from the Black Panther movement in the sixties were involved in James Perkins' campaign, and they called upon Geronimo, due to those relationships, to come down. Joe Smitherman, who had been the mayor of Selma since the march on the bridge and is the guy who went on national television and called Martin Luther King 'Martin Luther Coon', was still the mayor of Selma, Alabama. It was very clear that this guy was a local businessman: one of those guys who was counting that there'd be federal funds taking care of certain infrastructure, and you could sell to a largely illiterate public the idea that you had brought it to them. So this guy had been re-elected time and time again, largely based on the black vote – *despite* calling Martin Luther King 'Martin Luther Coon' . . . But there was evidence of a lot of trickery and money used for advantage throughout those years, and not really a contribution to the people of Selma. So, finally, there was a real opposition. And, sure enough, there was a car fire-bombed in front of Perkins' headquarters. So there was some discussion of whether the same people would bomb this church, and Geronimo said, 'Not if we go down there . . .' So we went down and spoke at the church that night, and it was a one-day sleepover at a motel outside of Selma, and Joe Smitherman got chucked out of office that year. And that was pretty cool.

I don't know how much that *night* had to do with it versus they were ready for a change. But I was glad to participate as one more person.

On 8 November 2000, following two terms of Democrat presidency, America decided once again. Earlier that year, in a shoot with photographer Dan Winters for Detour *magazine, Penn insisted on being framed with a Vote Gore button in his lapel. In the accompanying interview, he reflected: 'I think most of us who pay any attention realize that there's a case to be made that it doesn't matter who is President. There might even be a case to be made that if Bush won, it would be great, because it would actually force the Democratic party to be a unified left party again. But I can't quite get myself into this area of cynicism, and I'm going to vote for Gore . . .'[1]*

---

1 'The Burden of Integrity', Juan Morales, *Detour*, May 2000.

Courtesy of Sean Penn

67 The Candidate, 2000: Albert Gore, producer Michael Fitzgerald, Penn

SEAN PENN: I was very reluctant to get involved there: I didn't know what I felt about any of the candidates. And then Gore spoke to a group of people in San Francisco, and I just went along as an observer. And the minute the TV cameras left, they opened the floor to a Q&A, and suddenly I saw an Al Gore I'd never seen before; and I was very impressed by him. I met him, we spoke, and there were certainly issues that I disagreed with him on; but it wasn't hard to know that the opposition wasn't what I wanted. So I got a *little* bit involved in that campaign. But I went to the convention one night and, by then, clearly Joseph Lieberman was very much on board. And that was a little bit more confusing. I was a bit ashamed, later, of the connection to Lieberman. In terms of the debate about 'Are the Democrats any different to the Republicans?' – well, *he's* not. He's certainly a really significant foe of the arts. So when that choice was made, I was a bit shaken. And, as I look back on it, I probably would have changed my vote to Nader on the basis of that alone.

But I saw the shame of it on that night with Gore: if the cameras had just kept going, you would have seen a passionate, incredibly informed person, with great ideas and great love for his country – really . . .

WOODY HARRELSON: I was with Sean when the election went down in 2000 and Bush ultimately got in. At the time Sean was like, 'See? You voted for Nader and look what happened!'

PETER COYOTE: I voted for Ralph Nader: because I felt that if you're always forced to vote for the most mediocre Democrat to protect yourself against the most rapacious Republican, then our political life is on a downward spiral that's irretrievable. Nader was not supposed to run in swing states – he was going to try and get enough names on his petitions so that the Green Party could qualify for federal matching money. But the Democrats were so dismissive of the Greens – treated them like aberrant children and told them to come into the fold – that I think it made Nader a little nuts. And he ran. And although he can't be blamed for the vote getting as close as it got – Gore ran an extremely tepid campaign and lost his home state as well as Clinton's state of Arkansas – it's arguable that Nader *did* make a difference, and made it that much easier for George the Second to steal the election.

Penn and Harrelson were keeping company in that moment because of a shared theatrical endeavour: the first staging, in San Francisco, of The Late Henry Moss *by Sam Shepard. It was a piece Shepard had begun in 1990, then set aside: 'I was worried about the brother thing. I thought, "Jesus, who wants to see this again?"'.[2] The play concerns two combustible siblings in the wake of the death of their cussed, alcoholic father. The younger, Ray, is impelled to lay bare the circumstances surrounding the death, believing his older brother Earl knows more than he's letting on and that answers are buried in their shared past. Frustration turns to fury, borne on tides of booze.*

Shepard brought the piece to San Francisco's Magic Theatre, where he was once playwright-in-residence. Penn was his first recruit, as Ray. Nick Nolte followed as Earl. Shepard specialist James Gammon, he of the semi-legendary nicotine-scorched rasp, was the natural Henry Moss and brought in Cheech Marin as a devoted neighbour. Harrelson was drafted in as a cab driver who assists Ray through his reminiscences of an especially tortuous night in Henry's company.

WOODY HARRELSON: Seaner said, 'You gotta do this.' First I thought, 'Jeez, he's only in the second act of a three-act play.' But then later I realized there were some comic gems. Though, to be honest, I think Sam had in mind for it to be a little more dramatic. But it was a heavy, heavy play, so me and Cheech Marin were kind of the comic relief in it. I wouldn't have done Sean's part for the world, you know? Too sad.

2 'Sam Shepard Comes Home', Belinda Taylor, *Performing Arts*, November 2000.

I liked the experience just for having had it, but I didn't love doing it. I like a different relationship with a director than that had. But, you know, Sam was going through some stuff. A week into it, we all come in to rehearsal, Sam's not there. Comes in the next day, he'd had a major deal with his heart, angioplasty, and the doctor's told him he can't smoke any more cigarettes, but – *but* [*laughs*] – a glass of wine in the evening can help thin the blood, you know? Well, he didn't know who he was *dealing* with. Once the doctor opened that door for him, it was a whole different ball of wax . . .

JERRY HANNAN: T-Bone Burnett wrote music for the show that he'd play during the performance, but he couldn't be there the whole time, so he decided to train a guitar player to fill in. Sean suggested that I do it, and I said I'd love to.

I think it didn't evolve quite to where they had hoped it would. Sam used to say in rehearsal, 'Pardon me, but I'm still writing this play, so forgive me, and let's do this instead.' Plus they had a short time to rehearse, and it was cut even shorter.

ART WOLFF: I think it could have used some rewriting, and it could have used another eye too, in terms of directing. But it was an interesting production. We know the themes Sean is drawn to: children in peril, also fathers and sons, from *Heartland* to *At Close Range* . . . and many of his other films, even where the father isn't present, the father's presence in the life of the character is very strong.

The production was close to home, and that was Sean's deal – 'I'll do this play but only if it's in San Francisco, and I won't go to New York with it if you move.' But it was physically demanding. When I saw him in San Francisco he was like, '*Why* do I never remember what a pain in the ass is the daily coming-to-the-theatre, saying-the-same-lines . . .? It's like going to the dentist every night.'

JERRY HANNAN: I'd be at the side of the stage playing guitar. And there's one part where Sean had a monologue, describing how his dad had beat up his mom, and in describing it, he was beating up his brother. And you felt it every time – even though I'd seen them rehearse it, you thought you'd just seen a huge fight break out . . .

NEIL JORDAN: Abiding memories? I remember Sean Penn kicking Nick Nolte around a stage for about three hours. With great vigour [*laughs*]. And from Nick's perspective, it looked like it really hurt. It was an extraordinary play – kind of wayward, but a great night at the theatre, I thought.

DENNIS HOPPER: It was a hard one, man. Great, but hard. A long, long play. It's tough to stay in the theatre with people screaming at you for three and a half fucking hours. And they were killing each other up there. I had dinner with them afterwards, and Nick and Sean embraced, both of them sore and beaten up, and they kept saying, [*husky*] 'Only three more performances, three more performances . . .'

JOSEPH VITARELLI: Having Woody Harrelson and Sean and Nolte on the same stage – they're such major stars that I think, for the audience, it becomes something like a Lakers game. I mean, the Rolexes abound . . . people were buying annual subscriptions just to get seats for that show.

SEAN PENN: A starry show brings a certain kind of audience. And here, there was a *bunch* of us. The theatre audience is a theatre audience – if you have one. In Los Angeles it's that much tougher. But then it's in New York now too, as far as I can tell. There's a place for everything, but there's no place for drama on Broadway . . . Sam's play, I felt like we should have workshopped it with invited audiences, if this was what we were going to face, and really just explore the play, with Sam, for Sam. And then he could do what he wanted with it. But I'm not interested in doing a play again. [*sotto voce*] Except *Goose and Tomtom* . . .

The Pledge *had its Hollywood unveiling at the Egyptian Theatre on 9 January 2001.*

JON SCHEIDE: This was a movie about fate and the moment where your life hangs on a simple act, and you go from being a hero to an idiot stumbling around in a gas station that you bought at a cross-roads on some fucking mountain pass . . .

TONY DRAZAN: I think the end of *The Pledge* is funny. I said as much to a producer at the première in Hollywood, and he said, 'You really are a sick person.'

SEAN PENN: It was a different kind of movie than my first two. There was a kind of obligation to a form that I didn't have before. I'm not necessarily hung up on the idea of conventional story structure, but I didn't want to violate the conventions so as to make it distracting, so that was a balancing act. Interesting to do once or twice, but I don't think it'll fill out the rest of the movies I make.

DENNIS HOPPER: *The Pledge* didn't mean anything to me. Jack gave a brilliant performance, but I wasn't emotionally involved, and I should be. Maybe that's just old-fashioned, but I don't know enough about the character to care about him until the movie's almost over. And that just left me in a seat looking at pictures, giving me time to not be involved and pick it apart.

JOSEPH VITARELLI: Just seeing Jack's performance, the subtlety of it . . . it may sound ridiculous to say this, but Jack Nicholson seems almost underrated as an actor. He's this colossal movie star, nominated for a dozen Academy Awards, and yet I sometimes get the feeling that people don't realize how great this guy is.

JACK NICHOLSON: The last little while, I've been saying, 'Sean, you're so entertaining as an actor, now will you try with your next movie to do one where you're not *doomed* before you start to having a marginal audience?' Because there are movies you do and you know that either they're too literary and intelligent, or too tough – you'll have a *succès d'estime*, but with the numbers, you'll have problems. And if he's not interested, I respect that too. But I've been trying to [*mimes elbow to ribs*] – you know?

JAY CASSIDY: Sean's often said that he's gotten away with making three art films at ever increasing budgets. I think he's being too hard on himself, because *The Pledge* I think they ended up making money on.

WOODY ALLEN: I wrote to Sean after I saw *The Pledge*, because I thought that he did a wonderful job on it: I mean, I was riveted to the picture. And I thought his wife was wonderful in it; Nicholson, of course, is always wonderful, that's no news. But Sean has found his way. I think he's a very, very good director.

Having taken pay cuts for Hurlyburly *and* The Thin Red Line, *worked for scale with Woody Allen, and paid some* Pledge *bills from his own pocket for a while, Penn was, by the standards of the life he had made, somewhat strapped. At which point a project written by Kristine Johnson and director Jessie Nelson, to which he had been attached for three years without movement, unexpectedly came to life, and also remunerated him decently.*

387

JESSIE NELSON: Kris came to visit me after my daughter was born and had colic: it was a very challenging experience, those first three months with the baby. And Kris told me an idea she'd been researching for a movie about a disabled parent, and I said, 'Would you mind if I came aboard?' Being a new mother myself, I just felt it would be an interesting metaphor, exploring parenting through that character.

We did about a year's worth of research, meeting disabled parents and social workers, working at a non-profit centre called LA Goal, going through the legal system. And it sounds so schmaltzy when I say it, so I almost hate to – but the key ingredient in parenting is love; and it was so astounding to meet these phenomenally flawed and limited parents who just loved their children so fiercely that the children were blossoming, and forgiving them everything.

'Sam I Am' (later I Am Sam) told of Sam Dawson, a thirty-five-year-old man with the mental capacity of an eight-year-old, father of a seven-year-old daughter, Lucy, whom he conceived with a homeless woman who then took flight. He waits tables in a coffee house, has the friendship and support of a group of men with similar disabilities, and his bright, affectionate daughter adores him. But as she begins to cotton to his clear limitations in the spectrum of her future development, teachers and social services are several steps ahead of her, and so Sam faces a legal battle to retain custody of Lucy, for which he manages to enlist strident defence lawyer Rita.

JESSIE NELSON: We set it up at Fox where I had a deal to write and direct. They then went through the usual thing of 'We have to get Tom Cruise.' I had a very strong instinct about Sean, so I wrote and sent him a script, and we agreed to meet. I was heading to Italy on vacation, and he was in another village shooting *Up at the Villa*, so we thought, 'Why not take our first meeting in Italy?' At one point we were talking about shooting in San Francisco, with a scene of Sam walking over the Golden Gate Bridge, and Sean stood up in the restaurant we were in and did Sam's walk, how he imagined it. And I thought, 'Oh! There's the whole movie . . .'

What was then so fascinating was Fox kept telling me, 'Sean won't be sympathetic, he's too dark, he carries too much baggage with the public,' rather than seeing what he could bring to the film. Then Sean had his falling-out with Fox and wrote the letter to Rupert Murdoch . . . and the next day they said, 'You can't use Sean.' So that began a battle of my saying, 'I don't want to do it with anybody else,' and them telling me, 'Forget it'. At one point they even fired me off the movie in the hope they could get Brendan Fraser to do it. *George of the Jungle* had just been a hit . . . Finally, they gave me one week to set it up at another studio. And, God bless Mike De Luca and Claire Rudnick Polstein at New Line, they stepped up to the plate and we were out of jail.

Sean went very carefully through the script, examining how far he could go and what his limits were, so he could build the proper cage for himself. Then the big day for me was when I took him to LA Goal. And everybody there welcomed him. One guy said, 'Sean Penn! I can't believe you're here! I loved you in all the *Pink Panther* movies!' They were working on an assembly line, folding paper into envelopes, putting plastic cutlery into containers for airplanes. Sean just joined the line – no ego, no trying to entertain them or make them like him. And that day, I could see his eye gathering a gesture here and a walk there, hearing the phrasing of words. But he was almost invisible: very much like a sponge, soaking it in.

Then I was in the trailer with Sean and the barber, as he was slowly creating him: 'Take more off here, and more off *here*.' That kind of Bazooka Joe/Stan Laurel hairdo he ended up with, that was a very key thing for him. I remember that day watching his face and feeling like a real transformation was taking place. The same with the wardrobe, the choice he made to wear two shirts together like the guys at LA Goal, and his pants a certain height on his belly . . .

The concerns about directorial trust and editorial privilege that Penn had learned to take seriously in his early screen-acting career were a thing of the distant past when it came to dealing with a simpatico writer–director such as Nelson. In other respects of his craft, however, Penn remained professionally adamant: as in a sequence where Sam, visiting Lucy after she has been taken from him with a hearing pending, arrives late and encumbered with a cake-box.

JESSIE NELSON: Physically, Sean knows what he's capable of: he can go there and be safe. Maybe it's the surfing, I don't know . . . Anyway, this was not in the script, but right as we were setting up camera, he said, 'I think I'm gonna fall down the steps.' My producer and the stunt person said, 'Legally that's a stunt, you can't do that.' I'm thinking, 'As if *that'll* stop him . . .' They finally convinced him to wear knee pads. I was more scared of him going face-first and breaking his jaw. But I just quickly set up two cameras and prayed we got it in one. And of course he did. Same later on when he's sitting high up in a tree, watching Lucy. They wanted to harness him in so there'd be no insurance problem. Sean's like, 'Fuck no! I can't *act* if I'm harnessed.' Next thing you know, they're still arguing and Sean's shimmying up the tree.

One thing I learned, Sean loves the happy accident in the moment that keeps it fresh. And when you're working with kids and dogs and actors with disabilities, you get that all day long, non-stop.

As with The Pledge, *Penn asked that Art Wolff be engaged, this time to coach the excellent Dakota Fanning in her performance as Lucy.*

ART WOLFF: Dakota has that 'wise child' quality, and Lucy had to have that too in order to run this family. She already had the ability to seem to be observing the scene, but that was one of the things that disturbed Sean. He didn't want to be in a situation where she couldn't play with him: where she'd be frozen into line-readings and attitudes, cute when she had to be cute, sad when she had to be sad. We wanted the surprises – when you thought she'd be cute, she'd be angry, and when you expected anger, she'd be sad. Like life is, you know?

And we talked a lot about the double relationship she had with her father: the relationship as his child, and then also as a parent to him. I think one of the heartbreaking, tender things in the movie is the way she relates to Sean in this gentle way of his being a child. My favourite scene between them is in the booth at IHOP, and she's saying, 'Are you different? *Why* are you different?' And he says, 'What do you mean?' He can't get his mind around that. But he knows it, somehow.

Through the scenes of Sam with his loyal, albeit chaotic, peer-group buddies, Penn had the novel experience of working with two actors with disabilities: Brad Silverman, who has Down's Syndrome, and Joe Rosenberg, a man with autism.

SEAN PENN: It wasn't difficult. If anything, they were the ones who accepted my transition from whoever they considered 'Sean' to be to what 'Sam' was, and they did it without comment. And that had been what I was concerned about – one of the guys saying, 'What are you *doing*? Why are you *acting* like that?' But they saw the personality, so you could talk back and forth in any manner. There were certain areas that were inappropriate to get into, and there are issues specifically related to sexuality, which is often undeveloped. So that can be a confusing area. But it was very quickly not different from usual when we were all off-camera, in a trailer, having lunch or whatever. You would slow down your way of talking and be more economical in it, but you were talking about most of the same things: in terms of observations of how the day was going, thoughts about the scene to come, 'How's your food? What are you thinking about having for dessert?', 'Let's look at dailies from yesterday . . .'

Certain other cast members Penn was previously acquainted with: Bobby Cooper as the boss of the coffee-house where Sam works, and Dennis Fanning as a cop who arrests him when he's lured into social intercourse with a pushy hooker. As on previous occasions, Fanning had the pleasure of subjecting Penn to a thorough frisk.

DENNIS FANNING: The fun thing, where I actually started to learn how you could do that ad-lib shit, was when I squeezed Sean's nut-sack. The first time I just pretended, but then he said something smart-ass to me, so the next time I searched him I squeezed his nuts. I mean, I *squeezed*. That's when I saw the tear in his eye . . . And I felt for sure it would be one of those capers where it blew the scene and took him out of character. But he stayed in it. *That's* when you know a guy's good. So I had to stay with him. Then he says, 'You touched my *private* place . . .' And I could feel the laugh building in my chest. I wanted to bust up, but I couldn't . . .

JESSIE NELSON: There were five or six alumni of Peggy Feury's in the cast: Sean and Michelle Pfeiffer and a few others. I think that's part of why Michelle and Sean had such a good acting chemistry. And I think there's a shared addiction to the truth there. For Sean, any little untruth, be it the wrong prop, a bullshit moment from another actor, a sense the camera's in the wrong place, unnerves him so much. And if he's going ballistic over some prop . . . it's usually the wrong prop. Our dog-handler kept trying to make the dogs behave, and Sean said, 'I'm a disabled man walking six dogs, it's gonna be messy, let it be. Let them be dogs!'

ART WOLFF: One area in the script that was really off the deep end was an affair between Sean's and Michelle's characters – they were supposed to sleep together. You mention that to most people and they say, 'Oh, that's so bizarre. So wrong. You don't do that.' Well, yeah, but that's the whole point of what it brought up.

68 *I Am Sam*: Michelle Pfeiffer (Rita Harrison), Penn (Sam Dawson)

JESSIE NELSON: It was the night that Rita comes to Sam's house and he's built an origami wall, and she breaks the wall and they connect. And she's feeling so horrendous about herself as a parent, and her life . . . and at that point it happened and they came together. Hence 'Norwegian Wood' on the soundtrack. Then later on they stepped away from that moment, realized that they had to make their relationship professional. It's like the line of Sam's, 'When dealing with the customer, be friendly but not familiar.' It was that same feeling: that for her to help him and him to help her, they couldn't really go there. The people I did the research with at the centre read the script and had a lot of input about what was real and what wasn't, and they didn't want Kris and I to do that scene, felt that it was wrong and that Rita was taking advantage of Sean's character. But we fought very hard to keep it in. And when we shot it, it was very, very beautiful and very powerful.

The horrible courtroom scenes Sean had, where he had to weep on the stand, he would then do eight takes in a row for the other actors and be at the same level of intensity – very generous in that way. It's not easy for him, it's not like, 'Boom, I'll cry.' You can feel the pain he's in to get there, and you hope to shoot it quickly so you don't have to keep him in it too long. But it wasn't easy to watch. Sean sort of carries the energy of whatever scene he's shooting, and for the scenes that were gut-wrenching, he'd be fanning that fire all day long.

I couldn't get over how much laughter he'd bring, though. Sean loves to laugh and to make other people laugh. When we were shooting the intimate scene between Rita and Sam, obviously a big important scene, we cleared the set and they began to get in position to do it. Sean was supposed to be wearing pyjamas or something. And he took off his robe, and he was wearing a big Depends diaper . . . Once Michelle saw that, she relaxed. I relaxed, the whole crew relaxed. Sean had broken the ice. And I thought, 'OK, we're going to do fine now . . .'

The Pledge, however well received in the US, was a picture that stood to benefit from the kind of connoisseurial platform afforded by the leading international festivals. However, in early 2001, it suffered the indignity of being withdrawn from an official selection berth at Berlin, amid budget-related recriminations between Elie Samaha's Franchise Pictures and the German backer Intertainment. Nevertheless, Gilles Jacob readily stepped in with an invitation to the competition in Cannes that May. Jack Nicholson was not available for that particular press conference and red-carpet promenade, but he couldn't resist accompanying Penn and the picture on a jaunt to the Moscow Film Festival one month later.

JACK NICHOLSON: Oh, we had a wonderful time in Moscow. I'd always wanted to go. Nikky Mikhalkov, who runs the festival, is an old friend of mine, quite an extravagant and extreme individual. And it just felt right that this was the time to go.

Fascinating to see what's going on there. I could write a movie on the trip to Moscow. Because, of course, security is extreme. You get serious Russian guys, very austere and official, who are used to having it tougher: the average charging autograph hound might wind up with a broken *ass* if he charged too hard . . . One security guy gradually softened up and got friendly with us. He was a paramarine. Just before we left, he said, 'My cousin's going to be with you tomorrow, because I've been ordered on active duty. I'm going to Chechnya.' 'Really? Aw, that's too bad. How wonderful to know you and thanks for your help.' A week later, Michael Fitzgerald tells me, 'Did you hear what happened in Chechnya?' The day after our guy left, there was a huge firefight – he's right in the middle of it – thirty-four *hundred* casualties. So that would be my Moscow movie: this very quiet man, being nice

Courtesy of Sean Penn

69 Penn, Jack Nicholson and Vladimir Putin at Nikita Mikhalkov's country
residence, June 2001

to movie stars, and then heading off into *that*. To me, it said where
Russia was at that moment.

We had a great time out there, no doubt. The showing was beautiful, and we met with Putin out at Nikky's place in the country. I don't
know that he saw the picture, to tell you the truth. But we had a nice
talk with him and he was a very impressive man, very together, very
gracious. I got a good laugh out of him too. The photographer said,
'You must have got him a good one, he never laughs.' All I did was
offer him some mosquito repellent. Out in the country, you know,
you're always slapping . . .

*Penn's drive to maintain the momentum of his directorial career then
settled upon the idea of adapting David Rabe's spare and magisterial
stage play* A Question of Mercy, *derived from the journal of Dr
Richard Selzer and exploring the exquisite issue of doctor-assisted suicide
through the sufferings of a man stricken with AIDS and a retired sur-
geon to whom the fateful call for quietus is made. Among the actors
with whom Penn discussed participation were Warren Beatty, Aaron
Eckhart, and his director from* Sweet and Lowdown.

WOODY ALLEN: Sean asked me if I would play some kind of role: I

394

believe it was an elevator operator. I felt it was within my limited range to do it. And I was only too happy to say yes, and I couldn't care less whether or not he could pay me, because I have great respect for him as a director. And in certain cases, where people are serious and they're artists and they're really trying to *do* something, I'm happy to contribute in any way that I can.

DAVID RABE: Sean was going to direct it. I did a script, then went out in June, July, and worked with him. We kept thinking we were gonna get it on in the fall of 2001, but it didn't happen. It got right up to the point where you could swear it was gonna happen, and yet . . .

In late August 2001, Penn crossed the Atlantic and took The Pledge *and his family to the Edinburgh Film Festival by way of London, where he watched U2 play Earl's Court on 21 August, the day of the passing of Bono's father.*

BONO: It was such a blur. It was just enough that he was there for me. It's an interesting thing: I don't have this feeling about a lot of people, because for an insecure performer I'm pretty secure. I'm strong. But when Sean's around I feel stronger, if that makes any sense. If he *was* a musician . . . he probably sees himself as a kind of solo singer-songwriter type of thing – but I just think he'd be great in the band. In any capacity. Except for one: he's not gonna be the singer . . .

In Edinburgh Penn gave a characteristically combative press conference on abiding preoccupations: 'Most of my own generation just didn't make the cut as far as I'm concerned. They have no broader interest – everything is about entertainment and no politics.'

Politics was perhaps the watchword, an indication that Penn was once again making a thoughtful revision of his professional priorities. Acting had turned out to be insufficient. Writing and direction had more resonant claims. But the notion of political activism, what that might mean in his own life as well as amongst the coming generation, was abroad in his comments. 'I think it would be an enormously patriotic movement to invest in the possibility of revolution,' he told the press corps. 'There's a lot of stuff going on around the world and in the US as well, like the protests in Genoa and Seattle, and young people are putting themselves on the line. We're going to start seeing directors coming out of that group. I hope there are going to be people who care about things bigger than themselves . . .'

The following night, interviewed onstage before a public audience, Penn was asked the perennial favourite: 'If you weren't an actor and director, what would you want to be, and why?' 'This is the very first year in the history of my life when I could say this,' he pondered. 'But it would be President of the United States. As to why . . .' He made an open-handed gesture for which the amused audience required no elucidation. A questioner who had clearly read the coverage of the previous day's conference then asked him if he might be drawn to make a 'political' film?

'There's not a lot of music in it to me,' he said after some thought. 'It's something I'd be inclined to participate in as a citizen. I think it's part of our obligation to the degree we're able to fill it as people. I don't feel as a film-maker I'm literally politically inclined. But I would certainly be open to it if I was ever struck . . .'

On 11 September 2001, Penn was scheduled to begin work for two episodes' worth of cameo appearance on the NBC sit-com Friends, *his daughter's favourite TV show and one in which he admired the tight calibre of the comedic writing as well as the respectable pay cheque.*

SEAN PENN: It was my first day of rehearsal on *Friends*. I didn't rehearse that day. I got up that morning, drove straight to the studio and got turned around by security, no explanation. So I turned on the radio in my car, and that's how I found out about it.

The twin towers of the World Trade Center in New York had already collapsed, the Pentagon had been attacked, and flight 93 had crashed in Pennsylvania. As Penn later remarked to Variety, *'We were in such a new world in that minute.'*

DAVID BAERWALD: The night after September 11 – or maybe the night after the night after – I was just driving around Los Angeles, thinking, 'Oh my fucking god . . .' Sean calls me and says, 'Have you eaten dinner yet? Why don't you come meet me in Beverly Hills?' I told him that was really pretty far for me, and he said, 'You really ought to do this . . .' So I go to this place, and it's one of the weirdest post-9/11 gatherings of people you could imagine: Mariah Carey, Naomi Campbell, David Blaine, the magician from New York who's always piercing himself, two hot-shit record producers, a guy who's the second-string bookie for the Gotti mob, so he says . . . Nobody really knew each other, and everybody was having their own conversations. The bookie was talking about the glory days of Joe Namath; Naomi Campbell was talking about her weird little Blackberry communications device; Mariah Carey kept on jumping up and shouting, 'I'm forever fourteen!'

It kind of reminded me of *Grand Hotel*. You know, here we all are eating our crumpets while the howitzers line up. Sort of like the 'Boomtown' script . . .

THIRTEEN

2001–2003

Sean is batty as a loon and is prone to taking extraordinary risks in foreign towns . . .
Hunter S. Thompson, 'Page 2', ESPN.com, 6 December 2001

It had not been tough before the war for the US government to suss out conditions in Iraq. Electronic surveillance, satellite photography, interviews with refugees – all of this could have produced a picture of life within Iraq. Or the CIA could have asked Sean Penn . . .
David Corn, 'George Won't Be Reading This', LA Weekly, 24 October 2003

In November 2001, Penn's penchant for raving unabashedly about the new films and film-makers he most admired landed him yet another unusual gig. He did a single day's work in Vancouver on It's All About Love, *Danish director Thomas Vinterberg's immaculately styled retro–futuristic follow-up to his prize-winning Dogme 95 film* Festen/The Celebration.

THOMAS VINTERBERG: I had read some articles in which Sean said he was crazy about *The Celebration*. And I knew how courageous he is in the choice of work that he does. So I made contact with him and we talked, and I visited him at his house. He was really nice, very warm, very smart. I showed him the script for *It's All About Love*, and he said, 'I want to put my name in the hat for The Man in the Plane.' I said, 'Fine, it's yours.' The character is scared of flying, so he goes into therapy and is given pills that mean he can now *only* fly. So he's stuck on a plane, always on his mobile phone, watching over crazy events going on below.

I kept saying to people, 'If you need a tool for viewing this film, if you want to go on this journey, see it as a dream.' The first person who spotted that was Sean, actually, at the script stage. He told me he thought it had 'a drunken sleepwalk quality' that he really liked. And in a way, it was an anti-Dogme film that we were making: very lit-up, with artifice, an illusion. All the airline shots with Sean were done on computer. But Sean was very supportive. He told me to really go for my vision: he's a director himself, so he knows that you're alone out there . . .

I Am Sam had its Oscar-qualifying limited run in the last week of December 2001; it duly opened nationally in January. The film as released had some significant departures from what had been scripted, and perhaps envisaged, in style and content.

JESSIE NELSON: I had the intimate scene between Sam and Rita in my first cut, and I would say half-to-three-quarters of the audience, straighter people than I, couldn't get past it. It eclipsed the rest of the story. And I almost felt that as a writer I had written two different movies: one about getting over the taboo of sexuality, which I would have loved to explore, and the other about a father fighting for custody of his child and touching people on that journey. Ultimately what became important for me is that he touched her, whether that be sexually or emotionally or spiritually. It didn't ultimately matter to me whether it was sexual or not; it was important that it was meaningful.

SEAN PENN: The scene seemed weird; and it didn't serve Michelle's character. And there had been a lot of reluctance about it going in anyway – there had been discussions about not shooting it. I thought – like a lot of things I think – 'You never know what's going to work and what's not . . .'

It was bittersweet, that whole experience. We really had a great experience making the movie, we all really cared about it. It was one of those ones that was really made by a family. Most of the bittersweetness that I speak of is not related to the movie itself – because I think Jessie did some wonderful things – but in terms of the way in which post-production time could have been spent. I think we could have gone a lot tougher with the picture. But Jessie, who I really love, was up against a studio that was so unaware that the movie was going to work not on the basis of what flavour it advertised but on the nourishment that it gave; and that it wasn't going to make it a 'dark art-picture' if you shuffled the deck a little bit and allowed some things to get a little uncomfortable at times. But there was a lot of pressure on that, and I don't know how much it influenced the final sound, music, cutting.

JESSIE NELSON: I felt very grateful to New Line, as much as it was a challenging experience, because they agreed to make it with Sean. No other studio would, and I felt like they wanted the movie to reach a lot of people, so that was something I was weighing too. I was working at a studio that doesn't necessarily always make these kinds of movies, so it was kind of trying to find a way to get them to understand what this kind of movie is. They had put a certain amount into the movie in terms of actors' salaries and things like that; they weren't making a $4 million movie with me where you don't care if it only makes $5 million . . .

SEAN PENN: The tone of the picture became different than I had imagined. I was given some tougher scenes to approve, scenes that were not in the final picture, but I think some of them can be accessed on the DVD. I felt that the way they wanted to package the movie meant a lot of confectionery sort-of stuff was done to it. They sold it as a fucking old-style Disney movie or something, and had pushed for that in the tone. Nonetheless, I had a great experience, and I knew we shot a movie that I think could have worked on a much more sophisticated, edgy level.

ART WOLFF: Where it went wrong was in not truly dealing with the case for why there were problems in this kind of father/child relationship – the things Richard Schiff as the lawyer brings up: 'Now they're the same age. What are you gonna do when she's in tenth grade? When she hits puberty?' – and dealing with those issues honestly, rather than just saying, 'Oh, it doesn't matter, all you need is love,' and having it be just being an emotional love story between Sam and Lucy. Look at *My Left Foot* and imagine if that had not been made in the way it was. Granted, the advantage there was that it was about a real person. And this was a make-believe person, so they can say, 'Well, what if he did this?' Then you're really in trouble, if you don't have a sense of what I'd call the drama of truthful behaviour. Then the audience is thinking, 'Wait a minute, why is he . . .? Oh no, please, c'mon . . .' And it becomes a fable.

New Line certainly marketed the film aggressively, and it received a lot of the kinds of notices they clearly desired, though some of the broadsheet critics were, perhaps for the first time since Shanghai Surprise, unabashed in querying not only the basis of Penn's characterization but his very motivation for undertaking it. In February, he received his

*third Academy Award nomination for Best Actor (*Sweet and
Lowdown *was the second, in 2000), and made his third non-appear-
ance at the ceremony.*

BOBBY COOPER: Sean always says about going to the Oscars, 'It's like
being an extra in a bad TV show . . .'

JACK NICHOLSON: I thought he should have won it. He could just as
easily have won an Academy Award for *Sweet and Lowdown*: that
was as good as anything anyone's ever done, also. But I thought his
performance in *I Am Sam* was just tremendous – transcendent, really.
I really was very puzzled by any criticism of it. I didn't really get it.
'Oh, it's a person of less than full mental capacity . . .' But that's the
problem: you're *meant* to be good in that. So to find a new approach
to it as Sean did . . . I was completely in despair and tears, I was so
moved by it.

ELIZABETH MCGOVERN: Even though I thought the movie was so
stupid and I was sure I was going to hate it – I really loved *I Am Sam*,
I have to admit: I suppose because that heart that I love about Sean, I
could see it coming through . . .

Interviewed by Venice *magazine for* I Am Sam, *Penn was asked if he
felt the fall-out from the September 11 atrocity might influence what
American cinema audiences were drawn to: 'The level of this discomfort, tragedy and sadness has, I hope, raised the bar,' he answered, 'so
that instead of avoiding thoughtful things, perhaps they will seek them
out.'[1] A remarkable opportunity then arose. French producer Alain
Brigand conceived the idea of a portmanteau, 11'09"01: eleven short
films in response to that awful day, made by eleven directors from
eleven different countries, each lasting eleven minutes, nine seconds
and a single frame. Amid a set of veteran cineastes (Ken Loach, Idrissa
Ouedraogo) and brilliant newcomers (Danis Tanovic, Samira
Makhmalbaf), Penn was invited to represent America.*

JON SCHEIDE: Sean had been talking to me about *A Question of
Mercy*, but that didn't fly. Then I was at the Houston Film Festival
when Sato[2] called and said, 'Sean needs you to produce this short
film.' I say, 'OK.' No idea what it was: some kind of test, maybe? Then

---

1 *Venice*, February 2002, interview by Alex Simon.

this forty-five-page fax comes through. Fuck. It's a short film, yes, but it's certainly not a small film. This is *big*. Eleven international directors, and if you count up the Palme d'Ors and Golden Bears these directors have between them . . . And I'm supposed to produce the American contribution for Sean.

There were only three stipulations for the project: same budget, same amount of screen time, and basically that they not incite racial hatred or bigotry. Even that was pretty loose, but they didn't want people to take it as a soapbox and turn in an eleven-minute oration on the faults of Israel or Islamic fundamentalism or whatever.

SEAN PENN: To me, that meant, 'Don't make a bad movie' [*laughs*]. If you incite hatred, you made a bad movie, that's all I figured. They were looking for some kind of common-sense spirit: part of it was related to this event having recently occurred, and people having very strong feelings that were very emotional and maybe not digested. So basically they were saying, 'Don't take this opportunity to expose the worst of yourself.' Unlike, perhaps, certain administrations do . . .

The idea came pretty quickly. I knew somehow it was gonna be a kind of poem. I knew when I was gonna start pre-production. But I didn't feel any pressure. I just waited until the producers showed up, and I sat down on the couch and I said, 'I'm starting to see a story of a guy . . .' They seemed to like where I was going, and I started writing it the next day. Then we made improvements. I had a three-page script; I supplied them a one-page outline: 'Old man does this, then does that.' And they said, 'Go.'

JACK NICHOLSON: Sean's writing is very, very deeply observant – he articulates it well, he executes his thoughts beautifully. When he told me the idea for his short film, I just thought, 'This guy is really great.'

JON SCHEIDE: The first script was very much like the film: only three pages but we knew it was ultimately going to represent eleven minutes. 'In this part we'll see a sequence of a widower's life, in an apartment, cooking, cleaning . . .' The idea was that he was having conversations with his dead wife, and the audience had to try to figure where he was in terms of dementia and living in a fantasy. And then it's about how he has to give up that fantasy at the end in order for a miracle, a revelation, to happen. There's a cost to awareness and see-

2 Sato Masuzawa, personal assistant to Penn.

ing what's going on around you: you may have to give up something –
in his case, the fantasy that his wife is still alive.

As the widower sleeps in the subfusc of a Manhattan apartment sur-
rounded by the world's tallest structures, there is a slow pan from his
slumbering frame to a mute television screen, where the Twin Towers
burn. Then, as the first begins to collapse, light breaks through the
apartment window, and a pot of dead flowers burst into bloom and
colour. The widower, stirred awake, witnesses this in delight, then
snatches up the pot to carry to where he has lain his late wife's dress
on the sleeping berth beside him: 'Flowers, my dear!' His joy turns
swiftly to crestfallen realization and bitter tears. As the camera with-
draws through the window, the shadow of the second tower plummets
down the wall of the apartment building.

SEAN PENN: My DP Sam Bayer flew up here. We went to the local craft
store and bought some green foam-cord and some Exacto knives, and
started making a model of the apartment. We had a flashlight and we
shut the lights off and started playing around, because so much of it
was regarding light, seeing where shadows could go. And I would
leave Sam with his flashlight on the floor and come back to my desk
and write ideas, because I was starting to see the man in there.

JON SCHEIDE: Briefly, we had technical production conversations. Is it
a practical location or is it a build? How many days? How big is the
stage? How big does the set need to be? Does it need to be four-wall?
Do you want running water in both sinks? And then we jumped into
it. I said to the crew, 'This film is *the* American contribution to this
project.' And we lit up the phone lines around Hollywood. I had no
hesitation in waving the flag to vendors and dealers – I wasn't even
asking, I was *requiring* everybody's best deal. Then we built the set at
GMT in Culver City, a big space.

SEAN PENN: Let's say I was in a spat with another actor who I was considering: an actor who I felt might make the process extend beyond
our budget . . . And I was having a little trouble finding another idea
in my head for where I was. Around that time, Ernest Borgnine wrote
me a letter about *I Am Sam*, just like a fan letter, very sweet. And I just
got very excited when I saw his name; it jumped right out.

I went to meet him, and he was fucken great. He said, 'Hey, kid!' and
grabbed the script, sat there and read it without glasses on. And he was in.

JON SCHEIDE: When Sean told me Ernest was going to play the part, I thought, 'That's a spot-on call.' Here's a guy whose career goes from an Academy Award for *Marty*, two or three films with Peckinpah, and now he's the voice of Mermaid Man on *SpongeBob SquarePants*. How great is that? Eighty-five years old, and he kicked ass.

SEAN PENN: I had structured the script knowing that I had eleven minutes, nine seconds and one frame. It's basically just a day-in-the-life-of. There were points I knew I needed to come back to: I needed to establish the pattern of him laying a dress out for his wife every day. But the story, texture and detail aside, had to be no more than three quarters of it, so that you could let it breathe and live, and get takes of improvised stuff within certain behaviour patterns.

JON SCHEIDE: There were scenes where Sean and Ernest spoke very quietly for a few moments, then we would just roll. Sean had done his homework with Ernest, found out what some of his reminiscences were, and he's got a mind like a steel trap. So he'd be behind the camera asking Ernest questions: 'Remember that story you told me? Tell that story.'

© Galatee Films / Canal +

70 *11'09'01'*: Ernest Borgnine as the widower

SEAN PENN: He'd be sitting there saying, 'You know, I'll tell you something Frank Sinatra told me . . .' We dressed him up a nice dressing room and he never went in it: he just stayed on the set the whole day in his underpants and shirt. He's just one of those guys who makes you happy to see him. He's so happy to be fucken alive, I've never seen him in anything but a great mood. Except in my movie . . .

JON SCHEIDE: Then there were moments where Sean or Sam would roll sort of clandestinely – to get slices of life. We were all in on it; hair, make-up and wardrobe all knew that when Ernie was onstage, he needed to be shoot-able. But I don't think we got much past Ernest. Once people started dodging and diving out of the way, I think he understood what we were doing and thought, 'Oh, I'll let the kids have their game . . .' But Sean's not sitting behind a monitor thirty yards away; he's right there. He operated 40, 50 per cent of that film.

SEAN PENN: Sam I worked with very partner-like. We're looking for the same thing visually. He had one camera on his shoulder, I had another on mine, and we were just . . . dancing and getting pieces. We both knew this stuff was being shot for the lightning-in-the-bottle effect. Until the last sequence, which was certainly the most difficult piece: the TV set, the rising of light and the match-cutting to where that light would fall. That would be where I storyboarded some stuff.

JON SCHEIDE: I did ask Sean how the hell we were gonna get all 40,000 feet of film that he'd shot into the cut. He said, 'Don't you worry, I'm gonna use it . . .'

SEAN PENN: If anything, I felt there would be things lost that I'd like to keep [*laughs*]. I didn't feel I had to have the movie understood for all its details the first time you saw it – as long as they were there and you could find them.

JON SCHEIDE: Then, once we got it in the can, came the whole second layer of Sean's skill and his relationship with Jay Cassidy, who's a tremendous editor. Jay's abilities combined with Sam's beautiful imagery – the montage really pushed it to another level, the multiple cuts, the side-by-side images, the overt use of wipes.

We did what's called a digital intermediate. Normally you cut the negative, strike a new print, and then that goes through a photochemical bath and you have your answer print. But in the TV–commercial world, since you don't go back to film, there are a whole lot of other toys you can use to get the image you want. So we went to Cinesite, where they actually scan in each frame. Then Sean and Sam and Jay had the ability to get in there and play with nuances of texture and colour, bleaching or bringing the greens up, dialling some pink into a rack onto a faucet – the colour of rust, or Ernie's skin. Or slowing it down, or step printing, – all the things that, on a subconscious level, make the film more powerful. When you're doing that on one reel, that's reasonable: for an entire feature, it gets expensive. But it *is* the future.

SEAN PENN: No question about it. I would definitely want to do that, in terms of the look of a movie. It changes your cutting ways too: there are whole scenes that suddenly make sense that maybe wouldn't otherwise – or that you see better.

The only thing I don't think is productive is that, in the expense of that, you'd generally be forfeiting a work print. And there's nothing like screening a piece of film to see where you are, what the movie means, and to maintain, I think, the integrity of the big screen in terms of the storytelling. Also, what you can see is performance, always, and you can't really see that on a little screen electronically: not the kind of performances I'm looking for . . . They're not made for television. It's also very important to my process to have actors come to dailies every day. Having them come to my Avid suite? That ain't the thing. It's about a bucket of beers and a movie theatre. And that's something I'm not ready to detach from just yet.

At the end, Ernie says to his wife, 'You should have seen this . . .' And I think about my dad. I didn't want him to see that: I didn't want him to see those towers come down. Sure, I'd like to have him here and healthy, but . . . I was glad that it happened after his life, whenever that was going to be. He'd seen enough terrible things. You just have to look in yourself when you go back to that day. It was a rape. Alejandro's film brings me back to that day. That *is* the day . . .

Mexican director Alejandro González Iñárritu's contribution to 11'09"01 *is an insupportable experience evoking chaos and agony: a black screen interrupted by brief flashes of bodies falling from the towers, and a cacophonous soundtrack in which Mexican prayers for the dead mingle with radio news reports and the cell-phone messages left by those whom the hijacked planes were carrying to their deaths. Iñárritu was a director whose work Penn had previously encountered with an immediate embrace.*

ALEJANDRO GONZÁLEZ IÑÁRRITU: Friends of mine who'd been in Cannes or other places, they would tell me, 'Hey, I was in a press conference with Sean Penn and he kept talking about *Amores Perros*.' Then I did a press tour and a journalist told me Sean had told him in some interview that *Amores Perros* had helped him find some kind of new hope in cinema. So, to my understanding, it had a big impact on him.

Then one day he called me on his cell phone, and said he was Sean Penn. And I didn't believe him: he's always been for me one of the best actors in the world, so I was really shocked. So I said I was Marlon Brando, pleased to meet you . . . But we started a conversation, and he was extremely generous to me.

Sean was the one who convinced me to get into the *11'09"01* project. At first, I told him, 'Sean, I'm really affected by it but it's confusing and I don't know what to think . . .' But he really convinced me, and he was right, and I was glad I did it.

I didn't want to talk about politics in eleven minutes. I just wanted to concentrate on the human suffering, to explore about Cain and Abel and why we use God to justify these fucking atrocities we commit on each other.

For me it wasn't a short film, more an experimental video-art kind of thing. I think this piece would be very interesting in a museum: it was more designed for *that* kind of experience than for cinema. As a director I felt any fictional story would be stupid compared to the size of this, and I thought I had to take a step back. And at the same time I wanted to make a criticism of the media – so many voices and images and paranoia: for three days I thought I would die of a panic attack because they were saying bad guys would come in my house with chemical weapons, blah-blah-blah. I wanted to convey that in the audio and make people remember how much we were bombed that day in our minds and our spirits, to trigger images we already have, and for the people in the dark theatre to have a catharsis and cry.

Sean knew what the concept of my film was. I explained to him that I would be just using audio. And he told me he knew someone: he connected me with Jack Grandcolas, the husband of a woman who died that day. Sean talked to him and convinced him to let me use the love-message his wife left on his cell phone when she was on the plane.

'Honey, are you there? Jack? Pick up, sweetie. OK, well, I just

wanted to tell you that I love you. We're having a little problem on the plane. I – just love you more than anything, just know that . . .'

ALEJANDRO GONZÁLEZ IÑÁRRITU: When I heard that, I felt I had to make the piece. Because, at the end, that for me is redemption, you know? When you are in those circumstances and still you can leave a message of love to the ones you love – that for me is the greatness of human beings, the spirit of human beings. Sean was a key part of that; he really worked on it a lot and I owe him.

The teenage Penn had made Super-8 movies inspired by the songs of Peter Gabriel. In 2002, Gabriel readied 'The Barry Williams Show' as the lead single from his long-gestating album Up, *and asked Penn to concoct a promo video.*

JON SCHEIDE: Three weeks after we finished closing up *11'09"01*, just when I thought it was safe . . . the phone rings. It's Sean. 'Guess what? We're gonna do Peter Gabriel's next video.' Sean had a social relationship with Peter. Peter initially contacted him, then Sean showed him the *11'09"01* film and we were off and running. OK, cool. I figured, Peter Gabriel onstage, knock it off in a day? Oh no . . .

Of course, Peter Gabriel has a legacy of big conceptual videos that break new ground. So my fear of failure rears its head again – 'Oh great, I get to be the guy who made the wanky Peter Gabriel video . . .'

Barry Williams is a fictitious Jerry Springer-like talk-show host presiding over the everyday freaks of daytime TV. His audience develop stigmata and shed tears of blood until Williams finds himself all but drowned in a sanguinary tide.

JON SCHEIDE: Peter was genuinely wonderful, a nice, easygoing guy. He liked Sean's concept a lot, the darkness of it, the edginess of it. The whole thing was the metaphor of the reality talk-shows sort of bleeding the humanity out of society. So Sean went literal on that and started bleeding the audience. We had a custom-built thirty by thirty by eight-foot steel tank, rebuilt the studio set inside it and flooded it in real time. Stigmata and people and blood – just nuts, you know? The one thing I'll say is that the post-process in music videos and commercials is significantly different than in films. There is this committee, Standards and Practices, what you can get on air, and that was a process that was new and, let's just say, less comfortable for us as a team.

The label would look at raw footage and kept saying to me, 'This blood seems rather horrific.' I said, 'Oh no, it's kind of *ironic* blood.' That became a catchphrase as we went through production . . .

With eighteen months having elapsed since his last acting job on I Am Sam, *Penn now returned to work, and for an authentic icon of the American cinema.*

SEAN PENN: We've talked about what I guess you'd call my 'art-film' fancy of the seventies. There's another issue that comes in around age 12 or 13: there's wanting to have a detective's gold shield, and parade around San Francisco . . . And the only way I can describe my reaction to Clint Eastwood at that time is that I seem to share it with the popular consciousness – the iconic figure that he struck in a movie, which I found indelible, and quite exciting.

Then my interests in film moved, along with other things, but through the years, without being a big pursuer of his films, one couldn't avoid his presence in the culture; and there was always something that made me happy about it. I had some odd awareness of what seemed to be his politics at an earlier stage, but I think that I just chose to look the other way on that stuff, because I had a picture in my head and I wanted to keep it there.

Cut to – I see *Bird*, and I think it's tremendous; and I'm aware of his passion for that music.[3] So that's another lock in my head to go with the detective's gold shield – a cymbal flying through the air in *Bird*. Then, around 1990, Thom Mount brought me to an event where I met Clint, and he was very gracious.

Years pass. I get a call from my ex-agent John Burnham that Clint wants to meet me on this movie, *Blood Work*. I meet him in Carmel. I hadn't read the script at that point, and we didn't talk so much about the movie, because his attitude on these things is, 'Read it. If you like it, you'll do it, if you don't, you won't.' But we had a really good sit-down, a couple of beers, and I wanted the night to go on – I had a great time talking to him, about filmmaking and other things.

I started reading *Blood Work* and got a certain way in, but I felt there were two reasons not to do it. One, it was dealing with something that was very close thematically to *The Pledge*, in terms of

3 Eastwood's 1988 film on the life of jazz saxophonist Charlie Parker. A recurrent transitional image in the film is that of a cymbal hurled across the screen, referencing a humiliation suffered by the 16-year-old Parker when he was 'gonged off' stage in Kansas City.

Clint's character; and I had just spent a couple of years in that. Secondly, I didn't really see what I would do with the part I was being offered that I couldn't see others doing at least as successfully. So I called Clint and said it wasn't for me, and he said, 'Well, we'll find something else sometime . . .' Less than a year later, he called me up and said, 'I want you to read something.' And by page eight, I knew I was gonna do it. But I got to the last page before I called him and said, 'I'm in.'

The Boston crime novelist Dennis Lehane writes with a pungent sense of place, a solid grasp of police procedures and a good feel for class distinctions among America's ordinary Joes. As such, he quickly became a major figure in his genre in the mid-nineties. Clint Eastwood, who keeps an eye on such developments, liked Lehane's Mystic River *enough to buy it and commission a screenplay from Brian Helgeland. The novel was rich in threads one might trace out into Eastwood's body of directorial work: a grievous scene of violence, resurfacing from the past; vigilantism and revenge, bluntly enacted, however bitter the harvest.*

Jimmy Markum, Sean Devine and Dave Boyle are young friends in a working-class Boston neighbourhood, confronted one day by two dubious characters presenting themselves as cops. Dave is ordered into their car and meekly complies. He is then abducted and subjected to sexual abuse before escaping. Twenty-five years later, Jimmy is an ex-con running a grocery store; Sean a homicide detective; Dave a sheepish neighbourhood character with a wife and young son. One night Dave comes home bloodstained, telling his wife he may just have killed a mugger. The next morning, Jimmy's daughter Katie's dead body is discovered in a park. . .

Having had a handshake deal at Warners for decades, Eastwood gave them first look at financing. Chary, they let him shop it around, but no one else bit. So Eastwood plumped for what he knew, threw his salary in, and recruited Penn as Jimmy. Then a formidable cast came aboard, including Tim Robbins as Dave and Kevin Bacon as Sean. As Jimmy's criminal associates, the Savage brothers, Val and Nick, Eastwood cast Bostonian Kevin Chapman and Penn's old friend Adam Nelson.

© Warner Bros. Entertainment Inc.
Photo by Merie W. Wallace

71 *Mystic River*: Kevin Bacon (Sean Devine), Penn (Jimmy Markum)

ADAM NELSON: Clint had a lot of guts to tackle that piece. I didn't realize until after we shot it how much he was up against to even get it made. The studio was like, 'Ahh, this isn't something we're sure we want to touch.' They don't seem too unhappy now . . .

TIM ROBBINS: I had no problem with the darkness of it. It's a tragedy; and people don't see that very often. It's like – imagine you got an offer to do a movie written by Eugene O'Neill. All the characters have such meat on them, you can really go to an emotion and know that the script is gonna back it up, and the story you're telling is going to be one of depth and nuance and mystery – all the good stuff, you know? A real great opportunity. And none of us wanted to blow it or sell it short.

ADAM NELSON: It was a dream job for me because I'm from the northeast. Casting myself and Kevin Chapman, I think Clint went for people who knew that area and had a little taste for it . . .

KEVIN CHAPMAN: I grew up in Boston. I know these characters all too well. Dennis Lehane lives not even a half mile from my house. For me, Sean Penn is the Marlon Brando of my generation, but I knew that I had the home-court advantage . . . And Sean said to me about a week in, 'Any one of these actors doesn't stay close to you in my eyes is a fool, because we're trying to act like we're from Boston and you're the real thing.' I helped Sean with the accent; he'd have me read his lines into a recorder. And then he orchestrated table readings we would have once a week at the hotel. We'd sit in the big presidential suite, Sean would get food delivered, and we'd read through the script, start to finish. You found more beats in the material, things to make it pop a little more.

TIM ROBBINS: But I think the main reason we did them is we just felt guilty. We had the greatest job. Clint never starts before 9am, and he works a six or seven hour day. Alright! After work every night you'd see everyone in the gym, just because it felt like that was too short of a day . . . So the other thing was the readings: we so wanted to be able to pull it off for Clint, so that when we walked onto that set, we wanted to be ready. We wanted to get an idea of what the beginning, middle and end was, and find out who these people were, to some degree, before we went in and shot our one take . . .

SEAN PENN: Clint's crews are ready to move. He don't sit around. This crew knows that when Clint feels his actors are ready, you're shooting So it's like, 'Don't tell me you're gonna take two hours to change the lighting when we turn around on the other guy. They're in the middle of the scene *now* – not later.' He's not gonna show off at the risk of losing that, and I don't think he's interested in a movie that demands that. Granted, we're talking about a traditionalist approach to filmmaking: I think Clint's the last guy who'll tell you otherwise. His interest and his storytelling aren't dependent on the kind of cinematography that made *The Deer Hunter*, say. But if you have a script that is well-written and will be best told traditionally, and you have the right cast, you're not going to have a better movie than the one Clint Eastwood will make.

ADAM NELSON: Dennis Lehane says that writing is like a muscle, and once it's built, things start flowing. And I think that's where Sean's at: he's built his acting muscles up to a degree where his instrument is very highly tuned. But he worked hard on *Mystic*: he was at the gym practically every night. He knows what he has to do to look and behave the way he wants.

Penn's Jimmy is a doting father with grey in his hair and reading glasses, but he is also lethally muscle-bound, tattooed in various places and capable of shifting the air around a room in his displeasure. The discovery of his daughter's body about forty minutes in is the cue for Penn to play a scene of heartbreak with incomparable intensity. Kept from the crime scene by his old associate Sean Devine and a cordon of cops, Jimmy unleashes a howl of despair to crack heaven's vault.

ADAM NELSON: When I tried to talk to Sean about *Mystic River* before I was cast, there were certain scenes I'd say, 'Wow, this one's incredible.'

He didn't want to go there. He didn't say, 'Shut the fuck up,' but I took the hint . . . He was saving it for the day, the moment when it came time.

KEVIN CHAPMAN: Jimmy knows his daughter is in that hole. That's the most horrific pain can be inflicted on someone, the loss of your child you brought into this world and nurtured and loved. So he's gotta be thinking, 'One way or another, I'm getting in that hole to see Katie.' What that scene was to me: as kids we used to play Red Rover, two lines of human chains on either side of the street. Then someone calls out, 'Red rover, red rover, send Billy right over.' And your job is to run through the chain and break through to the other side. Clint says, 'They're all stunt guys, so don't be concerned . . .' And I knew Sean was gonna bring it. You pretty much know if you go into business with Sean Penn, he's coming to play. So I gotta bring it too, turn it on ten and pull the knobs off. I went in there first take, knocked a guy to the floor; they all fell on me, I clawed, I bit. But Sean saw that, and I like to think it helped him load in what he needed to load in.

Buddy Van Horn, the stunt co-ordinator, forty-odd years in the business, he knew exactly what he needed to do to arrest Sean physically. And he did it by just applying more bodies on him. By the end Sean must have had twenty-plus people on him, holding him down until he just couldn't move. Couldn't have done much more than three on that one; and Sean had to hit oxygen between takes – he was crazy.

The early theme that Eastwood draws out is the existential misery of 'If only . . .', voiced by Jimmy as he sits numbly with Sean after identifying Katie's body. What, he wonders, if they and not Dave had been so meek as to climb into a car with two evil perverts? Wouldn't they then be lesser men? But thereafter Jimmy's instinctual fear of how Dave's ordeal may have deformed him – linked to Dave's own borderline-psychotic behaviour – conspire to size Dave up for concrete boots. In fact, the real killers are elsewhere; but Jimmy himself is a killer, his lawless past not so deeply interred behind those grey tints and glasses. Blinded by grief, he makes a lethal judgement call, and Mystic River *then takes on an almost* film noir *fatalism, ending in Dave being lured to the river's edge by a kangaroo court of Jimmy and the Savages.*

KEVIN CHAPMAN: We all knew that was gonna be a powerful scene. It's my favourite line of the whole movie, Sean saying, 'I remember when I killed Just Ray over there. And God looked down at me and shook his head, not like he was disappointed, just the way you do at a puppy when he shits on your rug . . .' Sean delivered it so powerful. Jimmy's crazy, going, 'Say you did it and I'll spare your life.' And me and Adam, we're going, 'Do him!' But Sean, you could see the pain in his face. There's a moment there where I say, 'You're gonna let this piece of shit explain himself?' And then Jimmy turns: '*Shut* up, Val, *shut* up. It's *my* daughter.' Like, 'Let me determine whether he lives or dies.'

My trailer was next to Tim Robbins'. We were both walking in the door after we shot, and I looked over at Tim and said, 'You know something? That shit was *spooky* . . .'

SEAN PENN: Whatever positive instincts I had about Clint going in, whatever he advertised about himself – none of that ever had a second of diminishment. He surely was who he was. That's a very unusual experience, and a very life-affirming thing – that there are people out there who are who they are; and on top of that, such an impressive who-they-are. The guy, you feel that when he knows you, he knows you. No great effort. No theoretical analysis. You just go and do it the way you would do it at that time, and he's there rooting you on, this sort of pillar of wisdom and peace-of-mind. And a very good truth-detector, too – if he don't look at you like you've lost it, you ain't lost it [*laughs*]. It's an extremely comforting and inspiring thing, humanly as well as creatively. There's something about it one aspires to – not only in his particular personality of calm, but in the way that you realise the generosity of it in him. And after a twenty-five-year tumultuous life in this business, and playing roles that are sometimes extremely demanding, to then get an opportunity to play a *better* one of those roles – a better-*written* one, with a guy like that, this new kind of presence orchestrating it – was just like a reaffirmation of a lot of the things that I hoped to find in going into film. That was sort of the gift that Eastwood gave.

KEVIN CHAPMAN: After we finished *Mystic*, Sean said to me, 'I want you to come up to my house with your wife and daughter and spend some time, we'll have a nice Thanksgiving weekend.' And that was his way of saying goodbye: because, and he said to me, 'Life gets in the way; and I'll see you in the big world . . .'

The big world was now enduring an excruciating wait for a war to start: namely the attack on Iraq that had been an objective of President Bush and his circle upon taking office, and which had acquired an air of inevitability since the bombing of Afghanistan that ousted the Taliban earlier in 2002. In a speech of 7 October, Bush made his case, asserting a grave threat posed to the United States by Saddam Hussein's alleged weapons of mass destruction held in violation of UN resolutions. Bush posited a link between Saddam's regime and the potentially boundless terrorism of Al-Qaeda, warning that Iraq would have to disarm or face an enforced regime change.

On 11 October, the House and Senate voted to authorize the President's use of force. West Virginia Senator Robert Byrd was one of the few hold-outs, calling the pre-emptive unilateral action 'blind and improvident'.

TIM ROBBINS: Another thing that working with Clint gets you is a lot of time to write stuff . . . I even went to a protest rally one day in Boston Common, an early protest against the war, right down the street from our hotel.

KEVIN CHAPMAN: When we were in Boston, Sean was in the process of editing his letter to the *Washington Post* in reference to the administration's decision to go into Iraq. He read it to a couple of us, sitting around, asked us what we thought. I said, 'I think I see an IRS audit in your future . . .'

SEAN PENN: It had been building – from what I was reading in the media, particularly what I was seeing on television, all the talking heads; and from speeches by members of the administration, from the President down. And what had mostly been building is that I just started to feel my head look from right to left, like, 'Where's this all going? And where's America? And am I the only one feeling this?'

SUSAN SARANDON: To my knowledge, Sean's interest in politics is something that has grown kind of concurrently with his children. And if there's ever anything that will make you risk, it's the love of your child, your concern for their future, and your sense of responsibility for the world that they will claim. He showed me different drafts of his letter when I was up in Boston with Tim. Sean's clearly someone who asks questions and wants to know. And if you're a person who's sensitive to injustice and has any kind of empathy and imagination, as Sean clearly does, it's just a matter of time before something grabs you.

Penn's 'Open Letter to the President of the United States of America' was printed as a paid advertisement, at a cost of approximately $56,000, in the Washington Post *on 18 October 2002. Respectfully addressed, it nevertheless offered a critique of the Bush administration's drive to unilateral action, backed by the conservative media:*

'We know that Americans are frightened and angry. However, sacrificing American soldiers or innocent civilians in an unprecedented pre-emptive attack on a separate sovereign nation, may well prove itself a most temporary medicine . . .'

'How far have we come from understanding what it is to kill one man, one woman, or one child, much less the "collateral damage" of many hundreds of thousands. Your use of the words, "this is a new kind of war' is often accompanied by an odd smile . . ."

'There can be no justification for the actions of Al-Qaeda. Nor acceptance of the criminal viciousness of the tyrant, Saddam Hussein. Yet, that bombing is answered by bombing, mutilation by mutilation, killing by killing, is a pattern that only a great country like ours can stop . . .'

'Weapons of mass destruction are clearly a threat to the entire world in any hands . . .'

'Simply put, sir, let us re-introduce inspection teams, inhibiting offensive capability. We buy time, maintain our principles here and abroad and demand of ourselves the ingenuity to be the strongest diplomatic muscle on the planet . . .'

'I do understand what a tremendously daunting task it must be to stand in your shoes at this moment. As a father of two young children who will live their lives in the world as it will be affected by critical choices today, I have no choice but to believe that you can ultimately stand as a great president. History has offered you such a destiny. So again, sir, I beg you, help save America before yours is a legacy of shame and horror . . .'

MEEGAN OCHS: Sean always said my father was a true patriot, and that to love your country enough to criticize its government is a heavily patriotic thing to do. But he did it in a smart way. The letter wasn't: 'You're an asshole. Stop being such a bully.' He didn't rant, he was clear in giving a positive message. He empathized with Bush, he said,

'My father was a war veteran as yours was' and 'If you lead, we will follow.'

BONO: It's a venerable tradition in the United States to take your country to task for not being more like you. And I think it was brave, because on the Right at the time there *was* an attempt to gag all the stars. Now, we're all sick of celebrity – but let's be honest, the people in support of the war had the far bigger loudhailers. So some voices of dissent were necessary.

WOODY HARRELSON: And of course, all of the right-wing Murdochian rags went after him. But his karma shot through the roof [*laughs*]. And it probably needed a boost . . .

While in Boston, Penn had also firmed up his next filming commitment. Guillermo Arriaga, novelist and screenwriter of Amores Perros, *had composed another brilliant script for director Alejandro González Iñárritu, its title,* 21 Grams, *alluding to a mysterious loss of weight in the human body at time of death. The script drew three lives into a narrative that moved boldly back and forth through time, before and after a fatal moment when all three are enmeshed. Christina is a recovered drug addict, happily married to architect Michael, with two beautiful children. Paul is a mathematician with a critical heart ailment, trapped in a spent relationship. Jack is an ex-convict who has clutched Christianity to his heart and is desperately trying to keep himself pure. Three souls in isolation, until Jack is responsible for the death of Christina's young family in a hit-and-run; Michael's heart is transplanted into Paul's chest, renewing his life; Jack is condemned to a fresh hell of incarceration and guilt; Christina spirals into lonely despair; and Paul becomes obsessed by the veiled identity of his deceased donor/saviour.*

ALEJANDRO GONZÁLEZ IÑÁRRITU: 21 *Grams* was a very complicated script, and I didn't like to think of specific actors. But I always had an idea that Sean could be good to work with, knowing the mutual enthusiasm we had. Three, four months after the script was finished, I was thinking about who should play who: if Sean should play Jack and Benicio Del Toro should play Paul. And that was the toughest decision, because I felt Sean was a natural Jack, the kind of role he would normally fit. But then I thought, 'Well, I'd like to see the opposite, a Sean Penn who is tender and shows mercy and sweetness /

Finally I decided to send the script to him in San Francisco; he would be the first actor to read it. I was very nervous. My assistant called Sato, asked if Sean had received it. She said, 'Yes, he's just started to read.' So then I'm smoking one cigar after another . . . Twenty minutes later, my assistant says, 'Sean is calling,' and I'm thinking, 'I'm *fucked*. He will say this is ridiculous, stupid, what do you think I am?' He says, 'Hey, this is amazing. What's going to happen? Don't tell me the kids will die?' I said, 'Keep reading.' He said, 'I can't, I'm a nervous wreck.' He's like a kid. I say, 'Keep going.' Forty minutes after, he calls again. 'Oh my god, this is amazing, this could be a masterpiece.' And he was in.

I told him I needed some readings, especially for me and for Naomi Watts, just to warm up the scenes I was afraid of. He agreed. I had three big meetings with him, one in Boston when he was shooting *Mystic River*, and we talked long about the character, who he was, what Sean saw, what I expected of him. Always we were very close in what we felt. But, in my experience, Sean is a guy who doesn't want to analyze a character too much: he wants to *know* them very well, he wants to be *as* the character. Then we flew to Memphis, had two or three days' research, interviewed some guys waiting for heart transplants, and asked some doctors a lot of questions . . .

Back in the big world, the UN weapons inspectorate fronted by Dr Hans Blix had returned to Iraq, even as both proponents and opponents of war believed a conflagration was nigh. As executive director of the San Francisco-based Institute for Public Accuracy, Norman Solomon had made it his job to counter the mainstream media's more or less untrammelled support for the President's program. In mid-September, just prior to Dr Blix receiving his instructions, Solomon's Institute had sponsored a trip to Iraq by West Virginia Democrat congressman Nick Rahall.

NORMAN SOLOMON: When Representative Rahall returned to the US, he got a little bit of flak in his home district, but he also appeared on some major US TV networks and the tone of the coverage was good. So our institute immediately got in touch with dozens of Congressional offices: we were 'cautiously optimistic' that this could be the first of a number of high-level visits done as kind of quasi-'citizen diplomacy'. But scarcely two weeks later, there was a second Congressional visit to Baghdad, which we had nothing to do with, and they got very bad press. Jim McDermott did a live interview on ABC from Baghdad in which he said that he felt it was quite possible President Bush would mislead the American people in order to go to war. That was held by some conservative critics as an absolutely scurrilous thing to say on what they considered to be enemy territory. And in October, the tone of the responses from Congressional offices really shifted. Even some that had initially been warm were now basically telling us: 'Are you crazy? Why would we want to walk the gangplank by going to Iraq?'

Lo and behold, there was an open letter to President Bush that filled a full page of the *Washington Post*. The eloquence was clear, and I was moved by it . . .

So our institute sent a letter to Sean Penn, recounting what had happened with our delegation and inviting him to go. All the work I do is against the odds and optimistic – but I certainly thought this was a long shot: something akin to putting a message in a bottle and tossing it in the Pacific . . .

A rainy day in early December 2002, I got a call from Sato, who said that Sean would like to talk with me. His initial conversation was already on the basis that he was *very* interested in going. I certainly got the impression he had done a lot of reading about Iraq and a lot of reflection on the situation. So, pretty soon, the questions he was asking had to do with his calendar and the logistics, flights and visa issues. Towards the end of December it was pretty unrelenting because of a commitment he had, as I later found out, to be in Tennessee to begin the shooting of *21 Grams*.

ROBIN WRIGHT PENN: The idea came from nowhere, pretty much. But then I'm so used to that with Sean. Because he's not one to just sit back and let things happen, ever. I'd experienced it for fifteen years, so it was not a surprise. And my reaction was not a surprise, which was, '*What . . .!?*' And at the same time I knew he was going to go, but I'm still going to have that 'Are you out of your fucking mind?' reaction. And what I'm getting at is that you totally accept it in him. I believe in why he does things, in that context. It's that part in him of his dad, and I back it all the way.

NORMAN SOLOMON: I made some contact via phone and email with people in Baghdad. But it was really nip and tuck, because governments generally don't move fast, Baghdad being no exception. The scenario was that I would accompany Sean. He called one evening and invited me over to his house, and we talked about our hopes for the trip. I drove home late that evening, and the next morning when I got up around dawn and checked the email, there in the subject line from an Iraqi official was: 'Welcome to Baghdad.' And I called Sean with the news . . .

ADAM NELSON: So Sean calls me and says, 'I just wanna say, it's been nice knowing you. I'm going to Iraq tomorrow.' Talk about a rare occurrence in this world.

ROBIN WRIGHT PENN: Our children were the reason to go, yes, but also the reason not to go. There's always a conflict. He was like, 'I'm not going to be able to call you,' and I heard that a thousand times. So, yes, I've already gone through the fear that your life is in danger, and now you're just rubbing salt in the wound. At a certain point I just said, 'Just shut up and go. And when you get home we'll resume the conversation, because there's nothing really important between now and the time you get off the plane on US soil.' Of course, he called five times a day . . . It was almost overkill.

NORMAN SOLOMON: In a matter of a day, we were on a plane: the first leg being San Francisco Airport to Amsterdam, then on to Amman, then to Baghdad.

Now, we were going to be arriving in Baghdad and still there wasn't a single journalist who knew that's where Sean Penn was going. Later, a journalist told me, 'I saw this guy on the plane and I thought, 'God, that looks like Sean Penn, but it *couldn't* be . . .' As it happened, Sean hadn't shaved for a while, and he explained to me that was because his schedule for *21 Grams* first involved some hospital scenes where he would need some beard. But still he was pretty recognizable.

It was about dawn when the plane was flying into Baghdad, and the skies were grey.

We landed, got in a car and half an hour later we were at the Al-Rashid hotel. Sean had written a statement prior to arriving, and I called the Institute office in Washington to let them know we'd arrived, and it was at that point that Sean's statement was released: just a few sentences, but it seemed very important to establish clearly what his perspective was on why he was there.

SEAN PENN (Statement Released in Washington and Baghdad, Friday, 13 December 2002): *By the invitation of the Institute for Public Accuracy, I have the privileged opportunity to pursue a deeper understanding of this frightening conflict. I would hope that all Americans will embrace information available to them outside conventional channels. As a father, an actor, a film-maker, and a patriot, my visit to Iraq is for me a natural extension of my obligation (at least attempt) to find my own voice on matters of conscience.*

NORMAN SOLOMON: Within minutes after the statement went out, calls started coming in. I remember the first was from a BBC reporter, a woman, who said, 'I've just received this most *incredible* news release. Sean Penn is in Baghdad . . .?' Then we met up with Kathy Kelly from Voices in the Wilderness. Kathy is so down-to-earth and had so much experience.

A seasoned and dauntless non-violent peace activist, Kathy Kelly had been instrumental in a campaign protesting the UN/US sanctions against Iraq, helping to organize seventy delegations to the country in the period between 1996 and the eventual onset of 'Operation Shock and Awe' in March 2003.

KATHY KELLY: A number of us had been in Iraq in 1991, and by 1995 we were sort of ashamed: we could see that the war hadn't ended; it had turned into an economic war that was in fact a lot more devastating, and the targets of this war, it seemed, were the most vulnerable people: hundreds of thousands of children had died as a direct result of economic sanctions. So we decided we would go to Iraq as often as we could in open and public defiance of the sanctions, carrying medicines and medical relief. If one child's life was saved because we brought an antibiotic, then that certainly was valuable. But it would also raise a question: why is the United States government saying that a pair of grandparents from Kalamazoo, Michigan, committed a crime because they brought some medicines and a teddy bear over to children who were dying in an Iraqi hospital? By October 2002 we were going to places that we knew were crucial to civilian infrastructure – an electrical plant or a water-treatment facility – and posting huge banners saying, 'To bomb this site would be a war crime,' and citing the Geneva Convention. There wasn't enough to stop the war, but we were a motley crew who sort of got a ball rolling.

We were asked by one of Norm Solomon's colleagues to start working on an itinerary for Sean Penn. I'm sort of preternaturally out of it: my friends wrote to me and said, 'Sean Penn was married to Madonna, and we *don't* mean the mother of Jesus. Try to get this straight.' But I had seen *Dead Man Walking*, one of the very few films I've seen in the last decade. So we went to the Al-Rashid, and Sean sat and talked with us for about an hour. It seemed to me he was a very genuine person – didn't have any airs, didn't seem interested in making an impression on people about his own skills or personal history. And we admired him for saying he wasn't going to be anybody's poster boy: he just wanted to go and look and listen.

We felt it was important he be aware of what kind of impact the sanctions had had on ordinary people, and there are a number of places where that is immediately evident: certainly a hospital. The cure rate for cancer was nought per cent. Certainly Saddam Hussein's regime bore blame in that case, but also the sanctions. And those kids committed no crime – the doctors would wring their hands and say they felt more like social workers or psychiatrists, helping to get kids on the wards ready for the deaths of other children, and then for their own death.

NORMAN SOLOMON: The entire itinerary in Iraq was decided by Sean, and he decided that our first stop would be the Al-Mansour Children's Hospital.

We got there, and waiting at the kerb in front of the main entrance were a very assertive – and I can say aggressive – press corps: they were pressing in on the car, they wanted their photos and their questions answered. Sean's thought was to tell the reporters that he had just arrived and he didn't want to start making statements of any sort in front of cameras, so he made a request: 'I'd prefer if you could avoid following me around, but the last day I'm here, I'll be glad to do a news conference at the hotel and respond to questions.' And the press corps mostly left. Then we went to the cancer and leukaemia ward and visited with some of the children, and the director and some physicians talked with Sean. I couldn't help noticing that I couldn't recognize hardly any of the kids I had seen in September. And I remember at some point Sean saying, 'You don't even want someone to slam a *door* too loud around these children, let alone imagine a bomb exploding in the neighbourhood . . .'

The next day, we went to the UNICEF office and met with the Director. He was talking about low birth-weight as an indicator to the degraded health of children in Iraq; then the question of the impending war came up, which was obviously a menace to health, to put it mildly, and the Director somewhat apologetically mumbled something like, 'That's outside of our purview.' In a way, the politics of a possible war was the water's edge for UNICEF; and while Sean's concerns were basically the same as the Director's, Sean took the opportunity to deal with another link in the chain, and that was whether war could be avoided. And he did that publicly.

Then we went to what was then called Saddam City, now Sadr City, and visited a couple of schools, one of which had been repaired by UNICEF. The other, which hadn't, was in a really shocking condition: overflowing sewers in the courtyard, broken windows, sixty kids in a class, many sitting on the floor with coats on.

We were driving back, looking out the windows at the sidewalks and street stalls teeming with life. I said something like, 'There's a story on every block.' And Sean said, 'There's a story in every *person*.' I thought immediately: yes, that's the film-maker and the artist talking. As he said in the news conference, and was nicely quoted in *People* magazine: 'I needed to come here and see a smile, see a street, smell the smells, talk to the people and take that home with me.'

Our last official meeting that Sunday was with Tariq Aziz in a huge palatial office building. He was clearly eager to have the meeting, once somebody had explained to him who Sean Penn was. He's in his late sixties. I'd met him in September, and I thought he was quite courteous and very slick. He could spin as adroitly as anybody on Capitol Hill or Foggy Bottom in Washington. And I later thought of him as kind of epitomizing the urbanity of evil.

Afterwards Sean would often be asked, 'Don't you realize that the Iraqi government has agendas?' And he would say, 'I was born at night, but not last night' [*laughs*]. And, when you think about it, a great actor might well be inclined to understand that people have a variety of motivations . . .

Sean said to Tariq Aziz: 'The politics for me are a side note to concern about my children, and the children of the United States, and the children of this country.'

KATHY KELLY: Sean used his time persistently and used it well. What impressed me so much was that at the end – when I thought he should really be taking a nap, he was exhausted – he said to me, 'What about the woman you wanted me to meet? She could come up now.'

Ikbal l'artous is a schoolteacher and mother of four who, per Arab tradition, goes by the name Um Haider – mother of Haider, her first-born son. On 25 January 1999, she was in her kitchen when an 'errant' US missile rained down death upon the Al-Jamhuriyah district where she lived. She raced outdoors to where her older boys were playing and found Haider buried beneath rubble, already dead. Then she saw three-year-old Mustafa, alive but covered with blood, wounded in the head, legs and back, his hand partly severed. She took him in her arms and carried him to receive medical attention.

KATHY KELLY: Mustafa lost two fingers, and there wasn't a prosthesis that would make a difference. The shrapnel that was embedded in his back would cause irritation and sometimes little bits of it would move. So he grew up with a lot of pain and irritation and certainly traumatic memories.

Um Haider speaks English quite well, and she's a magnetic kind of woman, wearing the full *abaya*. Sean sat on the floor with her and Mustafa; it was a very sensitive, very genuine parent-to-parent time. In fact, he evoked something from her just in the course of that meeting. Mustafa had fallen asleep, and Sean tousled his head and asked Um Haider very sensitively, 'What about him? What does he remember from that day?' I've heard her interviewed so many times, but nobody had ever asked that question. And Um Haider said, 'Oh, yes, yes, this question very important. I ask him, and he tell me that day my son Haider is killed, he say one thing, "Mama". And that his last word . . .'

On Sunday, 15 December 2002, Penn opened a news conference at the Al-Rashid with a statement: 'I am privileged in particular to raise my children in a country of high standards in health, welfare and safety. I am also privileged to have lived a life under our Constitution that has allowed me to dream and prosper. In response to these privileges I feel, both as an American and as a human being, the obligation to accept some level of personal accountability for the policies of my government, both those I support and any that I may not. Simply put, if there is a war or continued sanctions against Iraq, the blood of Americans and Iraqis alike will be on our hands . . .'

Photo by Alan Pogue

72 Al-Rashid, Baghdad, December 15 2002: Norman Solomon and Penn

NORMAN SOLOMON: Then Sean flew straight to Memphis for 21 *Grams.* We left late Sunday night out of the Saddam Hussein International Airport, but Royal Jordanian Airlines was about three hours late in departing, which meant that when the flight arrived in Amman, Sean's connecting KLM flight to Amsterdam had left. So it was literally a dash for him to catch a back-up flight through Frankfurt and jerry-build a schedule in order to get there to start the film.

ALEJANDRO GONZÁLEZ IÑÁRRITU: Sean arrived in Memphis at 11 p.m. directly from Iraq, and we were due to start shooting at 6 a.m. the next day with him. He showed up for work, arrived at wardrobe and make-up, we turned the camera on. And he was Paul. The first scene I shot with him, he was playing with his computer; he stood up and went into the bathroom to have a smoke. And he was like a fucking ill guy dying from a bad heart. I think he had big jet-lag; it probably helped him be so distraught. It was like he did it on purpose . . . But the moment I saw him walking like that, breathing like that, embodying that spirit – I had been exploring those characters for three years, so Paul had become like my friend. And in those first ten minutes, I turned to Rodrigo Prieto, my DP, and our faces were like, 'Fuck! He did it . . .'

WOODY HARRELSON: I always really have admired Seaner – even when we were on the outs. But when he did that deal with Iraq, my admiration for him shot through the roof. I just thought that was one of the bravest moves ever. Of course, he got nothing but shit for it.

DR KATZ: Iraq? I called him up and I said, 'I can't believe you didn't take me.'

Rupert Murdoch's New York Post *contacted Republican congressman Pete King, who talked tough: 'The guy's lucky he can act and should leave it at that. It gives recognition to Hussein that he doesn't deserve. It gives an acknowledgement to Iraq that it doesn't deserve. You'd think these guys would have learned their lesson from Jane Fonda.'*[4]

NORMAN SOLOMON: Sean could have just hunkered down. The flak was pretty fierce after he got back, led by the Murdoch media empire, the Fox News Channel and the *New York Post*, and so forth. But I think he made sure every step he took felt like it was on solid ground, so there was never any need to retreat later on. The reporter who really picked up on that was John Burns of the *New York Times*. The article he wrote alluded to the contrast with Jane Fonda: I think he quoted Sean to the effect of, 'I don't imagine I'll be apologizing as she did at some far point in the future'.

On Thursday, 19 December 2002, the official Iraqi News Agency reported that Penn had in the course of his trip 'confirmed that Iraq is completely clear of weapons of mass destruction'.

NORMAN SOLOMON: It was certainly irksome to have the Iraqi government lying about what Sean had said. He had been so explicit all the way through that he wasn't going to speak outside of his expertise. And because I'd been on the trip, I made a statement to AP saying it was preposterous. Of course, looking at it a year later, the onus was on the Bush administration and the Rupert Murdoch gang to prove that this imputed statement that was never made actually would have been false . . .

DAVID BAERWALD: I was stunned by the negative response, personally. I think it's really much more a tribute to the demographics of

---

4 Jane Fonda visited North Vietnam in July 1972, criticizing US 'imperialism' and exhorting US troops to defy 'illegal orders'. In a 1988 TV interview she apologized to veterans: 'I was trying to help end the killing and the war, but there were times when I was thoughtless and careless about it . . . '

American talk radio than anything Sean actually did.

PETER COYOTE: I mean, what a spectacular display of hypocritical horseshit. We have a mass media that is dedicated to *every* single aspect of actors' lives. We have entire magazines dedicated to where celebrities *shop*. We follow their divorces, their drug treatments, the size of the engagement rings they give their betrothed. So everything about celebrities just fascinates us, except their political opinions. And it strikes me there's a very clear reason – because the political opinion of a celebrity can be a detriment to merchandising, because there's the possibility that those who don't agree with them will then not buy the product.

NORMAN SOLOMON: Sean's visit to Iraq in the pre-war period really resonated with people who were upset about the prospect of war, who had questions and doubts. And on that basis alone, it turned out to be a journey with some historic resonance – and perhaps some historic consequences.

KATHY KELLY: I know that we have to be on guard not to get devoured by a celebrity culture and think that only certain people who are celebrities can make the difference. On the other hand, in terms of activists' efforts towards peacemaking, it's very, *very* hard to try to communicate information that is necessary for democratic choices to be made when there's sort of a stranglehold on the part of many of the mainstream media people and some of the biggest lobbyists on Capitol Hill.

We needed a leg-up. And I think Sean Penn was casting light on the fact that no US senator had ever gone over there in all these years of an abysmally failed policy. I'm all in favour of person-to-person diplomacy. And, to my mind, if somebody like Sean Penn wants to use his platform as a means to educate or just speak up on these issues, that's great.

NORMAN SOLOMON: It must have been an incredible challenge to bear down on the film work of 21 *Grams* and still be in the here and now amid the political swirl with the war coming up. He did the *Larry King* show on a short break from the filming.

SEAN PENN (*Larry King*, January 11 2003): *We start by taking out a pad of paper, and every mother and father in the country – and they can do it while this interview goes on – writes down the words: 'Dear Mr and Mrs So-and-so, we regret to inform you that your son,*

John, has died in combat in Iraq.' And then you have to finish that letter in a way that will comfort you. If you can do that, then you have one side of the debate and I respect that position . . .

I think there's probably two legitimate places for Saddam Hussein: it's either Bellevue or a meat grinder. This man's a horror and a criminal, there's no question about it.
LARRY KING: *So you did not come back as any sort of spokesman for the Iraqi point of view?*
SEAN PENN: *Do I sound like it?. . . I don't think that ultimately it's going to be good business to go in. I think that in the short term it may be, and so I'm wondering how long- and short-term the agenda is of the establishment . . . The cost of the Gulf War was $82 billion . . . In this case, we're talking about $200 billion. I wonder who's going to pay for that? It's going to be you and me and everybody watching this show. And then what will be the costs afterwards?*

21 Grams *completed its business in Memphis on Valentine's Day 2003 and moved to Albuquerque to shoot the bleak desert landscape required for its death-stakes finale, scenes to be laced throughout the picture: Paul, implacably pulled to begin a sexual relationship with the vulnerable Christina, then must weigh her demand that he track down Jack and kill him. The couple locate him doing hard labour in the desert, but Paul cannot bring himself to pull the trigger, and so Jack pursues and half kills them both, a struggle broken only when Paul fires a bullet into his own chest.*

ALEJANDRO GONZÁLEZ IÑÁRRITU: Sometimes Sean can be a very chaotic person in different ways, but as a professional he's the most practical, common-sense, eloquent guy, very simple and to the point.

The only directions he needed were very, very subtle details. And he was always so receptive, so respectful. Ninety-eight per cent of his work is so well done that even his bad takes are, I will say, better than the average good takes of any actor. Whenever I wanted to talk to him about some emotion I wanted, I would try to explain it with my hands, because my English was not great at the beginning of the film. He would snap his fingers and say, 'I know what you mean.' Then we would roll, and he would get it exactly right. He has this intuition, he can smell what you want. And it's in the subtleties he surprises you on every level. So when you are editing, you have a range of takes where

73 On location for 21 Grams: Penn and Alejandro González Iñárritu

you're thinking, 'This one is perfect, because he's showing this emotion. But in this one, look at what he's doing with his eyes, or the little turn.' And it's in that detail that you get crazy, because you don't know which one is better . . .

BENICIO DEL TORO: I think Sean made everyone better on 21 Grams, even when he wasn't around. It's almost like you feel like he's watching. You know he cares. And he's not just thinking about his character and 'Let's get it done so we can go home.' He cares about the movie.

Sean's easy to work with. He's really a pushover [laughs]. There's no sense of competition or 'Wait a second, this is my moment.' He's there like The Catcher in the Rye, willing and ready to help you up if you fall. And then he forces that out of you, so you're there for him. He and Naomi, they worked together a lot. But he was helpful to everybody – to the sound guy, the catering service . . .

ALEJANDRO GONZÁLEZ IÑÁRRITU: And sometimes off-camera he can be playing better than on-camera, you know? We were doing the scene in the cafeteria where Paul is trying to flirt with Christina and be funny. His line is, 'Did you know that eating alone can seriously damage your kidneys?' But Naomi wasn't in the mood, she couldn't really laugh. Sean says to me, 'You need her to laugh? OK, don't worry.' So he was off-camera and he said to her, 'Did you know that eating alone can give you *volcanic* diarrhoea?' And the food *flew* from Naomi's mouth, then the whole fucking set was laughing and the mood was completely different. And then the next take Naomi got it. But he's a director too, you know?

One time I will never forget, we were in Memphis, bored, freezing our asses off: Sean and I, Naomi, our producer Robert Salerno, Martin Hernandez, my audio guy. And suddenly Sean said, 'I'll get a jet.' And he got it, we flew to New Orleans, he organized cars, and we ate in a restaurant and spent the night, a great New Orleans night. The next day we were having a coffee and suddenly Sean stands up and goes out, and for ten minutes no one can find him: what's going on? We have to go get the plane. And he returns with necklaces he's just bought for everybody, as a remembrance of the trip: 'This one is for you, and this colour's for *you*.' And that detail broke my heart, because he was like a kid, worried for his guests. So the generosity of his heart as a human being, it shows in *21 Grams*. That's why he is perfect for the role. He's so human.

Through the Eastwood and Iñárritu projects, Penn was feeling uncommonly good about his work, the material he was addressing, the company he was keeping.

In the big world, President Bush ordered US troops into Iraq on 20 March 2003.

Earlier that month, the Screen Actors' Guild issued a plea via its website asking Hollywood producers to avoid retaliation against actors who spoke out politically in the current climate. Was any kind of new blacklist conceivable? Penn had not ruled it out a couple of years previously: 'There's signs of it all the time. The one thing you can count on in Hollywood – across the board – is cowardice.'[5]

In Penn's case, the eeriest augur was in respect of his relations with Steve Bing, the well-heeled would-be writer/producer/director who had lately parted with decent-sized chunks of his wealth, settling a $1-billion suit he had filed against MGM head Kirk Kerkorian and making handsome paternity arrangements with Elizabeth Hurley to support the baby he first denied was his, on the order of a UK court.

In September 2002, it had been announced that Bing would write

---

5 'Give It Up for Sean Penn', James Kaplan, *Observer*, Sunday, 6 May 2001.

and direct Why Men Shouldn't Marry, *his company Shangri-La financing for Warners to distribute worldwide. Penn would play a tyre salesman who suffers a painful divorce and becomes an anti-marriage fanatic, despite the efforts of his best employee (Woody Allen), an oft-divorced man who still maintains his faith in the nuptial bond.*

WOODY ALLEN: *Why Men Shouldn't Marry* was a picture that was proposed to me to act in. Steve Bing was not a director with years and years of experience. But he had Sean in the lead, and that, of course, instantly conferred a real legitimacy on the project. So I was happy to be involved in it. And I think it would have been fun, because, you know, Sean and I get along, even though we're so opposite in personality and temperament. I think we would be funny in that situation . . .

Penn brought Allen on board to address Bing's script. Bing, controversially, was going to pay Penn $10 million, the like of which he'd never received before.

But in February 2003, the Los Angeles Superior Court saw a pair of vying lawsuits. Penn claimed breach of oral contract and asked for his alleged fee in damages. He argued that Bing was 'borrowing a page from the dark era of Hollywood blacklisting', having grown fearful of his investment owing to the public furore over the Baghdad trip. Bing in turn claimed civil extortion and asked for $15 million: he said Penn had lost interest in the project, but still wanted his money.

These were very disparate stories. Clearly only one set of facts could be accurate.

On Thursday, 8 May 2003, in what he described as 'an easy call', Superior Court Judge Irving Feffer upheld Penn's right to sue for $10 million. On Monday, 23 June 2003, Feffer ruled that Bing could not sue Penn for attempted civil extortion, the claim not existing in California law.

But then these were, as Dr Thompson might say, savage and twisted times. Oliver North, the second-rate Gordon Liddy of the eighties, once indicted for channelling funds to Nicaraguan contras from the proceeds of arms sales to Iran, was now shilling as a war correspondent for Fox News.

SEAN PENN: I still can't get it through my head that they had an issue with my going to Baghdad, but we've got a guy, Oliver North, who on the record lied to Congress, getting special access to do war stories on

TV. This is in any way, shape or form an anti-American thing to do. It is against *everything*, every principle that we have. There's never been a heroic moment in the life of Oliver North. He's a shameful human being, and there seem to be more and more of them. He personifies that kind of ugliness to me in a big way, much more significantly than somebody like Bill O'Reilly.

BOBBY COOPER: A friend of mine, an old Jewish guy, real pro-war – after 9/11, he said to me, 'Where's all your liberal friends now, huh? Where's Sean Penn? Where's Martin "Save the Homeless, boo-hoo!" Sheen?' Then when the inspections were going on in Iraq, he called me and said, 'We knew there was chemicals there. What does your little friend say about that, huh?' I told Sean this, and Sean called him a couple of times – he doesn't know it's Sean – and left a message on his machine . . .

The message was to the effect that this was UNICEF calling to thank the gentleman for his kindly offer to adopt a child orphaned by the war, and that the child would shortly be delivered to the gentleman's home, with instructions for his medical care and dietary requirements; but that for the first few months this child would have to be accompanied by a live-in Iraqi-speaking care-worker, so they were deeply grateful also for the gentleman's kind offer of additional accommodation . . .

Such commitments, however, were an onus other Americans were actually ready and willing to undertake. The case of Um Haider and her son Mustafa, whom Penn had met at the Al-Rashid in Baghdad, had generated great interest among the activist community, including LA-based writer and website designer Cole Miller.

KATHY KELLY: Mustafa might have been able to be treated in Baghdad, but we just weren't sure. We were keen on getting some kind of evaluation and research as to whether the shrapnel in his back might have a depleted uranium component. In the end, Cole Miller and Chris Doucot got involved and were able to help bring Um Haider and Mustafa from Amman to the US.

COLE MILLER: I went to a mosque in Los Angeles and met with a number of physicians, and they guaranteed they would provide whatever was needed if I got the people there. Then I went to Amman with Alan Pogue, a Vietnam veteran and a great documentary photographer. Chris Doucot of the Hartford *Catholic Worker* accompanied Um

Haider and Mustafa from Iraq to Amman. Then, every morning Alan and I went down to the US Embassy to get entry visas, and none materialized. I went in and met the consular official Larry Mitchell, and he had denied the visas once already to Chris. We had to gather all the information to show there was a medical need and that help couldn't be provided in Iraq. That wasn't hard. But then there was a State Department document concerning financial responsibility, which can be pretty onerous if they want to make trouble – they can require that you provide bank statements, tax records.

I contacted Sean Penn once and we spoke briefly – he was shooting a film. Then I left for the Middle East and others took over. But this was the last piece of the puzzle in putting the paperwork together, and it came in at the last minute: Sean Penn was kind enough to send us a fax that said, 'I will be responsible for anything extra that these folks can't take care of themselves.' And we appreciated that. Ultimately we covered the costs with donations, but Um Haider was very pleased. She said, 'I like Sean Penn! He is a man of his word, he help me and my Mustafa . . .'

Sean and his family ending up coming out to see them in Clairemont, where they were staying; then he invited Um Haider and Mustafa and myself to go spend Easter at his mother's house in Malibu. We were driving out there, and Mustafa started to shout. Um Haider quieted him and I asked her what was he saying? There was a plane flying overhead, and he'd said, 'They're going to bomb us, they know I am Iraqi . . .'

It was a small gathering down at the beach, with great food. And Mustafa went into the ocean – for the first time, I believe. He took off his clothes, and you could see the scars on his body. But he was running around with Sean's kids on the sand. Then we went up to his mother's house and talked, and I met Christopher Penn. Mustafa went into the pool, and it was amazing to sit there and watch him: in such a brief time he'd gone from Basra – where there's no electricity or clean water, danger everywhere, bombers flying overhead – to Sean Penn's mother's pool in Malibu, California . . .

Then Sean wanted us to speak to parents and teachers at his kids' school, and he paid for all of us to go up north. The school officials got paranoid, so finally we wound up having it in a rented space right across the street from where he lives. But we made the presentation: Alan Pogue came up, Chris Doucot. Kathy Kelly made it out, and she's a wonderful speaker. Then we went over to Sean's house and went up to his playroom and watched his $11'09''01$ film.

He just struck me as very intelligent and committed. He's put his money and his reputation where his mouth is – a fucken brave guy. He said a wonderful thing to me, I'll have to paraphrase: 'These people think I'm gonna back down because of all the flak they've given me. They have *no idea* . . .'

74 Penn, Mustafa Fartous and Ikbal Fartous/Um Haider,
Marin County, May 2003

FOURTEEN

2003–2004

SAM BYCK: I believe the life span of a human being would be a hundred years,
even a hundred and fifty years if everything could be done with honesty and
integrity instead of through lying and deceit.

The Assassination of Richard Nixon, screenplay by
Niels Mueller and Kevin Kennedy, 2003

DON PHILLIPS: Why is Sean so fascinated with this movie he's wanted
to do for the last couple of years about the guy who's deluded and
wants to assassinate Richard Nixon? Maybe because, metaphorically,
that's what *everybody* wants to do . . .

*In mid-May 2003, and after some years of consideration, Penn began
shooting* The Assassination of Richard Nixon *for first-time director Niels
Mueller, co-scripted by Mueller and Kevin Kennedy and based on an
infamous real event: on 23 February 1974, salesman Sam Byck tried to
commandeer an airliner to fly into the White House and kill the
President. He got as far as a cockpit, where he shot and killed a co-pilot,
but was himself wounded by an airport policeman and then took his own
life.*

*In the Mueller/Kennedy script, Byck is a man who just wants 'a lit-
tle piece of the American dream' but finds that 'words like "pure" and
"honest" don't mean a hell of a lot any more'. He lacks the mean,
plausible moxie to succeed as a furniture salesman; his boss urges self-
improvement upon him but what Sam truly yearns for are hugs
from his estranged wife. Browbeaten, he begins to wildly over-iden-
tify with righteous causes, addressing tape-recorded musings to
Marlon Brando and Muhammad Ali, even volunteering for the Black
Panthers. Meanwhile, as the bombing of Cambodia and the
Watergate break-in become public knowledge, Nixon's clammy
endurance in the White House builds before Byck's eyes into a form
of personal affront.*

Post-production on Mueller's film was completed in early 2004, and

*shortly thereafter it was officially selected for the Un Certain Regard
section of the Cannes Film Festival in May.*

On 30 May 2003, Penn paid for a full page in the New York Times *in
order to run a 4,500 word essay entitled 'Kilroy's Still Here': a reflection on the Baghdad trip, his motives in going, its reception in the
media, and subsequent developments in the region.*

BOB RAFELSON: The piece that Sean wrote to the *New York Times* I
thought was an absolutely amazing statement about his trip to Iraq:
how personal it was, how profoundly American it was. Even though
he opposed everything, he opposed it on the grounds of a very strong
and positive attitude about being an American.

*However respectfully Penn had addressed his 'Letter' of 18 October
2002, subsequent events had persuaded him to remove the bars in
regard to expressing his citizen's opinion of the President. He zeroed in
with maximum derision upon Bush's foolish 'Mission Accomplished'
stunt on the aircraft carrier* Abraham Lincoln, *an expensive attempt to
claim the victor's spoils on prime-time television while the lives of so
many American service people were still at stake: 'This is his debutante
ball, isn't it? This young man of privilege, who never had the curiosity
to set foot outside our country before becoming our President, was
dressed in his "top gun" jumper, flown in, onto the flight deck of the*
Lincoln. *I didn't need a second viewing of this one. Tom Cruise was
fine by me . . . '*

'If military intervention in Iraq has been a grave misjudgement,'
wrote Penn, 'it has been one resulting in thousands upon thousands of
deaths, and done so without any credible evidence of imminent threat
to the United States. Our flag has been waving, it seems, in servicing a
regime change significantly benefiting US corporations. What remains
to be seen is an effective plan for the rebuilding of the civilian
infrastructure, or any other benefit to the people of Iraq or the United
States . . .'

*Penn asserted that the Stars 'n' Stripes presented to his mother at
Leo's funeral service had come to symbolize for him his late father's
virtues: 'his great heart, his kindness, his courage, and yes, even his (I
was lucky) occasional human lapses'.*

*The effect of the war on Iraq, he decided, was to render the flag 'a
vulgar billboard, advertising our disloyalty to ourselves and our allies*

. . . The responsibility "for which it stands" is ours. That flag is my father and I want him back.'

Mystic River *opened in the US in October 2003, and had A. O. Scott of the* New York Times *reaching for staggering superlatives: 'Jimmy Markum is not only one of the best performances of the year, but also one of the definitive pieces of screen acting in the last half-century, the culmination of a realist tradition that began in the old Actor's Studio and begat Brando, Dean, Pacino and De Niro . . .'*[1]

Eastwood's rendering of Lehane's vigilante tragedy was generally well-received by critics and audiences alike: in interviews Penn attributed its success to a certain sombre public mood, an interest in dramas where 'people answered their grief by removing the culprit.'[2]

R. D. CALL: I was watching *Mystic River,* and there were moments there when I saw Sean's father – I saw Leo: just an expression or a mannerism or a look in his eye or the way he said a word. I don't know if he'll agree with that, whether it has anything to do with what he was doing. But he had a maturity about him that he didn't have. He's got a family, so it's another understanding that he has now. But he's got a power too that I think only comes with a certain age – it's there now. Having grey in his hair and glasses? I think he's been dying to do that for years . . .

At the gala finale of the Venice Festival on 6 September 2003, Penn was for the second time in his career awarded the Volpi Cup for Best Actor, for 21 Grams. *He accepted the solus distinction with a nod of deference to his collaborators: 'Everyone who saw the film knows the ensemble that I am part of.'*

ERIN DIGNAM: I thought 21 *Grams* was about more than most people make films about these days – the bigger things, the value of life, what death is. And I loved the structure, what it did with time, the way it folded into itself. Because time is bendable, and we repeat the same mistakes. People have said, 'Oh, it's so sad.' Sad is not the right word for me. I was saddened by what the characters went through. But I thought it showed connections being made between human beings, and a lot of hope.

1 'Dark Parable of Violence Avenged', *New York Times*, 3 October 2003.
2 John Clark, *San Francisco Chronicle*, Monday, 6 October 2003.

ALEJANDRO GONZÁLEZ IÑÁRRITU: I think it's a very hopeful film, a film about life. United States culture tries to deny that we die: that's why they have surgery to their faces and every woman gets the same tits from the same doctors. So most of the films too are not in touch with reality. In my country, we don't have any problem talking about death. It is the deal that we make when we get out of the bellies of our mothers: somebody says, 'OK, welcome. But you will have to go some day, that's for sure . . . '

In late November 2003, San Francisco Chronicle editor Phil Bronstein confirmed that he and Penn were in discussions about a return journey to Iraq in the form of a journalistic commission. As Penn would short- ly write, 'I felt a responsibility to change or reaffirm my position in the context of the new situation for our US soldiers, and Iraqi civilians as well.' Penn also suggested he might go hunting for certain Fox News foghorns, over-ready to claim expertise in the field. 'We know that two people in particular, Sean Hannity and Bill O'Reilly, know so much about the subject, and I know that they're there because they'd have to be there to know that.'[3]

NORMAN SOLOMON: In December 2003, a delegation left the United States for Iraq, including parents of US soldiers in Iraq, one of whom had died in March, some of whom were stationed there. A mother who went on the trip said something in a news release very similar to what Sean said when he was over there: 'I want to see the people there, and see them as people, what they're like, how they talk . . .'

Penn joined up with that same delegation, courtesy of the San Francisco human rights organization Global Exchange. Once again, he flew from San Francisco to Amsterdam to Amman, but there he parted ways with Global Exhange, and undertook a twelve-hour car ride into Baghdad.

ROBIN WRIGHT PENN: The second time, it was more dangerous. I knew. But again I completely understand why. People asked, 'Did you think about going with him?' And my only answer to that is, 'No, our children need *one* parent if it comes to it.' But these are huge priorities with Sean, huge, and I know that's what drives him in his life. And I also believe that's why he's here.

3 John Clark, *San Francisco Chronicle*, Monday, 6 October 2003.

© Hiwa Osman. Courtesy of Sean Penn

75 Baghdad, December 2003: Penn with US serviceman
and Iraqi youths

This time out, Penn met young patrolling US soldiers and relatives of
those murdered and made to disappear by Saddam; he saw the
marks of the indigenous resistance to 'de-Ba'athification', and the
damage inflicted on the occupying powers by a mounting Iraqi insur-
gency; he heard the new and welcome sounds of unfettered Iraqi
opinion, some sceptical of the US imperium and the prospect of elec-
toral democracy in a land with no history of the same. He met with
and was impressed by the thoughtfulness and eloquence of govern-
ing council member Sheikh Ghazi Ajil al-Yawar (a Sunni Arab who
subsequently, in June 2004, became Iraq's first post-Saddam president.)
A restaurant replete with women in floor-length Islamic dress also
afforded him a glimpse of a future Iraq 'as Iran would like to see it'. But
he also suffered a close encounter with representatives of the 'private
military corporation' Dyncorp, mercenaries by any other name, not
obviously possessed of any hearts-and-minds objectives. And he visited
the Al-Iskan children's hospital, only to find his hope for an improvement
in the care of young leukaemia sufferers dashed by miserable conditions
in 'a place you wouldn't bring a mangy dog for veterinary care'.

BONO: Sean told me after his second trip that some of his positions had
changed, from the meeting of US servicemen and his respect for them
and what they had pulled off, and for the sake of the lives of people
they were never going to meet. Again, that takes courage. That's not

very Irish, is it? [*laughs*] You could at least just take your position and pour some cement over it.

TIM ROBBINS: I find the most interesting people are the ones who are able to see the truth and walk in the face of resistance. And Sean is admirable in that respect. There's a great quote by Mark Twain: 'In the beginning of a change, the patriot is a scarce man, and brave, and hated and scorned. When his cause succeeds, the timid join him, for then it costs nothing to be a patriot.' It reminds me a lot of what's going on now.[4] A lot of people are just starting to question the war. Well, *none* of this stuff we didn't know last year.

Erin Dignam had lately done her own share of nerve-straining travel in Liberia, the setting of a new film she was due to start with Robin Wright Penn and Javier Bardem, a drama within the milieu of international aid-work entitled The Last Face.

ERIN DIGNAM: I picked Sean up at the airport and he was like, 'You go first,' and I was like, 'No, *you* go first.' He's like, 'OK, I had to drive twelve hours in.' 'Well, my plane was on fire when I landed in Freetown . . .'

We stayed up late together that night and I heard his stories. He told me how sad Baghdad was and how hopeful he felt. He was saying, 'If we could just rebuild the place and not be so concerned with our economic gain there . . .' And my mouth just dropped open. I said, 'But, Sean, you know better than anyone that's why we went.' He said, 'I know, but now we're there, we have to get past that.' That optimism, that hope, it's what a lot of Sean's political stuff is about for him: he just really believes the world can be better. He wants the best for people, from his friends to people halfway across the world – it's very deep in him. He's like a relentless energy. I mean, people bang their head against the wall and they give up. Sean never gives up.

Also proving himself to be no quitter was the principled Ohio congressman Dennis Kucinich, whose issue-driven campaign to be Democratic presidential nominee chugged onward in spite of the Party's collective slump into the arms of Massachusetts senator John Kerry. Penn hosted a fund-raising soiree for Kucinich at Mike Medavoy's residence in late February, and would join him on the stump in the following months. Whither then the cinema? Penn was

4 Robbins was speaking on 16 April 2004.

spinning several plates. He was writing a script for Sam Bayer to direct, an English-language remake of Orlow Seunke's 1982 Dutch film The Taste of Water. Harry Crews' The Knockout Artist had not evaded his attention, and another draft was in the works from another writer. The notion of adapting Hunter S. Thompson's marlin-fishing lark The Curse of Lono with Jack Nicholson as the good doctor had a mischievous appeal. Penn was also spending productive time with Paul Watson, the Canadian 'eco-warrior' who first came to public promi-nence by pursuing and ramming a rogue whaling ship with his own steel-hulled vessel in a Portuguese harbour in 1979. And Steve Zailllian was said to be seeking Penn to play Willie Stark in a second filming of Robert Penn Warren's All the King's Men. Then there was also the matter of Penn's own script, Unmoveable You, something of a veiled autobiography, which he was minded to direct.

First, though, a window of time opened, and Penn walked through it in February 2004, committing as an actor to the role of secret-service agent Tobin Keller opposite Nicole Kidman in The Interpreter, a Sydney Pollack-directed political thriller for Working Title and Universal. Kidman would play Silvia Broome, a South African interpreter at the United Nations in New York, who inadvertently overhears a death threat against an African head of state scheduled to address the General Assembly. Remarkably, the production was granted permission through Secretary-General Kofi Annan to shoot sequences inside UN headquarters; and for Penn, the script by Charles Randolph and Steve Zaillian had resonance not only with Pollack's Three Days of the Condor but also Alan Pakula's Klute – movies of the seventies, when each new picture promised something different to the one before . . .

Two outstanding performances in two strong pictures within one cal-endar year are always a useful reminder of an actor's calibre. Penn's work in 21 Grams and Mystic River earned him a solid stack of criti-cal and professional nominations and prizes. His fourth Academy Award nod duly came for the Eastwood picture: the bookies gradually installed him as joint-favourite with Bill Murray for Lost in Translation. Johnny Depp, winner of the Screen Actors Guild prize for Pirates of the Caribbean, was the cantering outsider. On the night of February 29 2004, Penn, accompanied by his wife and his mother, took up his seat in the Kodak Pavilion, somewhat in the teeth of widespread expectation that he would default.

Tim Robbins, the very first winner of the evening as Best Supporting Actor for Mystic River, *then had a prime seat for the dramas unfolding.*

TIM ROBBINS: It was great to win and get it out of the way, but then it was a matter of being nervous about Sean, you know? Because the weekend before that was the SAG Awards. And, I mean, we love Johnny Depp. But I think we were all shocked that Sean didn't win there. So after I got back to my seat, it all became about my nerves for Sean – mainly because I didn't want to hang out with him if he was going to be a drag that night [*laughs*]. I knew he would be so much more fun if he won.

PETER COYOTE: When I heard Sean's name announced, and watched him walking up there to get the award, I got goose-bumps – because I could see all the people behind his back standing up to applaud, and he couldn't see it. But I knew that once he turned around, he would. And I was thrilled for him, because that's a serious recognition, and deserved.

TIM ROBBINS: Then suddenly he's up there doing his speech, and we're so happy, and then you're just pulling for him to do a nice speech. And he did a *great* speech.

Penn managed to convey his regards both for his fellow nominees as well as some whose performances hadn't made the final cut: so underscoring his conviction that 'there is no such thing as 'best' in acting.'

SEAN PENN: Marlon said once, 'If you think that people sit around in tribal cultures and say, Here's to Johnny, he killed that bear. I don't think that anybody's quite killed a bear the way that Johnny did . . .' And if you're Johnny, it's okay. But it's like jokes, they're generally best for the teller. So, if you're feeling like the teller that night . . .

76 Marlon Brando 1924–2004

KEVIN SPACEY: I couldn't be happier that Sean's outside success has increased tenfold in the last couple of years. I think his work in *21 Grams* was remarkable, and equally worthy of awards in its year. And, you know, look – who doesn't love *Fast Times*? But you look from that to *Mystic River* and you think, 'Can that possibly be the same person?' And that's the joy of watching an actor grow and come into his own, wrestle with the issues he wrestles with as a man, and come to a place where he's just doing some of the finest work we've ever seen. And it just makes me very pleased for my friend. But he's the same man he's always been. So things may be changing on the outside, people may be perceiving, 'Oh, now he's more commercial', or whatever – in fact it's not true, it's just that people are finally figuring out that he's one of the great actors of all time.

JAMES RUSSO: I called Sean and said, 'It's about fucken time you won something.' I told him he should have got it for *Crackers* . . .

Fade Out

DR KATZ: He's had a good life. Never had a bad day. I got blown up two times in Vietnam, I was a POW for a couple of days . . . He's had a *good* life.

EILEEN RYAN PENN: I visited Sean on set when he was doing *Sweet and Lowdown*, and Woody said to me, 'Tell me about your son. I'd like to understand something about him.' Everyone had been tiptoeing around Woody on set, so they were looking at us as we talked, and I said something in his ear, and he started laughing. So I guess they all thought, 'What did Mrs Penn just say to Woody?' I said, 'Woody, I think Sean was always a bit embarrassed at having had a happy childhood . . .' I think he wanted to identify with the other side of the tracks, he felt bad for people who had a bad time, and he wanted to say, 'I know what you're going through, even if you don't think I could. I do, believe me.' But who knows? That's just what I think. Sean, I'm sorry. Maybe I'm completely wrong, and you can refute it.

SEAN PENN: I guess if there's any responsibility that anybody in film or any of the arts has, it's being aware of the times you live in and making things that address them, whether you're making a statement or just shining a light on it. Or questioning it for yourself.

JESSIE NELSON: At times I felt Sean's father's ghost a little on the set of *I Am Sam*. I think when you're doing such vulnerable work as Sean was, you can't help but pull up some of that feeling. We spoke a great deal, we came from similar backgrounds, both of our families had gone through blacklisting during that era. Both my parents were communists, my stepmother's first husband was a blacklisted musician, and we'd had the FBI come to our house at times. I actually think that's the unspoken level on which Sean and I connect, where you've been raised by people who know what it's like to fight for something they believe in for a better world. I think it's an incredible thing to be given as a kid, even if it makes you a little different from the other kids

... That someone would say, 'Everybody *should* have health care, and there *shouldn't* be the very rich and the very poor, this world *is* out of balance and what they're telling you on the news *is* bullshit and you've got to question it all.'

LINDA LEE BUKOWSKI: I think a lot of Sean's acting has been an opportunity to know himself, also to learn about the life he wanted to experience and know in a larger and more worldly sense. Each character he would take on, he would immerse himself in so strongly that he couldn't just leave them and just let it go – he extrapolated from those roles and those experiences, letting it go eventually, but taking the essence of it, why he did it in the first place. I admire that he did all that and took it on. To see him now, it seems like he's integrated a lot of the important points of these different experiences into his life, in a way that he can have an easier path that goes from his work to his family life to his marriage to his mother to every relationship he has. He's gaining more of an even keel in dealing with all of life's situations.

ALEJANDRO GONZÁLEZ IÑÁRRITU: I consider him, I can tell you, one of those friends who are really special in my life. I don't know, people can say I'm in love with Sean Penn, and I say, 'Maybe that's true . . .' Maybe if I was gay, I would marry him [*laughs*]. But, you know, Robin would kick me out . . .

EILEEN RYAN PENN: She's a lovely girl, Robin. And they fight, but they love each other. They're crazy about each other and they could kill each other, so . . .

BONO: He's a frontiersman, she's Calamity Jane. I think he found his match . . . The word that applies to them both is 'rigour'. That's a rare thing in these times, and they both have it. I love being in his company with Robin. I just *really* like that. They seem fluid in each other's company and with their kids. They don't need to look for each other out of the corner of their eye; they know where each other is in the room.

ERIN DIGNAM: Robin is extremely beautiful; and I don't just mean physically – the way she moves, the way she touches her children, she's an extremely beautiful woman. I'm sure that's important to Sean. He's extremely outgoing in the way he loves to meet people, and she's extremely *not* outgoing: but their personalities, they can entertain you, each of them – you don't need anybody else. And it always comes down to this brutal, *brutal* honesty.

JOSEPH VITARELLI: Sean's plenty self-deprecating. If not, Robin will take care of that. I think the prerequisite of being a great woman is the ability to cut the man you live with down to size. Or smaller . . . Robin's got the intelligence to do it, and does it routinely. They just don't make 'em any better than her. She's gorgeous, she has great taste, she's intelligent, funny, a phenomenal mother . . . Have I left something out?

SAMANTHA MORTON: Robin is one of my heroes, really, out of all the actresses in America of her age – I just think she's out of this world, mind-blowing.

ROBIN WRIGHT PENN: It's like, 'What is it you need for sustenance, so you can be the person that you are?' I'm sure I need to be around Sean because he's one who will push and push, and I'll be, 'Forget it, it's not worth the stress.' And he's like, 'It *is* worth the stress.' I'll do probably the same for him – 'You don't *need* the stress' – and help him back off of certain things. Maybe that's our scale, our balance. I don't know that we've 'changed' each other . . . but I think maybe just our beings, which are very different in many ways, have definitely moved – we've helped move each other into another way.

JAMES RUSSO: He's just very loving to her and the kids. Mr Tough Guy, it's nice to see that – makes him even more endearing . . .

EILEEN RYAN PENN: Hopper's cute as a button. He's just like Sean when he was little. I have pictures of the two of them and you can't tell them apart. You should see him on his skateboard. Scary. He took me out to the enormous ramp they have in the back of the property. I said, 'You go on that, Hopper?' He said, 'Oh *yeah*, Grandma . . .'

MEEGAN OCHS: I think it'll be harder for Sean with Dylan than Hopper, because Hopper's a guy, whereas there's just this tremendous feeling of protectiveness around the women in his life. Dylan's such a beauty; she's so strong-willed and smart, and he's not going to be able to keep her under his wing for ever. But I have to say, I think those punches Sean has thrown in his time are going to come in handy as firm reminders to anyone that they'd better treat Dylan with incredible kid gloves. Because Daddy is there, and he's not afraid to use force . . .

STANLEY JAFFE: Sean is what I want this industry to be. He stands for excellence. If I were a young actor starting, he'd be the person I'd be looking at real hard.

77 The family Penn, 2002

JOHN SYKES: He's like the pied piper of actors: he sits down and all of a sudden they begin to appear. We were out to a restaurant at the end of 2003 and the entire cast of *Lord of the Rings* was in town promoting the third in the trilogy, and it was almost surreal to see all of these characters come up to a table and just fawn over Sean . . .

BOB RAFELSON: There's nobody's performance I'd rather see, nobody's mistakes I would rather embrace, and nobody's ambition that is so pure and clear. I follow his career with a kind of awe: I want to know what movie he's making and why he's making it.

MIKE MEDAVOY: Somebody once said you know who were the pioneers by the guys who get arrows in the front as opposed to the back . . . I think Sean's doing what serves him best – what serves his conscience best, what serves him best artistically.

ART LINSON: Sean's fierce integrity is truly, *truly* a rare quality in Hollywood. Everybody talks about it, blah-blah-blah, but with Sean, it's in his DNA. And he maintains it, fiercely. So guys like that are important to all of us: he makes you want to do a little better. Not everybody, mind you. But certainly he's had that effect on me, as a producer. I've become a little more selective. In other words, I'm too embarrassed to do some of the stuff I've almost done, because I've thought Sean would say, 'Oh shit, you're really losing it . . .'

ERIN DIGNAM: He recoils from it, but he has so much to teach, actually, and I don't think he realizes that. I think that he thinks of it as being self-aggrandising, but when somebody is doing something on the level that Sean is achieving, I think it's a great thing to give some of the things you know about what you're doing to people growing up who are so passionate about acting.

SEAN PENN: You try to explain something that's hard to explain, not because of anything but that . . . it's not really meant to be explained [*laughs*].

I did a Q&A at the Screen Actors' Guild in Los Angeles the night before the premiere of *21 Grams*, and it was all actors. Afterwards, Robin was saying, 'You know, you ought to teach an acting class . . .' She's not correct. Because these are very abstract things, thematic ideas, about how I work or how I view acting. But I remember a good acting teacher . . . and I remember how she took a set of bona fide skills and applied them to me very personally. And I was able to take those things that had a foundation and build on them. But my foundation was strengthened specifically to my process. Nobody should have the *same* process. But there are great tools, from the classical theatre down to the Method, Stanislavsky, Boleslavsky, there are great things that come out of that stuff, particularly related to relaxation. And on the other side, the pragmatic side: script analysis and breakdown and how to ask questions. But it takes a certain repetition of thought before you're able to call on the things that will help *this* person now in *this* way of developing as an actor. Sometimes I feel I can be generous enough where I can refocus people on finding their way. But I can't supply building blocks too well: I don't have that skill. A great acting teacher does.

KEVIN CHAPMAN: I did a big movie for Disney in Baltimore with Joaquin Phoenix and John Travolta. We played firefighters. I'm ten days in, and I feel like the director's not covering me: I have these lines that are very important to the piece, but I'm in a three-shot, or a rake. So I call Sean on his cell: 'Seanie!' 'What's happening?' I tell him my problem. And as we're speaking, I can see what he's doing, in my head: he's in the car, driving eighty miles an hour, stereo on ten, he's got an American Spirit stuffed in his face, he's kind of lost because he's going somewhere he hasn't been, and he's got the cell phone under his ear. It's a three-ring circus in that car. But he's giving me advice. 'Listen to me, listen to me! [*honks horn*] Hey! Get of the way! No, *listen* to me. If you go to the director and tell him you want more coverage, he's no longer the director. You are. You've fallen into a trap. Actors, we think what we have to say is the most important piece in the movie, and that's a trap. But don't feel bad. Who's the lead?' 'Joaquin Phoenix.' 'OK, I want you to read the story as if you're Joaquin's character. And then I want you to assess the relationship of your character to Joaquin's through his eyes, look how much your character means to him. I want you to find those beats. And then when those beats come, and Joaquin comes anywhere remotely near your character, and the camera comes near you, you be ready to jump all over that scene. I want you to hit the cover off the ball like I know you can, and I guarantee things are gonna turn around.' Well, don't you know, by week two the director's putting the camera on me, saying, 'Gimme a cutaway, gimme something, anything!' Even the guys on the set were saying, 'How the hell did you make that happen?' I said, 'I have a friend who's a genius is how.'

SEAN PENN: You have to be aware in your choices as an actor in movies – especially as a famous or near-famous actor – of the way to allow people to see each new character. There's the inevitable baggage of a successful career. People get to know rhythms of that person that, in some cases, you loan out to piecing in a character within other choices. In other cases, you may fully embody something that is a variation of that thing. In other words, we all recognize idiosyncrasies of personality that are invested and used, and that – sometimes to great effect – have a through-connection with other characters. So the more you work, the more you have to grow and develop your own personality, so that it's not just that old one they've seen pieces of before.

AMY HECKERLING: Even when I was watching *Dead Man Walking*, every now and then you see these little glimpses of Spicoli . . . I mean, just because it's Sean and that's his face, it's not like he's not in character. It's just that you go, 'Oh my god, no, don't kill *him* . . .' But maybe that's just me. And in 21 *Grams*, even though you think he's gonna go kill somebody, I thought he was showing glimmers of that amazing charm he has, and you think, 'Ah, if he ever *decided* to pour it on . . . there wouldn't be a woman in the world wouldn't go crazy.'

DENNIS HOPPER: For an actor, the paralysis usually sets in only when you don't have any choices any more, and you have to take the work that's given you. Right now, Sean has choices he can make. And I wouldn't worry about his choices. He seems to be making good ones . . .

JACK NICHOLSON: Sean has no limitations as an actor. I mean, these are just the facts of the matter. There are certain things other actors can speak of with authority – there *rarely* are – but that's one of them: Sean doesn't have any limitations as an actor. I always say, 'Really good actors, if the time came, they could play their own grandmother.' And Sean's one of those.

But I hope he does keep directing, and keeps his emphasis there. It's hard, it's a tough row he's hoeing. But I really think he's too dedicated a man to do anything but.

CHRISTOPHER PENN: I think acting was an incredibly joyous means to an end, and the end was directing, because that's his thing. And he's as good as it gets. My dad, from heaven, is proud of Sean's directing.

ANGELICA HUSTON: He's probably more than capable of being a great director. I can't imagine, if that's something he wants to do and wants to pursue, that he won't be able to do exactly as he wants, ultimately. I do think sooner or later there's a demand that your movies make money, and so probably he'll have to figure that one out. But then I think maybe he won't – maybe he'll find a way around it [*laughs*], because I don't see Sean cowing to the system. And I think we *rely* on him not to cow to the system. As the Irish say, there's only a few of us left . . .

BENICIO DEL TORO: At this point, I think Sean is at a place that very few people get to. He knows every position – as an actor, as a director. But I think now that he's hitting his stride a little bit more than just as an actor – he's been evolving as a man, I think. He's become a leader, like the ambassadors of Hollywood, like Jack Nicholson and Marlon Brando. He's a leader of being free and independent; and that's what I love about him. I love that he can go for the big guy. He's no bully – he *goes* for the bully. And if he keeps that up . . .

R. D. CALL: For all the work Sean has done – I think his greatest work is still ahead of him. I think he has that maturity now, and that power. It's still out there. I hope he understands that. He has the capability and the wherewithal to make that happen – if he chooses. But I think everything else that has gone before, as great as it may be . . . it's just prologue.

WOODY HARRELSON: One thing I do want to say: there is definitely still a public opinion of Sean; people who don't know him have an image of him as a tough guy. Maybe it's a Brando-esque toughness, where he can show that vulnerable side sometime. And nobody doubts his genius, I guess . . . But the thing I wish is, there have been *so* many nights I've had in Sean's company that I wish I had videotape of, where you see Sean as he really is – which is this big kid, you know? He has his pranks, and he loves to stir things up. He'll get excited, and tell all these great stories. Or he'll launch into his poems, or get up and do a whole hysterical pantomime of a first date between two people . . .

MATT PALMIERI: Or he'll be right in the middle of a big group and all of a sudden he'll say, 'Let me just do a little interpretive *dance* for you all . . .' Then he turns around and becomes this fey, strange guy, and does a dance for everybody. Which is always a showstopper . . .

WOODY HARRELSON: That playfulness that comes out of him, I mean . . . I've got a lot of really fun friends, and when they're on their game, it's amazing. But it's hard to imagine having more fun than when Sean's having fun. That's the guy who I see as my brother. And I wish everybody could see that playful, joyful, fun loving – and truly genius – character. The real Sean, you know?

Acknowledgements

Naturally, the foremost debt of gratitude is to Sean Penn himself, for consenting to and co-operating with this lengthy inquiry, in the midst of what was, even by his own exacting standards, an exceptionally busy period in respect of personal and professional commitments.

Even so, precious little would have been possible thereafter without Sato Masuzawa at Clyde Is Hungry Films, indefatigably helpful in the midst of innumerable commitments of her own. Nor would the logistics of the project have been remotely achievable without my host in Los Angeles, Bill Higgins, a true stand-up guy and a man who holds the keys to the city. Hercules Belville, who is welcomed the world over, made possible a number of interviews that otherwise could hardly have been hoped for. Mara Buxbaum at ID-PR also kindly made a number of contacts on my behalf. And Paula Jalfon, Colin MacCabe, and Lizzie Francke each helped to create the very circumstances whereby this project could become a reality.

Gratitude is owed to every individual who gave of their time to speak for the book and the many individuals – too numerous, I fear, to list – who assisted in the arrangements of the same. Thomas Vinterberg was interviewed on my behalf by Kaleem Aftab.

Walter Donohue commissioned the book and, as always, patiently and insightfully aided its progress. Lesley Felce did a terrific job as desk editor of these pages, and I am grateful too to Ron Costley and Ian Bahrami. Thanks are also owed to Anna Pallai, Tara Hiatt and Jon Riley at Faber, and to Jamie Byng at Canongate.

A pair of documentary projects to which Sean Penn provided voice-over are not discussed in these pages: with apologies to their makers, one heartily recommends *Dear America: Letters Home from Vietnam* (1987) and *Dogtown and Z-Boys* (2001).

Extracts from *Goose and Tomtom* and *Hurlyburly* by David Rabe are reprinted courtesy of Mr. Rabe, © Ralako Corp.

The majority of the images in these pages were supplied by Sean Penn and Clyde Is Hungry Films. Meegan Ochs, too, was hugely helpful with the provision of illustrations. Thanks also in this line to Art Wolff, Matt Palmieri, Linda Lee Bukowski, Alan Pogue, Joseph Vitarelli, and Gisela Getty.

Every effort was made to correctly identify the photographers and copyright holders of the images. If any errors or omissions have been made, apologies – they will be set right for further editions. Key to the paper-research process were both the Library and the Stills, Posters, and Designs department of the British Film Institute; The Performing Arts Library at the Lincoln Centre in New York; and The Margaret Herrick Library of the Academy of Motion Picture Arts and Sciences in Los Angeles.

Richard T. Kelly

June 2004

Index

All films and stage plays with which Sean Penn was involved are indexed under Penn, Sean.
References to photos and illustrations are in bold type